OLD
PATH
WHITE
CLOUDS

This is for you. I can't put in words how much your family means to me. You have a good soul. You taken me places that I never been. You made me smile when I needed it. You listen when no one would. Thank you for rubbing my back and holding my head up.

This book was given to me from my aunt she meant the world t

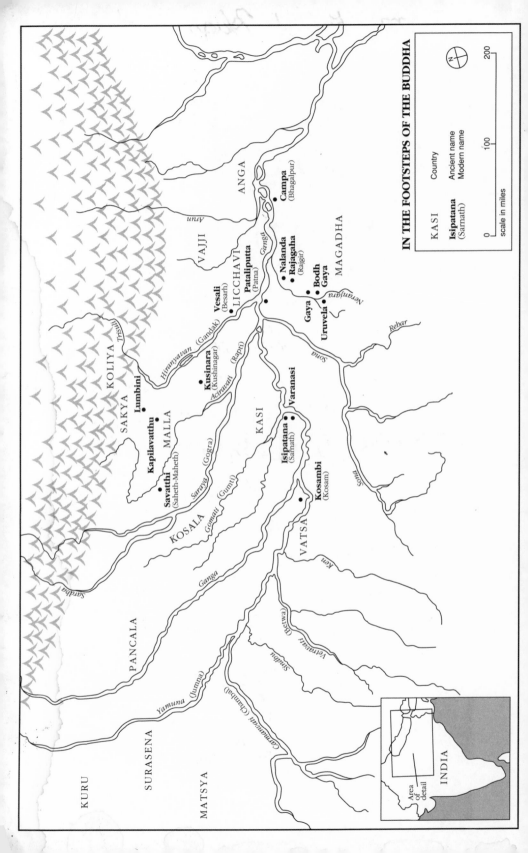

IN THE FOOTSTEPS OF THE BUDDHA

KASI   Country

Isipatana   Ancient name
(Sarnath)   Modern name

scale in miles

0   100   200

ANGA

VAJJI

Campa
(Bhagalpur)

LICCHAVI

Nalanda

Pataliputta
(Patna)

Rajagaha
(Rajgir)

MAGADHA

Vesali
(Besarh)

**Bodh
Gaya**

Gaya

Uruvela

Neranjara

Arun

Ganga

Rehar

Hiranyavan (Gandak)

Trisuli

SAKYA

KOLIYA

Lumbini

Kapilavatthu

MALLA

Kusinara
(Kushinagar)

Aciravati

Sona

Savatthi
(Saheth-Maheth)

Varanasi

Isipatana
(Sarnath)

KASI

Saraya (Gogra)

Rapti

Gomati (Gumti)

KOSALA

Kosambi
(Kosam)

VATSA

Ken

Sona

Sardha

PANCALA

Ganga

Sindhu

Betwa

Vetravati (Betwa)

KURU

SURASENA

Yamuna (Jumna)

Cavanwati (Chambal)

MATSYA

Area
of
detail

INDIA

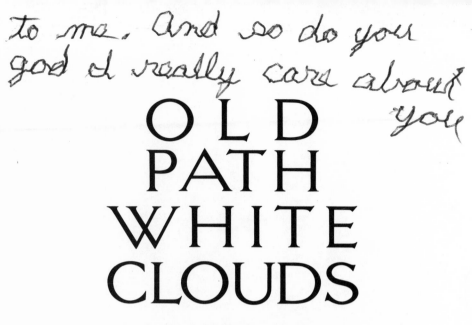

to me. And so do you
god I really care about
you

OLD
PATH
WHITE
CLOUDS

WALKING IN THE FOOTSTEPS
OF THE BUDDHA

THICH NHAT HANH

If you ever need to talk
I'll listen

Love
Elaine

Parallax Press
Berkeley, California

Parallax Press
P.O. Box 7355
Berkeley, California 94707

Parallax Press is the publishing division of Unified Buddhist
Church, Inc.

Translated from the Vietnamese by Mobi Ho.
Drawings by Nguyen Thi Hop.
Map and Cover Design by Gay Reineck.
Photo on back cover by James D. Gollin.

Library of Congress Cataloging-in-Publication Data
Nhât Hanh, Thích
[Duòng xua mây trang: English]
Old path white clouds: walking in the footsteps of the Buddha /
Thich Nhat Hanh.
p. cm.
Translation of Duòng xua mây trang.
Includes bibliographical references.
ISBN 0-938077-26-0 (pbk.)
1. Gautama Buddha. I. Title
BQ882.N4813 1991
294.3'63—dc20   90-21483
                                           CIP

01 02 03 04 05 / 15 14 13 12 11

Contents

Book One

Book Two

Book Three

Appendix

One dollar from the sale of each copy of *Old Path White Clouds*
will be donated to organizations which help children
in India and other Third World countries.

BOOK ONE

Chapter One
Walking Just to Walk

Under the shadows of the green bamboo, the young *bhikkhu*, Svasti, sat cross-legged, concentrating on his breath. He had been meditating for more than an hour in the Bamboo Forest Monastery, while hundreds of other bhikkhus were also practicing under the shade of the bamboo trees or in their own thatched huts.

The great teacher Gautama, whom people affectionately called the "Buddha," lived in the monastery with nearly four hundred disciples. Although crowded, it was very peaceful. Forty acres surrounded the monastery, and many varieties of graceful bamboo from all over Magadha were planted there. Just a thirty minutes' walk north of the capital city of Rajagaha, the Bamboo Forest Monastery had been given to Buddha and his community by King Bimbisara seven years earlier.

Svasti rubbed his eyes and smiled. His legs were still tender as he slowly uncrossed them. Twenty-one years old, he had been ordained three days earlier by the Venerable Sariputta, one of the Buddha's senior disciples. During the ordination ceremony, Svasti's thick brown hair was shaved off.

* * *

Svasti was very happy to be part of the Buddha's community. Many bhikkhus were of noble birth, such as the Venerable Nanda, the Buddha's brother, and Devadatta, Anuruddha, and Ananda. Although Svasti had not yet been introduced to these men, he had noticed them from afar. Even in faded robes, their noble bearing was unmistakable.

"It will be a long time before I can be friends with men of such noble birth," thought Svasti. And yet, even though the Buddha himself was the son of a king, Svasti felt no gulf between them. Svasti was an "untouchable," lower than the lowest and poorest caste according to the system of discrimination among the people of India at that time. For more than ten years, he had tended water buffalo, but for two weeks now, he was living and practicing with monks from all castes. Everyone was very kind to him, offering him warm smiles and deep bows, but he did not yet feel at ease. He suspected it might take years before he could feel completely comfortable.

Suddenly, a broad smile emerged from deep within him, as he thought of Rahula, the Buddha's eighteen-year-old son. Rahula had been a novice in the community since the age of ten, and in just two weeks Rahula and Svasti had become best friends. It was Rahula who taught Svasti how to follow his breath during meditation. Rahula understood the Buddha's teachings well, even though he was not yet a bhikkhu. He needed to wait until he was twenty before he could receive full ordination.

* * *

Svasti reflected on the time, just two weeks before, when the Buddha came to Uruvela, his small village near Gaya, to invite him to become a monk. When the Buddha arrived at his home, Svasti was out with his brother, Rupak, taking care of the buffaloes. His two sisters, Bala, age sixteen, and Bhima, age twelve, were there, and Bala recognized the Buddha right away. She began to run out to find Svasti, but the Buddha told her it wasn't necessary. He said that he and the monks traveling with him, including Rahula, would walk to the river to find her brother. It was late afternoon when they came upon Svasti and Rupak scrubbing down their nine buffaloes in the Neranjara River. As soon as they saw the Buddha, the young men ran up the bank of the river, joined their palms to form a lotus bud, and bowed deeply.

"You've grown so much," the Buddha said, smiling warmly at Svasti and his brother. Svasti was speechless. Seeing the Buddha's peaceful face, his warm and generous smile, and his brilliant, penetrating eyes, moved him to tears. The Buddha wore a saffron robe made of patches sewn together in the pattern of a rice field. He still walked barefoot as he had ten years before, when Svasti first met him not far from this very spot. Ten years before they had spent hours sitting together on the banks of the Neranjara and beneath the shade of the bodhi tree, just ten minutes' walk from the riverbank.

Svasti glanced at the twenty bhikkhus behind the Buddha and saw that they, too, were barefoot and clad in patched robes of the same color. Looking more closely, Svasti saw that the Buddha's robe was a hand-length longer than those of the others. Standing next to the Buddha was a novice about Svasti's age who looked at him directly and smiled. Buddha gently placed his hands on Svasti and Rupak's heads and told them he had stopped by to visit on his way back to Rajagaha. He said he would be happy to wait while Svasti and Rupak finished bathing the buffaloes so they could all walk to Svasti's thatched hut together.

During the walk back, Buddha introduced Svasti and Rupak to his son Rahula, the young novice who had smiled so beautifully at Svasti. Rahula was three years younger than Svasti, but they were the same height. Rahula was a *saman-era*, a novice, but he dressed much the same as the older bhikkhus. Rahula walked between Svasti and Rupak, handing his alms bowl to Rupak and placing his arms lovingly around the shoulders of his two new friends. He had heard so much about Svasti and his family from his father that he felt he already knew them. The brothers basked in the warmth of Rahula's love.

As soon as they arrived at Svasti's home, the Buddha invited him to join the bhikkhu community and study the Dharma with him. Ten years earlier, when Svasti had first met the Buddha, he expressed his wish to study with him, and the Buddha had agreed to accept Svasti as a disciple. Now that Svasti was twenty-one, the Buddha had returned. He had not forgotten his promise.

Rupak led the buffaloes back to Mr. Rambhul, their owner. The Buddha sat outside Svasti's hut, on a small stool, while the bhikkhus stood behind him. With earthen walls and a thatched roof, Svasti's tiny home was not large enough for everyone to come inside. Bala told Svasti, "Brother, please go with the Buddha. Rupak is even stronger than you were when you began tending the buffaloes, and I am quite capable of taking care of the house. You have looked after us for ten years, and now we are ready to be on our own."

Sitting next to the rainwater barrel, Bhima looked up at her big sister without saying a word. Svasti looked at Bhima. She was a lovely young girl. When Svasti met the Buddha, Bala was six years old, Rupak three, and Bhima only an infant. Bala cooked for the family while Rupak played in the sand.

Six months following their father's death, their mother passed away in childbirth. Just eleven years old, Svasti became the head of the household. He found a job tending water buffaloes, and because Svasti was a good worker, he earned enough to feed his family. He was even able to bring buffalo milk home for little Bhima.

Realizing that Svasti was asking her about her feelings, Bhima smiled. She hesitated a moment and then spoke softly, "Brother, go with the Buddha." She turned her face away to hide the tears. Bhima had heard Svasti mention his wish to study with Buddha so many times and she truly wanted him to go, but now that the moment had arrived she could not hide her sadness.

The Buddha sat outside Svasti's hut, on a small stool.

Just then, Rupak returned from the village, and hearing Bhima's words, "Go with the Buddha," he understood that the time had come. He looked at Svasti and said, "Yes, brother, please go with the Buddha," and the whole family fell silent. Rupak looked at the Buddha and said, "Venerable Sir, I hope you will permit my brother to study with you. I am old enough to care for our family." Rupak turned to Svasti and, holding back his tears, said, "But brother, please ask the Buddha if you can come back and visit us from time to time."

The Buddha stood up and gently stroked Bhima's hair. "Children, please eat now. Tomorrow morning, I will return for Svasti so we can walk together to Rajagaha. The bhikkhus and I will rest beneath the bodhi tree tonight."

As the Buddha reached the gate, he looked back at Svasti and said, "Tomorrow morning, you do not need to bring anything. The clothes you are wearing are enough."

That night the four siblings stayed up late. Like a departing father, Svasti gave them his last advice on taking care of each other and the household. He embraced each of them for a long time. Unable to hold back her tears, little Bhima sobbed while her oldest brother held her. But then she looked up, breathed deeply, and smiled at him. She didn't want Svasti to feel sad. The oil lamp cast a dim light, but it was enough for Svasti to see her smile, and he appreciated it.

Early the next morning, Sujata, Svasti's friend, came to say goodbye. The evening before, she had seen the Buddha when she was on her way to the riverbank, and he told her that Svasti would be joining the order of monks. Sujata, the daughter of the village head, was two years older than Svasti, and she, too, had met Gautama before he became the Buddha. Sujata gave Svasti a small jar of herbal medicines to take with him. They spoke only briefly, and then the Buddha and his disciples arrived.

Svasti's brother and sisters were already awake to see their brother off. Rahula spoke gently to each of them, encouraging them to be strong and to take care of each other. He promised that whenever he was nearby, he would stop in Uruvela to visit them. Svasti's family and Sujata walked with the Buddha and the bhikkhus to the riverbank, and there they joined their palms to say goodbye to the Buddha, the monks, Rahula, and Svasti.

Svasti was overcome with both fear and joy. There was a knot in his stomach. This was the first time he had ever left Uruvela. The Buddha said it would take ten days to reach Rajagaha. Most people traveled more quickly, but the Buddha and his bhikkhus walked slowly and with great ease. As Svasti's pace slowed down, his heart quieted. He was wholeheartedly immersing himself in the Buddha, the Dharma, and the Sangha, and this was his path. He turned around for one last glimpse of the only land and people he knew, and he saw Sujata and his family as mere specks merging with the shadows of the forest trees.

It seemed to Svasti that the Buddha walked just to enjoy the walking, unconcerned about arriving anywhere at all. So it was with all the bhikkhus. No one seemed anxious or impatient to reach their destination. Each man's steps were slow, balanced, and peaceful. It was as if they were taking a pleasant stroll together. No one ever appeared tired, and yet they covered a good distance each day.

Each morning they would stop in the nearest village to beg for food. They walked along the streets in a single line with the Buddha at the head. Svasti came last, just behind Rahula. They walked with quiet dignity, observing each breath and each step. Once in a while, they would stop while villagers placed offerings of food in their bowls. Some villagers knelt by the side of the road in respect. As the bhikkhus received the food, they quietly recited prayers for the people.

When they finished begging, they slowly left the village to find a place beneath some trees or in a grassy meadow where they could eat. They sat in a circle and divided the food equally, careful to fill anyone's bowl that was still empty. Rahula filled a jug with water from a nearby stream and respectfully carried it to the Buddha. After the Buddha joined his palms together to form what looked like a lotus flower, Rahula poured the water over the Buddha's hands and rinsed them clean. He did the same for everyone else, coming last to Svasti. As Svasti did not yet have a bowl, Rahula placed half of his own food on a fresh banana leaf and gave it to his new friend. Before eating, the bhikkhus joined their palms and chanted together. Then they ate in silence, mindful of each bite.

When they finished, some bhikkhus practiced walking meditation, some did sitting meditation, and others took a short nap. When the hottest part of the day had passed, they took to the road again, and they walked until it was nearly dark. The best places to rest for the night were undisturbed forests, and they walked until they found a good place. Each bhikkhu had his own cushion, and many sat cross-legged in the lotus position for half the night before spreading out their robes and going to sleep. Each bhikkhu carried two robes, the one he was wearing and another to use as protection against wind and cold. Svasti sat in meditation like the others and learned to sleep upon the earth using a tree root for a pillow.

When Svasti awoke the next morning, he saw the Buddha and many of the bhikkhus already sitting peacefully in meditation, radiating profound calm and majesty. As soon as the sun rose over the horizon, each bhikkhu folded his extra robe, picked up his bowl, and began the day's journey.

Walking by day and resting by night, it was ten days before they reached Rajagaha, the capital of Magadha. It was the first time Svasti had seen a city. Horse carts pressed through streets lined with crowded dwellings; shouts and laughter echoed everywhere. But the silent procession of the bhikkhus continued, as peacefully as when they strolled along the quiet riverbanks or between country rice fields. A few of the city dwellers paused to watch them, and a few, recognizing the Buddha, bowed deeply to show their respect.

The bhikkhus continued their calm procession until they reached the Bamboo Forest Monastery, just beyond the city.

News spread quickly throughout the monastery that the Buddha had returned, and within moments, nearly four hundred bhikkhus gathered to welcome him back. The Buddha did not say much but asked about everyone's well-being and meditation practice. He entrusted Svasti to Sariputta, who was also Rahula's spiritual instructor. Sariputta was the novice master of Bamboo Forest Monastery and watched over the studies of nearly fifty young monks, all of whom had been in the community for less than three years. The abbot of the monastery was a monk named Kondanna.

Rahula was asked to introduce Svasti to the ways of monastery life—how to walk, sit, stand, greet others, do walking and sitting meditation, and observe his breathing. He also showed Svasti how to wear the monk's robe, beg for food, recite prayers, and wash his bowl. For three continuous days, Svasti did not leave Rahula's side, so that he could learn these things well. Rahula put his whole heart into instructing Svasti, yet Svasti knew it would take years of practicing before he would be able to do these things in a relaxed and natural way. After this basic instruction, Sariputta invited Svasti into his hut and explained the precepts of a bhikkhu.

A bhikkhu was one who left his family in order to follow the Buddha as a teacher, the Dharma as the path which leads to awakening, and the Sangha as the community that supports one along the path. A bhikkhu's life was simple and humble. Begging for food helped foster humility and was also a means to be in contact with others and help them see the Way of Love and Understanding which the Buddha taught.

Ten years earlier beneath the bodhi tree, Svasti and his friends had listened to the Buddha speak about the path of awakening as the path of love and understanding, so it was easy for him to grasp all that Sariputta told him. Though Sariputta's face appeared serious, his eyes and smile radiated great warmth and compassion. He told Svasti that there would be a precepts ceremony to formally accept him into the community of bhikkhus, and he taught Svasti the words he would need to recite.

Sariputta himself presided over the precepts ceremony. About twenty bhikkhus attended. The Buddha and Rahula were there, adding to Svasti's happiness. Sariputta silently recited a gatha, and then shaved off several locks of Svasti's hair. He then gave the razor to Rahula, who completed the task of shaving Svasti's head. Sariputta gave Svasti three robes, a bowl, and a water filter. Because he had already been taught by Rahula how to wear the robe, Svasti put it on without difficulty. He bowed before the Buddha and the other bhikkhus present to express his deep gratitude.

Later that morning, Svasti practiced begging for the first time as an ordained bhikkhu. The monks of Bamboo Forest Monastery walked into Rajagaha in several small groups, and Svasti was part of the group led by Sariputta. After taking just a few steps out of the monastery, Svasti reminded himself that begging was a vehicle to practice the Way. He observed his breathing and took each step quietly and in mindfulness. Rahula walked behind him. Although he was now a bhikkhu, Svasti knew that he had considerably less experience than Rahula. He resolved with all his heart to nurture humility and virtue within himself.

Chapter Two
Tending Water Buffaloes

The day was cool. After eating the noon meal in mindfulness, each bhikkhu washed his own bowl and placed his cushion on the earth to sit facing the Buddha. The many squirrels that lived in Bamboo Forest mingled freely with the monks, and some climbed up into bamboo trees to gaze down at the gathering. Svasti saw Rahula sitting directly in front of the Buddha, and he quietly tiptoed there and placed his cushion next to Rahula's. They sat together in the lotus position. In that serene and dignified atmosphere, no one spoke. Svasti knew that each bhikkhu was following his breath mindfully, waiting for the Buddha to speak.

The Buddha's bamboo platform was high enough for everyone to see him clearly. The Buddha had a relaxed yet majestic air like that of a lion prince. His eyes filled with loving compassion as he looked out over the assembly. When his eyes came to rest on Svasti and Rahula, the Buddha smiled and began to speak:

"Today I wish to tell you about the work of tending water buffaloes—what a good buffalo boy must know and what he must be able to do. A boy who cares well for water buffaloes is a boy who easily recognizes each buffalo under his care, knows the characteristics and tendencies of each one, knows how to scrub them, care for their wounds, chase mosquitoes away with smoke, find safe paths for them to walk, love them, find safe and shallow places for them to cross the

river, seek fresh grass and water for them, preserve the grazing meadows, and let the older buffaloes serve as good models
for the younger ones.

"Listen Bhikkhus, just as a buffalo boy recognizes each of
his own buffaloes, a bhikkhu recognizes each of the essential
elements of his own body. Just as a buffalo boy knows the
characteristics and tendencies of each buffalo, a bhikkhu
knows which actions of body, speech, and mind are worthy
and which are not. Just as a buffalo boy scrubs his animals
clean, a bhikkhu must cleanse his mind and body of desires,
attachments, anger, and aversions."

As he spoke, the Buddha's eyes did not leave Svasti.
Svasti felt that he himself was the source of the Buddha's
words. He recalled how, years before, while sitting at the
Buddha's side, the Buddha would ask him to describe in detail his work of tending water buffaloes. How else could a
prince raised in a palace know so much about buffaloes?

Though the Buddha spoke in a normal voice, each sound
rose clear and distinct and no one missed a word: "Just as a
buffalo boy cares for his buffaloes' wounds, a bhikkhu
watches over his six sense organs—eyes, ears, nose, tongue,
body, and mind—so that they do not become lost in dispersion. Just as a buffalo boy protects his buffaloes from mosquito
bites by building fires to create smoke, the bhikkhu uses the
teaching of becoming awake to show those around him how to
avoid the afflictions of body and mind. Just as the boy finds a
safe path for the buffaloes to walk, the bhikkhu avoids
those paths that lead to desire for fame, wealth, and sexual
pleasure—places such as taverns and theaters. Just as a buffalo boy loves his buffaloes, the bhikkhu cherishes the joy
and peace of meditation. As the boy finds a safe, shallow
place in the river for the buffaloes to cross, the bhikkhu relies on the Four Noble Truths to negotiate this life. As the
boy finds fresh grass and water for his buffaloes, the
bhikkhu knows that the Four Establishments of Mindfulness
are the nourishment leading to liberation. As the boy pre-
serves the fields by not overgrazing them, the bhikkhu is

"As a buffalo boy finds fresh grass for his buffaloes, so a bhikkhu knows that the Four Establishments of Mindfulness lead to liberation."

careful to preserve the relationships with the nearby community as he begs offerings. As the boy lets the older buffaloes serve as models for the younger ones, the bhikkhu depends on the wisdom and experience of their elders. O bhikkhus, a bhikkhu who follows these eleven points will attain arhatship in the span of six years of practice."

Svasti listened in astonishment. The Buddha had remembered everything he had told him ten years before, and was able to apply each detail to a bhikkhu's practice. Though Svasti knew the Buddha was teaching the entire assembly of monks, he also had the distinct impression that the Buddha was addressing him directly. The young man's eyes did not wander even once from the Buddha's countenance.

These were words to hold in one's heart. Of course, there were terms such as "six sense organs," "Four Noble Truths," "Four Establishments of Mindfulness," which Svasti did not yet understand. He would ask Rahula later to explain these terms, but he knew he understood the essential meaning of the Buddha's words.

Buddha continued to speak. He told the assembly about choosing a safe path for the buffaloes to walk. If the path was overgrown with thorns, the buffaloes would get cuts which could become infected. If the buffalo boy did not know how to take care of wounds, his buffaloes could become feverish and even die. Practicing the Way was the same. If a bhikkhu did not find a proper path, he could become wounded in mind and body. Greed and anger could further poison his wounds until they grew so infected that the way to enlightenment became hindered.

The Buddha paused. He motioned for Svasti to come up and stand beside him. Svasti stood with his palms joined while Buddha, smiling, introduced Svasti to the assembly:

"Ten years ago I met Svasti in the forest near Gaya, just before I realized the Way. He was then eleven years old. It was Svasti who gathered armfuls of kusa grass which I used for a cushion to sit beneath the bodhi tree. Everything I have taught about water buffaloes, I learned from him. I knew he

was a good buffalo boy, and I know he will be a fine
bhikkhu."

Everyone's eyes were on Svasti, and he could feel his ears
and cheeks tingling and becoming very red. The men all joined
their palms and bowed to him, and he bowed back to them.
The Buddha then concluded the Dharma talk by asking
Rahula to recite the sixteen methods of conscious breathing.
Rahula stood, placed his palms together, and recited each
method in a voice as bright and clear as a bell. When he finished, he bowed to the community, and the Buddha stood up
and slowly walked back to his hut. After he did so, all the
monks in the assembly took their own cushions and walked
slowly to their own spot in the forest. Some of the monks
lived in huts, but many slept and meditated outdoors, beneath the bamboo trees. Only when it rained very hard did
they pick up their cushions and seek shelter in the residen-
tial huts or lecture halls.

Svasti's teacher, Sariputta, had assigned him to share a
space outdoors with Rahula. When Rahula was younger, he
had to sleep in a hut with the teacher who served as his
guardian, but now he had a spot under the trees. Svasti was
happy to be with Rahula.

Late that afternoon after sitting meditation, Svasti practiced walking meditation alone. He selected an empty path
to avoid encountering others, but he found it difficult to remain concentrated on his breathing. His thoughts were filled
with longing for his brother and sisters and the village at
home. The image of the path leading to the Neranjara River
rose clearly in his mind. He saw little Bhima lowering her
head to hide her tears and Rupak caring for Rambhul's water
buffaloes alone. He tried to chase these images away and focus on nothing but his steps and breathing, but the images continued to flood him. He felt ashamed that he could not devote himself to his practice, and he felt unworthy of the
Buddha's trust. After walking meditation, he thought, he
would ask Rahula for help. There were also several things
the Buddha had said in his Dharma talk that morning that

he had not fully grasped, and he was sure Rahula could explain them to him. Just thinking about Rahula encouraged and calmed him, and he found it easier to follow his breathing and each slow step.

Svasti had not yet had a chance to look for Rahula, when Rahula came looking for him. He led Svasti to a seat beneath a bamboo tree, and said, "This afternoon I met the elder Ananda. He would like to hear all about how you first met the Buddha."

"Who is Ananda, Rahula?"

"He's a prince of the Sakya line and the Buddha's cousin. He became a monk seven years ago and now he is one of the best disciples. The Buddha loves him dearly. It is he who looks after the master's health. Ananda has invited us to come to his hut tomorrow evening. I too want to hear all about the time the Buddha was living in the Gaya Forest."

"Hasn't the Buddha already told you?"

"Yes, but not in detail. I'm sure you have a lot of stories to tell."

"Well, there isn't really much, but I will tell all I remember. Rahula, what is Ananda like? I feel a little nervous."

"Don't worry. He's very kind and friendly. I told him about you and your family, and he was delighted. Shall we meet in this spot tomorrow morning when we go begging for food? Now I must wash my robe so it will be dry in time."

As Rahula stood to leave, Svasti tugged lightly at his robe, "Can you sit for just a while longer? There are some things I want to ask you. This morning the Buddha spoke about eleven points a bhikkhu must follow, but I can't recall all eleven. Can you repeat them for me?"

"I can only remember nine myself. But don't worry, tomorrow we can ask Ananda."

"Are you sure the elder Ananda will remember all of them?"

"Positive! If it had been one hundred eleven, Ananda would still remember. You don't know Ananda yet, but everyone here admires his memory. It's incredible. He can repeat flawlessly everything the Buddha has said without leaving out even one tiny detail. Around here, everyone calls him the most learned of all the Buddha's disciples. So whenever someone forgets something the Buddha has said, they seek out Ananda. Sometimes the community organizes study sessions in which Ananda goes over the Buddha's basic teachings."

"Then we're very lucky. We'll wait and ask him tomorrow. But there is something else I want to ask you—how do you quiet your mind during walking meditation?"

"Do you mean to say that during your walking meditation other thoughts came into your mind? Like thoughts of missing your family?"

Svasti grasped his friend's hand, "How did you know? That's exactly what happened! I don't know why I miss my family so much this evening. I feel terrible, but I don't seem to have enough resolve to practice the Way. I feel ashamed before you and the Buddha."

Rahula smiled. "Don't be ashamed. When I first joined the Buddha, I missed my mother, my grandfather, and my aunt. Many nights I buried my face in my cushion and cried alone. I knew that my mother, grandfather and aunt missed me, too. But after a while, it was better."

Rahula helped Svasti up to a standing position and gave him a friendly hug.

"Your brother and sisters are lovely. It's only natural for you to miss them. But you'll get used to your new life. We've got lots of work to do here—we must practice and study. But listen, when we get a chance, I'll tell you about my family, all right?"

Svasti held Rahula's hand in his own two hands and nodded. Then they parted, Rahula to wash his robe and Svasti to find a broom to sweep the paths clear of bamboo leaves.

Chapter Three
An Armful of Kusa Grass

Before falling asleep, Svasti sat beneath a bamboo tree and recalled the months he had first met the Buddha. He was just eleven years old then, and his mother had recently died, leaving him in charge of his three younger siblings. His youngest sister, an infant, had no milk to drink. Luckily, a man in the village named Rambhul hired Svasti to tend his water buffaloes—four grown buffaloes and one calf. And so Svasti was able to milk a buffalo cow everyday and feed his baby sister. He tended the water buffaloes with utmost care, for he knew that he had to keep his job or his siblings would starve. Since his father's death, their roof had not been rethatched, and every time it rained, Rupak had to scurry about placing stone jars beneath the gaping holes to catch the rainwater. Bala was only six years old but had to learn to cook, care for her baby sister, and gather firewood in the forest. Though just a small child, she could knead flour into chappati bread for her siblings to eat. Rarely could they buy even a bit of curry powder. When Svasti led the buffaloes back to their stable, the tantalizing fragrance of curry drifting from Rambhul's kitchen made his mouth water. Chappati dipped in curry sauce cooked with meat had been an unknown luxury since his father died. The children's clothes were little more than rags. Svasti owned but one worn dhoti. When it was cold he wrapped an old brown cloth around his shoulders. It was threadbare and faded, but precious to him, nonetheless.

Svasti had to find good grazing spots for the buffaloes, for if he returned them to their stable hungry, he knew he would be beaten by Mr. Rambhul. In addition, he had to carry home a sizable bundle of grass every evening for the buffaloes to eat throughout the night. On evenings when the mosquitoes were thick, Svasti lit a fire to chase them away with the smoke. Rambhul paid him in rice, flour, and salt every three days. Some days, Svasti was able to bring home a few fish that he had caught along the edges of the Neranjara River for Bhima to cook.

One afternoon, after he had bathed the buffaloes and cut a bushel of grass, Svasti felt like spending a quiet moment alone in the cool forest. Leaving the buffaloes grazing at the forest's edge, Svasti looked about for a tall tree to rest against. Suddenly he stopped. There was a man sitting silently beneath a pippala tree, no more than twenty feet away. Svasti gazed at him in wonder. He had never before seen anyone sit so beautifully. The man's back was perfectly straight, and his feet rested elegantly upon his thighs. He held himself with utmost stability and inner purpose. His eyes appeared to be half-closed, and his folded hands rested lightly on his lap. He wore a faded yellow robe which left one shoulder bare. His body radiated peace, serenity, and majesty. Just one look at him, and Svasti felt wondrously refreshed. His heart trembled. He did not understand how he could feel something so special for a person he hadn't even met, but he stood immobile in utter respect for a long moment.

Then the man opened his eyes. He did not see Svasti at first, as he uncrossed his legs and gently massaged his ankles and the soles of his feet. Slowly he stood up and began to walk. Because he walked in the opposite direction, he still did not see Svasti. Without making a sound, Svasti watched the man take slow, meditative steps along the forest floor. After seven or eight such steps, the man turned around, and it was then that he noticed Svasti.

He smiled at the boy. No one had ever smiled with such gentle tolerance at Svasti before. As though drawn by an invisible force, Svasti ran towards the man, but when he was within a few feet, he stopped in his tracks, remembering that he had no right to approach anyone of higher caste.

Svasti was an untouchable. He did not belong to any of the four social castes. His father had explained to him that the *brahmana* caste was the highest, and people born into this caste were priests and teachers who read and understood the *Vedas* and other scriptures and made offerings to the gods. When Brahma created the human race, the brahman issued from his mouth. The *kshatriya* were the next highest caste. They could hold political and military positions, as they had issued from Brahma's two hands. Those of the *vaishya* caste were merchants, farmers, and craftspeople who had sprung from Brahma's thighs. Those of the *shudra* caste had come from Brahma's feet and were the lowest of the four castes. They did only the manual labor not performed by the higher castes. But Svasti's family members were "untouchables," those who had no caste at all. They were required to build their homes outside of the village limits, and they did the lowest kinds of work such as collecting garbage, spreading manure, digging roads, feeding pigs, and tending water buffaloes. Everyone had to accept the caste into which he or she was born. The sacred scriptures taught that happiness was the ability to accept one's position.

If an untouchable like Svasti touched a person of a higher caste, he would be beaten. In the village of Uruvela, an untouchable man had been beaten severely for touching a brahman with his hand. A brahman or kshatriya touched by an untouchable was considered polluted and had to return home to fast and do penance for several weeks in order to cleanse himself. Whenever Svasti led the buffaloes home, he took great pains not to pass near any person of high caste on the road or outside Rambhul's house. It seemed to Svasti that even the buffaloes were more fortunate than he, because a brahman could touch a buffalo without being polluted. Even if, through no fault of the untouchable, a person of higher caste accidentally brushed against him, the untouchable could still be ruthlessly beaten.

Here, before Svasti, stood a most attractive man, and it was clear from his bearing that he did not share the same social status. Surely someone with so kind and tolerant a smile would not beat Svasti even if he did touch him, but Svasti did not want to be the cause of pollution of someone so special, and that was why he froze when he and the man were a few steps apart. Seeing Svasti's hesitation, the man stepped forward himself. Svasti stepped back to avoid coming in contact with the man, but the man was quicker, and in the blink of an eye had grasped Svasti by the shoulder with his left hand. With his right hand, he gave Svasti a tender pat on the head. Svasti stood motionless. No one had ever touched him on the head in so gentle and affectionate way, and yet he felt suddenly panic-stricken.

"Don't be afraid, child," the man said in a quiet and reassuring voice.

At the sound of that voice, Svasti's fears disappeared. He lifted his head and gazed at the man's kind and tolerant smile. After hesitating for a moment, he stammered, "Sir, I like you very much."

The man lifted Svasti's chin in his hand and looked into the boy's eyes. "And I like you also. Do you live nearby?"

Svasti did not answer. He took the man's left hand in his own two hands and asked the question that was troubling him, "When I touch you like this, aren't you being polluted?"

The man laughed and shook his head. "Not at all, child. You are a human being and I am a human being. You can't pollute me. Don't listen to what people tell you."

He took Svasti's hand and walked with him to the edge of the forest. The water buffaloes were still grazing peacefully. The man looked at Svasti and asked, "Do you tend these buffaloes? And that must be the grass you have cut for their dinner. What is your name? Is your house nearby?"

Svasti offered Siddhartha an armful of kusa grass to use as a cushion.

Svasti answered politely, "Yes, Sir, I care for these four buffaloes and that one calf, and that is the grass I cut. My name is Svasti and I live on the other side of the river just beyond the village of Uruvela. Please, Sir, what is your name and where do you live? Can you tell me?"

The man answered kindly, "Certainly. My name is Siddhartha, and my home is far away, but at present I am living in this forest."

"Are you a hermit?"

Siddhartha nodded. Svasti knew that hermits were men who usually lived and meditated up in the mountains.

Though they had just met and exchanged no more than a few words, Svasti felt a warm bond with his new friend. In Uruvela, no one had ever treated him in so friendly a way or spoken to him with such warmth. A great happiness surged within him, and he wanted to somehow express his joy. If only he had some gift he could offer Siddhartha! But there was no penny in his pocket, not even a piece of sugar cane or rock candy. What could he offer? He had nothing, but he summoned the courage to say,

"Mister, I wish I had something to give you as a gift, but I have nothing."

Siddhartha looked at Svasti and smiled. "But you do. You have something I would like very much."

"I do?"

Siddhartha pointed to the pile of kusa grass. "That grass you have cut for the buffaloes is soft and fragrant. If you could give me a few handfuls I shall make a sitting cushion for my meditation beneath the tree. That would make me very happy."

Svasti's eyes shone. He ran to the pile of grass, gathered a large bundle in his thin arms, and offered it to Siddhartha.

"I just cut this grass down by the river. Please accept it. I can easily cut more for the buffaloes."

Siddhartha placed his hands together like a lotus bud and accepted the gift. He said, "You are a very kind boy. I thank you. Go and cut some more grass for your buffaloes before it grows too late. If you have a chance, please come and see me tomorrow afternoon in the forest again."

Young Svasti bowed his head in farewell and stood watching as Siddhartha disappeared back into the forest. Then he picked up his sickle and headed for the shore, his heart filled with the warmest of feelings. It was early autumn. The kusa grass was still soft and his sickle was newly sharpened. It wasn't long at all before Svasti had cut another large armful of kusa grass.

Svasti led the buffaloes to Rambhul's home, guiding them to cross a shallow section of the Neranjara River. The calf was reluctant to leave the sweet grass along the shore and Svasti had to coax her along. The bushel of grass on his shoulder was not heavy and Svasti waded across the river together with the buffaloes.

Chapter Four

The Wounded Swan

Early the next morning, Svasti led his buffaloes to graze. By noon he had cut enough grass to fill two baskets. Svasti liked to let the buffaloes graze on the side of the river which bordered the forest. That way, when he finished gathering grass, he could stretch out in the cool breeze and not worry about the buffaloes wandering into someone's rice fields. He carried only his sickle, the tool by which he earned his living. Svasti opened the small fistful of rice Bala had wrapped in a banana leaf for his lunch, but as he was about to eat, his thoughts turned to Siddhartha.

"I could take this rice to the hermit, Siddhartha," he thought. "Surely he won't find my rice too humble." Svasti wrapped the rice, and, leaving the buffaloes at the forest's edge, followed the path to where he had met Siddhartha the day before.

From a distance he saw his new friend sitting beneath the great pippala tree. But Siddhartha was not alone. Before him sat a girl just about Svasti's age, dressed in a fine white sari. There was food already placed before him, and Svasti stopped abruptly. But Siddhartha looked up and called to him, "Svasti!" He motioned for the boy to join them.

The girl in the white sari looked up, and Svasti recognized her as someone he had often passed on the village road. As Svasti approached, she moved to her left to make a place for him, and Siddhartha gestured him to sit down. In front of Siddhartha was a banana leaf which held a fistful of rice and a small amount of sesame salt. Siddhartha divided the rice into two portions.

"Have you eaten yet, child?"

"No, Mister, I haven't."

"Well then, let's share this."

Siddhartha handed Svasti half the rice, and Svasti joined his palms together in thanks, but refused the rice. He took out his own humble rice and said, "I've also brought some."

He opened his banana leaf to reveal coarse grains of brown rice, unlike the soft white grains on Siddhartha's leaf. He had no sesame salt. Siddhartha smiled at the two children and said, "Shall we put all our rice together and share it?"

He took half the white rice, dipped it in sesame salt and handed it to Svasti. Then he broke off half of Svasti's rice ball and began to eat it with obvious delight. Svasti felt awkward, but seeing Siddhartha's naturalness, he began to eat as well.

"Your rice is so fragrant, Mister."

"Sujata brought it," answered Siddhartha.

"So her name is Sujata," thought Svasti. She looked a bit older than Svasti, perhaps a year or two. Her large black eyes twinkled. Svasti stopped eating and said, "I've seen you before on the village road, but I didn't know your name was Sujata."

"Yes, I am the daughter of the village chief of Uruvela. Your name is Svasti, isn't it? Teacher Siddhartha was just telling me about you," she said, adding gently, "Svasti, it is more correct to call a monk, 'Teacher,' than 'Mister.'"

Svasti nodded.

Siddhartha smiled. "Well then, I don't need to introduce you two. Do you know, children, why I eat in silence? These grains of rice and sesame are so precious, I like to eat silently so that I can appreciate them fully. Sujata, have you ever had a chance to taste brown rice? Even if you've already eaten, please taste a bit of Svasti's rice. It is quite delicious.

Siddhartha, Svasti, and Sujata shared a meal in mindfulness.

Now then, we can eat together in silence, and when we've finished, I'll tell you a story."

Siddhartha broke off a piece of brown rice and handed it to Sujata. She joined her palms like a lotus and respectfully accepted it. The three of them ate quietly in the deep calm of the forest.

When the rice and sesame were gone, Sujata gathered the banana leaves. She took a jug of fresh water from her side and poured some into the only cup she had brought. She lifted the cup to offer water to Siddhartha. He took it in his two hands and offered it to Svasti. Flustered, Svasti blurted, "Please, Mister, I mean, Teacher, please, you take the first drink."

Siddhartha answered in a soft voice, "You drink first, child. I want you to have the first drink." Again he lifted and offered the cup to Svasti.

Svasti felt confused but didn't know how to refuse such an unaccustomed honor. He joined his palms in thanks and took the cup. He drank all the water in one long gulp. He handed the cup back to Siddhartha. Siddhartha asked Sujata to pour a second cup. When it was full he raised it to his lips and sipped the water slowly, with reverence and deep enjoyment. Sujata's eyes did not stray from Siddhartha and Svasti during this exchange. When Siddhartha finished drinking, he asked Sujata to pour a third cup. This one he offered to her. She put down the water jug, joined her palms, and accepted the cup of water. She lifted it to her lips and drank in slow, small sips, just as Siddhartha had done. She was aware that this was the first time she had ever drunk from the same cup as an untouchable. But Siddhartha was her Teacher, and if he had done so, why shouldn't she? And she noticed that she had no feeling whatsoever of being polluted. Spontaneously, she reached out and touched the buffalo boy's hair. It was such a surprise, Svasti didn't have a moment to move out of the way. Then Sujata finished drinking her water. She placed the empty cup on the ground and smiled at her two companions.

Siddhartha nodded. "You children have understood. People are not born with caste. Everyone's tears are salty, and everyone's blood is red. It is wrong to divide people into castes and create division and prejudice among them. This has become very clear to me during my meditation."

Sujata looked thoughtful and she spoke, "We are your disciples and we believe your teaching. But there does not seem to be anyone else like you in this world. Everyone else believes that the sudras and the untouchables came forth from the Creator's feet. Even the scriptures say so. No one dares to think differently."

"Yes, I know. But the truth is the truth whether anyone believes it or not. Though a million people may believe a lie, it is still a lie. You must have great courage to live according to the truth. Let me tell you a story about when I was a boy.

"One day, when I was nine years old and strolling alone in the garden, a swan suddenly dropped from the sky and writhed on the ground in front of me in great pain. I ran to pick it up, and I discovered that an arrow had deeply penetrated one of its wings. I clasped my hand firmly around the arrow's shaft and yanked it out, and the bird cried as blood oozed from its wound. I applied pressure to the wound with my finger to stop the bleeding, and took the bird inside the palace to find princess Sundari, the lady in waiting. She agreed to pick a handful of medicinal leaves and make a poultice for the bird's wound. The swan shivered, so I took off my jacket and wrapped it around her. Then I placed her close to the royal fireplace."

Siddhartha paused for a moment to look at Svasti. "Svasti, I did not tell you yet, but when I was young I was a prince, the son of King Suddhodana in the city of Kapilavatthu. Sujata knows this already. I was about to go find some rice for the swan when my eight-year-old cousin, Devadatta, burst into the room. He was clutching his bow and arrows, and he asked excitedly, 'Siddhartha, did you see a white swan fall down near here?'

"Before I could answer, Devadatta saw the swan resting by the fireplace. He ran towards it, but I stopped him.

"'You may not take the bird.'

"My cousin protested, 'That bird is mine. I shot it myself.'

"I stood between Devadatta and the swan, determined not to let him have it. I told him, 'This bird is wounded. I'm protecting it. It needs to stay here.'

"Devadatta was quite stubborn and not about to give in. He argued, 'Now listen, cousin, when this bird was flying in the sky, it didn't belong to anyone. As I'm the one who shot it out of the sky, it rightfully belongs to me.'

"His argument sounded logical, but his words made me angry. I knew there was something wrong with his reasoning, but I couldn't quite put my finger on it. So I just stood there, speechless, becoming more upset. I felt like punching him. Why I didn't, I don't know. Then, I saw a way to answer him.

"'Listen, cousin,' I told him, 'Those who love each other live together, and those who are enemies live apart. You tried to kill the swan, so you and she are enemies. The bird cannot live with you. I saved her, bandaged her wound, warmed her, and was on my way to find food for her when you arrived. The bird and I love each other, and we can live together. The bird needs me, not you.'"

Sujata clapped her hands together, "That's right! You were right!"

Siddhartha looked at Svasti. "And what do you think, child, of my statement?"

Svasti thought for a moment and then answered slowly, "I think you were right. But not many people would agree. Most people would side with Devadatta."

Siddhartha nodded. "You are right. Most people do follow Devadatta's view.

"Let me tell you what happened next. As we couldn't agree on our own, we decided to take our concern to the adults. That day there was a meeting of the government in the palace, so we scurried to the hall of justice, where they were meeting. I held the swan and Devadatta clasped his bow and arrows. We presented our problem to the ministers and asked them to render judgment. The affairs of state came to a halt as the men listened, first to Devadatta and then to me. They discussed the matter at length, but they also were unable to agree. The majority seemed to be leaning towards Devadatta, when my father, the king, suddenly cleared his throat and coughed a few times. All the ministers suddenly stopped speaking, and—tell me if you don't think this is odd—with total accord, they agreed that my argument was correct and that the bird should be given to me. Devadatta was beside himself with anger, but of course, there was nothing he could do.

"I had the bird, but I wasn't really happy. Even though I was still young, I knew that my victory had been less than honorable. I was given the bird because the ministers wanted to please my father, not because they saw the truth of what I said."

"That's sad," Sujata said and frowned.

"Yes, it was. But turning my thoughts to the bird, I took comfort in the fact that she was safe. Otherwise she surely would have ended up in a cooking pot.

"In this world, few people look with the eyes of compassion, and so we are cruel and merciless toward each other. The weak are always oppressed by the strong. I still see that my reasoning that day was correct, for it arose from love and understanding. Love and understanding can ease the suffering of all beings. The truth is the truth, whether or not it is accepted by the majority. Therefore, I tell you children, it takes great courage to stand up for and protect what is right."

"What happened to the swan, Teacher?" asked Sujata.

"For four days, I cared for her. When I saw that her wound had healed, I released her, after warning her to fly far away lest she be shot again."

Siddhartha looked at the two children, their faces quiet and serious. "Sujata, you must return home before your mother begins to worry. Svasti, isn't it time for you to return to your buffaloes and cut more grass? The armful of kusa grass you gave me yesterday made a perfect cushion for meditation. Last night and this morning, I sat upon it and my meditation was very peaceful. I saw many things clearly. You have been a great help, Svasti. As my understanding deepens, I shall share the fruit of my meditation with both you children. Now I will continue sitting."

Svasti looked down at the grass which Siddhartha had shaped into a cushion. Though the grasses were packed firm, Svasti knew they were still fragrant and soft. He would bring his teacher a fresh armful of grass every three days to make a new cushion. Svasti stood up and, with Sujata, joined his palms and bowed to Siddhartha. Sujata set out for home and Svasti led his buffaloes to graze further along the riverbank.

Chapter Five
A Bowl of Milk

Every day Svasti went into the forest to visit Siddhartha. When he was able to cut two bundles of grass by midday, he had lunch with Siddhartha. But as the dry season continued and fresh grass became more and more scarce, it was often late afternoon before he could visit his friend and teacher. Sometimes when Svasti arrived, Siddhartha was sitting in meditation, and the boy sat silently for a brief moment, and then left the forest, not wanting to disturb his teacher's meditation. But when he found Siddhartha walking slowly along the forest path, he joined him, sometimes sharing simple conversation. Svasti also met Sujata frequently in the forest. Every day, she brought Siddhartha a rice ball with one condiment, such as sesame salt, peanuts, or a bit of curry. She also brought him milk or rice porridge or rock candy. The children had many occasions to talk with each other at the edge of the forest while the buffalo grazed. Sometimes Sujata brought her friend Supriya, a young girl Svasti's age. Svasti wanted to bring his brother and sisters to meet Siddhartha. He was sure they could cross the river at its most shallow point without difficulty.

Sujata told Svasti how she first met Siddhartha several months earlier, and how she had since brought him food every day around noon. It was on a full moon day. At her mother's request, she had put on a new pink sari and carried a platter of food to offer to the forest gods. There were cakes,

"Child, please pour me a little more milk."

milk, congee, and honey. The noon sun blazed. As Sujata neared the river, she saw a man lying unconscious on the road. She put down her platter and ran to him. He was barely breathing and his eyes were tightly closed. His cheeks had the sunken look of someone who had not had food for a long time. From his long hair, tangled beard, and ragged garment, Sujata knew he was a mountain ascetic who must have fainted from hunger. Without hesitating, she poured a cup of milk and eased it against the man's lips, spilling a few drops on them. At first he did not respond, but then his lips quivered and parted slightly. Sujata slowly poured milk into his mouth. He began to drink and before long the cup was empty.

Sujata then sat along the riverbank to see if the man would regain consciousness. Slowly he sat up and opened his eyes. Seeing Sujata, he smiled. He pulled the end of his garment back up over his shoulder and folded his legs in a lotus position. He began to breathe, first shallowly and then more deeply. His sitting was stable and beautiful. Thinking that he must be a mountain god, Sujata joined her palms and began to prostrate herself before him, but the man motioned for her to stop. Sujata sat up, and the man spoke to her in a soft voice, "Child, please pour me a little more milk."

Happy to hear him speak, Sujata poured another cup and he drank it all. He felt how truly nourishing it was. Less than an hour before, he thought he was about to breathe his last. Now his eyes shone and he smiled gently. Sujata asked him how he had fainted on the road.

"I have been practicing meditation in the mountains. Harsh ascetic discipline has left my body weak, so today I decided to walk down to the village to beg for some food. But I lost all my strength getting here. Thanks to you, my life has been saved."

They sat along the riverbank together and the man told Sujata about himself. He was Siddhartha, the son of a king who reigned over the country of the Sakya clan. Sujata listened carefully as Siddhartha told her, "I have seen that abusing the body cannot help one to find peace or understanding. The body is not just an instrument. It is the temple of the spirit, the raft by which we cross to the other shore. I will no longer practice self-mortification. I will go into the village each morning to beg for food."

Sujata joined her palms. "Honorable hermit, if you allow me, I will bring you food each day. There is no need for you to interrupt your meditation practice. My home is not far from here, and I know my parents would be happy for me to bring you your meal."

Siddhartha was silent for a moment. Then he answered, "I am glad to accept your offer. But from time to time, I would also like to go into the village to beg in order to meet the villagers. I would like to meet your parents and other children in the village as well."

Sujata was very happy. She joined her palms and bowed in gratitude. The thought of Siddhartha visiting her home and meeting her parents was wonderful. She knew, too, that bringing him food every day would be no hardship, as her family was one of the wealthiest in the village. She did not mention this to Siddhartha. She only understood that this monk was important and that offering food to him was more beneficial than making a dozen offerings to the forest gods. If Siddhartha's meditation deepened, she felt, his love and understanding could help relieve much suffering in the world.

Siddhartha pointed out the Dangsiri mountain where he had lived in the caves. "Beginning today, I will not return there. This forest is cool and refreshing. There is a magnificent pippala tree which I shall make the place of my practice. Tomorrow when you come with the food offering, please bring it there. Come, I will show you the spot."

Siddhartha led Sujata across the river into the cool forest that bordered the other bank of the Neranjara River. He showed her the pippala tree under which he would meditate. Sujata admired its massive trunk and raised her head to gaze at the leafy branches which spread out like an enormous canopy. It was a kind of banyan tree with leaves shaped like hearts with long pointed tails. The leaves were as big as Sujata's hand. She listened to the birds chirping happily among the branches. It was a truly peaceful and refreshing spot. In fact, she had been to this tree before with her parents to make food offerings to the forest gods.

"This is your new home, Teacher." Sujata looked at Siddhartha with her round black eyes. "I will visit you here every day."

Siddhartha nodded. He walked Sujata back out of the forest and said goodbye to her at the riverbank. Then he returned alone to the pippala tree.

From that day on, Sujata brought rice or chappatis to offer to the monk, just before the sun began to cast shadows. Sometimes she also brought milk or congee. Once in a while, Siddhartha would carry his begging bowl into the village. He met Sujata's father, the village chief, and her mother, who was wearing a beautiful yellow sari. Sujata introduced him to other children in the village and took him to the barber so he could have his head and beard shaved. Siddhartha's health recovered rapidly, and he told Sujata that his meditation practice was beginning to bear fruit. Then came the day that Sujata met Svasti.

That day Sujata had come early. She listened as Siddhartha told her about meeting Svasti the day before. She had just said that she wished to meet Svasti herself when he appeared. Afterward, whenever she met Svasti, she never forgot to ask about his family. She and her servant, Purna, even went to visit Svasti's hut. Purna was hired to work in Sujata's household when her predecessor, Radha, died of typhoid fever. On these visits, Sujata brought used clothes still full of good wear for Svasti's family to use. And much to Purna's surprise, Sujata lifted baby Bhima in her arms. Afterwards, she cautioned Purna not to tell her parents that she had held an untouchable child.

One day, a number of children decided to go and visit Siddhartha together. All of Svasti's family came. Sujata brought her girlfriends Balagupta, Vijayasena, Ulluvillike, and Jatilika. She also invited her sixteen-year-old cousin Nandabala, who brought her younger brothers Nalaka, who was fourteen, and Subash, who was nine. Eleven children sat in a semi-circle around Siddhartha, and they ate lunch together in silence. Svasti had instructed Bala and Rupak beforehand how to eat with quiet dignity. Even baby Bhima, sitting on Svasti's lap, ate without making a sound, her eyes open wide.

Svasti brought a new armful of fresh grass for Siddhartha. He had asked his friend Gavampati, also a buffalo boy, to watch over Mr. Rambhul's buffaloes so that he could have lunch with Siddhartha. In the fields, the sun blazed, but within the forest, Siddhartha and the children were refreshed by the cool shade of the pippala tree. Its leafy branches extended over an area wider than a dozen houses. The children shared their food with one another, and Rupak and Bala especially enjoyed chappati with curry and fragrant white rice dipped in peanuts and sesame salt. Sujata and Balagupta brought enough water for everyone to drink. Svasti's heart overflowed with happiness. The atmosphere was still and quiet, yet alive with the greatest joy. On that day, at Sujata's request, Siddhartha told them the story of his life. The children listened enraptured from beginning to end.

Chapter Six
Beneath a Rose-Apple Tree

W hen he was nine years old, Siddhartha was told about the dream his mother had before giving birth to him. A magnificent white elephant with six tusks descended from the heavens surrounded by a chorus of beatific praises. The elephant approached her, its skin white as mountain snow. It held a brilliant pink lotus flower in its trunk, and placed the flower within the queen's body. Then the elephant, too, entered her effortlessly, and all at once she was filled with deep ease and joy. She had the feeling she would never again know any suffering, worry, or pain, and she awoke uplifted by a sensation of pure bliss. When she got up from her bed, the ethereal music from the dream still echoed in her ears. She told her husband, the king, of the dream, and he, too, marvelled at it. That morning, the king summoned all the holy men in the capital to come and divine the meaning of the queen's dream.

After listening intently to the dream's content, they responded, "Your majesty, the queen will give birth to a son who will be a great leader. He is destined to become either a mighty emperor who rules throughout the four directions, or a great Teacher who will show the Way of Truth to all beings in Heaven and Earth. Our land, your majesty, has long awaited the appearance of such a Great One."

King Suddhodana beamed. After consulting the queen, he ordered that provisions from the royal storehouses be distributed to the ill and unfortunate throughout the land. Thus the citizens of the kingdom of Sakya shared the king and queen's joy over the news of their future son.

Siddhartha's mother was named Mahamaya. A woman of great virtue, her love extended to all beings—people, animals, and plants. It was the custom in those days for a woman to return to her parents' home to give birth there. Mahamaya was from the country of Koliya, so she set out for Ramagama, the capital of Koliya. Along the way, she stopped to rest in the garden of Lumbini. The forest there was filled with flowers and singing birds. Peacocks fanned their splendid tails in the morning light. Admiring an ashok tree in full bloom, the queen walked towards it, when suddenly, feeling unsteady, she grabbed a branch of the ashok tree to support her. Just a moment later, still holding the branch, Queen Mahamaya gave birth to a radiant son.

The prince was bathed in fresh water and wrapped in yellow silk by Mahamaya's attendants. As there was no longer any need to return to Ramagama, the queen and the newborn prince were carried home in their four-horse carriage. When they arrived home, the prince was again bathed in warm water and placed next to his mother.

Hearing the news, King Suddhodana hurried in to see his wife and son. His joy was boundless. His eyes sparkled and he named the prince "Siddhartha," "the one who accomplishes his aim." Everyone in the palace rejoiced, and one by one they came to offer their congratulations to the queen. King Suddhodana wasted no time in summoning the soothsayers to tell him of Siddhartha's future. After examining the baby's features, they all agreed that the boy bore the marks of a great leader and would no doubt rule over a mighty kingdom that spread in all four directions.

One week later a holy man named Asita Kaladevala paid a visit to the palace. His back was bent with age, and he needed a cane to descend the mountain where he lived. When the palace guards announced Master Asita's arrival, King Suddhodana personally came out to greet him. He ushered

King Suddhodhana's joy was boundless, as he hurried in to see his wife and newborn son.

him in to see the baby prince. The holy man gazed at the prince for a long time without uttering a word. Then he began to weep, his trembling body supported by his cane. Streams of tears fell from his eyes.

King Suddhodana grew alarmed and asked, "What is it? Do you forebode some misfortune for the child?"

Master Asita wiped the tears with his hands and shook his head. "Your majesty, I see no misfortune at all. I weep for myself, for I can clearly see that this child possesses true greatness. He will penetrate all the mysteries of the universe. Your majesty, your son will not be a politician. He will be a great Master of the Way. Heaven and Earth will be his home and all beings his relations. I weep because I will pass away before I have a chance to hear his voice proclaim the truths he will realize. Majesty, you and your country possess great merit to have given birth to such a one as this boy."

Asita turned to leave. The king pleaded for him to stay, but it was of no use. The old man began walking back to his mountain. Master Asita's visit sent the king into a frenzy. He did not want his son to become a monk. He wanted him to assume his throne and extend the borders of their kingdom. The king thought, "Asita is only one among hundreds, even thousands of holy men. Perhaps his prophecy is mistaken. Surely the other holy men who said Siddhartha would become a great emperor were correct." Clinging to this hope, the king was comforted.

After having attained sublime joy giving birth to Siddhartha, Queen Mahamaya died eight days later, and all the kingdom mourned her. King Suddhodana summoned her sister Mahapajapati, and asked her to become the new queen. Mahapajapati, also known as Gotami, agreed, and she cared for Siddhartha as if he were her own son. As the boy grew older and asked about his real mother, he understood how much Gotami had loved her sister and how she more than anyone else in the world could love him as much as his own mother. Under Gotami's care, Siddhartha grew strong and healthy.

One day, as Gotami watched Siddhartha play in the garden, she realized he was old enough to learn the graces of wearing gold and precious gems. She instructed her attendants to bring forth precious jewels to try on Siddhartha, but to her surprise, none rendered Siddhartha more handsome than he already was. As Siddhartha expressed discomfort at wearing such things, Gotami ordered the jewels to be returned to their cases.

When Siddhartha reached school age, he studied literature, writing, music, and athletics with the other princes of the Sakya dynasty. Among his schoolmates were his cousins Devadatta and Kimbila and the son of a palace dignitary, a boy named Kaludayi. Naturally intelligent, Siddhartha mastered his lessons quickly. His teacher Vishvamitra found the young Devadatta a sharp student, but never in his teaching career had he taught a student more impressive than Siddhartha.

One day when he was nine years old, Siddhartha and his schoolmates were allowed to attend the ritual first plowing of the fields. Gotami herself dressed Siddhartha right down to the fine slippers on his feet. Attired in his royal best, King Suddhodana presided over the ceremonies. High ranking holy men and brahmans paraded in robes and headdresses of every color imaginable. The ceremony was held next to the finest fields in the kingdom, not far from the palace itself. Flags and banners waved from every gate and along every roadside. Colorful displays of food and drink were laid out on altars crowded along the roads. Minstrels and musicians strolled among the throngs of people, adding mirth and merriment to the bustling festivities. Holy men chanted with utmost solemnity as Siddhartha's father and all the dignitaries of the court stood facing the unfolding ritual. Siddhartha stood towards the back with Devadatta and Kaludayi at his sides. The boys were excited because they had been told that when the rituals were over, everyone would enjoy a feast spread out on the grassy meadow. Siddhartha did not often go on picnics, and he was delighted. But the holy men's chanting went on and on for what seemed like forever, and the young boys grew restless. Unable to endure any more, they wandered off. Kaludayi held onto Siddhartha's sleeve, and off they went in the direction of the music and dancing. The hot sun blazed and the performers' costumes grew wet with perspiration. Beads of sweat shone on the dancing girls' foreheads. After running about among the scenes of entertainment, Siddhartha, too, grew hot and he left his friends to seek the shade of the rose-apple tree alongside the road. Beneath the cool branches, Siddhartha felt pleasantly refreshed. At that moment, Gotami appeared and, spotting her son, she said, "I've been looking all over for you. Where have you been? You should return now for the conclusion of the ceremony. It would please your father."

"Mother, the ceremony is too long. Why must the holy men chant so long?"

"They are reciting the *Vedas,* my child. The scriptures have a profound meaning, handed down by the Creator Himself to the brahmans countless generations ago. You will study them soon."

"Why doesn't Father recite the scriptures instead of having the brahmans do it?"

"Only those born into the brahmana caste are permitted to recite the scriptures, my child. Even kings who wield great power must depend on the services of the brahmans for priestly duties."

Siddhartha thought over Gotami's words. After a long pause, he joined his palms and entreated her, "Please, Mother, ask Father if I may stay here. I feel so happy sitting beneath this rose-apple tree."

Giving in good-naturedly to her child, Gotami smiled and nodded. She stroked his hair, and then returned down the path.

At last the brahmans concluded their prayers. King Suddhodana stepped down into the fields and, together with two military officers, began to plow the first row of the season, as cheers resounded among the crowd. Then the farmers followed the king's example and began to plow their fields. Hearing the people's cheers, Siddhartha ran to the edge of the fields. He watched a water buffalo straining to pull a heavy plow, followed by a robust farmer whose skin was bronzed from long work in the sun. The farmer's left hand steadied the plow while his right hand wielded a whip to urge the buffalo on. Sun blazed and the man's sweat poured in streams from his body. The rich earth was divided into two neat furrows. As the plow turned the earth, Siddhartha noticed that the bodies of worms and other small creatures were being cut as well. As the worms writhed upon the ground, they were spotted by birds who flew down and grabbed them in their beaks. Then Siddhartha saw a large bird swoop down and grasp a small bird in its talons.

Utterly absorbed in these events, standing beneath the burning sun, Siddhartha, too, became drenched in sweat. He ran back to the shade of the rose-apple tree. He had just witnessed so many things strange and unknown to him. He sat cross-legged and closed his eyes to reflect on all he had seen. Composed and erect, he sat for a long time, oblivious to all the singing, dancing, and picnicking taking place around him. Siddhartha continued to sit, absorbed by the images of the field and the many creatures. When the king and queen passed by sometime later, they discovered Siddhartha still sitting in deep concentration. Gotami was moved to tears seeing how beautiful Siddhartha looked, like a small, still statue. But King Suddhodana was seized with sudden apprehension. If Siddhartha could sit so solemnly at such a young age, might not the holy man Asita's prophecy come true? Too disturbed to remain for the picnic, the king returned alone to the palace in his royal carriage.

Some poor, country children passed by the tree speaking and laughing happily. Gotami motioned them to be quiet. She pointed to Siddhartha sitting beneath the rose-apple tree. Curious, the children stared at him. Suddenly, Siddhartha opened his eyes. Seeing the queen, he smiled.

"Mother," he said, "reciting the scriptures does nothing to help the worms and the birds."

Siddhartha stood up and ran to Gotami and clasped her hand. He then noticed the children observing him. They were about his own age, but their clothes were tattered, their faces soiled, and their arms and legs piteously thin. Aware of his princely attire, Siddhartha felt embarrassed, and yet he wanted very much to play with them. He smiled and hesitantly waved, and one boy smiled back. That was all the encouragement Siddhartha needed. He asked Gotami for permission to invite the children to the picnic feast. At first she hesitated, but then she nodded in assent.

Chapter Seven
White Elephant Prize

When Siddhartha was fourteen years old, Queen Gotami gave birth to a son, Nanda. All the palace rejoiced, including Siddhartha, who was very happy to have a younger brother. Every day after his studies, he ran home to visit Nanda. Although Siddhartha was already of an age to be concerned with other matters, he often took little Nanda on walks, accompanied by Devadatta.

Siddhartha had three other cousins that he liked very much, named Mahanama, Baddhiya, and Kimbila. He often invited them to play with him in the flower gardens behind the palace. Queen Gotami enjoyed watching them play as she sat on the wooden bench beside the lotus pond. Her attendant was always ready to respond to her requests to bring drinks and snacks for the children.

With each passing year, Siddhartha grew ever more adept in his studies and Devadatta had a hard time concealing his jealousy. Siddhartha mastered every subject with ease, including the martial arts. Although Devadatta was stronger, Siddhartha was more agile and alert. In math, the other boys yielded to Siddhartha's brilliance. Arjuna, his math teacher, spent hours answering Siddhartha's advanced questions.

Siddhartha was especially gifted in music. His music teacher gave him a rare and precious flute and on summer evenings Siddhartha would sit alone in the garden and play his new instrument. Sometimes his songs were sweet and soft, while other times the sound was so sublime that listeners felt as though they were being carried high above the clouds. Gotami often sat outside as the evening shadows fell in order to listen to her son's music. She experienced deep contentment as she allowed her heart to drift with the sound of Siddhartha's flute.

As befitted his age, Siddhartha concentrated more intensely in his religious and philosophical studies. He was instructed in all the *Vedas*, and he pondered the meanings of the teachings and beliefs they expounded. He devoted special study to the *Rigveda* and *Atharveda* scriptures. From the time he was very small, Siddhartha had seen the brahmans recite scriptures and perform rituals. Now he himself began to penetrate the subject matter contained in these sacred teachings. Great importance was given to the sacred writings of Brahmanism. The words and the sounds themselves were seen to hold great power which could influence and even change the affairs of people and the natural world. The positions of the stars and the unfolding of the seasons were intimately connected to prayers and ritual offerings. The brahmans were regarded as the only ones capable of understanding the hidden mysteries of heaven and earth. They alone could use prayer and ritual to bring proper order to the realms of humans and the natural world.

Siddhartha was taught that the cosmos emanated from a Supreme Being known as Purusha or Brahman, and that all castes in society had issued from various parts of the Creator's body. Every person contained part of the essence of the transcendental Creator and that universal essence comprised a person's basic nature or soul.

Siddhartha devoted serious study, as well, to all the other brahmana texts, including the *Brahmanas* and the *Upanishads*. His teachers wanted only to instruct their charges in the traditional beliefs, but Siddhartha and his companions insisted on asking questions that forced their teachers to address contemporary ideas that did not always seem to accord with tradition.

On the days the boys were off from school, Siddhartha persuaded them to visit and discuss these matters with well-known priests and brahmans in the capital. Thanks to these encounters, Siddhartha learned that there were a number of movements in the country which openly challenged the absolute authority of the brahmans. Members of these movements were not only discontented laymen who wished to share some of the power that had long belonged exclusively to the brahmana caste, but they included reform-minded members of the brahmana caste as well.

Since the day young Siddhartha had been given permission to invite a few poor country children to his royal picnic, he had also been allowed to visit from time to time the small villages that surrounded the capital. On these occasions, he was always careful to wear only simple garments. By speaking directly with the people, Siddhartha learned many things that he had never been exposed to in the palace. He was aware, of course, that the people served and worshipped the three deities of Brahmanism—Brahman, Vishnu, and Shiva. But he also learned that they were manipulated and oppressed by the brahmana priests. In order to have the proper rituals for births, marriages, and funerals, families were forced to pay the brahmans in food, money, and physical labor, regardless of how impoverished they were.

One day while passing a straw hut, Siddhartha was startled by mournful cries from within. He asked Devadatta to enter and inquire what was the matter. They learned that the head of the household had recently died. The family was wretchedly poor. The wife and children were piteously thin and dressed in tattered rags. Their house was on the verge of collapse. Siddhartha learned that the husband had desired the services of a brahman to purify the earth before rebuilding their kitchen, but before providing these services, the brahman demanded the man work for him. Throughout several days the brahman had ordered him to haul large rocks and chop wood. During this time the man became ill and the brahman permitted him to return home, but halfway home, the man collapsed on the road and died.

As a result of his own reflections, Siddhartha began to question some of the fundamental teachings of Brahmanism: why had the *Vedas* been given exclusively to the brahmana caste, why was Brahman the Supreme Ruler of the universe, and what was the omnipotent power that prayers and rituals possessed. Siddhartha sympathized with those priests and brahmans who dared to directly challenge these dogmas. His interest never waned, and Siddhartha never missed a class or discussion on the *Vedas*. He also pursued the studies of language and history.

Siddhartha liked very much to meet and have discussions with hermits and monks, but as his father disapproved, he had to find excuses to go on other excursions in the hope of encountering such men. These monks cared nothing for material possessions and social status, unlike the brahmans who openly vied for power. Rather, these monks abandoned everything in order to seek liberation and to cut the ties that bound them to the sorrows and worries of the world. They were men who had studied and penetrated the meaning of the *Vedas* and the *Upanishads*. Siddhartha knew that many such hermits lived in Kosala, the neighboring kingdom to the west, and in Magadha which lay to the south. Siddhartha hoped that one day he would have a chance to visit these regions and study seriously with men such as these.

Of course, King Suddhodana was aware of Siddhartha's aspirations. He dreaded that his son might one day leave the palace and become a monk, and he confided his worries to his younger brother, Dronodanaraja, the father of Devadatta and Ananda.

"The country of Kosala has long had its eye on our territory. We must count on the talents of our young people, such as Siddhartha and Devadatta, to protect the destiny of our country. I greatly fear Siddhartha may decide to become a monk, as the Master Asita Kaladevala predicted. If this comes to pass, it is likely that Devadatta will follow in Siddhartha's footsteps. Do you know how much they like to go out and meet with these hermits?"

Dronodanaraja was taken aback by the king's words. After pondering a moment, he whispered in the king's ear, "If you ask me, I think you should find a wife for Siddhartha. Once he has a family to occupy him, he will abandon this desire to become a monk." King Suddhodana nodded.

That night he confided his concerns to Gotami, who promised she would arrange for Siddhartha to marry in the near future. Even though she had just recently given birth to a girl, a princess named Sundari Nanda, soon after, she began to organize a number of gatherings for the young people in the kingdom. Siddhartha joined these evenings of music, athletic events, and field trips with enthusiasm. He made many new friends, both young men and young women.

King Suddhodana had a younger sister named Pamita whose husband was King Dandapani of Koliya. The couple kept residences in both Ramagama, the capital of Koliya, and in Kapilavatthu. Sakya and Koliya were separated only by the Rohini River and their peoples had been close for many generations. Their capitals were but a day's journey apart. At Gotami's request, the king and queen of Koliya agreed to organize a martial arts competition on the large field that bordered Kunau Lake. King Suddhodana person-ally presided over the event to encourage the young people of his kingdom to develop their strength and increase their fighting skills. All the young people of the capital were in-vited to attend, girls as well as boys. The young women did not engage in the athletic contests but encouraged the young men with their praise and applause. Yasodhara, the daugh-ter of Queen Pamita and King Dandapani, was responsible for welcoming all the guests. She was a lovely and charming young woman, her beauty natural and fresh.

Siddhartha placed number one in all the events, including archery, swordsmanship, horse racing, and weightlifting, and it was Yasodhara who presented him with his prize, a

Siddhartha placed number one in all the events. Yasodhara presented him with his prize, a white elephant.

white elephant. With her palms joined and her head slightly bowed, in a voice noble and serene, she declared, "Please accept this elephant, Prince Siddhartha, for your well deserved victory. And please accept my heartfelt congratulations."

The princess' movements were graceful and unaffected, and her manner of dress elegant and refined. Her smile was as fresh as a half-opened lotus. Siddhartha bowed and looked into her eyes, saying in a quiet voice, "Thank you, princess."

Devadatta stood behind Siddhartha, unhappy to have won only second place. Upset that Yasodhara had not even noticed him, he grabbed the elephant's trunk and viciously struck it in a sensitive spot. Overcome with pain, the elephant dropped to its knees.

Siddhartha looked severely at Devadatta, "Cousin, that was outrageous."

Siddhartha rubbed the tender place on the elephant's trunk and spoke soothingly to it. Gradually the elephant stood up again and bowed its head in respect to the prince. The spectators applauded loudly. Siddhartha climbed upon the elephant's back and the victory procession began. Under the guidance of its trainer, the white elephant carried Siddhartha around the capital of Kapilavatthu, and the people cheered. Yasodhara walked beside them with slow, graceful steps.

Chapter Eight
The Jewelled Necklace

As he grew into his teens, Siddhartha came to find palace life stifling, so he began making excursions beyond the city limits to see what life was like outside. He was always accompanied by Channa, his faithful attendant, and sometimes also by his friends or brothers. Channa was responsible for Siddhartha's horse carriage, and he and Siddhartha took turns holding the reins. As Siddhartha never used a whip, Channa did not either.

Siddhartha visited every corner of the Sakya kingdom, from the rugged foothills of the Himalayan mountains in the north to the great southern plains. The capital, Kapilavatthu, was located in the richest, most populated region of the lowlands. Compared with the neighboring kingdoms of Kosala and Magadha, Sakya was quite small, but what it lacked in area it more than made up in its ideal location. The Rohini and Banganga Rivers which began in the highlands, flowed down to irrigate its rich plains. They continued southwards and joined the Hiranyavati River before emptying into the Ganga. Siddhartha loved to sit on the banks of the Banganga and watch the water rush by.

The local villagers believed that the waters of the Banganga could wash away one's bad karma, from both present and past lives, and so they often submerged themselves in the water, even at near freezing temperatures. One day, while sitting along the riverbank with his attendant, Siddhartha asked, "Channa, do you believe this river can wash away bad karma?"

"It must, your highness, otherwise why would so many people come here to wash themselves?"

Siddhartha smiled. "Well then, the shrimp, fish, and oysters who spend their entire lives in these waters must be the purest and most virtuous beings of all!"

Channa replied, "Well, at least I can say that bathing in this river will wash away the dirt and dust from one's body!"

Siddhartha laughed and patted Channa on the shoulder. "With that, I certainly agree."

On another day, as he was returning to the palace, Siddhartha was surprised to see Yasodhara in a small, poor village, with one of her maid servants, tending to the village children who were suffering from eye diseases, influenza, skin disorders, and other ailments. Yasodhara was dressed simply, yet she appeared to be as a goddess who had appeared among the poor. Siddhartha was deeply moved to see the daughter of a royal family placing her own comfort aside so that she could care for the destitute. She rinsed their infected eyes and skin, dispensed medicine, and washed their soiled clothes.

"Princess, how long have you been doing this?" asked Siddhartha. "It is beautiful to see you here."

Yasodhara looked up from washing a little girl's arm. "For almost two years, your highness. But this is only the second time I have been in this village."

"I often stop here. The children know me well. Your work must give you a great feeling of satisfaction, princess."

Yasodhara smiled without answering. She bent over to continue washing the girl's arm.

That day, Siddhartha had a chance to speak with Yasodhara for a longer time. He was surprised to learn that she shared many of his own ideas. Yasodhara was not content to remain in her lady's quarters blindly obeying tradition. She, too, had studied the *Vedas* and secretly opposed society's in-

Siddhartha was deeply moved to see Yasodhara caring for the destitute child.

justices. And like Siddhartha, she did not feel truly happy being a privileged member of a wealthy, royal family. She loathed the power struggles among the courtiers and even among the brahmans. She knew that as a woman she could not effect great social change, so she found ways to express her convictions through charitable work. She hoped that her friends might see the value of this through her example.

Since the day he first saw her, Siddhartha had felt a special affinity for Yasodhara. Now he found himself drawn to every word she spoke. His father had expressed a desire that he marry soon. Perhaps Yasodhara was the right woman. During the musical and athletic gatherings, Siddhartha had met many charming young women, but Yasodhara was not only the most beautiful, she was the one with whom he felt ease and contentment.

One day, Queen Gotami decided to organize a reception for all the young women of the capital. She asked Pamita, Yasodhara's mother, to help with the preparations. The young women of Kapilavatthu were invited, and each was to be presented with fine jewelry. Queen Pamita suggested that Siddhartha himself present each gift, much in the same spirit that Yasodhara had welcomed the guests that attended the martial arts contest. King Suddhodana and the members of the royal family would be present.

The party took place on a delightfully cool evening. Food and drinks were set out throughout the palace halls, while musicians entertained the guests. Beneath the bright, flickering lights of flowered lanterns, graceful young women arrived, wearing colorful saris shimmering with gold thread. One by one they passed before the royal dignitaries, including the king and queen. Siddhartha, dressed in princely garb, stood to the left behind a table covered with pearl necklaces and gold and precious gems to present to nearly a thousand young ladies.

At first Siddhartha had refused to present the gifts personally, but Gotami and Pamita had beseeched him. "It would be a great honor and happiness for any person to receive a gift directly from you. You should understand that," said Pamita with a convincing smile. Siddhartha did not want to refuse to provide happiness to others, and so he complied. But now, standing before the thousands of guests, Siddhartha did not know how he could possibly choose a fitting gift for each lady. Every young woman passed in full view of all the guests before approaching Siddhartha. The first young woman to be presented was Soma, daughter of a prince. As instructed by Pamita, she mounted the stairs of the royal dais, stopped to bow to the king and queen and all the distinguished guests, and then walked slowly towards Siddhartha. When she reached him, she bowed her head, and Siddhartha bowed in return. Then he offered her a strand of jade beads. The guests applauded their approval, and Soma bowed. She spoke her thanks so softly that Siddhartha could not understand her words.

The next woman was Rohini, named after the river. Siddhartha did not try to distinguish among the young women by selecting different jewels to match their particular grace and beauty. He picked up whichever ornament was next on the table and offered it to the next young woman. Thus the presentation of gifts proceeded quickly even though there were so many young women. By ten at night, most of the jewelry had been given away. Everyone believed a young woman named Sela was the last in line. But just as Siddhartha thought he had completed his task, another young woman appeared from the audience and slowly made her way to the dais. It was Yasodhara. She was dressed in an ivory colored sari as simple and light as a cool morning breeze. She bowed to the king and queen. Ever graceful and natural, she approached Siddhartha, smiled, and asked, "Does your highness have anything left for me?"

Siddhartha looked at Yasodhara and then confusedly at the ornaments remaining on the table. He appeared flustered—there was nothing on the table worthy of Yasodhara's beauty. Suddenly he smiled. He removed the necklace around his own neck and held it out to Yasodhara. "This is my gift to you, princess."

Yasodhara shook her head. "I came here to honor you. How can I take away your own necklace?"

Siddhartha answered, "My mother, Queen Gotami, often says that I look better without jewelry. Please, princess, accept this gift."

He motioned her to step closer so that he could place the shining beads around her neck. The guests burst into applause, and it seemed as if the cheers would never end. They all rose to their feet to express their joyous approval.

Chapter Nine

The Path of Compassion

Siddhartha and Yasodhara's wedding took place the following autumn. It was an occasion of great joy and celebration
for the entire kingdom. The capital, Kapilavatthu, was
decked with flags, lanterns, and flowers, and there was music
everywhere. Wherever Siddhartha and Yasodhara went in
their carriage, they were greeted with resounding cheers.
They also visited outlying hamlets and villages, bringing
gifts of food and clothing to many poor families.

King Suddhodana supervised the building of three palaces
for the young couple, one for each season. The summer palace
was built on a beautiful hillside in the highlands, while the
rainy season and winter palaces were in the capital city.
Each palace had lotus pools, some for pale blue lotuses, some
for pink, and some for white. The couple's fine garments and
slippers, and the fragrant sandalwood they lit every day,
were ordered specially from Varanasi, the capital of the
Kasi kingdom to the southwest.

King Suddhodana was at peace, now that Siddhartha had
followed the path he had wished his son to follow. He personally selected the finest musicians and dancers in the kingdom to provide continual and pleasant entertainment for his
young son and daughter-in-law.

But happiness for Siddhartha and Yasodhara was not to
be found in a pampered life of wealth and status. Their happiness came from opening their hearts and sharing their

Siddhartha and Yasodhara's wedding was an occasion of great joy and celebration for the entire kingdom.

deepest thoughts with each other. They weren't moved by exquisite and savory foods or fancy silken clothes. While they could appreciate the artistry of the dancers and musicians, they were not carried away by the pleasures they offered. They had their own dreams—to find answers concerning the spiritual quest and the renewal of society.

The following summer, as they were driven to their summer palace by faithful Channa, Siddhartha's boyhood attendant, Siddhartha introduced Yasodhara to places throughout the kingdom she did not yet know. They stayed several days at each location, sometimes spending the night in the homes of country folk, sharing their simple foods and sleeping upon their woven string beds. They learned a great deal about the way of life and the customs of each place they visited.

At times they encountered terrible misery. They met families with nine or ten children, every child racked with disease. No matter how hard the parents toiled day and night, they could not earn enough to support so many children. Hardship went hand in hand with the life of the peasants. Siddhartha gazed at children with arms and legs as thin as matchsticks and bellies swollen from worms and malnutrition. He saw the handicapped and infirm forced to beg in the streets, and these scenes robbed him of any happiness. He saw people caught in inescapable conditions. In addition to poverty and disease, they were oppressed by the brahmans, and there was no one to whom they could complain. The capital was too distant and even if they went there, who would help them? He knew that even a king had no power to change the situation.

Siddhartha had long understood the inner workings of the royal court. Every official was intent on protecting and fortifying his own power, not on alleviating the suffering of those in need. He had seen the powerful plot against each other, and he felt nothing but revulsion for politics. He knew that even his own father's authority was fragile and restricted—a king did not possess true freedom but was imprisoned by his position. His father was aware of many officials' greed and corruption, but was forced to rely on these same individuals to maintain the stability of his reign. Siddhartha realized that if he stood in his father's place, he would have to do the same. He understood that only when people overcame greed and envy in their own hearts would conditions change. And so his desire to seek a path of spiritual liberation was reignited.

Yasodhara was bright and intuitive. She understood Siddhartha's longings, and she had faith that if Siddhartha resolved to find the path of liberation he would succeed. But she was also quite practical. Such a search could last months, even years. In the meantime, sufferings would continue to daily unfold around them. And so she believed it was important to respond right in the present moment. She discussed with Siddhartha ways to ease the suffering of the poorest members of society. She had been doing work like that for several years, and her efforts eased some of the people's misery and brought some measure of peace and happiness to her own heart as well. She believed that with Siddhartha's loving support she could continue such work for a long time.

From Kapilavatthu came pouring all manner of goods and servants to provide for the couple's summer needs. Siddhartha and Yasodhara sent home most of the servants, retaining only a few to assist them with the gardens, cooking, and housekeeping. And, of course, they retained the services of Channa. Yasodhara organized their daily life as simply as possible. She personally entered the kitchen to direct the cooking of simple meals pleasing to Siddhartha, and she cared for his garments with her own hands. She sought Siddhartha's guidance concerning the relief projects she intended to continue when they returned to the capital. Siddhartha understood her need to engage in social action, and he never failed to express his support. Because of this, Yasodhara placed even deeper trust in her husband.

But although Siddhartha understood the value of Yasodhara's work, he felt that her path alone could not bring true peace. People were entrapped not only by illness and unjust social conditions, but by the sorrows and passions they themselves created in their own hearts and minds. And if in time, Yasodhara fell victim to fear, anger, bitterness, or disappointment, where would she find the energy needed to continue her work? Siddhartha had himself experienced suspicion, frustration, and pain when he saw how things worked in the palace and in society. He knew that the attainment of inner peace would be the only basis for true social work, but he did not confide these thoughts to Yasodhara, because he feared that they would only cause her uncertainty and worry.

When the couple returned to their winter palace, they entertained a constant stream of guests. Yasodhara welcomed family members and friends with great warmth and respect, but she was most attentive when Siddhartha spoke with them about philosophy and religion and their relation to politics and society. Even while going back and forth to direct the servants, Yasodhara never missed a word of these conversations. She had hoped to discover among their friends some who might like to join her work for the poor, but few expressed interest in such pursuits. Most were more interested in feasting and having a good time. Yet Siddhartha and Yasodhara patiently received them all.

In addition to Siddhartha, there was one other person who understood and wholeheartedly supported Yasodhara's efforts—Gotami, the Queen Mahapajapati. The queen was most attentive to her daughter-in-law's happiness, for she knew that if Yasodhara was happy, Siddhartha would be happy as well. But that was not the sole reason she supported Yasodhara's good work. Gotami was a woman of compassion and from the first time she accompanied Yasodhara on a visit to a poor village, she understood at once the true value of Yasodhara's work. It was not just the material goods given to the poor, such as rice, flour, cloth, and medicine, but the kind glances, helping hands, and loving heart of one willing to respond directly to those who suffer.

Queen Mahapajapati was not like other women in the palace. She frequently told Yasodhara that women possessed as much wisdom and strength as men and needed to shoulder the responsibilities of society also. While women did possess a special ability to create warmth and happiness in their families, there was no reason for them to remain only in the kitchen or in the palace. Gotami found in her daughter-in-law a woman with whom she could share true friendship, for like herself, Yasodhara was thoughtful and independent. Not only did the queen offer Yasodhara her approval, but she worked alongside Yasodhara as well.

Chapter Ten
Unborn Child

During this time, King Suddhodana expressed the desire to have Siddhartha spend more time at his side so that he could instruct his son in political and courtly affairs. The prince was invited to attend many official meetings, sometimes alone with the king, at other times with the king's court. Siddhartha gave his full attention to these affairs, and he came to understand that the political, economic, and military problems that beset any kingdom had their roots in the selfish ambitions of those involved in politics. Concerned only with protecting their own power, it was impossible for them to create enlightened policies for the common good. When Siddhartha saw corrupt officials feign virtue and morality, anger filled his heart. But he concealed it, as he did not have any alternatives to offer.

"Why don't you contribute ideas at court instead of always sitting so silently?" King Suddhodana asked one day after a long meeting with several officials.

Siddhartha looked at his father. "It is not that I haven't ideas, but it would be useless to state them. They only point to the disease. I do not yet see a cure for the selfish ambitions of those in the court. Look at Vessamitta, for example. He holds an impressive amount of power at court, yet you know he is corrupt. More than once he has tried to encroach upon your authority, but you are still forced to depend on his services. Why? Because you know if you don't, chaos will break loose."

King Suddhodana looked at his son silently for a long moment. Then he spoke. "Siddhartha, you know well that in order to maintain peace in one's family and country, there are certain things one must tolerate. My own power is limited, but I am sure that if you prepared yourself to be king, you would do far better than I have. You possess the talent needed to purge the ranks of corruption while preventing chaos in our homeland."

Siddhartha sighed. "Father, I do not think it is a question of talent. I believe the fundamental problem is to liberate one's own heart and mind. I too am trapped by feelings of anger, jealousy, fear, and desire."

Similar exchanges between father and son made King Suddhodana grow increasingly anxious. He recognized that Siddhartha was a person of unusual depth, and he saw how differently he and his son viewed the world. Still, he fostered the hope that over time, Siddhartha would come to accept his role and fill it in a most worthy way.

In addition to his duties at court and assisting Yasodhara, Siddhartha continued to meet and study with well-known brahmans and monks. He knew that the pursuit of religion was not just the study of the holy scriptures but included the practice of meditation to attain liberation for one's heart and mind, and he sought to learn more about meditation. He applied all that he learned in these studies to his own life in the palace, and he shared these insights with Yasodhara.

"Gopa," Siddhartha liked to call Yasodhara affectionately, "perhaps you should also practice meditation. It will bring peace to your heart and enable you to continue your work for a long time."

Yasodhara followed his advice. No matter how busy her work kept her, she reserved time for meditation. Husband and wife often sat together silently. At such times, their attendants left them alone, and the couple asked their musicians and dancers to go perform elsewhere.

Husband and wife often sat together silently.

From the time he was small, Siddhartha had been taught the four stages of a brahman's life. In youth, a brahman studied the Vedas. In the second stage, he married, raised a family, and served society. In the third stage, when his children were grown, he could retire and devote himself to religious studies. And in the fourth stage, released from every tie and obligation, a brahman could live the life of a monk. Siddhartha thought about it and concluded that by the time one was old, it would be too late to study the Way. He did not want to wait that long.

"Why can't a person live all four ways at once? Why can't a man pursue a religious life while he still has a family?"

Siddhartha wanted to study and practice the Way in the very midst of his present life. Of course, he could not refrain from thinking about famous teachers in distant places such as Savatthi or Rajagaha. He was sure that if he could find a way to study with such masters, he would make much more progress. The monks and teachers he frequently met had all mentioned the names of certain great masters such as Alara Kalama and Uddaka Ramaputta. Everyone aspired to study with such masters and each day, Siddhartha felt his own desire grow ever more urgent.

One afternoon Yasodhara came home, her face filled with grief. She did not speak to anyone. A young child she had tended for more than a week had just died. Despite all her efforts, she could not rescue the child from death's grasp. Overcome with sadness, she sat in meditation while tears streamed down her cheeks. It was impossible to hold back feelings. When Siddhartha returned from a meeting at court, she again burst into tears. Siddhartha held her in his arms and tried to console her.

"Gopa, tomorrow I will go with you to the funeral. Cry now, it will lessen the pain in your heart. Birth, old age, sickness, and death are heavy burdens each of us carries in this life. What has happened to the child could happen to any of us at any moment."

Yasodhara spoke between sobs, "Each day, I see how true all the things you have said are. My two hands are so small compared to the immensity of suffering. My heart is constantly filled with anxiety and sorrow. O husband, please show me how I can overcome the suffering in my heart."

Siddhartha embraced Yasodhara tightly in his arms. "My wife, I myself am seeking a path to overcome the suffering and anxiety in my own heart. I have seen into the situation of society and human beings, but despite all my efforts, I have not yet seen the way to liberation. Yet I feel sure that one day I will find a way for all of us. Gopa, please have faith in me."

"I have never been without faith in you, my darling. I know that once you have resolved to accomplish something, you will pursue it until you succeed. I know that one day you will leave all your wealth and privileges behind in order to seek the Way. Only, please, my husband, do not leave me just now. I need you."

Siddhartha raised Yasodhara's chin and looked into her eyes, "No, no, I won't leave you now. Only when, when..."

Yasodhara placed her hand over Siddhartha's mouth. "Siddhartha, please say no more. I want to ask you something—if you were to have a child with me, would you want it to be a boy or a girl?"

Siddhartha was startled. He looked carefully at Yasodhara. "What are you saying, Gopa? Do you mean, can you be..."

Yasodhara nodded. She pointed to her belly and said, "I am so happy to be carrying the fruit of our love. I want it to be a boy who looks just like you, with your intelligence and kind virtue."

Siddhartha put his arms around Yasodhara and held her close. In the midst of his great joy, he felt the seeds of worry. Still, he smiled and said, "I will be just as happy if it is a boy or a girl, just so long as the baby has your compassion and wisdom. Gopa, have you told Mother?"

"You are the only one I have told. This evening, I will go to the main palace and tell Queen Gotami. At the same time, I will ask her advice on how best to care for our unborn child. Tomorrow I will go tell my own mother, Queen Pamita. I'm sure everyone will be very happy."

Siddhartha nodded. He knew that his mother would pass the news on to his father as soon as she learned of it. The king would be overjoyed and would no doubt organize a great banquet to celebrate. Siddhartha felt the ties that bound him to life in the palace tightening.

Chapter Eleven
Moonlight Flute

Udayin, Devadatta, Kimbila, Bhadya, Mahanama, Kaludayi, and Anuruddha were Siddhartha's friends who visited most often to discuss such things as politics and ethics. In addition to Ananda and Nanda, they would be Siddhartha's closest advisors when he became king. They liked to begin their debates after several glasses of wine. Giving in to his friend's wishes, Siddhartha often kept the royal musicians and dancers performing far into the night.

Devadatta could wax endlessly about political matters, and Udayin and Mahanama debated tirelessly every point Devadatta made. Siddhartha spoke little. Sometimes in the middle of a dance or song, Siddhartha would look over to find Anuruddha nodding, half-asleep, and obviously wearied by the evening's activities. He would nudge Anuruddha and the two would steal outside where they could watch the moon and listen to the nearby stream. Anuruddha was Mahanama's younger brother. Their father was Prince Amritodana, Siddhartha's paternal uncle. Anuruddha was an affable, handsome fellow, much admired by the court ladies, though he himself was not inclined to pursue romance. Sometimes Siddhartha and Anuruddha would sit in the garden until midnight. By then their friends had become too intoxicated or tired to discuss any more and had retired to the guest rooms, and Siddhartha would take out his flute and play beneath the bright moonlight. Gopa would place a small in-

Siddhartha played his flute for Anuruddha beneath the bright moonlight.

cense burner on a rock, and sit quietly nearby, listening to the soft music rise and fall in the warm night air.

Time flew, and the day for Yasodhara to give birth approached. Queen Pamita told her daughter she did not need to return home to give birth, as Pamita herself was then living in Kapilavatthu. With Queen Mahapajapati, Pamita selected the finest midwives in the capital to assist Yasodhara. On the day Yasodhara went into labor, both Queen Gotami and Queen Pamita were there. A solemn and expectant atmosphere pervaded the palace. Although King Suddhodana did not show his presence, Siddhartha knew that the king anxiously awaited news of the birth in his own quarters.

When Yasodhara's labor pains began in earnest, she was led into the inner chamber by her attendants. It was only the noon hour, but suddenly the sky grew dark with clouds, as though a deity's hand had obscured the sun. Siddhartha sat outside. Although he was separated from his wife by two walls, he could clearly hear her cries. With each passing moment, his anxiety increased. Yasodhara's moans now followed one upon another, and he was beside himself. Her cries tore at his heart until it was impossible to sit still. He stood and paced the floor. At times Yasodhara's groans were so intense he could not quell his panic. His mother, Queen Mahamaya, had died as a result of giving birth to him, and that was a sorrow he could never forget. Now it was Yasodhara's turn to give birth to his own child. Childbirth was a passage most married women experienced, a passage fraught with danger, including the possibility of death. Sometimes both mother and child died.

Reminding himself what he had learned from a monk a number of months earlier, Siddhartha sat down in a lotus position and began to take hold of his mind and heart. This time of passage was a true test. He must maintain a calm heart even in the midst of Yasodhara's cries. Suddenly, the image of a newborn child arose in his mind. It was the image of his own child. Everyone had hoped he would have a child and would be happy for him once he did. He himself had hoped for a child. But now in the intensity of the actual event, he understood how immensely important the birth of a child is. He had not yet found his own path, he did not yet know where he was going, and yet here he was having a child—was it not a pity for the child?

Yasodhara's cries abruptly stopped. He stood up. What had happened? He could feel his own heartbeat. He observed his breath again in order to regain his calm. Just at that moment, the cries of an infant arose. The baby was born! Siddhartha wiped the sweat from his forehead.

Queen Gotami opened the door and looked in at him. She smiled and Siddhartha knew that Yasodhara was safe. The queen sat down before him and said, "Gopa has given birth to a boy."

Siddhartha smiled and looked at his mother with gratitude.

"I will name the child Rahula."

That afternoon, Siddhartha entered the room to visit his wife and son. Yasodhara gazed at him, her shining eyes filled with love. Their son lay by her side, swaddled in silk, and Siddhartha could see only his plump little face. Siddhartha looked at Yasodhara as if to ask something. Understanding, she nodded her assent and gestured for Siddhartha to pick Rahula up. Siddhartha lifted the infant in his arms as Yasodhara watched. Siddhartha felt as though he were floating, and yet his heart was heavy with worry.

Yasodhara rested for several days. Queen Gotami took care of everything from preparing special foods to tending the fireplace to keep mother and child warm. One day after they returned home, Siddhartha visited his wife and son, and as he held Rahula in his arms, he marvelled at how precious and fragile a human life was. He recalled the day he and Yasodhara had attended the funeral of a poor child, four years old. The body still lay upon its deathbed when Siddhartha and Yasodhara arrived. All signs of life had vanished, and the child's skin was pale and waxen, its body no more than skin and bones. The child's mother knelt beside the bed wiping her tears and then crying again. A moment later, a brahman arrived to perform the funeral rites. Neighbors who had kept an all-night vigil, lifted the child's corpse onto a bamboo stretcher they had made to carry the body to the river. Siddhartha and Yasodhara followed the procession of poor villagers. A simple funeral pyre had been set up by the riverbank. Following the brahman's instructions, the people carried the stretcher down to the river and submerged the body. They then lifted it back up and left it on the ground for the water to drain away. This was a purification rite, for the people believed that the waters of the Banganga River could cleanse bad karma. A man poured perfume over the funeral pyre and then the child's body was placed upon it. The brahman held a lit torch and walked around the pyre while chanting. Siddhartha recognized the passages from the *Vedas*. After the brahman had circled the pyre three times, he lit it, and it soon burst into flames. The child's mother, brothers, and sisters wailed. Before long, the fire consumed the little boy's corpse. Siddhartha looked at Yasodhara and saw her eyes were filled with tears. Siddhartha felt like crying, too. "Child, O Child, where now do you return?" he thought.

Siddhartha handed Rahula back to Yasodhara. He went outside and sat alone in the garden until the evening shadows fell. A servant came looking for him. "Your highness, the queen asked me to find you. Your royal father has come to visit."

Siddhartha went back inside. The palace torches had all been lit and flickered brightly.

Chapter Twelve

Kanthaka

Yasodhara quickly regained her strength and soon was able to return to her work, while also spending much time with baby Rahula. One spring day, at Queen Gotami's insistence, Channa drove Siddhartha and Yasodhara out into the countryside for an outing. They brought Rahula along and a young servant girl named Ratna to help care for him.

Pleasant sunlight streamed down upon tender green leaves. Birds sang on the blossoming branches of ashok and rose-apple trees. Channa let the horses trot at a leisurely pace. Country folk, recognizing Siddhartha and Yasodhara, stood and waved in greeting. When they approached the banks of the Banganga River, Channa pulled on the reins and brought the carriage to a sudden halt. Blocking the road before them was a man who had collapsed. His arms and legs were pulled in towards his chest and his whole body shook. Moans escaped from his half-open mouth. Siddhartha jumped down, followed by Channa. The man lying in the road looked less than thirty years old. Siddhartha picked up his hand and said to Channa, "It looks as though he's come down with a bad flu, don't you think? Let's massage him and see if it helps."

Channa shook his head. "Your highness, these aren't the symptoms of a bad flu. I'm afraid he's contracted something far worse—this is a disease for which there is no known cure."

"Are you sure?" Siddhartha gazed at the man. "Couldn't we take him to the royal physician?"

"Your highness, even the royal physician can't cure this disease. I've heard this disease is highly infectious. If we take him in our carriage, he might infect your wife and son, and even yourself. Please, your highness, for your own safety, let go of his hand."

But Siddhartha did not release the man's hand—he looked at it and then at his own. Siddhartha had always enjoyed good health, but now looking at the dying man no older than himself, all he had taken for granted suddenly vanished. From the riverbank came cries of mourning. He looked up to see a funeral taking place. There was the funeral pyre. The sound of chanting intertwined with the grief-stricken cries and the crackling of fire as the funeral pyre was lit.

Looking again at the man, Siddhartha saw that he had stopped breathing. His glassy eyes stared upwards. Siddhartha released his hand and quietly closed the eyes. When Siddhartha stood up, Yasodhara was standing close behind him. How long she had been there, he did not know.

She spoke softly, "Please, my husband, go and wash your hands in the river. Channa, you do the same. Then we will drive into the next village and notify the authorities so they can take care of the body."

Afterwards, no one had the heart to continue their spring outing. Siddhartha asked Channa to turn around, and on the way back no one spoke a word.

That night, Yasodhara's sleep was disturbed by three strange dreams. In the first, she saw a white cow on whose head was a sparkling jewel, as bright as the North Star. The cow strolled through Kapilavatthu headed for the city gates. From the altar of Indra resounded a divine voice, "If you can't keep this cow, there will be no light left in all the capital." Everyone in the city began chasing after the cow yet no one was able to detain it. It walked out the city gates and disappeared.

In her second dream, Yasodhara watched four god-kings of the skies, atop Mount Sumeru, projecting a light onto the city of Kapilavatthu. Suddenly the flag mounted on Indra's altar flapped violently and fell to the ground. Flowers of every color dropped like rain from the skies and the sound of celestial singing echoed everywhere throughout the capital. In her third dream, Yasodhara heard a loud voice that shook the heavens. "The time has come! The time has come!" it cried. Frightened, she looked over at Siddhartha's chair to discover he was gone. The jasmine flowers tucked in her hair fell to the floor and turned to dust. The garments and ornaments which Siddhartha had left on his chair transformed into a snake which slithered out the door. Yasodhara was filled with panic. All at once, she heard the bellowing of the white cow from beyond the city gates, the flapping of the flag upon Indra's altar, and the voices of heaven shouting, "The time has come! The time has come!"

Yasodhara awoke. Her forehead was drenched with sweat. She turned to Siddhartha and shook him. "Siddhartha, Siddhartha, please wake up."

He was already awake. He stroked her hair to comfort her and asked, "What did you dream, Gopa? Tell me."

She recounted all three dreams and then asked him, "Are these dreams an omen that you will soon leave me in order to go and seek the Way?"

Siddhartha fell silent, then consoled her, "Gopa, please don't worry. You are a woman of depth. You are my partner, the one who can help me to truly fulfil my quest. You understand me more than anyone else. If in the near future I must leave and travel far from you, I know you possess the courage to continue your work. You will care for and raise our child well. Though I am gone, though I am far away from you, my love for you remains the same. I will never stop loving you, Gopa. With that knowledge, you will be able to endure our separation. And when I have found the Way, I will return to you and to our child. Please now, try to get some rest."

Siddhartha's words, spoken so tenderly, penetrated Yasodhara's heart. Comforted, she closed her eyes and slept.

The following morning, Siddhartha went to speak to his father. "My royal father, I ask your permission to leave home and become a monk in order to seek the path of enlightenment."

King Suddhodana was greatly alarmed. Though he had long known this day might arrive, he had certainly not expected it to take place so abruptly. After a long moment, he looked at his son and answered, "In the history of our family, a few have become monks, but no one has ever done it at your age. They all waited until they were past fifty. Why can't you wait? Your son is still small, and the whole country is relying on you."

"Father, a day upon the throne would be like a day of sitting on a bed of hot coals for me. If my heart has no peace, how can I fulfil your or the people's trust in me? I have seen how quickly time passes, and I know my youth is no different. Please grant me your permission."

The king tried to dissuade his son. "You must think of your homeland, your parents, Yasodhara, and your son who is still an infant."

"Father, it is precisely because I do think of all of you that I now ask your permission to go. It is not that I wish to abandon my responsibilities. Father, you know that you cannot free me from the suffering in my heart any more than you can release the suffering in your own heart."

The king stood up and grabbed his son's hand. "Siddhartha, you know how much I need you. You are the one on whom I have placed all my hopes. Please, don't abandon me."

"I will never abandon you. I am only asking you to let me go away for a time. When I have found the Way, I will return."

A look of pain crossed King Suddhodana's face. He said no more and retired to his quarters.

Later on, Queen Gotami came to spend the day with Yasodhara, and in the early evening, Udayin, one of Siddhartha's friends, came to visit with Devadatta, Ananda, Bhadya, Anuruddha, Kimbila, and Bhadrika. Udayin had organized a party and had hired one of the finest dancing troupes in the capital to perform. Festive torches brightened the palace.

Gotami told Yasodhara that Udayin had been summoned by the king and given the task to do everything he could think of to entice Siddhartha to remain in the palace. The evening's party was the first of Udayin's plans.

Yasodhara instructed her attendants to prepare food and drinks for all the guests before retiring to her quarters with Gotami. Siddhartha himself went out and welcomed his guests. It was the full moon day of the month of Uttarasalha. As the music began, the moon appeared above a row of trees in the southeastern sky.

Gotami confided her thoughts to Yasodhara until it was late and then excused herself to return to her own residence. Yasodhara walked with her to the veranda where she saw the full moon now suspended high in the night sky. The party was still in full swing. Sounds of music, talking, and laughter drifted from within. Yasodhara led Gotami to the front gate and then went on her own to find Channa. He was already asleep when she found him. Yasodhara awoke him and whispered, "It is possible the prince will require your services tonight. Prepare Kanthaka to ride. And saddle another horse for yourself."

"Your highness, where is the prince going?"

"Please don't ask. Just do as I have said because the prince may need to ride tonight."

Channa nodded and entered the stable while Yasodhara returned inside the palace. She readied clothes suitable for traveling and placed them on Siddhartha's chair. She took a light blanket to cover Rahula and then lay upon the bed herself. As she lay there she listened to the sounds of music, talking, and laughter. It was a long time before the sounds faded then disappeared. She knew the guests had retired to their quarters. Yasodhara lay quietly as silence returned to the palace. She waited a long time, but Siddhartha did not return to their room.

He was sitting alone outside, gazing at the radiant moon and stars. A thousand stars twinkled. He had made up his mind to leave the palace that very night. At long last, he entered his chamber and changed into the traveling clothes awaiting him there. He pulled back the curtain and gazed upon the bed. Gopa was lying there, no doubt asleep. Rahula was by her side. Siddhartha wanted to enter and speak words of parting to Yasodhara, but he hesitated. He had already said everything that was essential. If he woke her now, it would only make their parting more painful. He let the curtain drop and turned to leave. Again he hesitated. Once more he lifted back the curtain to take a last look at his wife and son. He looked at them deeply as though to imprint on his memory that familiar and beloved scene. Then he released the curtain and walked out.

As he passed the guest hall, Siddhartha saw the slumbering, dancing girls sprawled across the carpets. Their hair was undone and dishevelled, their mouths hanging open like dead fish. Their arms, so soft and supple during the dance, now looked as stiff as boards. Their legs were tangled across each other's bodies like victims on a battlefield. Siddhartha felt as though he were crossing a cemetery.

He made his way to the stables and found Channa still awake.

"Channa, please saddle and bring Kanthaka to me."

Channa nodded. He had prepared everything. Kanthaka was already bridled and saddled. Channa asked, "May I accompany you, prince?"

Siddhartha nodded and Channa entered the stable for his own horse. They led the horses out of the palace grounds. Siddhartha stopped and stroked Kanthaka's mane. "Kanthaka," he spoke, "this is a most important night. You must give me your best for this journey."

After preparing Kanthaka for a long journey, Channa asked Siddhartha, "May I accompany you?"

He mounted Kanthaka and Channa mounted his horse. They walked them to avoid making any loud noise. The guards were fast asleep, and they passed through the city gates easily. Once well beyond the city gates, Siddhartha turned for a last look at the capital, now lying quietly beneath the moonlight. It was there that Siddhartha had been born and raised, the city where he had experienced so many joys and sorrows, so many anxieties and aspirations. In the same city now slept everyone close to him—his father, Gotami, Yasodhara, Rahula, and all the others. He whispered to himself, "If I do not find the Way, I will not return to Kapilavatthu."

He turned his horse towards the south and Kanthaka broke into a full gallop.

Chapter Thirteen
Beginning Spiritual Practice

Even at a full gallop, they did not reach the border of Sakya until daybreak. Before them flowed the Anoma River, which they followed downstream until they found a shallow place to cross over with the horses. They rode for another spell before coming to the edge of a forest. A deer flitted in and out among the trees. Birds flew close by, undisturbed by the men's presence. Siddhartha dismounted. He smiled and stroked Kanthaka's mane.

"Kanthaka, you are wonderful. You have helped bring me here, and for that, I thank you."

The horse lifted his head and looked lovingly at his master. Siddhartha pulled out a sword tucked in his horse's saddle and then grasping his own long locks of hair in his left hand, cut them off with his right. Channa dismounted his own horse. Siddhartha handed him the hair and sword. He then removed his jeweled necklace.

"Channa, take my necklace, sword, and hair and give them to my father. Please tell him to have faith in me. I have not left home to selfishly avoid my responsibilities. I go now on behalf of all of you and all beings. Please, console the king and queen for me. Console Yasodhara. I ask this of you."

As Channa took the necklace, tears streamed from his eyes. "Your highness, everyone will suffer terribly. I don't know what I will say to the king and queen or to your wife,

Yasodhara. Your highness, how will you sleep beneath the trees like an ascetic when all your life you've known nothing but a warm bed and soft blankets?"

Siddhartha smiled. "Don't worry, Channa. I can live the way others do. You must return to tell everyone of my decision before they begin to worry about my disappearance. Leave me here alone now."

Channa wiped his tears. "Please, your highness, let me stay here to serve you. Have mercy on me and don't make me bear such sorrowful news to ones I love!"

Siddhartha patted his attendant on the shoulder. His voice grew serious. "Channa, I need you to return and inform my family. If you truly care for me, please do as I say. I don't need you here, Channa. No monk has need of a personal attendant! Please, return home now!"

Channa reluctantly obeyed the prince. He carefully placed the hair and necklace inside his jacket and tucked the sword in Kanthaka's saddle. He grasped Siddhartha's arm in his two hands and beseeched him, "I will do as you say, but please, your highness, remember me, remember us all. Don't forget to return after you have found the Way."

Siddhartha nodded and smiled reassuringly at Channa. He stroked Kanthaka's head. "Kanthaka, my friend, now return home."

Channa held Kanthaka's reins and mounted his own steed. Kanthaka turned to look at Siddhartha one last time, his eyes filled with tears no less than Channa's.

Siddhartha waited until Channa and the two horses were out of sight before he turned toward the forest to enter his new life. The sky would now serve as his roof and the forest as his home. A sense of ease and contentment welled within him. Just at that moment a man came walking out of the forest. At first glance, Siddhartha thought he was a monk, for he was wearing the customary robe. But on closer inspection, Siddhartha saw the man was carrying a bow, and a quiver of arrows was slung across his back.

"You are a hunter, are you not?" asked Siddhartha.

"That is correct," the man answered.

"If you are a hunter, why are you dressed as a monk?"

The hunter smiled and said, "Thanks to this robe the animals do not fear me and I am thus easily able to shoot them."

Siddhartha shook his head. "Then you are abusing the compassion of those who follow a spiritual path. Would you agree to trade your robe for my garments?"

The hunter looked at Siddhartha and saw he was wearing royal garments of inestimable value.

"Do you really want to trade?" the hunter asked.

"Absolutely," said Siddhartha. "You could sell these garments and have enough money to stop hunting and begin a new trade. As for me, I wish to be a monk and have need of a robe like yours."

The hunter was overjoyed and after exchanging his robe for Siddhartha's handsome clothes, he hurried off. Siddhartha now had the appearance of a real monk. He stepped into the forest and found a tree to sit beneath. For the first time as a homeless monk, he sat in meditation. After a long final day in the palace and an autumn night spent on the back of a horse, Siddhartha now experienced a marvelous ease. He sat in meditation to savor and nurture the feeling of release and freedom that had filled him the moment he entered the forest.

Sunlight filtered through the trees and came to rest on Siddhartha's eyelashes. He opened his eyes and saw standing before him, a monk. The monk's face and body were thin and worn by a life of austerities. Siddhartha stood up and joined his palms together in greeting. He told the monk he had only just abandoned his home and had not yet had the chance to be accepted by any teacher. He expressed his intent to travel south to find the spiritual center of Master Alara Kalama and there ask to be accepted as a disciple.

The monk told Siddhartha that he himself had studied under Master Alara Kalama and that at present the Master had started a center just north of the city Vesali. More than four hundred disciples were gathered there for his teaching.

The monk knew how to get there and said he would be glad to take Siddhartha.

Siddhartha followed him through the forest to a path which wound up a hill and entered another forest. They walked until noon, when the monk showed Siddhartha how to gather wild fruits and edible greens. The monk explained that it was sometimes necessary to dig roots to eat when there were no edible fruits or greens to be found. Siddhartha knew he would be living in the forests a long time and so he asked the names of all the edible foods and carefully noted everything the monk told him. He learned that the monk was an ascetic who lived on nothing but wild fruits, greens, and roots. His name was Bhargava. He told Siddhartha that Master Alara Kalama was not an ascetic and in addition to wild foraging, his monks begged for food or accepted what was brought as offerings to them from neighboring villages.

Nine days later, they reached the forest center of Alara Kalama, near Anupiya. They arrived as Master Alara was giving a talk to more than four hundred disciples. He looked about seventy years old and, though he appeared thin and frail, his eyes shone and his voice resounded like a copper drum. Siddhartha and his companion stood outside the circle of disciples and quietly listened to the Master's teaching. When he finished speaking, his disciples scattered throughout the forest to pursue their practice. Siddhartha approached him and after introducing himself, respectfully said, "Venerable Teacher, I ask you to accept me as one of your disciples. I wish to live and study under your guidance."

The master listened and looked intently at Siddhartha, and then expressed his approval. "Siddhartha, I would be happy to accept you. You may stay here. If you practice according to my teachings and methods, you will realize the teachings in a short time."

Siddhartha prostrated himself to express his happiness.

Master Alara lived in a straw hut made for him by several of his disciples. Scattered here and there in the forest were the straw huts of his followers. That night, Siddhartha found a level place to sleep, using a tree root for his pillow. Because he was exhausted from the long journey, he slept soundly until morning. When he awoke, the sun had already risen and the songs of birds filled the forest. He sat up. The other monks had finished their morning meditation and were preparing to go down into the city to beg for food. Siddhartha was given a bowl and shown how to beg.

Following the other monks, he held his bowl and entered the city of Vesali. Holding a bowl to beg for the first time, Siddhartha was struck by how closely linked the life of a monk was to that of the laity—the monks were dependent on the lay community for food. He learned how to hold his bowl properly, how to walk and stand, how to receive the food offerings, and how to recite prayers in order to thank those who made the offerings. That day Siddhartha received some rice with curry sauce.

He returned with his new companions to the forest, and they all sat down to eat. When he had finished, he went to Master Alara to receive spiritual instruction. Alara was sitting in deep meditation when Siddhartha found him, and so he sat down before the master, quietly trying to focus his own mind. After a long time, Alara opened his eyes. Siddhartha prostrated himself and asked Master Alara to teach him.

Alara spoke to the new monk about faith and diligence and showed him how to use his breathing to develop concentration. He explained, "My teaching is not a mere theory. Knowledge is gained from direct experience and direct attainment, not from mental arguments. In order to attain different states of meditation, it is necessary to rid yourself of all thoughts of past and future. You must focus on nothing but liberation."

Siddhartha asked about how to control the body and the sensations, and then respectfully thanked his teacher and walked away slowly to find a place in the forest where he could practice. He gathered branches and leaves and constructed a small hut beneath a sal tree where his meditation practice could ripen. He practiced diligently and, every five or six days, he returned to ask Alara's advice concerning whatever difficulties he was experiencing. In a short time, Siddhartha made considerable progress.

While sitting in meditation he was able to let go of thoughts and even of clinging to his past and future, and he attained a state of wondrous serenity and rapture, although he felt the seeds of thought and attachment still present in him. Several weeks later, Siddhartha reached a higher state of meditation, and the seeds of thought and attachment dissolved. Then he entered a state of concentration in which both rapture and non-rapture ceased to exist. It felt to him as though the five doors of sense perception had completely closed, and his heart was as still as a lake on a windless day.

When he presented the fruits of his practice to Master Alara, the teacher was impressed. He told Siddhartha that he had made remarkable progress in a short time, and he taught Siddhartha how to realize the meditative state called *the realm of limitless space*, in which the mind becomes one with infinity, all material and visual phenomena cease to arise, and space is seen as the limitless source of all things.

Siddhartha followed his teacher's instructions and concentrated his efforts on achieving that state, and in less than three days, he succeeded. But Siddhartha still felt that even the ability to experience infinite space had not liberated him from his deepest anxieties and sorrows. Dwelling in such a state of awareness, he still felt hindrances, so he returned to Alara for assistance. The master told him, "You must go one step further. *The realm of limitless space* is of the same essence as your own mind. It is not an object of your consciousness, but your very consciousness itself. Now you must experience *the realm of limitless consciousness*."

Siddhartha returned to his spot in the forest, and in just two days, he realized *the realm of limitless consciousness*. He saw that his own mind was present in every phenomenon in the universe. But even with this attainment, he still felt oppressed by his deepest afflictions and anxieties. So Siddhartha returned to Master Alara and explained his difficulty. The master looked at him with eyes of deep respect and said, "You are very close to the final goal. Return to your hut and meditate on the illusory nature of all phenomena. Everything in the universe is created by our own mind. Our mind is the source of all phenomena. Form, sound, smell, taste, and tactile perception such as hot and cold, hard and soft—these are all creations of our mind. They do not exist as we usually think they do. Our consciousness is like an artist, painting every phenomenon into being. Once you have attained the state of *the realm of no materiality*, you will have succeeded. *The realm of no materiality* is the state in which we see that no phenomenon exists outside of our own mind."

The young monk joined his palms to express his gratitude to his teacher, and returned to his corner of the forest.

While Siddhartha studied with Alara Kalama, he made the acquaintance of many other monks. Everyone was attracted by Siddhartha's kind and pleasant manner. Often, before Siddhartha had a chance to seek food for himself, he found food waiting for him by his hut. When he came out of meditation, he would find a few bananas or a rice ball secretly left for him by another monk. Many monks liked to befriend Siddhartha in order to learn from him, as they had heard their own master praise Siddhartha's progress.

Master Alara had once asked about Siddhartha's background and so learned of Siddhartha's life as a prince. But Siddhartha only smiled when other monks asked him about his royal past. He answered modestly, "It's nothing of importance. It would be best if we spoke only about our experiences of practicing the Way."

In less than a month, Siddhartha attained *the state of the realm of no materiality*. Happy to have achieved this state of awareness, he spent the following weeks trying to use it to dissolve the deepest obstructions in his mind and heart. But although *the realm of no materiality* was a profound state of meditation, it, too, was unable to help him. Finally, he returned to ask the advice of Master Alara Kalama.

Alara Kalama sat and listened intently to Siddhartha. His eyes shone. Expressing deepest respect and praise, he said, "Monk Siddhartha, you are profoundly gifted. You have attained the highest level I can teach. All I have attained, you have attained as well. Let us join together to guide and lead this community of monks."

Siddhartha was silent as he contemplated Alara's invitation. While *the realm of no materiality* was a precious fruit of meditation, it did not help resolve the fundamental problem of birth and death, nor did it liberate one from all suffering and anxiety. It did not lead to total liberation. Siddhartha's goal was not to become the leader of a community, but to find the path of true liberation.

Siddhartha joined his palms and answered, "Venerable Teacher, the state of *the realm of no materiality* is not the final goal I am seeking. Please accept my gratitude for your support and care, but now I must ask your permission to leave the community in order to seek the Way elsewhere. You have taught me with all your heart these past months and I will be forever grateful to you."

Master Alara Kalama looked disappointed, but Siddhartha had made up his mind. The next day, Siddhartha again took to the road.

Chapter Fourteen
Crossing the Ganga

Siddhartha crossed the Ganges River, known as Ganga, and entered deep into the kingdom of Magadha, a region renowned for its accomplished spiritual teachers. He was determined to find someone who could teach him how to overcome birth and death. Most of the spiritual teachers lived in remote mountains or forests. Tirelessly, Siddhartha inquired the whereabouts of these masters, and sought out each of them, no matter how many mountains and valleys he had to cross. He continued his search through rain and sun, from one month to the next.

Siddhartha met ascetics who refused to wear any clothes, and others who refused to accept any food offerings, living on only the fruits, greens, and roots that grew wild in the forests. Exposing their bodies to the elements, these ascetics believed that by enduring extreme austerities they would enter heaven after they died.

One day Siddhartha said to them, "Even if you are reborn in Heaven, the suffering on Earth will remain unchanged. To seek the Way is to find a solution to life's sufferings, not to escape life. Granted, we cannot accomplish much if we pamper our bodies like those who live for sensual pleasure, but abusing our bodies is no more helpful."

Siddhartha continued his search—remaining in some spiritual centers for three months and in others for six. His powers of meditation and concentration increased, but he was still unable to find the true path of liberation from birth and death. The months passed quickly, and soon it was more than three years since Siddhartha had left home. Sometimes, as he sat in meditation in the forests, images arose in Siddhartha's mind of his father, Yasodhara, and Rahula, and of his childhood and youth. Although it was difficult for him to avoid feeling impatient and discouraged, his strong faith that he would find the Way allowed him to continue his search.

During one period, Siddhartha dwelled alone on the hillside of Pandava, not far from the capital city of Rajagaha. One day he took his bowl and went down the hillside to beg in the capital. His walk was slow and dignified, his countenance serene and resolute. People on both sides of the street stopped to gaze at this monk who walked as elegantly as a lion passing through a mountain forest. The royal carriage of King Bimbisara of Magadha happened to pass by, and the king ordered his driver to stop so that he could have a good look at Siddhartha. He asked his attendant to offer the monk food and to follow him to see where he lived.

The next afternoon, King Bimbisara rode to Siddhartha's dwelling. Leaving his carriage at the foot of the hill, he mounted the path with one of his attendants. When he saw Siddhartha sitting beneath a tree, he approached to greet him.

Siddhartha stood up. He could tell by his visitor's dress that he was the king of Magadha. Siddhartha joined his palms together and then motioned for the king to sit on a large rock nearby. Siddhartha sat on another rock and faced the king.

King Bimbisara was noticeably impressed by the monk's noble bearing and elevated manner. He said, "I am the king of Magadha. I wish to invite you to come to the capital with me. I would like you by my side so that I may benefit from your teaching and virtue. With you at my side, I am sure the kingdom of Magadha would enjoy peace and prosperity."

King Bimbisara was noticeably impressed by the monk's noble bearing and elevated manner.

Siddhartha smiled. "Great King, I am more used to living in the forest."

"This is too harsh a life. You have no bed, no attendant to assist you. If you agree to come with me, I will give you your own palace. Please return with me to teach."

"Great King, palace life is not well suited to me. I am endeavoring to find a path of liberation to free myself and all beings from suffering. Palace life is not compatible with the heart's quest of this monk."

"You are still young, as I am. I have need of a friend with whom I can truly share. From the moment I saw you, I felt a natural connection with you. Come with me. If you accept, I will reserve half of my kingdom for you, and when you are older, you can return to the life of a monk. It won't be too late."

"I thank you for your generous heart and offer of patronage, but I truly have but one desire, and that is to find the path which can liberate all beings from suffering. Time passes quickly, Great King. If I don't use the strength and energy I now possess as a young man, old age will arrive too soon and I will feel deep regret. Life is so uncertain—sickness or death can occur at any moment. The flames of inner turmoil caused by greed, anger, hatred, passion, jealousy, and pride continue to burn in my heart. Only when the Great Way is discovered, will liberation be possible for all beings. If you truly feel affection for me, you will allow me to continue the path I have long pursued."

King Bimbisara was even more impressed after hearing Siddhartha speak. He said, "It gives me great joy to hear your words so filled with determination. Dear monk, allow me to ask where you are from and what your family name is."

"Great King, I come from the kingdom of Sakya. My family name is Sakya. King Suddhodana who presently rules in Kapilavatthu is my father, and my mother was Queen Mahamaya. I was the prince, heir to the throne, but because I wished to become a monk in order to seek the Way, I left my parents, wife, and son, more than three years ago."

King Bimbisara was astonished. "Then you yourself are of royal blood! I am most honored to meet you, noble monk! The royal families of Sakya and Magadha have long been on very close terms. How foolish of me to try to impress you with my position and wealth in order to persuade you to return with me. Please forgive me! Let me ask only this—from time to time, come to my palace and allow me to offer you food, and when you have found the Great Way, return in compassion to teach me as your disciple. Will you promise that?"

Siddhartha joined his palms and answered, "I promise that when I have discovered the path, I will return to share it with your highness."

King Bimbisara bowed low before Siddhartha and returned down the hill with his attendant.

Later that day the monk Gautama abandoned his dwelling place to avoid the interruptions he feared would result from the young king bringing frequent offerings. Heading south, he looked for another place conducive to practice. He learned of the spiritual center of Uddaka Ramaputta, a great teacher who was said to have attained very deep levels of understanding. Three hundred monks were in residence at his center, located not far from Rajagaha, and four hundred other disciples practiced nearby. Siddhartha made his way there.

Chapter Fifteen

Forest Ascetic

Master Uddaka was seventy-five years old. He was venerated by all as though he were a living god. Uddaka required all new disciples to begin at the most elementary levels of practice, so Siddhartha began again with the simplest meditation techniques. But in just a few weeks, he demonstrated to his new teacher that he had already attained to *the realm of no materiality*, and Master Uddaka was impressed. He saw in this young man of noble bearing a potential spiritual heir, and he taught Siddhartha with utmost care.

"Monk Siddhartha Gautama, in *the state of no materiality*, emptiness is no longer the same as empty space, nor is it what is usually called consciousness. All that remains are perception and the object of perception. Thus, the path to liberation is to transcend all perception."

Siddhartha respectfully asked, "Master, if one eliminates perception, what is left? If there is no perception, how do we differ from a piece of wood or a rock?"

"A piece of wood or a rock is not without perception. Inanimate objects are themselves perception. You must arrive at a state of consciousness in which both perception and non-perception are eliminated. This is *the state of neither perception nor non-perception*. Young man, you must now attain that state."

Siddhartha left to return to his meditation. In just fifteen days, he realized the *samadhi* called *neither perception nor non-perception.* Siddhartha saw that this state allowed one to transcend all ordinary states of consciousness. But whenever he came out of this meditative state, he saw that in spite of its extraordinariness, it did not provide a solution to the problem of life and death. It was a most peaceful state to dwell in, but it was not the key to unlock reality.

When Siddhartha returned to Master Uddaka Ramaputta, the Master praised him highly. He grasped Siddhartha's hand and said, "Monk Gautama, you are the best student I have ever had. You have made enormous progress in such a short time. You have attained the highest level I have. I am old and not long for this world. If you will remain here, we can guide this community together and when I die, you can take my place as Master of the community."

Once again, Siddhartha politely declined. He knew that *the state of neither perception nor non-perception* was not the key to liberation from birth and death, and that he had to move on. He expressed his deepest gratitude to the Master and to the community of monks, and took his leave. Everyone had come to love Siddhartha, and all were sad to see him go.

During his stay at Uddaka Ramaputta's center, Siddhartha made friends with a young monk named Kondanna. Kondanna was very fond of Siddhartha and regarded him as a teacher as well as a good friend. No one else in the community except Siddhartha had attained *the state of no materiality*, not to mention *the state of neither perception nor non-perception*. Kondanna knew that the Master considered Siddhartha worthy to be his spiritual heir. Just looking at Siddhartha gave Kondanna faith in his own practice. He often approached Siddhartha to learn from him, and a special bond grew between them. Kondanna regretted his friend's departure. He accompanied Siddhartha down the mountain and waited until he was no longer in sight before returning back up the mountain.

Siddhartha had accomplished so much with the masters reputed to be the two best meditation teachers in the land, and yet the fundamental issue of liberation from suffering was still burning inside him. He realized that he probably would not be able to learn much more from any of the other teacher-sages throughout the land, and so he knew that he had to seek the key to enlightenment on his own.

Walking slowly west, between rice fields and across a long stretch of muddy lagoons and streams, Siddhartha reached the Neranjara River. He waded across it and walked until he reached Dangsiri Mountain, half a day's walk from Uruvela village. The steep and rocky slopes ended in saw-toothed peaks and concealed many caves. Boulders as large as the homes of poor villagers perched on the mountainside. Siddhartha resolved to remain here until he discovered the Way to Liberation. He found a cave in which he could sit in meditation for long hours, and while sitting, he reviewed all the practices he had done for what was now more than five years. He remembered how he had advised the ascetics not to abuse their bodies, telling them that that would ´only add to the suffering of a world already filled with suffering. But now as he considered their path more carefully, he thought to himself, "You can't make a fire with soft, wet wood. The body is the same. If physical desires are not mastered, it is difficult for the heart to attain enlightenment. I will practice self-mortification in order to attain liberation."

Thus, the monk Gautama began a period of extreme asceticism. On dark nights, he entered the deepest and most wild reaches of the forest, the mere thought of which was enough to make a person's hair stand on end, and there he remained throughout the night. Even as fear and panic engulfed his mind and body, he sat without stirring. When a deer approached with its rustling sounds, his fear told him that these were demons coming to kill him, but he did not budge. When a peacock broke a piece of dead twig, his fear told him it was a python coming down from a tree, yet he still did not move, even as fear shot through him like the sting of red ants.

He tried to overcome all physical fears. He believed that once his body was no longer enslaved by fear, his mind would break the chains of suffering. Sometimes he sat with his teeth clenched while pressing his tongue against the roof of his mouth, using his willpower to suppress all fear and horror. Even when he broke into a cold sweat and his whole body became drenched, he did not move. At other times, he held his breath for long stretches until a roar like thunder or a blazing furnace pounded in his ears, and his head felt as though someone had taken an axe and cleaved it in two. Sometimes he felt as though his head was being squeezed by a steel band and his stomach slashed open like a goat's by a butcher. And at times, he felt as if his body was being roasted over an open fire. Through these austere practices, he was able to consolidate his courage and discipline, and his body was able to endure unspeakable pain, but his heart was still without peace.

The monk Gautama practiced austerities in this way for six months. For the first three of these months, he was alone on the mountain, but during the fourth month, he was discovered by five disciples of Master Uddaka Ramaputta, led by his old friend Kondanna. Siddhartha was happy to see Kondanna again, and he found out that just one month after Siddhartha left the meditation center, Kondanna himself had attained *the state of neither perception nor non-perception*. Seeing there was nothing more he could learn from Master Uddaka, Kondanna persuaded four friends to join him in seeking Siddhartha. After several weeks, they were lucky enough to find him, and they expressed their desire to stay and practice with him. Siddhartha explained to them why he was exploring the path of self-mortification, and the five young men, Kondanna, Vappa, Bhaddiya, Assaji, and Mahanama, resolved to join him. Each monk found a cave to live in, not far from one another, and every day one of them went into town to beg for food. When he returned, the food was divided into six portions so that none of them had more than a small handful each day.

Days and months went by, and the six monks grew thin and gaunt. They left the mountain and moved east toward the village of Uruvela, on the bank of the Neranjara, and continued to practice in the same way. But Siddhartha's austerities began to alarm even his five companions, and they found it impossible to keep up with him. Siddhartha ceased bathing in the river or even taking his share of the food. On some days he ate just a shrivelled guava he happened to find on the ground or a piece of dried buffalo manure. His body had become terribly wasted—it was little more than loose flesh hanging on protruding bones. He had not cut his hair or beard in six months, and when he rubbed his head, handfuls of hair fell out as though there was no longer any space for it to grow on the bit of flesh still clinging to his skull.

And then one day, while practicing sitting meditation in a cemetery, Siddhartha realized with a jolt how wrong the path of self-mortification was. The sun had set and a cool breeze gently caressed his skin. After sitting all day beneath the blazing sun, the breeze was delightfully refreshing, and Siddhartha experienced an ease in his mind unlike anything he had felt during the day. He realized that body and mind formed one reality which could not be separated. The peace and comfort of the body were directly related to the peace and comfort of the mind. To abuse the body was to abuse the mind.

He remembered the first time he sat in meditation when he was nine years old, beneath the cool shade of a rose-apple tree on the day of the year's first plowing. He remembered how the refreshing ease of that sitting had brought him a sense of clarity and calm. He recalled, as well, his meditation in the forest right after Channa had left him. He thought back to his first days with Master Alara Kalama— those initial sessions of meditation had nourished both body and mind, creating in him a deep ability to concentrate and focus. But after that, Master Alara Kalama had told him to transcend the joys of meditation in order to attain to states that existed beyond the material world, states such as *the realms of limitless space and limitless consciousness,* and *the state of no materiality.* Later, there had been *the state of neither per-*

ception nor non-perception. Always the goal had been to find a means to escape the world of feeling and thought, the world of sensation and perception. He asked himself, "Why follow only the traditions laid down in scripture? Why fear the joyful ease that meditation brings? Such joys have nothing in common with the five categories of desire which obscure awareness. To the contrary, the joys of meditation can nourish body and mind and provide the strength needed to pursue the path to enlightenment."

The monk Gautama resolved to regain his health and to use his meditation to nourish both body and mind. He would beg for food again starting the next morning. He would be his own teacher, not depending on the teachings of anyone else. Happy with this decision, he stretched out on a mound of earth and peacefully drifted off to sleep. The full moon had just risen in a cloudless sky, and the Milky Way stretched clear and radiant across the heavens.

The monk Gautama awoke the next morning to the sound of birds singing. He stood up and recalled his decisions of the previous night. He was covered with dirt and dust, and his robe was so tattered and threadbare it no longer covered his body. He remembered seeing a corpse in the cemetery the day before, and he guessed that today or tomorrow people would lift it down to the river to perform the cremation ceremony, and the brick-colored cloth that covered it would no longer be needed. He approached the corpse and, reflecting quietly on birth and death, respectfully removed the cloth from the body. The corpse was that of a young woman, her body swollen and discolored. Siddhartha would use the brick-colored cloth as a new robe.

He walked to the river to bathe himself and at the same time to wash the cloth. The water was cool, and Siddhartha found it overwhelmingly refreshing. He enjoyed the pleasant feeling of the water on his skin, welcoming the sensation with a new state of mind. He took a long time bathing, and then he scrubbed and wrung out his new robe. But as he went to climb out of the water, his strength failed him. He did not

But as Siddhartha went to climb out of the water, his strength failed him.

have enough energy to pull himself onto the bank. He stood quietly and breathed calmly. To one side he saw a tree branch leaning over the water, its leaves skimming the surface. He walked towards it slowly and grabbed onto it to support himself while he climbed out of the water.

He sat down to rest on the riverbank as the sun climbed higher into the sky. He spread out the cloth to dry in the hot sun, and when the cloth was dry, Siddhartha wrapped it around himself and set out for the village of Uruvela. But before he had walked even half-way, his strength failed him, and, unable to catch his breath, he collapsed.

He lay unconscious for some time before a young girl from the village appeared. Thirteen-year-old Sujata had been sent by her mother to carry rice-milk, cakes, and lotus seeds to offer to the forest gods. When she saw the monk lying unconscious on the road, barely breathing, she knelt down and placed a bowl of milk to his lips. She knew he was an ascetic who had fainted from weakness.

When the drops of milk moistened his tongue and throat, Siddhartha responded immediately. He could taste how refreshing the milk was, and he slowly drank the entire bowlful. After a few dozen breaths he was revived enough to sit up, and he motioned Sujata to pour him another bowlful of milk. It was remarkable how quickly the milk restored his strength. That day he decided to abandon austerity practice and go to the cool forest across the river to practice there.

During the days that followed, he gradually began to eat and drink normally. Sometimes Sujata brought him food offerings, sometimes he took his bowl into the village to beg. Every day he practiced walking meditation along the riverbank, and the rest of the time he devoted to sitting meditation. Every evening he bathed in the Neranjara River. He abandoned all reliance on tradition and scripture in order to find the Way on his own. He returned to himself to learn from his own successes and failures. He did not hesitate to let meditation nourish his mind and body, and a sense of peace and ease grew within him. He did not distance himself or try to escape his feelings and perceptions, but maintained mindfulness in order to observe them as they arose.

He abandoned the desire to escape the world of phenomena, and as he returned to himself, he found he was completely present to the world of phenomena. One breath, one bird's song, one leaf, one ray of sunlight—any of these might serve as his subject of meditation. He began to see that the key to liberation lay in each breath, each step, each small pebble along the path.

The monk Gautama went from meditating on his body to meditating on his feelings, and from meditating on his feelings to meditating on his perceptions, including all the thoughts which rose and fell in his own mind. He saw the oneness of body and mind, that each and every cell of the body contained all the wisdom of the universe. He saw that he needed only to look deeply into a speck of dust to see the true face of the entire universe, that the speck of dust was itself the universe and if it did not exist, the universe could not exist either. The monk Gautama went beyond the idea of a separate self, of *atman*, and, with a start, realized that he had long been dominated by a false view of atman as expounded in the *Vedas*. In reality, all things were without a separate self. Non-self, or *anatman*, was the nature of all existence. Anatman was not a term to describe some new entity. It was a thunderbolt that destroyed all wrong views. Taking hold of non-self, Siddhartha was like a general raising his sharp sword of insight on the battlefield of meditation practice. Day and night he sat beneath the pippala tree, as new levels of awareness awoke in him like bright flashes of lightning.

During this time, Siddhartha's five friends lost faith in him. They saw him sitting along the river bank eating food offerings. They watched him speak and smile to a young girl, enjoy milk and rice, and carry his bowl down into the village. Kondanna said to the others, "Siddhartha is no longer someone we can rely on. He has abandoned the path half-way. He now concerns himself only with idly feeding his body. We should leave him and seek another place to continue our practice. I see no reason to continue here."

Only after his five friends had departed, did Siddhartha notice their absence. Encouraged by his new insights, Siddhartha had devoted all his time to meditation and had not yet taken the time to explain this to his friends. He thought, "My friends have misunderstood me, but I can't worry now about convincing them otherwise. I must devote myself to finding the true path. Once I have found it, I will share it with them." Then he returned to his daily practice.

During those same days in which he made such great progress along the path, the young buffalo boy Svasti appeared. Siddhartha cheerfully accepted the handfuls of fresh grass the eleven-year-old boy offered him. Though Sujata, Svasti, and their friends were still children, Siddhartha shared with them some of his new understanding. He was happy to see how unschooled children from the countryside could easily understand his discoveries. He was greatly heartened, for he knew that the door of complete enlightenment would soon open wide. He knew he held the wondrous key—the truth of the interdependent and non-self nature of all things.

Chapter Sixteen
Was Yasodhara Sleeping?

Because he was from a poor family, Svasti had, of course, never gone to school. Sujata taught him a few basics, but he still lacked skill with words, and while recounting his story about the Buddha, he sometimes halted, unable to find the right words. His listeners assisted him. In addition to Ananda and Rahula, two others came to listen to his story. One was an elderly nun named Mahapajapati and the other was a monk in his early forties named Assaji.

Rahula introduced them both to Svasti, who was deeply touched to learn that Mahapajapati was herself Queen Gotami, the Buddha's aunt who had raised him from infancy. She was the first woman to be accepted as a nun in the Buddha's sangha, and she now served as abbess to more than seven hundred nuns. She had just traveled from the north to visit the Buddha and to consult with him concerning precepts for the bhikkhunis. Svasti learned that she had arrived only the previous evening, and her grandson, Rahula, knowing how much she would enjoy hearing all Svasti had to say about the Buddha's days in Uruvela forest, had invited her to join them. Svasti placed his palms together and bowed low before the abbess. Remembering all the Buddha had told him about her filled his heart with deep affection and respect. Mahapajapati looked at Svasti with the same loving warmth as she looked at her own grandson, Rahula.

Rahula introduced Assaji to Svasti, and Svasti's eyes lit up when he learned that Assaji was one of the five friends who had practiced self-mortification with the Buddha near Svasti's own home. The Buddha had told him back then that when his friends saw he had abandoned austerities to drink milk and eat rice, they left him to practice elsewhere. Svasti wondered how Assaji had come to be one of the Buddha's disciples, living here at Bamboo Forest Monastery. He would ask Rahula about it later.

Bhikkhuni Gotami assisted Svasti the most in his efforts to tell his tale. She asked questions about details that didn't seem important to him but were of obvious interest to her. She asked where he had cut the kusa grass he offered the Buddha for a meditation cushion and how often he had provided new bundles of grass for the Buddha. She wanted to know if after giving the Buddha the grass, the buffaloes still had enough to eat at night. And she asked if he was ever beaten by the buffaloes' owner.

Much remained to be told, but Svasti asked permission to stop there for the evening and promised to continue the following day. But before taking his leave, he wondered if he could ask Bhikkhuni Gotami a few questions that he had held in his heart for ten years. She smiled at him and said, "Go ahead and ask. If I am able to answer your questions, I will be most happy to."

There were several things Svasti wanted to know. First of all, had Yasodhara really been sleeping or only pretending to be asleep the night Siddhartha pulled back the curtain before his departure? Svasti also wanted to know what the king, queen, and Yasodhara thought and said when Channa returned with Siddhartha's sword, necklace, and locks of hair. What happened in the lives of the Buddha's family in the six years of his absence? Who first heard the news that the Buddha had attained the Way? Who first welcomed the Buddha back, and did all the city come out to greet him when he returned to Kapilavatthu?

"You do have a lot of questions!" exclaimed Bhikkhuni Gotami. She smiled kindly at Svasti. "Let me try to answer them briefly. First of all, was Yasodhara truly asleep or not? If you want to know for certain, you should ask Yasodhara, but if you ask me, I don't believe she was. Yasodhara herself had prepared Siddhartha's garments, hat, and shoes, and placed them on his chair. She told Channa to saddle and ready Kanthaka. She knew that the prince would leave that very night. How could she sleep on such a night? I believe she only pretended to be asleep in order to avoid a painful parting for Siddhartha and herself. You do not yet know Yasodhara, Svasti, but Rahula's mother is a woman of great determination. She understood Siddhartha's intent and quietly gave him her wholehearted support. I know this more clearly than anyone else, for of all those close to Yasodhara, I was the closest, next to Siddhartha."

Bhikkhuni Gotami told Svasti that the following morning when it was discovered that Siddhartha had left, everyone, except Yasodhara, was in a state of shock. King Suddhodana flew into a rage and yelled at everyone, blaming them for not preventing the prince from leaving. Queen Gotami ran at once to find Yasodhara. She found her sitting quietly and weeping. Official search parties were sent out on horseback in all four directions with orders to return with the prince if they found him. The southbound party met Channa returning with the riderless Kanthaka. Channa stopped them from going any further. He said, "Leave the prince in peace to follow his spiritual path. I have already wept and pleaded with him, but he is intent on seeking the Way. Anyway, he has entered the deep forests which lie in another country's territory. You cannot seek him there."

When Channa returned to the palace, he lowered his head to the ground three times as a sign of remorse and took the sword, necklace, and locks of hair to give to the king. At that moment, Queen Gotami and Yasodhara were by the king's side. Seeing Channa's tears, the king did not rebuke him, but slowly asked about all that had taken place. He told Channa to give the sword, necklace, and hair to Yasodhara for safekeeping. The atmosphere in the palace was dreary. Losing the prince was like losing the light of day. The king retired to his quarters and refused to come out for many days. His minister Vessamitta was obliged to handle all palace matters on his behalf.

After being returned to his stall, Kanthaka refused to eat or drink, and died a few days later. Overcome with grief, Channa asked Yasodhara's permission to provide a ritual cremation for the prince's horse.

Bhikkhuni Gotami had recounted events up to that point when the bell for meditation rang. Everyone looked disappointed, but Ananda said they should not skip meditation, no matter how good the stories were. He invited them all to return the following day to his hut. Svasti and Rahula joined their palms and bowed to Bhikkhuni Gotami, Ananda and Assaji before returning to the hut of their teacher, Sariputta. The two young friends walked side by side without speaking. The slow reverberations of the bell gained momentum like waves breaking one upon another. Svasti followed his breath and silently recited the *gatha* for hearing the bell: "Listen, listen, this wonderful sound brings me back to my true self."

Chapter Seventeen
Pippala Leaf

Beneath the pippala tree, the hermit Gautama focused all of his formidable powers of concentration to look deeply at his body. He saw that each cell of his body was like a drop of water in an endlessly flowing river of birth, existence, and death, and he could not find anything in the body that remained unchanged or that could be said to contain a separate self. Intermingled with the river of his body was the river of feelings in which every feeling was a drop of water. These drops also jostled with one another in a process of birth, existence, and death. Some feelings were pleasant, some unpleasant, and some neutral, but all of his feelings were impermanent: they appeared and disappeared just like the cells of his body.

With his great concentration, Gautama next explored the river of perceptions which flowed alongside the rivers of body and feelings. The drops in the river of perceptions intermingled and influenced each other in their process of birth, existence, and death. If one's perceptions were accurate, reality revealed itself with ease; but if one's perceptions were erroneous, reality was veiled. People were caught in endless suffering because of their erroneous perceptions: they believed that which is impermanent is permanent, that which is without self contains self, that which has no birth and death has birth and death, and they divided that which is inseparable into parts.

Gautama next shone his awareness on the mental states which were the sources of suffering—fear, anger, hatred, arrogance, jealousy, greed, and ignorance. Mindful awareness blazed in him like a bright sun, and he used that sun of awareness to illuminate the nature of all these negative mental states. He saw that they all arose due to ignorance. They were the opposite of mindfulness. They were darkness—the absence of light. He saw that the key to liberation would be to break through ignorance and to enter deeply into the heart of reality and attain a direct experience of it. Such knowledge would not be the knowledge of the intellect, but of direct experience.

In the past, Siddhartha had looked for ways to vanquish fear, anger, and greed, but the methods he had used had not borne fruit because they were only attempts to suppress such feelings and emotions. Siddhartha now understood that their cause was ignorance, and that when one was liberated from ignorance, mental obstructions would vanish on their own, like shadows fleeing before the rising sun. Siddhartha's insight was the fruit of his deep concentration.

He smiled, and looked up at a pippala leaf imprinted against the blue sky, its tail blowing back and forth as if calling him. Looking deeply at the leaf, he saw clearly the presence of the sun and stars—without the sun, without light and warmth, the leaf could not exist. This was like this, because that was like that. He also saw in the leaf the presence of clouds—without clouds there could be no rain, and without rain the leaf could not be. He saw the earth, time, space, and mind—all were present in the leaf. In fact, at that very moment, the entire universe existed in that leaf. The reality of the leaf was a wondrous miracle.

Though we ordinarily think that a leaf is born in the springtime, Gautama could see that it had been there for a long, long time in the sunlight, the clouds, the tree, and in himself. Seeing that the leaf had never been born, he could see that he too had never been born. Both the leaf and he himself had simply manifested—they had never been born and were incapable of ever dying. With this insight, ideas of birth and death, appearance and disappearance dissolved, and the true face of the leaf and his own true face revealed themselves. He could see that the presence of any one phenomenon made possible the existence of all other phenomena. One included all, and all were contained in one.

The leaf and his body were one. Neither possessed a separate, permanent self. Neither could exist independently from the rest of the universe. Seeing the interdependent nature of all phenomena, Siddhartha saw the empty nature of all phenomena—that all things are empty of a separate, isolated self. He realized that the key to liberation lay in these two principles of interdependence and non-self. Clouds drifted across the sky, forming a white background to the translucent pippala leaf. Perhaps that evening the clouds would encounter a cold front and transform into rain. Clouds were one manifestation; rain was another. Clouds also were not born and would not die. If the clouds understood that, Gautama thought, surely they would sing joyfully as they fell down as rain onto the mountains, forests, and rice fields.

Illuminating the rivers of his body, feelings, perceptions, mental formations, and consciousness, Siddhartha now understood that impermanence and emptiness of self are the very conditions necessary for life. Without impermanence and emptiness of self, nothing could grow or develop. If a grain of rice did not have the nature of impermanence and emptiness of self, it could not grow into a rice plant. If clouds were not empty of self and impermanent, they could not transform into rain. Without an impermanent, non-self nature, a child could never grow into an adult. "Thus," he thought, "to accept life means to accept impermanence and emptiness of self. The source of suffering is a false belief in permanence and the existence of separate selves. Seeing this, one understands that there is neither birth nor death, production nor destruction, one nor many, inner nor outer, large nor small, impure nor pure. All such concepts are false distinctions created by the intellect. If one penetrates into the empty nature of all things, one will transcend all mental barriers, and be liberated from the cycle of suffering."

From one night to the next, Gautama meditated beneath the pippala tree, shining the light of his awareness on his body, his mind, and all the universe. His five companions had long abandoned him, and his co-practitioners were now the forest, the river, the birds, and the thousands of insects living on the earth and in the trees. The great pippala tree was his brother in practice. The evening star which appeared as he sat down in meditation each night was also his brother in practice. He meditated far into the night.

The village children came to visit him only in the early afternoons. One day Sujata brought him an offering of rice porridge cooked with milk and honey, and Svasti brought him a fresh armful of kusa grass. After Svasti left to lead the buffaloes home, Gautama was seized with a deep feeling that he would attain the Great Awakening that very night. Only the previous night he had had several unusual dreams. In one he saw himself lying on his side, his head pillowed by the Himalaya Mountains, his left hand touching the shores of the Eastern Sea, his right hand touching the shores of the Western Sea, and his two feet resting against the shores of the Southern Sea. In another dream, a great lotus as large as a carriage wheel grew from his navel and floated up to touch the highest clouds. In a third dream, birds of all colors, too many to be counted, flew towards him from all directions. These dreams seemed to announce that his Great Awakening was at hand.

Early that evening, Gautama did walking meditation along the banks of the river. He waded into the water and bathed. When twilight descended, he returned to sit beneath his familiar pippala tree. He smiled as he looked at the newly spread kusa grass at the foot of the tree. Beneath this very tree he had already made so many important discoveries in his meditation. Now the moment he had long awaited was approaching. The door to Enlightenment was about to open.

Slowly, Siddhartha sat down in the lotus position. He looked at the river flowing quietly in the distance as soft breezes rustled the grasses along its banks. The night forest was tranquil yet very much alive. Around him chirped a thousand different insects. He turned his awareness to his breath and lightly closed his eyes. The evening star appeared in the sky.

Chapter Eighteen

The Morning Star Has Risen

Through mindfulness, Siddhartha's mind, body, and breath were perfectly at one. His practice of mindfulness had enabled him to build great powers of concentration which he could now use to shine awareness on his mind and body. After deeply entering meditation, he began to discern the presence of countless other beings in his own body right in the present moment. Organic and inorganic beings, minerals, mosses and grasses, insects, animals, and people were all within him. He saw that other beings were himself right in the present moment. He saw his own past lives, all his births and deaths. He saw the creation and destruction of thousands of worlds and thousands of stars. He felt all the joys and sorrows of every living being—those born of mothers, those born of eggs, and those born of fission, who divided themselves into new creatures. He saw that every cell of his body contained all of Heaven and Earth, and spanned the three times—past, present, and future. It was the hour of the first watch of the night.

Gautama entered even more deeply into meditation. He saw how countless worlds arose and fell, were created and destroyed. He saw how countless beings pass through countless births and deaths. He saw that these births and deaths were but outward appearances and not true reality, just as millions of waves rise and fall incessantly on the surface of the sea, while the sea itself is beyond birth and death. If the waves understood that they themselves were water, they would transcend birth and death and arrive at true inner peace, overcoming all fear. This realization enabled Gautama to transcend the net of birth and death, and he smiled. His smile was like a flower blossoming in the deep night which radiated a halo of light. It was the smile of a wondrous understanding, the insight into the destruction of all defilements. He attained this level of understanding by the second watch.

At just that moment thunder crashed, and great bolts of lightning flashed across the sky as if to rip the heavens in two. Black clouds concealed the moon and stars. Rain poured down. Gautama was soaking wet, but he did not budge. He continued his meditation.

Without wavering, he shined his awareness on his mind. He saw that living beings suffer because they do not understand that they share one common ground with all beings. Ignorance gives rise to a multitude of sorrows, confusions, and troubles. Greed, anger, arrogance, doubt, jealousy, and fear all have their roots in ignorance. When we learn to calm our minds in order to look deeply at the true nature of things, we can arrive at full understanding which dissolves every sorrow and anxiety and gives rise to acceptance and love.

Gautama now saw that understanding and love are one. Without understanding there can be no love. Each person's disposition is the result of physical, emotional, and social conditions. When we understand this, we cannot hate even a person who behaves cruelly, but we can strive to help transform his physical, emotional, and social conditions. Understanding gives rise to compassion and love, which in turn give rise to correct action. In order to love, it is first necessary to understand, so understanding is the key to liberation. In order to attain clear understanding, it is necessary to live mindfully, making direct contact with life in the present moment, truly seeing what is taking place within and outside of oneself. Practicing mindfulness strengthens the ability to look deeply, and when we look deeply into the heart of anything, it will reveal itself. This is the secret treasure of mindfulness—it leads to the realization of liberation and enlightenment. Life is illuminated by right understanding, right thought, right speech, right action, right livelihood, right effort, right mindfulness, and right concentration. Siddhartha called this the Noble Path: *aryamarga*.

Looking deeply into the heart of all beings, Siddhartha attained insight into everyone's minds, no matter where they were, and he was able to hear everyone's cries of both suffering and joy. He attained to the states of divine sight, divine hearing, and the ability to travel across all distances without moving. It was now the end of the third watch, and there was no more thunder. The clouds rolled back to reveal the bright moon and stars.

Gautama felt as though a prison which had confined him for thousands of lifetimes had broken open. Ignorance had been the jailkeeper. Because of ignorance, his mind had been obscured, just like the moon and stars hidden by the storm clouds. Clouded by endless waves of deluded thoughts, the mind had falsely divided reality into subject and object, self and others, existence and non-existence, birth and death, and from these discriminations arose wrong views—the prisons of feelings, craving, grasping, and becoming. The suffering of birth, old age, sickness, and death only made the prison walls thicker. The only thing to do was to seize the jailkeeper and see his true face. The jailkeeper was ignorance. And the means to overcome ignorance were the Noble Eightfold Path. Once the jailkeeper was gone, the jail would disappear and never be rebuilt again.

The hermit Gautama smiled, and whispered to himself, "O jailer, I see you now. How many lifetimes have you confined me in the prisons of birth and death? But now I see your face clearly, and from now on you can build no more prisons around me."

Looking up, Siddhartha saw the morning star appear on the horizon, twinkling like a huge diamond. He had seen this star so many times before while sitting beneath the pippala tree, but this morning it was like seeing it for the first time. It was as dazzling as the jubilant smile of Enlightenment. Siddhartha gazed at the star and exclaimed out of deep compassion, "All beings contain within themselves the seeds of Enlightenment, and yet we drown in the ocean of birth and death for so many thousands of lifetimes!"

Siddhartha knew he had found the Great Way. He had attained his goal, and now his heart experienced perfect peace and ease. He thought about his years of searching, filled with disappointments and hardships. He thought of his father, mother, aunt, Yasodhara, Rahula, and all his friends. He thought of the palace, Kapilavatthu, his people and country, and of all those who lived in hardship and poverty, especially children. He promised to find a way to share his discovery to help all others liberate themselves from suffering. Out of his deep insight emerged a profound love for all beings.

Along the grassy riverbank, colorful flowers blossomed in the early morning sunlight. Sun danced on leaves and sparkled on the water. His pain was gone. All the wonders of life revealed themselves. Everything appeared strangely new. How wondrous were the blue skies and drifting white clouds! He felt as though he and all the universe had been newly created.

Just then, Svasti appeared. When Siddhartha saw the young buffalo boy come running towards him, he smiled. Suddenly Svasti stopped in his tracks and stared at Siddhartha, his mouth wide open. Siddhartha called, "Svasti!"

The boy came to his senses and answered, "Teacher!"

Svasti joined his palms and bowed. He took a few steps forward but then stopped and gazed again at Siddhartha in awe. Embarrassed by his own behavior, he spoke haltingly, "Teacher, you look so different today."

Siddhartha motioned for the boy to approach. He took him into his arms and asked, "How do I look different today?"

Svasti joined his palms and said, haltingly, "Teacher, you look so different today."

Gazing up at Siddhartha, Svasti answered, "It's hard to say. It's just you look so different. It's like, like you were a star."

Siddhartha patted the boy on the head and said, "Is that so? What else do I look like?"

"You look like a lotus that's just blossomed. And like, like the moon over the Gayasisa Peak."

Siddhartha looked into Svasti's eyes and said, "Why, you're a poet, Svasti! Now tell me, why are you here so early today? And where are your buffaloes?"

Svasti explained that he had the day off as all the buffaloes were being used to plow the fields. Only the calf had been left in its stall. Today his only responsibility was to cut grass. During the night he and his sisters and brother were awakened by the roar of thunder. Rain pounded through their leaky roof, soaking their beds. They had never experienced a storm so fierce, and they worried about Siddhartha in the forest. They huddled together until the storm subsided and they could fall back asleep. When day broke, Svasti ran to the buffaloes' stall to fetch his sickle and carrying pole, and made his way to the forest to see if Siddhartha was alright.

Siddhartha grasped Svasti's hand. "This is the happiest day I have ever known. If you can, bring all the children to come see me by the pippala tree this afternoon. Don't forget to bring your brother and sisters. But first go and cut the kusa grass you need for the buffaloes."

Svasti trotted off happily as Siddhartha began to take slow steps along the sun-bathed shore.

Chapter Nineteen

Tangerine of Mindfulness

W hen Sujata brought Siddhartha's food that noon, she found him sitting beneath the pippala tree as beautiful as a young morning. His face and body radiated peace, joy, and equanimity. She had seen him sitting solemnly and majestically beneath the pippala tree over a hundred times, and yet today there was something different about him. Looking at Siddhartha, Sujata felt all her sorrows and worries vanish. Happiness as fresh as a spring breeze filled her heart. She felt there was nothing else she needed or wanted on this Earth, that everything in the universe was already good and beneficial, and that no one needed to worry or despair anymore. Sujata took a few steps forward and placed the food before Siddhartha. She bowed before him. She felt the peace and joy within Siddhartha enter herself.

Siddhartha smiled at her and said, "Here, sit down with me. I thank you for bringing me food and water these past months. Today is the happiest day of my life because last night I found the Great Way. Please enjoy this happiness too. In the near future I will go teach this path to all others."

Sujata looked up with surprise. "You will be going? You mean you will leave us?"

Siddhartha smiled kindly. "Yes, I must leave, but I won't abandon you children. Before I leave, I will show you the path I have discovered."

Sujata was not very reassured. She wanted to ask him more, but he spoke first, "I will remain with you children for at least several more days in order to share what I have learned with you. Only then will I take to the road. But that doesn't mean I will be apart from you forever. From time to time, I will return to visit you children."

Sujata felt comforted. She sat down and opened the banana leaf to reveal the offering of rice. She sat silently at Siddhartha's side as he ate. She watched as he broke off pieces of rice and dipped them in sesame salt. Her heart was filled with inexpressible happiness.

When he finished eating, Siddhartha asked Sujata to return home. He said he wanted to meet with the village children that afternoon in the forest.

Many children came, including Svasti's brother and sisters. The boys had all bathed and put on clean clothes. The girls wore their loveliest saris. Sujata's sari was ivory colored, Nandabala wore a sari the color of banana shoots, and Bhima's sari was pink. The children, looking as fresh and colorful as flowers, sat around Siddhartha beneath the pippala tree.

Sujata brought a basketful of coconut and chunks of palm sugar as a special treat. The children scooped out the tasty coconut meat and ate it with the delicious sugar. Nandabala and Subash brought a basketful of tangerines. Siddhartha sat with the children, his happiness complete. Rupak offered him a chunk of coconut with a piece of palm sugar on a pippala leaf. Nandabala offered him a tangerine. Siddhartha accepted their offerings and ate with the children.

They were still enjoying their lunch when Sujata made an announcement, "Dear friends, today is the happiest day our Teacher has ever known. He has discovered the Great Way. I feel this is also a very important day for me. Brothers and sisters, let us consider this a day of great jubilation for us all. We are here today to celebrate the Enlightenment of our Teacher. Respected Teacher, the Great Path has been found. We know you cannot stay with us forever. Please teach us the

In mindfulness, the children passed around the basket of tanger-ines.

things you think we might be able to understand."

Sujata joined her palms together and bowed to Gautama to express her respect and devotion. Nandabala and the other children also joined their palms and bowed with deepest sincerity.

Siddhartha quietly gestured for the children to sit back up and he said, "You are all intelligent children and I am sure you will be able to understand and practice the things I will share with you. The Great Path I have discovered is deep and subtle, but anyone willing to apply his or her heart and mind can understand and follow it.

"When you children peel a tangerine, you can eat it with awareness or without awareness. What does it mean to eat a tangerine in awareness? When you are eating the tangerine, you are aware that you are eating the tangerine. You fully experience its lovely fragrance and sweet taste. When you peel the tangerine, you know that you are peeling the tangerine; when you remove a slice and put it in your mouth, you know that you are removing a slice and putting it in your mouth; when you experience the lovely fragrance and sweet taste of the tangerine, you are aware that you are experiencing the lovely fragrance and sweet taste of the tangerine. The tangerine Nandabala offered me had nine sections. I ate each morsel in awareness and saw how precious and wonderful it was. I did not forget the tangerine, and thus the tangerine became something very real to me. If the tangerine is real, the person eating it is real. That is what it means to eat a tangerine in awareness.

"Children, what does it mean to eat a tangerine without awareness? When you are eating the tangerine, you do not know that you are eating the tangerine. You do not experience the lovely fragrance and sweet taste of the tangerine. When you peel the tangerine, you do not know that you are peeling the tangerine; when you remove a slice and put it in your mouth, you do not know that you are removing a slice and putting it in your mouth; when you smell the fragrance or taste the tangerine, you do not know that you are smelling the fragrance and tasting the tangerine. Eating a tangerine in such a way, you cannot appreciate its precious and wonderful nature. If you are not aware that you are eating the tangerine, the tangerine is not real. If the tangerine is not real, the person eating it is not real either. Children, that is eating a tangerine without awareness.

"Children, eating the tangerine in mindfulness means that while eating the tangerine you are truly in touch with it. Your mind is not chasing after thoughts of yesterday or tomorrow, but is dwelling fully in the present moment. The tangerine is truly present. Living in mindful awareness means to live in the present moment, your mind and body dwelling in the very here and now.

"A person who practices mindfulness can see things in the tangerine that others are unable to see. An aware person can see the tangerine tree, the tangerine blossom in the spring, the sunlight and rain which nourished the tangerine. Looking deeply, one can see ten thousand things which have made the tangerine possible. Looking at a tangerine, a person who practices awareness can see all the wonders of the universe and how all things interact with one another. Children, our daily life is just like a tangerine. Just as a tangerine is comprised of sections, each day is comprised of twenty-four hours. One hour is like one section of tangerine. Living all twenty-four hours of a day is like eating all the sections of a tangerine. The path I have found is the path of living each hour of the day in awareness, mind and body always dwelling in the present moment. The opposite is to live in forgetfulness. If we live in forgetfulness, we do not know that we are alive. We do not fully experience life because our mind and body are not dwelling in the here and now."

Gautama looked at Sujata and said her name.

"Yes, Teacher?" Sujata joined her palms.

"Do you a think a person who lives in awareness will make many errors or few?"

"Respected Teacher, a person who lives in awareness will make few errors. My mother always tells me that a girl should pay attention to how she walks, stands, speaks, laughs, and works, in order to avoid thoughts, words, and actions that might cause sorrow to herself or others."

"Just so, Sujata. A person who lives in awareness knows what she is thinking, saying, and doing. Such a person can avoid thoughts, words, and actions that cause suffering for herself and others.

"Children, living in awareness means to live in the present moment. One is aware of what is taking place within one's self and in one's surroundings. One is in direct contact with life. If one continues to live in such a way, one will be able to deeply understand one's self and one's surroundings. Understanding leads to tolerance and love. When all beings understand one another, they will accept and love one another. Then there will not be much suffering in the world. What do you think, Svasti? Can people love if they are unable to understand?"

"Respected Teacher, without understanding love is most difficult. It reminds me of something that happened to my sister Bhima. One night she cried all night long until my sister Bala lost her patience and spanked Bhima. That only made Bhima cry more. I picked Bhima up and sensed that she was feverish. I was sure her head ached from the fever. I called Bala and told her to place her hand on Bhima's forehead. When she did that she understood at once why Bhima was crying. Her eyes softened and she took Bhima into her arms and sang to her with love. Bhima stopped crying even though she still had a fever. Respected Teacher, I think that was because Bala understood why Bhima was upset. And so I think that without understanding, love is not possible."

"Just so, Svasti! Love is possible only when there is understanding. And only with love can there be acceptance. Practice living in awareness, children, and you will deepen your understanding. You will be able to understand yourselves, other people, and all things. And you will have hearts of love. That is the wonderful path I have discovered."

Svasti joined his palms. "Respected Teacher, could we call this path the 'Path of Awareness'?"

Siddhartha smiled, "Surely. We can call it the Path of Awareness. I like that very much. The Path of Awareness leads to perfect Awakening."

Sujata joined her palms to ask permission to speak. "You are the awakened one, the one who shows how to live in awareness. Can we call you the 'Awakened One'?"

Siddhartha nodded. "That would please me very much."

Sujata's eyes shone. She continued, "'Awaken' in Magadhi is pronounced '*budh.*' A person who is awakened would be called '*Buddha*' in Magadhi. We can call you 'Buddha.'"

Siddhartha nodded. All the children were delighted. Fourteen-year-old Nalaka, the oldest boy in the group, spoke, "Respected Buddha, we are very happy to receive your teaching on the Path of Awareness. Sujata has told me how you have meditated beneath this pippala tree for the past six months and how just last night you attained the Great Awakening. Respected Buddha, this pippala tree is the most beautiful one in all the forest. Can we call it the 'Tree of Awakening,' the 'Bodhi Tree'? The word '*bodhi*' shares the same root as the word 'buddha' and also means awakening."

Gautama nodded his head. He was delighted, too. He had not guessed that during this gathering with the children the path, himself, and even the great tree would all receive special names. Nandabala joined his palms. "It is growing dark and we must return to our homes, but we will come back to receive more of your teaching soon." The children all stood and joined their palms like lotus buds to thank the Buddha. They strolled home chattering like a flock of happy birds. The Buddha was happy, too. He decided to stay in the forest for a longer period of time in order to explore ways to best sow the seeds of Awakening and to allow himself, as well, special time to enjoy the great peace and joy that attaining the path had brought him.

Chapter Twenty
The Deer

Every day the Buddha bathed in the Neranjara River. He did walking meditation along the riverbanks and along the small forest paths his own steps had created. He sat in meditation on the shore beside the flowing river or beneath the bodhi tree while hundreds of birds chirped among its branches. He had realized his vow. He knew he must return to Kapilavatthu where so many awaited news of his quest. He recalled, as well, King Bimbisara in the city of Rajagaha. He felt a special affinity for the young king and wished to visit him also. There were also his five former companions. He knew they each possessed the ability to attain liberation quickly, and he wanted to find them. No doubt they still dwelled nearby.

River, sky, moon and stars, mountains, forest, every blade of grass, and every mote of dust were transformed for the Buddha. He knew that the long years he wandered in search of the Way had not been wasted. Indeed, thanks to his trials and hardships, he had finally discovered the Way in his own heart. Every living being possessed the heart of enlightenment. The seeds of enlightenment existed in everyone. Living beings did not need to seek enlightenment outside of themselves because all the wisdom and strength of the universe was already present in them. This was the Buddha's great discovery and was cause for all to rejoice.

The children came to visit him often. The Buddha was happy to see that the way of liberation could be expressed simply and naturally. Even poor country children who had never attended school could understand his teaching. This greatly encouraged him.

One day the children arrived with a basketful of tangerines. They wanted to eat the tangerines in awareness in order to practice the very first lesson the Buddha had taught them. Sujata bowed gracefully before the Buddha and then held the basket before him. He joined his palms together like a lotus bud and took a tangerine. Sujata offered the basket to Svasti, who was sitting by the Buddha's side. He too joined his palms together and took a tangerine. She offered the basket to each child until everyone had a tangerine. She sat down and placed her palms together before taking a tangerine for herself. All the children sat silently. The Buddha told them to follow their breath and smile. Then he lifted his tangerine in his left hand and looked deeply at it. The children followed his example. He slowly peeled his tangerine and the children began to peel theirs. Teacher and students enjoyed their tangerines in silent awareness. When everyone was finished eating, Bala gathered up the peels. The children had greatly enjoyed eating their tangerines mindfully with the Buddha. The Buddha took great pleasure in sharing such a practice with the children.

The children visited the Buddha in the afternoons. He showed them how to sit still and to follow their breath in order to calm their minds when they felt sad or angry. He taught them walking meditation to refresh their minds and bodies. He taught them to look deeply at others and at their own actions in order to be able to see, to understand, and to love. The children understood all he taught them.

Nandabala and Sujata spent an entire day sewing a new robe to offer the Buddha. It was the color of bricks, similar to the cloth of the Buddha's old robe. When Sujata learned he had to take the cemetery cloth used to cover the corpse of her former household servant, Radha, who died of typhoid fever, she wanted to weep.

The Buddha was sitting beneath the bodhi tree when the two girls arrived to offer him the robe. They waited quietly for him to emerge from his meditation. When they presented him with the new robe he was very happy.

"I have need of this robe," he said. He told them he would keep the old cloth, as well, in order to have something to wear whenever he washed his new robe. Nandabala and Sujata privately resolved to sew him another robe soon.

One day, Sujata's twelve-year-old girlfriend, Balagupta, asked the Buddha to speak to them about friendship. Just the day before, Balagupta had had an argument with her closest friend, Jatilika. She had not wanted to stop by Jatilika's house on her way to see the Buddha the following day and only did so at Sujata's insistence. Jatilika only agreed to join them because Sujata was there. When the girls arrived at the bodhi tree, Balagupta and Jatilika sat far apart from one another.

The Buddha told the children about the friendship shared by a deer, a bird, and a turtle. He told them that the story had taken place several thousand years before, when he was a deer in a past life. The children looked surprised but he explained, "In previous lives, we have all been earth, stones, dew, wind, water, and fire. We have been mosses, grasses, trees, insects, fish, turtles, birds, and mammals. I have seen this most clearly in my meditations. Thus, in one life, I was a deer. This is quite an ordinary thing. I can still remember a life in which I was a jagged rock upon a mountain peak and another life in which I was a plumeria tree. It is the same for all of you. The story I am going to tell you is about a deer, a bird, a turtle, and a hunter. Perhaps one of you was the bird and another the turtle.

"We have all existed in times when there were not yet any humans, or even birds and mammals on Earth. There were only plants beneath the seas and trees and vegetation on the Earth's surface. In those times we may have been stones, dew, or plants. Afterwards we experienced lives as birds, as all kinds of animals, and finally as human beings. Right now we are more than just human beings. We are rice plants, tangerines, rivers, and air, because without these things we could not be. When you children look at rice plants, coconuts, tangerines, and water, remember that in this life you depend upon many other beings for your existence. These other beings are part of you. If you can see that, you will experience true understanding and love.

"Although the story I'm about to tell you took place several thousand years ago, it could just as easily take place this very moment. Listen carefully and see whether or not you have something in common with the animals in this story."

Then the Buddha began to tell his tale. At that time the Buddha was a deer who lived in a forest which had a clear lake where the deer liked to drink. A turtle lived in the lake's waters and a magpie lived in the branches of a willow tree beside the lake. Deer, Turtle, and Magpie were very close friends. One day, a hunter followed day old tracks left by Deer that led to the edge of the lake. There he left a trap made of strong ropes before returning to his hut on the outskirts of the forest.

Later that day when Deer came for a drink of water, he was caught by the trap. He cried out and was heard by Turtle and Magpie. Turtle crawled out of the water and Magpie flew down from her nest. They discussed how best to help their friend get out of his predicament. Magpie said, "Sister Turtle, your jaws are sturdy and strong. You can use them to chew and cut through these ropes. As for me, I'll find a way to prevent the hunter from coming back here." Magpie then flew off in haste.

Turtle began to gnaw at the ropes. Magpie flew to the hunter's hut and perched on a mango branch outside his front door all night to wait for him. When day broke, the hunter took a sharp knife and walked out his door. As soon as she saw him, Magpie flew into his face with all her might. Struck in the face by the bird, the hunter was momentarily dazed and went back inside his hut. He lay down on the bed to rest a moment. When he got up he paused for a moment and then, still clutching his sharp knife, went out the back door of his hut. But clever Magpie had outguessed him. She was waiting at the back perched on a jackfruit branch. Again she flew into his face, smacking him hard. Struck in the face twice by a bird, the hunter went back into his house to think things over. He decided it was an unlucky day and that perhaps it would be best to remain home until the morrow.

The next morning he rose early. He picked up his sharp knife and, as a precaution, covered his face with a hat before he walked out the door. Seeing she could no longer attack the hunter's face, Magpie sped back to the forest to warn her friends.

"The hunter is on his way!"

Turtle had almost chewed through the last of the ropes. But the last rope seemed as hard as steel. Her jaws were raw and bloody from chewing nonstop throughout two nights and a day. Still she did not stop. Just then the hunter appeared. Frightened, Deer gave a mighty kick which broke through the last rope and set him free. Deer ran into the forest. Magpie flew high into the willow tree. But Turtle was so exhausted from her efforts that she could not move. The hunter was angry to see the deer escape. He picked up the turtle and tossed her in his leather sack which he left hanging on a branch of the willow tree. Then he went off to find Deer.

Deer stood concealed behind some bushes and so saw Turtle's predicament. "My friends risked their lives for me," he thought, "now it is time for me to do the same for them." Deer stepped out in full view of the hunter. He pretended to stumble as though very tired and then he turned away and hobbled weakly down the path.

The hunter thought, "The deer is almost out of strength. I will stalk it and soon kill it with my knife."

The hunter pursued Deer deeper and deeper into the forest. Deer managed to stay just out of the hunter's reach. When they were far from the lake, Deer suddenly broke into a run

until he was out of the hunter's sight. He covered his hoof-
prints and then returned to the lake. He used his antlers to
lift the leather bag off the branch and to shake Turtle out.
Magpie joined her two friends.

"You both saved me from sure death today at the hunter's
hand!" said Deer. "I fear he will return here before long.
Magpie, fly to a safer spot in the forest. Sister Turtle, crawl
back into the water and hide. I will run back into the forest."

When the hunter arrived back at the lake, he found his
leather sack on the ground, empty. Frustrated, he picked it
up and still clutching his knife, trudged home.

The children had listened to the Buddha's tale with
wide-eyed interest. When the Buddha described how raw
and bloody Turtle's jaws had become from chewing the ropes
to save her friend, Rupak and Subash almost cried. The Buddha asked the children, "What do you think, children? Long
ago, I was Deer. Were any of you Turtle?"

Four children raised their hand, including Sujata.

The Buddha then asked, "And who among you was Magpie?"

Svasti raised his hand as did Jatilika and Balagupta.

Sujata looked at Jatilika and then at Balagupta. "If you
were both Magpie, that makes you one person. What good is
it for Magpie to be mad at Magpie? Can't our friendship
equal that of Magpie, Turtle, and Deer?"

Balagupta stood up and walked over to Jatilika. She took
her friend's hand in her own two hands. Jatilika pulled Balagupta into her arms and then slid over to make a place for
Balagupta to sit.

The Buddha smiled. "You children understand the story
well. Remember that tales like the one I have just recounted
are taking place all the time right in our own daily lives."

The Buddha lifted his robe to wade across the river, and then walked in meditation to a lotus pond that he liked very much.

Chapter Twenty-One
The Lotus Pond

After the children returned home, the Buddha did walking meditation. He lifted his robe to wade across the river, and then followed a path between two rice fields that led to a lotus pond he liked very much. There he sat down and contemplated the beautiful lotuses.

As he looked at the lotus stems, leaves, and flowers, he thought of all the different stages of a lotus' growth. The roots remained buried in mud. Some stems had not risen above the surface of the water while others had barely emerged to reveal leaves still curled tightly shut. There were unopened lotus flower buds, those with petals just beginning to peek out, and lotus flowers in full bloom. There were seed pods from which all the petals had fallen. There were white lotus flowers, blue ones, and pink ones. The Buddha reflected that people were not very different from lotus flowers. Each person had his or her own natural disposition. Devadatta was not like Ananda, Yasodhara was not the same as Queen Pamita; Sujata was not like Bala. Personality, virtue, intelligence, and talent varied widely among people. The Path of Liberation which the Buddha had discovered needed to be expounded in many ways to suit many kinds of people. Teaching the village children was so pleasant, he thought, because he could speak to them in such a simple way.

Different teaching methods were like gates by which different kinds of people could enter and understand the teaching. The creation of "Dharma gates" would result from direct encounters with people. There were no ready-made methods miraculously received under the bodhi tree. The Buddha saw that it would be necessary to return to society in order to set the wheel of Dharma in motion and to sow the seeds of liberation. Forty-nine days had passed since his Awakening. It was now time to depart from Uruvela. He decided to leave the following morning, parting from the cool forest by the banks of the Neranjara River, the bodhi tree, and the children. He wanted first to seek out his two teachers, Alara Kalama and Uddaka Ramaputta. He was confident that they would attain Awakening in no time at all. After assisting these two venerable men, he would find the five friends who had practiced austerities with him. Then he would return to Magadha to see King Bimbisara.

The next morning, the Buddha put on his new robe and walked into Uruvela while the morning air was still misty. He went to Svasti's hut and told the young buffalo boy and his family that the time had come for him to depart. The Buddha patted each of the children gently on the head, and together they walked to Sujata's house. Sujata cried when she learned the news.

The Buddha said, "I must leave in order to fulfil my responsibilities. But I promise that I will return to visit you whenever I have a chance. You children have helped me greatly, and I am grateful. Please remember and practice the things I have shared with you. That way I will never be far from you. Sujata, dry your tears now and give me a smile."

Sujata wiped her tears with the edge of her sari and tried to smile. Then the children walked with the Buddha to the edge of the village. The Buddha was turning to say farewell, when he noticed a young ascetic walking towards them. The ascetic joined his palms in greeting and looked curiously at the Buddha. After a long moment, he said, "Monk, you look most radiant and peaceful. What is your name and who is your Master?"

The Buddha answered, "My name is Siddhartha Gautama. I have studied with many teachers, but no one is my teacher now. What is your name, and where are you coming from?"

The ascetic answered, "My name is Upaka. I have just left the center of Master Uddaka Ramaputta."

"Is Master Uddaka in good health?"

"Master Uddaka died just a few days ago."

The Buddha sighed. He would not have a chance to help his old teacher after all. He asked, "Have you ever studied with Master Alara Kalama?"

Upaka answered, "Yes. But he, too, has recently died."

"Do you by any chance know of a monk named Kondanna?"

Upaka said, "Yes, indeed. I heard about Kondanna and four other monks when I was living at Master Uddaka's center. I heard they are living and practicing together at the Deer Park in Isipatana, near the city of Varanasi. Gautama, if you will excuse me, I will continue on my way. I have a long day's journey ahead."

The Buddha joined his palms to bid Upaka farewell, and then he turned to the children. "Children, I will follow the road to Varanasi to find my five friends. The sun has risen. Please return home now."

The Buddha joined his palms in farewell. Then he followed the river northwards. He knew it would be a longer route but easier to travel. The Neranjara River led northwards to where it emptied into the Ganga. If he followed the westward course of the Ganga, he would reach the village of Pataligrama within a few days. There he could cross to the other side of the Ganga and reach Varanasi, the capital of Kasi.

The children gazed at him until he was out of sight. They were filled with terrible sadness and longing. Sujata cried, and Svasti felt like crying too, but he did not want to cry in front of his brother and sisters. After a long moment, he said, "Sister Sujata, I need to get ready to tend the buffaloes. We should all head home. Bala, remember to give Rupak a bath today. Here, I'll carry Bhima."

They followed the riverbank back towards the village. No one spoke another word.

* * *

The elder Ananda was gentle and friendly, as well as unusually handsome. And he did indeed possess an uncanny memory. He remembered every detail of every discourse the Buddha gave. He repeated the eleven points the Buddha had elaborated in the *Sutra on Tending Water Buffaloes,* to Svasti and Rahula's gratitude. Svasti realized that Ananda would remember everything Svasti had just recounted about the Buddha's time in the forest near Uruvela.

While Svasti recounted his story, he glanced often at Bhikkhuni Gotami. Her sparkling eyes told him how much she enjoyed listening to all he was saying. He made a special effort to include as many details as he could remember. Bhikkhuni Gotami especially enjoyed hearing about all the children in Uruvela, like the time they ate tangerines mindfully with the Buddha in the forest.

It was easy to see how much Rahula enjoyed hearing what Svasti had to say. Although the elder Assaji had not made any comments during the two days Svasti told his story, it was clear he was enjoying it also. Svasti knew that Assaji was one of the five friends who had practiced self-mortification with the Buddha. Svasti was most curious to know what happened when the Buddha met them after six months of separation, but he was too shy to ask. As if she could read his thoughts, Bhikkhuni Gotami said, "Svasti, would you like to hear the elder Assaji tell us what happened after the Buddha left Uruvela? Assaji has been with the Buddha for ten years now, but I don't think he has ever spoken about what happened in the Deer Park at Isipatana. Master Assaji, would you consent to tell us about the Buddha's first Dharma talk and some of what has taken place in the past ten years?"

Assaji joined his palms and responded, "No need to call me Master, Bhikkhuni Gotami. Today we have already heard a great deal from Bhikkhu Svasti, and it is almost time for meditation. Why don't you all come to my hut tomorrow, and I will tell you all that I remember."

Kondanna took Siddhartha's begging bowl, Mahanama brought him water, Bhaddiya pulled up a stool, Vappa fanned him with a palm leaf, while Assaji stood to one side, not knowing what to do.

Turning the Wheel of Dharma

Assaji was practicing the austere way in the Deer Park. One day after his sitting meditation, he noticed a monk approaching from off in the distance. As the stranger came closer, he realized it was none other than Siddhartha, and he quickly told his four friends.

Bhaddiya said, "Siddhartha abandoned the path halfway. He ate rice, drank milk, and visited with the village children. He really let us down. I say we shouldn't even greet him." So the five friends agreed not to meet Siddhartha by the gate to the park. They also decided not to stand and greet him if he should enter the Deer Park by himself. But what actually took place was entirely different.

When Siddhartha entered the gate, the five ascetic companions were so impressed by his radiant bearing that they all stood up at once. Siddhartha seemed to be surrounded by an aura of light. Each step he took revealed a rare spiritual strength. His penetrating gaze undermined their intention to snub him. Kondanna ran up to him and took his begging bowl. Mahanama fetched water so that Siddhartha could wash his hands and feet. Bhaddiya pulled up a stool for him to sit on. Vappa found a fan of palm leaves and began to fan him. Assaji stood to one side, not knowing what to do.

After Siddhartha washed his hands and feet, Assaji realized he could fill a bowl with cool water and offer it to him. The five friends sat in a circle around Siddhartha, who looked kindly at them and said, "My brothers, I have found the Way, and I will show it to you."

Assaji half-believed and half-doubted Siddhartha's words. Perhaps the others felt the same, for no one spoke for a long moment. Then Kondanna blurted out, "Gautama! You abandoned the path halfway. You ate rice, drank milk, and spent time with the village children. How can you have found the path to liberation?"

Siddhartha looked into Kondanna's eyes and asked, "Friend Kondanna, you have known me a long time. During all that time, have I ever lied to you?"

Kondanna admitted that he had not. "Indeed, Siddhartha, I have never heard you speak anything but the truth."

The Buddha said, "Then please listen, my friends. I have found the Great Way, and I will show it to you. You will be the first to hear my Teaching. This Dharma is not the result of thinking. It is the fruit of direct experience. Listen serenely with all your awareness."

The Buddha's voice was filled with such spiritual authority that his five friends joined their palms and looked up at him. Kondanna spoke for them all, "Please, friend Gautama, show us compassion and teach us the Way."

The Buddha began serenely, "My brothers, there are two extremes that a person on the path should avoid. One is to plunge oneself into sensual pleasures, and the other is to practice austerities which deprive the body of its needs. Both of these extremes lead to failure. The path I have discovered is the Middle Way, which avoids both extremes and has the capacity to lead one to understanding, liberation, and peace. It is the Noble Eightfold Path of right understanding, right thought, right speech, right action, right livelihood, right effort, right mindfulness, and right concentration. I have followed this Noble Eightfold Path and have realized understanding, liberation, and peace.

"Brothers, why do I call this path the Right Path? I call it the Right Path because it does not avoid or deny suffering, but allows for a direct confrontation with suffering as the means to overcome it. The Noble Eightfold Path is the path of living in awareness. Mindfulness is the foundation. By practicing mindfulness, you can develop concentration which enables you to attain Understanding. Thanks to right concentration, you realize right awareness, thoughts, speech, action, livelihood, and effort. The Understanding which develops can liberate you from every shackle of suffering and give birth to true peace and joy.

"Brothers, there are four truths the existence of suffering, the cause of suffering, the cessation of suffering, and the path which leads to the cessation of suffering. I call these the Four Noble Truths. The first is the existence of suffering. Birth, old age, sickness, and death are suffering. Sadness, anger, jealousy, worry, anxiety, fear, and despair are suffering. Separation from loved ones is suffering. Association with those you hate is suffering. Desire, attachment, and clinging to the five aggregates are suffering.

"Brothers, the second truth is the cause of suffering. Because of ignorance, people cannot see the truth about life, and they become caught in the flames of desire, anger, jealousy, grief, worry, fear, and despair.

"Brothers, the third truth is the cessation of suffering. Understanding the truth of life brings about the cessation of every grief and sorrow and gives rise to peace and joy.

"Brothers, the fourth truth is the path which leads to the cessation of suffering. It is the Noble Eightfold Path, which I have just explained. The Noble Eightfold Path is nourished by living mindfully. Mindfulness leads to concentration and understanding which liberates you from every pain and sorrow and leads to peace and joy. I will guide you along this path of realization."

While Siddhartha was explaining the Four Noble Truths, Kondanna suddenly felt a great light shining within his own heart. He could taste the liberation he had sought for so long. His face beamed with joy. The Buddha pointed at him and cried, "Kondanna! You've got it! You've got it!"

Kondanna joined his palms and bowed before the Buddha. With deepest respect, he spoke, "Venerable Gautama, please accept me as your disciple. I know that under your guidance, I will attain the Great Awakening."

The other four monks also bowed at the Buddha's feet, joined their palms, and asked to be received as disciples. The Buddha motioned his friends to rise. After they took their places again, he said, "Brothers! The children of Uruvela village gave me the name 'the Buddha.' You, too, may call me by that name if you like."

Kondanna asked, "Doesn't 'Buddha' mean 'one who is awakened'?"

"That is correct. And they call the path I have discovered 'the Way of Awakening.' What do you think of this name?"

"'One who is awakened'! 'The Way of Awakening'! Wonderful! Wonderful! These names are true, yet simple. We will happily call you the Buddha and the path you have discovered the Way of Awakening. As you just said, living each day mindfully is the very basis of spiritual practice." The five monks were of one mind to accept Gautama as their teacher and to call him the Buddha.

The Buddha smiled at them. "Please, brothers, practice with an open and intelligent spirit, and in three months you will have attained the fruit of liberation."

The Buddha stayed in Isipatana to guide his five friends. Following his teaching, they gave up their practice of austerities. Every day three monks went begging for food and returned to share the offerings with the other three. The Buddha gave them individual attention, enabling each monk to make rapid progress.

The Buddha taught them about the impermanent and nonself nature of all things. He taught them to look at the five aggregates as five constantly flowing rivers which contained nothing that could be called separate or permanent. The five aggregates were the body, feelings, perceptions, mental formations, and consciousness. By meditating on the five aggregates within themselves, they came to see the intimate and wondrous connection between themselves and all in the universe.

Thanks to their diligence, they all realized the Way. The first to attain Awakening was Kondanna, followed two months later by Vappa and Bhaddiya. Shortly afterwards, Mahanama and Assaji also attained Arhatship.

In great joy, the Buddha told them, "Now we have a real community, which we will call our Sangha. The sangha is the community of those who live in harmony and awareness. We must take the seeds of awakening and sow them in all places."

*It was the Buddha's custom to walk in meditation each morning
among the forest trees.*

Chapter Twenty-Three
Dharma Nectar

It was the Buddha's custom to rise early and to sit in meditation, and then do walking meditation among the forest
trees. One morning while walking, he saw a handsome, elegantly dressed man in his late twenties, half-hidden in the
morning mist. The Buddha sat on a large rock, and when the
man approached quite close to the rock, still unaware of the
Buddha, he mumbled, "Disgusting! Repulsive!"

The Buddha spoke up, "There is nothing disgusting. There
is nothing repulsive."

The man stopped in his tracks. The Buddha's voice was
clear and soothing, and the man looked up to see the Buddha
sitting there, relaxed and serene. The young man removed his
sandals and bowed deeply before the Buddha. Then he sat on
a nearby rock.

The Buddha asked, "What is so disgusting? What is so repulsive?"

The young man introduced himself as Yasa, the son of one
of the wealthiest and most reputable merchants in Varanasi.
Yasa had always enjoyed a life of splendor and ease. His
parents catered to his every whim, providing him with every
kind of pleasure, including a handsome manor, jewels, money,
wine, courtesans, banquets, and parties. But Yasa, a sensitive
and thoughtful young man, had begun to feel suffocated by
this life of pleasure and could no longer find any contentment
in it.

He was like a person locked in a room without windows; he longed for some fresh air, for a simple, wholesome life. The night before, Yasa and some friends had gathered to feast, drink, play music, and be entertained by lovely young courtesans. In the middle of the night, Yasa woke up and looked at his friends and the young women sprawled out asleep. At that moment he knew he could not continue to live that way. He threw a cloak over his body, slipped on a pair of sandals, and walked out the front gate, not even knowing where he would go. He had wandered aimlessly all night until by chance he found himself in the Deer Park of Isipatana. And now as the sun rose, he sat facing the Buddha.

The Buddha counselled him, "Yasa, this life is filled with suffering, but it is also filled with many wonders. To drown in sensual pleasures is bad for the health of both body and mind. If you live simply and wholesomely, not ruled by desires, it is possible to experience the many wonders of life. Yasa, look around you. Can you see the trees standing in the morning mists? Are they not beautiful? The moon, the stars, the rivers, the mountains, the sunlight, the songs of birds, and the sounds of bubbling springs are all manifestations of a universe which can provide us with endless happiness.

"The happiness we receive from these things nourishes mind and body. Close your eyes, and breathe in and out a few times. Now open them. What do you see? Trees, mist, sky, rays of sunlight. Your own two eyes are wonders. Because you have been out of touch with wonders like these, you have come to despise your mind and body. Some people despise their own minds and bodies so much they want to commit suicide. They see only the suffering in life. But suffering is not the true nature of the universe. Suffering is the result of the way we live and of our erroneous understanding of life."

The Buddha's words touched Yasa like fresh drops of cool dew to soothe his parched heart. Overcome with happiness, he prostrated before the Buddha and asked to become a disciple.

The Buddha helped him up and said, "A monk lives a simple and humble life. He has no money. He sleeps in a grass hut or beneath the trees. He eats only what he receives from begging, and he eats only one meal a day. Can you live such a life?"

"Yes, Master, I would be happy to live such a life."

The Buddha continued, "A monk devotes his mind and body to realize liberation, in order to help himself and all others. He concentrates his efforts to help relieve suffering. Do you vow to follow such a path?"

"Yes, Master, I vow to follow such a path."

"Then I accept you as my disciple. A disciple in my community is known as a *bhikkhu*, a beggar. Every day you will go to beg your food in order to nourish yourself, to practice humility, and to be in touch with others in order to show them the Way."

Just then the Buddha's five friends and first disciples appeared. Yasa stood up and respectfully greeted each one. The Buddha introduced them to Yasa and then turned to Kondanna, "Kondanna, Yasa wishes to become a bhikkhu. I have accepted him. Please show him how to wear a robe, carry a begging bowl, observe his breath, and do sitting and walking meditation."

Yasa bowed to the Buddha and then followed Kondanna, who led him to his hut, where he shaved Yasa's hair and gave him instruction according to the Buddha's wishes. Kondanna happened to have an extra robe and bowl which had been offered to him but which he had never used. He gave these to Yasa.

That afternoon Yasa's father came looking for him. All morning long the household had frantically been seeking Yasa at his father's orders. One servant followed Yasa's footprints to the Deer Park, and there he found Yasa's golden sandals abandoned by a large rock. After making inquiries, he learned that his young master was staying there with some monks. He returned in haste to inform Yasa's father.

When Yasa's father arrived, he found the Buddha sitting serenely on a rock. He joined his palms and respectfully asked, "Revered monk, have you seen my son Yasa?"

The Buddha motioned to a nearby rock and invited Yasa's father to be seated. He said, "Yasa is in the hut and will be out shortly."

Yasa's father listened as the Buddha recounted all that had taken place that morning. The Buddha helped him understand Yasa's inner thoughts and aspirations. "Yasa is a bright and sensitive young man. He has found the path of liberation for his heart. He now has faith, peace, and joy. Please be happy for him," the Buddha said.

The Buddha also told Yasa's father how it was possible to live in a way that could reduce suffering and anxiety and create peace and joy for oneself and all those around one. The merchant felt lighter with each word the Buddha spoke. He stood up and joined his palms together to ask to be accepted as a lay disciple.

The Buddha was silent for a moment and then he spoke, "My disciples strive to live simply with awareness, avoid killing, shun adultery, speak truthfully, and avoid alcohol and stimulants which cloud the mind. Sir, if you feel you can follow such a path I will accept you as a lay disciple."

Yasa's father knelt before the Buddha and joined his palms. "Allow me to take refuge in your teaching. Please show me the way in this life. I vow to remain faithful to your teaching all my days."

The Buddha helped the merchant back to his feet. Yasa joined them. He was clad in a bhikkhu's robe and his head was shaven. The new bhikkhu smiled with rare joy. He joined his palms to make a lotus bud and then bowed to his father. Yasa looked radiant. His father had never seen him so happy. Yasa's father bowed to his son and said, "Your mother is at home, and she is very worried about you."

Yasa answered, "I will visit her to relieve her worries. But I have taken vows to follow the Buddha and to live a life of service to all beings."

Yasa's father turned to the Buddha, "Please, Master, allow me to invite you and your bhikkhus to have a meal at my house tomorrow. We would be deeply honored if you would come instruct us on the Path of Awakening."

The Buddha turned and looked at Yasa. The new bhikkhu's eyes sparkled. Then the Buddha nodded his acceptance.

The following day, the Buddha and his six bhikkhus ate at the home of Yasa's parents. Yasa's mother wept, so overcome was she to see her son both safe and happy. The Buddha and his bhikkhus were invited to sit on cushioned chairs. Yasa's mother served them herself. As the bhikkhus ate in silence, no one spoke, not even the household servants. When the meal was finished and the begging bowls had been washed, Yasa's parents bowed to the Buddha and then sat on low stools placed before him. The Buddha taught them the five precepts which formed the foundation of practice for lay disciples.

"The first precept is do not kill. All living beings fear death. If we truly follow the path of understanding and love, we will observe this precept. Not only should we protect the lives of humans, we should protect the lives of animals as well. Observing this precept nourishes compassion and wisdom.

"The second precept is do not steal. We do not have the right to steal the property of others, nor to gain wealth by taking advantage of the labor of others. We must find ways to help others support themselves.

"The third precept is do not engage in sexual misconduct. Do not violate the rights and commitments of others. Always remain faithful to your spouse.

"The fourth precept is do not say untruthful things. Do not utter words that distort the truth or cause discord and hatred. Do not spread news that you do not know to be certain.

"The fifth precept is do not use alcohol or any other stimulants.

"If you live by the spirit of the five precepts, you will avoid suffering and discord for yourself, your family, and your friends. You will find your happiness in life multiplied many times over."

As Yasa's mother listened to the Buddha, she felt as though a gate of happiness had just opened in her heart. She was happy to know that her husband had already been accepted as a lay disciple by the Buddha. She knelt before the Buddha and joined her palms. She, too, was accepted as a lay disciple.

The Buddha and his six bhikkhus returned to Isipatana.

Chapter Twenty-Four
Taking Refuge

News of Yasa becoming a bhikkhu spread quickly among his friends. His closest companions—Vimala, Subahu, Punnaji, and Gavampati—decided to visit him at Isipatana. On the way there Subahu said, "If Yasa has decided to become a monk, his Master must really be extraordinary and the path he teaches most lofty. Yasa is very discriminating."

Vimala retorted, "Don't be so certain. Perhaps he became a monk on a whim, and it won't last long. After six months or a year, he may very well abandon such a life."

Gavampati disagreed. "You're not taking Yasa seriously enough. I have always found him to be quite serious, and I'm sure he wouldn't do anything like this without sincerely intending it."

When they found Yasa at the Deer Park, he introduced them to the Buddha. "Teacher, these four friends of mine are all fine persons. Please have compassion and open their eyes to the path of liberation."

The Buddha sat down to talk with the four young men. At first Vimala was the most skeptical, but the more he heard the more impressed he became. Finally, he suggested to the other three that they all ask the Buddha to accept them as bhikkhus. The four young men knelt before the Buddha. Recognizing their sincerity, the Buddha accepted them on the spot. He asked Kondanna to give them basic instruction.

Yasa had several hundred other friends who soon heard how Yasa and his four closest companions had all become bhikkhus. One hundred twenty of these young men, all in their twenties, met outside Yasa's home and decided to visit Isipatana that very morning. Yasa was informed of their arrival and he came out to greet them. He spoke about his decision to become a bhikkhu and then he led them to have an audience with the Buddha.

Surrounded by the young men, the Buddha spoke about the path which can end suffering and lead to peace and joy. He told them about his own search and how he had vowed to find the Way while he was still a young man. The one hundred twenty young men listened as if entranced. Fifty of them requested to become bhikkhus at once. Many of the other seventy also wanted to become bhikkhus but could not abandon their responsibilities as sons, husbands, and fathers.

Yasa asked the Buddha to accept his fifty friends, and the Buddha agreed. Overjoyed, Yasa said, "With your permission, tomorrow I will pass by my parents' home when I am out begging. I can ask them if they might like to offer robes and bowls to these new bhikkhus."

The Buddha now had sixty bhikkhus living with him at the Deer Park. He remained there for three additional months in order to guide the community. During that time, several hundred men and women were accepted by the Buddha as lay disciples.

The Buddha taught the bhikkhus how to practice observing their body, feelings, perceptions, mental formations, and consciousness. He taught them about the interdependent nature of all things and explained that meditating on interdependence was very important. He explained that all things depend on each other for their arising, development, and decline. Without dependent co-arising, nothing could exist. Within one thing existed all things. "The meditation on dependent co-arising," he said, "is a gate which leads to liberation from birth and death. It has the power to break through fixed and narrow views such as the belief that the universe has been created either by some god or from some element such as earth, water, fire, or air."

The Buddha understood his responsibility as a teacher. He cared for and guided the sixty bhikkhus like a loving elder brother. He also shared a lot of responsibility with his first five disciples. Kondanna guided twenty young men, while Bhaddiya, Vappa, Mahanama, and Assaji each helped guide ten young men. All the bhikkhus made great progress along the path.

When the Buddha saw this, he called the community together and said, "Bhikkhus, please listen. We are totally free, not bound by anything. You understand the path now. Proceed with confidence and you will make great strides. You can leave Isipatana whenever you like. Walk as free persons and share the Way of Awakening with others. Please sow the seeds of liberation and enlightenment to bring peace and joy to others. Teach the path of liberation which is beautiful from beginning to end, in form and content. Countless others will benefit from your work of spreading the Dharma. As for me, I will leave soon. I plan to head east. I want to visit the bodhi tree and the children in Uruvela village. Afterwards I will go to visit a special friend in Rajagaha."

After listening to the Buddha's words, a large number of bhikkhus, clad in brick-colored robes and carrying just their begging bowls, left to go spread the teaching. Only twenty bhikkhus remained in Isipatana.

Before long, many people in the kingdoms of Kasi and Magadha heard about the Buddha and his disciples. They knew that a prince of the Sakya clan had attained liberation and was teaching his path in Isipatana, near the city of Varanasi. Many monks, who up to then had not yet attained the fruits of liberation, felt greatly encouraged, and they came from all directions to Isipatana. After hearing the Buddha speak, most took vows to become bhikkhus. The bhikkhus who had left Isipatana to spread the teaching brought back many more young men who also wished to become monks. The number of disciples soon swelled.

One day the Buddha gathered the sangha in the Deer Park and said, "Bhikkhus! It is no longer necessary for me personally to ordain every new bhikkhu or for everyone who wishes to be ordained to come to Isipatana. Those who wish to receive ordination should be able to do so in their own villages, in the presence of their friends and families. And, like you, I too would like to be free to remain here and to travel from here. Henceforth, when you meet a sincere and aspiring new bhikkhu, you may ordain him wherever you may be."

Kondanna stood up and joined his palms. "Master, please show us the way to organize a ceremony of ordination. Then we can do it by ourselves in the future."

The Buddha answered, "Please do as I have done in the past."

Assaji stood up and said, "Master, your presence is so formidable, you do not need to perform a formal ceremony. But for the rest of us, a formal procedure is needed. Brother Kondanna, perhaps you can suggest a form. The Buddha is here with us and he can add to your suggestions."

Kondanna was silent for a moment. Then he spoke, "Respected Buddha, I think the first step should be to have the aspiring bhikkhu allow his hair and beard to be shaved. Then he can be instructed in the manner of wearing the robe. After he has put on his robe, he can expose his right shoulder in the customary manner, and kneel before the monk giving the ordination. It is proper to kneel as the monk giving the ordination is serving as the representative of the Buddha. The one being ordained can hold his palms together like a lotus bud and recite three times, 'I take refuge in the Buddha, the one who shows me the way in this life. I take refuge in the Dharma, the way of understanding and love. I take refuge in the Sangha, the community that lives in harmony and awareness.' After repeating these refuges, he will be considered a bhikkhu in the community of the Buddha. But this is only my poor suggestion. Please, Teacher, correct it."

The Buddha answered, "It is most fine, Brother Kondanna. Reciting the three refuges three times while kneeling before an already ordained bhikkhu shall be sufficient to become an ordained bhikkhu."

The community was happy with this decision.

A few days later the Buddha put on his robe, lifted his bowl, and left Isipatana on his own. It was an especially beautiful morning. He headed towards the Ganga River to return to Magadha.

Chapter Twenty-Five
Music's Lofty Peaks

The Buddha had traveled the road from Varanasi to Raja-gaha before. He walked slowly and enjoyed the surrounding forests and rice fields. Towards noon, he stopped to beg in a small hamlet by the roadside. He then entered the forest to eat quietly, and then did walking meditation right there. When he was finished, he sat beneath a shady tree to meditate. He enjoyed being alone in the forest. After he had meditated for some hours, a group of well-dressed young men passed by, obviously agitated over something. Several of them clutched musical instruments. The young man at the head of their party bowed his head to greet the Buddha and then asked, "Monk, did you see a girl run by here?"

The Buddha asked, "Why do you wish to find her?"

The young man recounted their story from the beginning. They were from the city of Varanasi and had entered the forest that morning on a pleasure outing, bringing with them their musical instruments and a young woman to entertain them. When they had finished singing, dancing, and feasting, they stretched out on the forest floor to take a nap. But when they awoke, they discovered that the young girl had stolen their jewelry and disappeared. They had been chasing after her ever since.

The Buddha looked calmly at the young men and asked, "Tell me, friends, is it better in this moment to find the young woman or to find your own selves?"

The young men were startled. The Buddha's radiant appearance and his unusual question brought them back to themselves. The first young man answered, "Respected Teacher, perhaps we should try to find ourselves first."

The Buddha said, "Life can be found only in the present moment, but our minds rarely dwell in the present moment. Instead we chase after the past or long for the future. We think we are being ourselves, but in fact we almost never are in real contact with ourselves. Our minds are too busy chasing after yesterday's memories or tomorrow's dreams. The only way to be in touch with life is to return to the present moment. Once you know how to return to the present moment, you will become awakened, and at that moment, you will find your true self.

"Look at these tender leaves caressed by the sunlight. Have you ever really looked at the green of the leaves with a serene and awakened heart? This shade of green is one of the wonders of life. If you have never really looked at it, please do so now."

The young men grew very quiet. With their eyes following the Buddha's pointing finger, each of them looked at the green leaves gently swaying in the afternoon breeze. A moment later, the Buddha turned to the youth sitting on his right and said, "I see you have a flute. Please play something for us."

The youth felt shy, but he lifted his flute to his lips and began to play. Everyone listened attentively. The flute's sound was like the lamenting cry of a disappointed lover. The Buddha's eyes did not waver from the young man playing the flute. When he finished his song, sadness seemed to veil the afternoon forest. Still no one spoke, until suddenly the young man held out his flute to the Buddha and said, "Respected Monk, please play for us."

The Buddha smiled, as several of the young men burst out laughing, taking their friend for a real fool. Who ever heard of a monk playing the flute? But to their surprise, the Buddha took the flute in his hands. The young men all turned their eyes to the Buddha, unable to mask their curiosity. The Buddha took several deep breaths, and then raised the flute to his lips.

The image of a young man playing the flute long ago in the royal gardens of Kapilavatthu arose in the Buddha's mind. It was a full moon night. He could see Mahapajapati sitting on a stone bench quietly listening. And there was Yasodhara with her freshly lit incense holder of fragrant sandalwood. The Buddha began to play the flute.

The sound was as delicate as a thin strand of smoke curling gently from the roof of a simple dwelling outside Kapilavatthu at the hour of the evening meal. Slowly the thin strand expanded across space like a gathering of clouds which in turn transformed into a thousand-petalled lotus, each petal a different shimmering color. It seemed that one flutist suddenly had become ten thousand flutists, and all the wonders of the universe had been transformed into sounds—sounds of a thousand colors and forms, sounds as light as a breeze and quick as the pattering of rain, clear as a crane flying overhead, intimate as a lullaby, bright as a shining jewel, and subtle as the smile of one who has transcended all thoughts of gain and loss. The birds of the forest stopped singing in order to listen to this sublime music, and even the breezes ceased rustling the leaves. The forest was enveloped in an atmosphere of total peace, serenity, and wonder. The young men sitting around the Buddha felt completely refreshed, and they now dwelled completely in the present moment, in touch with all the wonders of the trees, the Buddha, the flute, and each other's friendship. Even after the Buddha put the flute down, they could still hear the music. Not one of the young men thought about the young woman or the jewels she had stolen.

No one spoke for a long while. Then the young man to whom the flute belonged asked the Buddha, "Master, you play so wonderfully! I've never heard anyone who could play so well. Who did you study with? Would you accept me as your student so that I could learn flute from you?"

The Buddha smiled and he said, "I learned to play the flute when I was a boy, but I have not played in nearly seven years. My sound, however, is better than it was before."

"How can that be, Master? How can your playing have improved if you have not practiced in seven years?"

"Playing the flute does not depend solely on practicing the flute. I now play better than in the past because I have found my true self. You cannot reach lofty heights in art if you do not first discover the unsurpassable beauty in your own heart. If you would like to play the flute truly well, you must find your true self on the Path of Awakening."

The Buddha explained the path of liberation, the Four Noble Truths, and the Noble Eightfold Path. The young men listened intently, and when the Buddha was finished speaking, every one of them knelt down and asked to be accepted as a disciple. The Buddha ordained them all. He then instructed them to make their way to Isipatana and introduce themselves to the bhikkhu Kondanna who would give them guidance in the practice of the Way. The Buddha told them he would see them again before long.

That night the Buddha slept alone in the forest. The next morning he crossed the Ganga and headed east. He wanted to visit the children of Uruvela before making his way to Rajagaha to see King Bimbisara.

Water Rises, Too

Seven days later, the Buddha was happy to find himself back in the forest of the bodhi tree. He rested the night there. In the morning he surprised Svasti by the banks of the Neranjara River. They sat for a long while along the shore before the Buddha told Svasti he should continue cutting the kusa grass needed by the buffaloes. He also helped Svasti cut some grass. Then, bidding Svasti good-bye, he walked to the village to beg.

The next afternoon the village children came to visit the Buddha in the forest. All of Svasti's family was there. Sujata brought along all her friends. The children were very happy to see the Buddha again. They listened intently while he told them all that had happened to him in the past year. The Buddha promised Svasti that when Svasti was twenty years old, the Buddha would accept him as a bhikkhu. By that time, Svasti's sisters and brother would be old enough to care for themselves.

The children told the Buddha that over the past few months a spiritual community led by a brahman had settled nearby. There were five hundred devotees in all. They did not shave their heads like the bhikkhus. Instead their hair was braided and then piled on top of their heads. They worshipped the god of Fire. The brahman's name was Kassapa. He was deeply revered by all who met him.

The following morning, the Buddha crossed the river and found Master Kassapa's community. His devotees lived in simple huts made from leafy branches and wore clothes made from the bark of trees. They did not enter the village to beg but accepted offerings brought to them by the villagers. In addition, they raised their own animals for food and for making sacrifices. The Buddha stopped to speak with one of Kassapa's followers who told him that Kassapa was deeply versed in the *Vedas* and lived a life of utmost virtue. Kassapa, he explained, also had two younger brothers who also led communities of fire worship. All three brothers held fire to be the original essence of the universe. Uruvela Kassapa was deeply loved by his two brothers, Nadi Kassapa who lived with three hundred devotees along the Neranjara about a day's travel north, and Gaya Kassapa who led two hundred devotees in Gaya.

Kassapa's disciple led the Buddha to his master's hut so that the Buddha could have an audience with him. Although Kassapa was no longer a young man, he was still quick and alert. When he saw the young teacher's extraordinary bearing, he felt immediately drawn to him and treated him as a special guest. Kassapa invited the Buddha to sit on a stump outside the hut, and the two enjoyed a long conversation. Kassapa marvelled at how deeply versed the Buddha was in the *Vedas*. He was further astounded to discover that this young monk had grasped certain concepts in the *Vedas* which had eluded his own understanding. The Buddha helped explain certain of the most profound passages in the *Atharveda* and *Rigveda* scriptures which Kassapa thought he had understood but discovered he had not yet truly grasped. Even more amazing was the young monk's knowledge of history, doctrine, and brahmanic rituals.

That noon the Buddha accepted Uruvela Kassapa's invitation to have a meal with him. The Buddha neatly folded his outer robe into a cushion and sat upon it, eating in mindful silence. So impressed was Uruvela Kassapa by the Buddha's serene and majestic countenance that he did not break the silence.

That afternoon they continued their conversation. The Buddha asked, "Master Kassapa, can you explain to me how worshipping fire can lead a person to liberation?"

Uruvela Kassapa did not answer right away. He knew very well that a superficial or ordinary response would not suffice for this extraordinary young monk. Kassapa began by explaining that fire was the basic essence of the universe. It had its source in Brahma. The main altar of the community, the Fire Sanctuary, always kept a sacred fire burning. That fire was itself the image of Brahma. The *Atharveda* scripture spoke of fire worship. Fire was life. Without fire there could be no life. Fire was light, warmth, and the source of the sun which enabled plants, animals, and people to live. It chased away dark shadows, conquered the cold, and brought joy and vitality to all beings. Food was made edible by fire, and thanks to fire, people were reunited with Brahma at death. Because fire was the source of life it was Brahma himself. Agni, the god of fire, was one of the thousands of manifestations of Brahma. On the Fire Altar, Agni was portrayed as having two heads. One symbolized the daily uses of fire and the other symbolized the fire of sacrifice and returning to the source of life. The fire worshippers performed forty sacrificial rites. A devotee in their community had to observe precepts, practice austerities, and pray diligently in order to follow the path that would one day lead to liberation.

Kassapa was strongly opposed to those brahmans who used their position in society to acquire wealth and lose themselves in pursuit of sensual pleasures. He said that such brahmans only performed rituals and recited the scriptures in order to become rich. Because of that the reputation of the traditional brahmanic path had become tarnished.

The Buddha asked, "Master Kassapa, what do you think of those who regard water as the fundamental essence of life, who say that water is the element which purifies and returns people to union with Brahma?"

Kassapa hesitated. He thought of the hundreds of thousands of people, right at that very moment, who were bathing themselves in the waters of Ganga and other sacred rivers to purify themselves.

"Gautama, water cannot really help one attain liberation. Water naturally flows down. Only fire rises. When we die, our body rises in smoke thanks to fire."

"Master Kassapa, that is not accurate. The white clouds floating above are also a form of water. Thus, water rises too. Indeed, smoke itself is no more than evaporated water. Both clouds and smoke will eventually return to a liquid state. All things, as I'm sure you know, move in cycles."

"But all things share one fundamental essence and all things return to that one essence."

"Master Kassapa, all things depend on all other things for their existence. Take, for example, this leaf in my hand. Earth, water, heat, seed, tree, clouds, sun, time, space—all these elements have enabled this leaf to come into existence. If just one of these elements was missing, the leaf could not exist. All beings, organic and inorganic, rely on the law of dependent co-arising. The source of one thing is all things. Please consider this carefully. Don't you see that this leaf I am now holding in my hand is only here thanks to the interpenetration of all the phenomena in the universe, including your own awareness?"

It was already evening and beginning to grow dark. Kassapa invited the Buddha to sleep in his own hut. It was the first time he had ever made such an offer to anyone, but then he had never before met such an extraordinary monk. But the Buddha refused, saying that he had grown accustomed to sleeping alone at night. He said he would like to sleep in the Fire Sanctuary if that would be all right.

The brahman said, "For the past several days, an enormous snake has taken refuge in the Fire Sanctuary. All efforts to chase it away have failed. You must not sleep there, friend Gautama. It might be dangerous. We have even been holding our ceremonies outside for fear of the snake. Please sleep in my hut for your own safety."

The Buddha replied, "Don't worry. I want to sleep in the Fire Sanctuary. I will not be in any danger."

The Buddha recalled all the months he had practiced austerities in the wild jungles. Wild beasts passed him by without harming him. Sometimes while he sat in meditation enormous snakes slithered in front of him. He knew that if you took care not to frighten such animals, they would not harm you.

Seeing that the Buddha could not be dissuaded, Kassapa said, "If you wish to sleep in the Fire Sanctuary, you shall. You may sleep there as many nights as you like."

That night the Buddha entered the Fire Sanctuary. On the central altar burned a great fire fed by many candles. On one side of the room was a pile of sandalwood logs, which were used for outdoor ceremonies. The Buddha guessed that the snake was probably curled up in the wood pile, so he sat in meditation on the other side of the room, using his folded robe as a cushion. He meditated deep into the night. Towards the end of his meditation, he saw the great snake coiled in the center of the room looking at him. The Buddha spoke softly to it, "Dear friend, return to the jungle for your own safety."

The Buddha's voice was filled with love and understanding. The snake slowly uncoiled itself and crept out the door. The Buddha stretched out and fell asleep.

When he awoke, brilliant moonlight poured through the window onto his sleeping place. The eighteenth day moon was unusually bright. He thought how pleasant it would be to do walking meditation beneath its light. He shook off the dust from his outer robe and put it on before walking out of the Fire Sanctuary.

In the early hours of the morning, the Sanctuary somehow caught on fire. Those who saw it first shouted to all the others. Everyone filled buckets with water at the river's edge, but to no avail. The water came too late to extinguish the raging fire. At last, the five hundred devotees could do no more than stand and watch their Sanctuary burn to the ground.

Uruvela Kassapa stood with his followers. His heart was heavy with grief as he thought of the virtuous and talented young monk he had met only the day before. The young monk had surely perished in the fire. If only Gautama had consented to sleep in his hut, he would still be alive. Just as he was thinking this, the Buddha appeared. The Buddha had seen the fire from where he had been walking in the hills and he had returned to see if he could be of any assistance.

Overcome with relief and joy, Kassapa ran to the Buddha and grasped his hand. "Thank goodness, you are alive, friend Gautama! Nothing has happened to you! I am so happy!"

The Buddha placed his hands on the brahman's shoulders and smiled. "Thank you, my friend. Yes, I am all right."

The Buddha knew that on that day Uruvela Kassapa would give a discourse and that in addition to his own five hundred disciples, at least a thousand others would attend from the neighboring villages. The lecture would take place after the noon meal. Sensing that his presence during the lecture might cause Kassapa some discomfort, the Buddha went begging down in the village. After receiving food offerings he walked to the lotus pond, ate his meal there, and spent the entire afternoon at that pleasant place.

Late in the afternoon, Kassapa came looking for him. When he found him by the pond, he said, "Friend Gautama, we waited for you at the noon meal but you never appeared. Why didn't you join us?"

The Buddha responded that he had wished to be absent during the lecture.

"Why did you not wish to attend the lecture?" asked Uruvela Kassapa.

The Buddha only smiled gently. The brahman did not say anything else. He knew that the young monk had read his thoughts. How tactful and considerate Gautama was!

atman is a falsehood

They sat by the lotus pond and conversed. Kassapa said, "Yesterday you said that the presence of a leaf resulted from the coming together of many different conditions. You said that humans, too, exist only because of the coming together of many other conditions. But when all these conditions cease to be, where does the self go?"

The Buddha answered, "For a long time humans have been trapped by the concept of *atman*, the concept of a separate and eternal self. We have believed that when our body dies, this self continues to exist and seeks union with its source, which is Brahma. But, friend Kassapa, that is a fundamental misunderstanding which has caused countless generations to go astray.

"You should know, friend Kassapa, that all things exist because of interdependence and all things cease to be because of interdependence. This is because that is. This is not because that is not. This is born because that is born. This dies because that dies. This is the wonderful law of dependent co-arising which I have discovered in my meditation. In truth, there is nothing which is separate and eternal. There is no self, whether a higher or a lower self. Kassapa, have you ever meditated on your body, feelings, perceptions, mental formations, and consciousness? A person is made up of these five aggregates. They are continuously changing rivers in which one cannot find even one permanent element."

Uruvela Kassapa remained silent for a long moment. Then he asked, "Could one say then that you teach the doctrine of non-being?"

The Buddha smiled and shook his head. "No. The concept of non-being is one narrow view among a whole forest of narrow views. The concept of non-being is just as false as the concept of a separate, permanent self. Kassapa, look at the surface of this lotus pond. I do not say that the water and lotus do not exist. I only say that the water and the lotus arise thanks to the presence and interpenetration of all other elements, none of which are separate or permanent."

Kassapa lifted his head and looked into the Buddha's eyes. "If there is no self, no atman, why should one practice a spiritual path in order to attain liberation? Who will be liberated?"

The Buddha looked deeply into the eyes of his brahmana friend. His gaze was as radiant as the sun and as gentle as the soft moonlight. He smiled and said, "Kassapa, look for the answer within yourself."

They returned together to Kassapa's community. Uruvela Kassapa insisted on giving the Buddha his hut for the night, and went to sleep himself in the hut of one of his senior disciples. The Buddha could see how deeply Kassapa's disciples revered their teacher.

Chapter Twenty-Seven
All Dharmas Are on Fire

Every morning Kassapa brought the Buddha some food and so the Buddha did not need to go begging in the village. After his daily meal, he walked alone on forest paths or down to the lotus pond. In the later afternoons, Kassapa would join him for discussion beneath the trees or beside the pond. The more time he spent with the Buddha, the more Kassapa understood how wise and virtuous the Buddha was.

One night it rained so heavily that by morning the Neranjara River had overflowed its banks. Nearby fields and dwellings were quickly submerged by floodwaters. Boats desperately went out to try to rescue people. Kassapa's community was able to climb to higher land in time, but no one could find Gautama. Kassapa sent several boats to look for him. At last he was found standing on a distant hill.

The water subsided as quickly as it had risen. The next morning the Buddha took his begging bowl and went down into the village to see how the villagers had fared in the flood. Luckily no one had drowned. The people told the Buddha that because they did not own many possessions in the first place, the flood had not robbed them of much.

Kassapa's disciples began to rebuild the Fire Sanctuary which had been destroyed by fire and to rebuild their huts washed away by the flood.

One afternoon, while the Buddha and Kassapa stood along the banks of the Neranjara, Kassapa said, "Gautama, the other day you spoke about the meditation on one's body, feelings, perceptions, mental formations, and consciousness. I have been practicing that meditation and I have begun to understand how one's feelings and perceptions determine the quality of one's life. I also see that there is no permanent element to be found in any of the five rivers. I can even see that the belief in a separate self is false. But I still don't understand why one should follow a spiritual path if there is no self? Who is there to be liberated?"

The Buddha asked, "Kassapa, do you accept that suffering is a truth?"

"Yes, Gautama, I accept that suffering is a truth."

"Do you agree that suffering has causes?"

"Yes, I accept that suffering has causes."

"Kassapa, when the causes of suffering are present, suffering is present. When the causes of suffering are removed, suffering is also removed."

"Yes, I see that when the causes of suffering are removed, suffering itself is removed."

"The cause of suffering is ignorance, a false way of looking at reality. Thinking the impermanent is permanent, that is ignorance. Thinking there is a self when there is not, that is ignorance. From ignorance is born greed, anger, fear, jealousy, and countless other sufferings. The path of liberation is the path of looking deeply at things in order to truly realize the nature of impermanence, the absence of a separate self, and the interdependence of all things. This path is the path which overcomes ignorance. Once ignorance is overcome, suffering is transcended. That is true liberation. There is no need for a self for there to be liberation."

Uruvela Kassapa sat silently for a moment and then said, "Gautama, I know you speak only from your own direct experience. Your words do not simply express concepts. You have said that liberation can only be attained through the efforts of meditation, by looking deeply at things. Do you think that all ceremonies, rituals, and prayers are useless?"

The Buddha pointed to the other side of the river and said, "Kassapa, if a person wants to cross to the other shore, what should he do?"

"If the water is shallow enough, he can wade across. Otherwise he will have to swim or row a boat across."

"I agree. But what if he is unwilling to wade, swim, or row a boat? What if he just stands on this side of the river and prays to the other shore to come to him? What would you think of such a man?"

"I would say he was being quite foolish!"

"Just so, Kassapa! If one doesn't overcome ignorance and mental obstructions, one cannot cross to the other side to liberation, even if one spends one's whole life praying."

Suddenly Kassapa burst into tears and prostrated himself before the Buddha's feet. "Gautama, I have wasted more than half my life. Please accept me as your disciple and give me the chance to study and practice the way of liberation with you."

The Buddha helped Kassapa stand back up and said, "I would not hesitate to accept you as my disciple, but what of your five hundred devotees? Who will guide them if you leave?"

Kassapa answered, "Gautama, give me a chance to speak with them this morning. Tomorrow afternoon I will let you know of my decision."

The Buddha said, "The children in Uruvela village call me the Buddha."

Kassapa was surprised. "That means the Awakened One, doesn't it? I will call you the same."

The next morning, the Buddha went begging in Uruvela village. Afterwards he went to the lotus pond to sit. Late that afternoon, Kassapa came looking for him. He told the Buddha that all five hundred of his devotees agreed to become disciples under the Buddha's guidance.

The next day, Uruvela Kassapa and all his followers shaved their heads and beards, and threw the locks of hair into the Neranjara River along with all the liturgical objects they had used for fire worship. They bowed before the Buddha and recited three times, "I take refugee in the Buddha, the one who shows me the way in this life. I take refuge in the Dharma, the way of understanding and love. I take refuge in the Sangha, the community that lives in harmony and awareness." Their recitation of the three refuges echoed throughout the forest.

When the ordination was completed, the Buddha spoke to the new bhikkhus about the Four Noble Truths and how to observe one's breath, body, and mind. He showed them how to beg for food and how to eat in silence. He asked them to release all the animals they had once raised for food and sacrifices.

That afternoon the Buddha met with Kassapa and ten of Kassapa's senior students to teach them the fundamentals of the Way of Awakening as well as to discuss how to best organize the sangha. Kassapa was a talented organizer and leader, and, with the Buddha, he assigned capable senior students to train the younger bhikkhus, just as the Buddha had done in Isipatana.

The next day Nadi Kassapa, Uruvela Kassapa's younger brother, arrived with his disciples in a state of shock. The day before, he and his three hundred devotees who lived downstream from Uruvela had seen hundreds of braids and liturgical objects floating in the river and they feared some terrible catastrophe had befallen the community of his elder brother. When Nadi Kassapa reached Uruvela it was the hour of begging and so he was unable to find anyone. His worst fears seemed to be confirmed. But slowly bhikkhus began to return from begging and they explained how they had all taken vows to follow a monk named Gautama. Uruvela Kassapa returned from begging with the Buddha and was most happy to see his younger brother. He invited him for a walk in the forest. They were gone for a good length of time, and when they returned Nadi Kassapa announced that he and his three hundred devotees would also take refuge in the Buddha. Both brothers agreed to send someone to summon their brother, Gaya Kassapa. Thus, in the space of only seven days, the two hundred devotees of Gaya Kassapa were also ordained as bhikkhus. The Kassapa brothers were well known for their brotherly love and sharing of common ideals. Together they became deeply devoted students of the Buddha.

One day after all the bhikkhus had returned from begging, the Buddha summoned them to gather on the slopes of the mountain in Gaya. Nine hundred bhikkhus ate in silence with the Buddha and the three Kassapa brothers. When they were finished eating, they all turned their gaze to the Buddha.

Sitting serenely upon a large rock, the Buddha began to speak, "Bhikkhus, all dharmas are on fire. What is on fire? The six sense organs—eyes, ears, nose, tongue, body and mind—are all on fire. The six objects of the senses—form, sound, smell, taste, touch, and objects of mind—are all on fire. The six consciousnesses—sight, hearing, smell, taste, feeling, and thought—are all on fire. They are burning from the flames of desire, hatred, and illusion. They are burning from the flames of birth, old age, sickness, and death, and from the flames of pain, anxiety, frustration, worry, fear, and despair.

"Bhikkhus, every feeling is burning whether it is an unpleasant, pleasant, or neutral feeling. Feelings arise and are conditioned by the sense organs, objects of the sense organs, and the sense-consciousnesses. Feelings are burning from the flames of desire, hatred, and illusion. Feelings are burning from the flames of birth, old age, sickness, and death, and from the flames of pain, anxiety, frustration, worry, fear, and despair.

"Bhikkhus, do not allow yourselves to be consumed by the flames of desire, hatred, and illusion. See the impermanent and interdependent nature of all dharmas in order not to be enslaved by the cycle of birth and death created by the sense organs, objects of the senses, and the sense-consciousnesses."

Nine hundred bhikkhus listened intently. Each man was deeply moved. They were happy to know they had found the path that taught how to look deeply in order to attain liberation. Faith welled in the heart of every bhikkhu there.

The Buddha remained in Gayasisa for three months to teach the new bhikkhus, and the bhikkhus made great progress. The Kassapa brothers were talented assistants to the Buddha, and they helped him guide and teach the sangha.

Chapter Twenty-Eight
Palm Forest

The morning had arrived for the Buddha to depart from Gayasisa and make his way to Rajagaha. Uruvela Kassapa asked the Buddha to allow the entire sangha to accompany him. The Buddha was reluctant, but Kassapa explained how easily nine hundred bhikkhus could travel together. There would be many forests around Rajagaha where the bhikkhus could dwell. They could beg in the many villages there, as well as in the capital city itself, making contact with many local people. Moreover, added Kassapa, the number of bhikkhus was now too large for the population of Gaya to support. Everything would be easier in Rajagaha. Seeing how knowledgeable Uruvela Kassapa was about the situation in Magadha, the Buddha agreed to let the nine hundred bhikkhus join him.

The Kassapa brothers divided the sangha into thirty-six groups of twenty-five bhikkhus. Each group was led by a senior student. This arrangement allowed the bhikkhus to make ever greater progress on the path.

Ten days were needed for them all to reach Rajagaha. Each morning, they begged in small villages and ate silently in the forests or fields. When they finished eating, they began to walk again, traveling in their own small groups. The sight of the bhikkhus walking quietly and slowly made a deep impression on all who saw them.

When they neared Rajagaha, Uruvela Kassapa led them to Palm Forest, where the Supatthita temple was located. Palm Forest was only two miles south of the capital. The next morning the bhikkhus took their bowls and went begging in the city. They walked single file in their small groups, taking calm, slow steps. They held their bowls serenely while their eyes looked straight ahead. Following the Buddha's instructions, they stood before each house without discriminating whether it belonged to rich or poor. If no one appeared after a few moments, they moved on to the next house. While silently waiting for food offerings to be made, they mindfully observed their breath. When they received a food offering, they bowed in thanks. They never made any comments about whether the food looked good or bad. Sometimes the layperson making the offering asked the bhikkhu a few questions about the Dharma, and the bhikkhu answered thoughtfully to the best of his ability. The bhikkhu explained that he belonged to the sangha of Gautama the Buddha. He would speak about the Four Noble Truths, the five precepts for the laity, and the Noble Eightfold Path.

The bhikkhus always returned to Palm Forest by noon to share their meal in silence before listening to a discourse on the Dharma given by the Buddha. Afternoons and evenings were reserved for meditation practice. Thus after the noon hour, no one in the city saw the saffron-robed bhikkhus.

By the end of two weeks, most of the city was aware of the presence of the Buddha's sangha. On cool afternoons, many laypersons came to Palm Forest to meet the Buddha and to learn about the Way of Awakening. Before the Buddha had had a chance to visit his friend, the young King Seniya Bimbisara had already learned of the Buddha's presence. Sure that this new teacher was the same young monk he had met on the mountain, he mounted his carriage and ordered it driven to Palm Forest. Many other carriages followed his for he had invited over a hundred highly regarded brahmana teachers and intellectuals to join him. When they reached the edge of the forest, the king stepped out of his carriage, accompanied by the queen and their son, Prince Ajatasattu.

When the Buddha was informed of the king's arrival, he and Uruvela Kassapa personally went out to greet him and all his guests. All the bhikkhus were seated in great circles on the earth waiting to hear the Buddha's Dharma talk. The Buddha invited the king, queen, prince, and other guests to be seated, too. King Bimbisara introduced as many of the guests as he could remember names, but sometimes had to ask a brahman to introduce himself. Among the guests were many scholars well-versed in the *Vedas* and belonging to many different schools of religious thought.

Most of these men had heard the name of Uruvela Kassapa. A number of them had even met him before. But no one had ever heard of the Buddha. They were surprised to see how reverently Kassapa treated the Buddha, even though Gautama Sakya was so much younger than Kassapa. They whispered to one another, trying to figure out whether Gautama was Kassapa's disciple or Kassapa was Gautama's disciple. Aware of their confusion, Uruvela Kassapa stood up and approached the Buddha. He joined his palms and spoke clearly and with respect, "Gautama, the Enlightened One, Most Precious Teacher in this life—I am Uruvela Kassapa, your disciple. Allow me to offer you my most profound respect." Then he prostrated himself before the Buddha three times. The Buddha helped Kassapa stand up again and asked him to sit by his side. There were no more whispers among the brahmans. Indeed, their respect increased as they looked out over the nine hundred saffron-robed bhikkhus sitting with awe-inspiring solemnity.

The Buddha spoke about the Way of Awakening. He spoke about the impermanent and interdependent nature of all things in life. He said that the Path of Awakening could help one overcome false views and transcend suffering. He spoke about how observing the precepts could help one attain concentration and understanding. His voice resounded like a great bell. It was as warm as spring sunshine, as gentle as a light rain, and as majestic as the rising tide. More than one thousand people listened. No one dared to breathe too loudly or rustle their robes for fear of disturbing the sound of the Buddha's wondrous voice.

King Bimbisara's eyes grew brighter by the moment. The more he listened, the more he felt his heart open. So many of his doubts and troubles vanished. A radiant smile appeared on his face. When the Buddha concluded his Dharma talk, King Bimbisara stood up and joined his palms. He said, "Lord, from the time I was young, I had five wishes. I have now fulfilled them all. The first wish was to receive coronation and become king. That has been fulfilled. The second wish was to meet in this very life an enlightened teacher. That has also been fulfilled. The third wish was to have a chance to show respect to such a teacher. That wish has now been fulfilled. The fourth wish was to have such a teacher show me the true path. That wish has now been fulfilled. And the fifth wish was to be able to understand the teaching of the Enlightened One. Master, this wish has just been fulfilled. Your wondrous teaching has brought me much understanding. Lord, please accept me as your lay disciple."

The Buddha smiled his acceptance.

The king invited the Buddha and all nine hundred of his bhikkhus to have a meal at the palace on the day of the full moon. The Buddha gladly accepted.

All the other guests stood up to thank the Buddha. Twenty of them expressed the desire to be accepted as the Buddha's disciples. The Buddha and Uruvela Kassapa accompanied the king, queen, and little prince Ajatasattu back to the edge of the forest.

The Buddha knew that in less than a month, the rainy season would begin, and it would be impossible to return to his homeland. Therefore, he resolved to remain with the nine hundred bhikkhus in Palm Forest for another three months. He knew that after three months of practice, the sangha would be strong and stable enough for him to depart.

He would leave in the spring, the season of clear skies and tender new plants.

King Seniya Bimbisara began at once to prepare for the reception of the Buddha and his bhikkhus. He planned to serve them in the great palace court paved with fine bricks. He called to his people to deck the streets with lanterns and flowers to welcome the Buddha and his sangha. He invited a great many other people to attend, including all the members of the government and their families. Children close to the age of twelve-year-old Prince Ajatasattu were invited, too. Knowing that the Buddha and his bhikkhus did not allow others to kill for their sake, he ordered that only delicious vegetarian foods be prepared. They had ten days to prepare for the reception.

Chapter Twenty-Nine
Dependent Co-Arising

Throughout the following weeks, many seekers came to the Buddha and asked to be ordained as bhikkhus. Many of them were highly educated young men from wealthy families. The Buddha's senior students performed the ordination ceremonies and gave the new bhikkhus basic instruction in the practice. Other young people, women as well as men, came to Palm Forest and took the three refuges.

One day Kondanna gave the three refuges to a gathering of nearly three hundred young people. After the ceremony, he spoke to them about the three precious gems—the Buddha, the Dharma, and the Sangha.

"The Buddha is the Awakened One. An awakened person sees the nature of life and the cosmos. Because of that, an awakened person is not bound by illusion, fear, anger, or desire. An awakened person is a free person, filled with peace and joy, love and understanding. Master Gautama, our Teacher, is a completely awakened person. He shows us the way in this life so that we may overcome forgetfulness and become awakened ourselves. Every one of us contains *Buddha-nature*. We can all become a Buddha. Buddha-nature is the capacity to awaken and transcend all ignorance. If we practice the way of awareness, our Buddha-nature will shine more brightly every day until one day, we, too, shall attain total freedom, peace, and joy. We must each find the Buddha within our own heart. The Buddha is the first precious gem.

"The Dharma is the path which leads to Awakening. It is the path which the Buddha teaches, the path which helps us to transcend the prisons of ignorance, anger, fear, and desire. This path leads to freedom, peace, and joy. It enables us to love and understand all others. Understanding and love are the two most beautiful fruits of the Path of Awakening. The Dharma is the second precious gem.

"The Sangha is the community of persons practicing the Way of Awakening, those who travel this path together. If you want to practice the way of liberation, it is important to have a community to practice with. If you are all alone, difficulties along the path may hinder your realization of awakening. It is important to take refuge in the Sangha, whether you are an ordained bhikkhu or a lay person. The Sangha is the third precious gem.

"Young people, today you have taken refuge in the Buddha, the Dharma, and the Sangha. With the support of these refuges, you will not wander aimlessly but will be able to make real progress on the Path of Enlightenment. It has been two years since I took refuge in the three gems myself. Today you have vowed to travel the same path. Let us rejoice together that we have taken refuge in the three precious gems. Of course, these gems have been present in our own hearts from beginningless time. Together we will practice the way of liberation to allow these three gems to shine from within us."

The young people were greatly encouraged by Kondanna's words. They all felt a new source of vitality surge within their hearts.

During those same days, the Buddha received two exceptional new disciples, Sariputta and Moggallana, into his sangha of bhikkhus. They were both disciples of the famous ascetic Sanjaya, who lived in Rajagaha. Sanjaya's devotees were called *parivrajakas*. Sariputta and Moggallana were close friends, respected for their intelligence and open-mindedness. They had promised each other that whoever attained the Great Way first would immediately inform the other.

One day Sariputta saw the bhikkhu Assaji begging in Rajagaha, and he was immediately drawn by Assaji's relaxed and serene bearing. Sariputta thought to himself, "This appears to be someone who has attained the Way. I knew such persons could be found! I will ask him who his Teacher is and what his teaching is."

Sariputta quickened his pace to catch up with Assaji but then stopped himself, not wanting to disturb the bhikkhu while he was silently begging from house to house. Sariputta resolved to wait until Assaji was finished begging before approaching him. Without making himself noticed, Sariputta followed Assaji. When Assaji's bowl was filled with offerings and he turned to leave the city, Sariputta joined his palms in respectful greeting and said, "Monk, you radiate such peace and calm. Your virtue and understanding shine in the way you walk, in the expression on your face, and in your every gesture. Please allow me to ask who your Teacher is and at what practice center you reside. What methods does your teacher teach?"

Assaji looked at Sariputta for a moment and then smiled in a most friendly manner. He answered, "I study and practice under the guidance of the Master Gautama of the Sakya clan who is known as the Buddha. He is presently dwelling near Supatthita Temple in Palm Forest."

Sariputta's eyes brightened. "What is his teaching? Can you share it with me?"

"The Buddha's teaching is deep and lovely. I have not grasped it fully yet. You should come and receive the teachings directly from the Buddha."

But Sariputta implored Assaji, "Please, can't you share with me even a few words of the Buddha's teaching? It would be so precious to me. I will come for more teaching later."

Assaji smiled and then recited a short *gatha*:

"From interdependent origins
all things arise
and all things pass away.
So teaches the
Perfectly Enlightened One."

Sariputta suddenly felt his heart open as though it were being flooded by bright light. A flawless glimpse of true Dharma flashed before him. He bowed to Assaji and quickly ran to seek his friend Moggallana.

When Moggallana saw Sariputta's radiant face, he asked, "My brother, what has made you so happy? Can you have found the true path? Please tell me, brother!"

Sariputta related what had just happened. When he recited the gatha for Moggallana to hear, Moggallana also felt a sudden flash of light illuminate his heart and mind. Suddenly he saw the universe as an interconnected net. This was because that was, this arose because that arose, this was not because that was not, this passed away because that passed away. The belief in a creator of all things vanished in this understanding of dependent co-arising. He now understood how one could cut through the endless cycle of birth and death. The door of liberation opened before him.

Moggallana said, "Brother, we must go to the Buddha at once. He is the Teacher we have been waiting for."

Sariputta agreed, but reminded him, "What of the two hundred fifty parivrajaka brothers who have long placed their faith and trust in us as elder brothers of the community? We can't just abandon them. We must go and inform them of our decision first."

The two friends made their way to the parivrajaka main gathering place and explained to their fellow practitioners their decision to leave the community and become disciples of the Buddha. When the parivrajakas heard that Sariputta and Moggallana were about to leave them, they were grieved. The community would not be the same without these two elder brothers. And so, they all expressed their desire to follow them and become disciples of the Buddha, too.

Sariputta and Moggallana went to Master Sanjaya and told him of the decision of the community. He entreated them to stay, saying "If you remain here, I will transfer the leadership of the community to you both." He said this three times, but Sariputta and Moggallana had made up their minds.

They said, "Respected Master, we embarked on the spiritual path in order to find liberation, and not to become religious leaders. If we do not know the true path, how can we lead others? We must seek out the Master Gautama for he has attained the path we have long sought for."

Sariputta and Moggallana prostrated themselves before Sanjaya and then departed, followed by the other parivrajakas. They walked to Palm Forest where they all prostrated before the Buddha and asked to be ordained. The Buddha spoke to them about the Four Noble Truths and accepted them as bhikkhus in his sangha. After the ordination ceremony, the number of bhikkhus in Palm Grove numbered 1,250.

Here ends Book One.

BOOK TWO

Chapter Thirty

Bamboo Forest

It was the full moon day. The Buddha took his bowl and entered the city of Rajagaha with his 1,250 bhikkhus. They walked silently with slow, calm steps. The streets of the capital were decorated with lanterns and fresh flowers. Crowds flanked both sides of the streets to welcome the Buddha and his sangha. When the bhikkhus came to the main crossroads, the crowd was so thick that it was impossible for the Buddha and his bhikkhus to proceed.

Uruvela Kassapa was wondering what to do, when a handsome young fellow appeared, singing and playing a sixteen-string sitar. His voice resonated like a clear bell. As he walked through the crowds singing, the people moved to the sides to let him pass. There was now a path for the Buddha and his bhikkhus to continue walking. Kassapa recognized the musician, who had taken the three refuges with him less than a month earlier. His song expressed his deep feelings:

"On this fresh spring morning,
the Enlightened One passes through our city
with the noble community of 1,250 disciples.
All are walking with slow, calm, and radiant steps."

The crowds listened to the young musician as if entranced, and they looked from him to the Buddha passing before them. The singer smiled and continued to sing:

"Grateful for this chance to be his student,
let me praise his endless love and wisdom,

the path that leads to self-contentment,
and the Sangha which follows the True Way
to Awakening."

The young man continued to sing and open up a path until the Buddha and all the bhikkhus reached the palace gates. Then he bowed to the Buddha and disappeared back into the crowds as quickly as he had appeared.

King Bimbisara, accompanied by six thousand attendants and guests, came out to welcome the Buddha. The king led the Buddha and the bhikkhus to the royal courtyard where spacious tents had been set up to shade the guests from the hot sun. The Buddha was given the place of honor at the center of the courtyard. All the places for the bhikkhus had been prepared with utmost care. Once the Buddha was seated, King Bimbisara invited everyone else to be seated. The king and Uruvela Kassapa sat on either side of the Buddha.

Prince Ajatasattu carried a basin of water and a towel to the Buddha for him to wash his hands and feet. Other attendants brought water and towels for all the bhikkhus. After that, the vegetarian feast was laid upon the tables. The king personally placed food into the Buddha's bowl while Queen Videhi directed servants to serve the bhikkhus. The Buddha and the bhikkhus recited special gathas before eating. King Bimbisara and his royal guests maintained perfect silence throughout the meal. All six thousand guests were impressed by the calm and joyous countenance of the Buddha and his bhikkhus.

When the Buddha and all of the 1,250 bhikkhus were finished eating, their bowls were taken and washed and then returned. King Bimbisara turned towards the Buddha and joined his palms. Understanding the king's wishes, the Buddha began to teach the Dharma. He spoke about the five precepts as the way to create peace and happiness for one's family and all the kingdom.

"The first precept is do not kill. Observing this precept nourishes compassion. All living beings fear death. As we

King Bimbisara, accompanied by six thousand attendants and guests, came out to welcome the Buddha.

cherish our own lives, we should cherish the lives of all other beings. Not only should we refrain from taking human life, we should strive to avoid taking the lives of other species. We must live in harmony with people, animals, and plants. If we nourish a heart of love, we can reduce suffering and create a happy life. If every citizen observes the precept not to kill, the kingdom will have peace. When the people respect each other's lives, the country will prosper and be strong, and it will be safe from invasion by other countries. Even if the kingdom possesses great military force, there will be no reason to use it. Soldiers can devote time to such worthy tasks as building roads, bridges, marketplaces, and dams.

"The second precept is do not steal. No one has the right to take away the possessions that another has earned by his own labor. Attempting to seize another's goods violates this precept. Do not cheat others or use your influence and power to encroach on other's goods. Making profits from the sweat and labor of others violates this precept, as well. If the citizens observe this precept, social equality will flower and robbing and killing will quickly cease.

"The third precept is avoid sexual misconduct. Sexual relations should only take place with your spouse. Observing this precept builds trust and happiness in the family, and prevents unnecessary suffering to others. If you want happiness and the time and will to help your country and people, abstain from having several concubines.

"The fourth precept is do not lie. Do not speak words that can create division and hatred. Your words should be in accord with the truth. Yes means yes. No means no. Words have the power to create trust and happiness, or they can create misunderstanding and hatred and even lead to murder and war. Please use words with the greatest care.

"The fifth precept is do not drink alcohol or use other intoxicants. Alcohol and intoxicants rob the mind of clarity. When someone is intoxicated he can cause untold suffering to himself, his family, and others. Observing this precept is to preserve health for the body and mind. This precept should be observed at all times.

"If your majesty and all high-ranking officials study and observe these five precepts, the kingdom will benefit greatly. Your majesty, a king stands at the helm of his country. He must live with awareness and know all that is happening in his kingdom at all times. If you see to it that those under your charge understand and observe the five precepts, the five principles of living in peace and harmony, the country of Magadha will thrive."

Overcome with joy, King Bimbisara stood and bowed before the Buddha. Queen Videhi approached the Buddha, holding the hand of her son, Prince Ajatasattu. She showed the prince how to join his palms like a lotus bud and respectfully greet the Buddha. She said, "Lord Buddha, Prince Ajatasattu and four hundred other children are present today. Can you teach them about the Way of Awareness and Love?"

The queen bowed before the Buddha. The Buddha smiled. He reached out and clasped the young prince's hand. The queen turned around and motioned for the other children to come forward. They were the children of noble and wealthy families and were dressed in the finest of garments. Boys as well as girls wore golden bracelets around their wrists and ankles. The girls were dressed in shimmering saris of many colors. Prince Ajatasattu sat down by the feet of the Buddha. The Buddha thought of the poor country children he shared a picnic with so long ago beneath the rose-apple tree in Kapilavatthu. He silently promised himself that when he returned home he would seek out such children and share the teaching with them, too.

The Buddha spoke to the children before him. "Children, before I was a human being, I lived as earth and stones, plants, birds, and many other animals. You, too, have had past lives as earth and stones, plants, birds, and animals. Perhaps you are here before me today because of some connection we shared in a past life. Perhaps in another life we brought one another joy or sorrow.

"Today I would like to tell you a story that took place several thousand lifetimes ago. It is the story of a heron, a crab, a plumeria tree, and many small shrimp and fish. In that life, I was the plumeria tree. Perhaps one among you was the heron or the crab or one of the shrimp. In this story, the heron was a wicked and deceitful creature who caused death and suffering to many others. The heron made me, the plumeria tree, suffer, too. But from that suffering, I learned a great lesson and that was—if you deceive and harm others, in turn, you will be deceived and harmed.

"I was a plumeria tree growing close to a fragrant, cool lotus pond. No fish lived in that pond. But not far from that pond was a shallow and stagnant pond in which many fish and shrimp and one crab lived. A heron flying overhead saw the crowded situation of the fish and shrimp and devised a scheme. He landed at the edge of their pond and stood there with a long, sad face.

"The fish and shrimp asked him, 'Mister Heron, what are you thinking about so seriously?'

"'I'm thinking about your poor lot in life. Your pond is muddy and foul. You lack adequate food. I feel terrible pity for your hard lives.'

"'Do you know of any way to help us, Mister Heron?' asked the small creatures.

"'Well, if you would allow me to carry each one of you over to the lotus pond not far from here, I could release you in the cool waters there. There is plenty to eat over there.'

"'We would like to believe you, Mister Heron, but we have never heard that herons care anything about the lot of fish or shrimp. Perhaps you only want to trick us in order to eat us up.'

"'Why are you so suspicious? You should think of me as a kind uncle. I have no reason to deceive you. There really is a large lotus pond not far from here filled with plenty of fresh, cool water. If you don't believe me, let me fly one of you over there to see for himself. Then I'll fly him back to tell you whether or not I'm telling the truth.'

"The shrimp and fish discussed the matter at some length before at last agreeing to allow one of the elder fish to go with the heron. This fish was tough and bristly, his scales as hard as stones. He was a swift swimmer who could also maneuver well on sand. The heron picked him up in his beak and flew him to the lotus pond. He released the old fish into the cool waters and let him explore every nook and cranny of the pond. The pond was indeed spacious, cool, refreshing, and a plentiful source of food. When the heron returned him to the old pond, the fish reported all he had seen.

"Convinced of the heron's good intentions, the shrimp and fish begged him to fly them to the pond one by one. The crafty heron agreed. He picked up a fish in his beak and flew off. But this time, instead of releasing the fish into the pond, he landed near the plumeria tree. He placed the fish in a fork of the tree and ripped off its flesh with his beak. He tossed its bones by the plumeria's roots. Then he returned to transport another fish. He devoured it as well, and discarded its bones by the foot of the plumeria tree.

"I was that plumeria, and I witnessed all this taking place. I was enraged, but there was nothing I could do to stop the heron. A plumeria's roots are firmly anchored in the earth. There is nothing a plumeria can do but grow branches, leaves, and flowers. It cannot run anywhere. I could not call out and warn the shrimp and fish about what was really happening. I could not even stretch my branches to prevent the heron from eating the helpless creatures. I could only witness the horrible scene. Every time the heron brought a fish in its beak and began to tear at its flesh, I was filled with pain. I felt as though my sap would dry up and my branches break. Drops of moisture like tears collected on my bark. The heron did not notice. Over a number of days, he continued to bring the fish over to devour them. When all the fish were gone, he began to eat the shrimp. The pile of bones and shells that piled up by my roots could have filled two large baskets.

"I knew that as a plumeria tree my job was to beautify the forest with my fragrant flowers. But at that moment I suffered terribly from not being able to do anything to save the shrimp and fish. If I had been a deer or a person I could have done something. But anchored by my roots to the ground, I could not move. I vowed that if I were reborn as an animal or a human in a future life, I would devote all my efforts to protect the weak and helpless from the strong and powerful.

"When the heron had devoured all the shrimp and fish, only the crab remained. Still hungry, the heron said to the crab, 'Nephew, I have carried all the fish and shrimp to the lotus pond where they now live happily. You are all alone here now. Let me take you to the new pond, too.'

"'How will you carry me?' asked the crab.

"'In my beak, just as I carried all the others.'

"'What if I slipped out and fell? My shell would shatter into a hundred pieces.'

"'Don't worry. I'll carry you with utmost care.'

"The crab thought carefully. Perhaps the heron had kept his word and truly carried all the shrimp and fish to the lotus pond. But what if he had deceived them and eaten them all? The crab devised a plan to insure his own safety. He said to the heron, 'Uncle, I'm afraid your beak is not strong enough to hold me securely. Let me wrap my claws around your neck to hold on while you fly.'

"The heron agreed. He waited for the crab to crawl onto his neck and then he spread his wings and flew into the air. But instead of carrying the crab to the lotus pond, he landed by the plumeria tree.

"'Uncle, why don't you put me down by the lotus pond? Why did we land here instead?'

"'What heron would be so stupid as to carry a bunch of fish to a lotus pond? I am no benefactor, nephew. Do you see all those fish bones and shrimp shells at the foot of the plumeria? This is where your life will end, as well.'

"'Uncle, the fish and shrimp may have been easily fooled, but you can't trick me so easily. Take me to the lotus pond at once or I will cut off your head with my claws.'

"The crab began to dig his sharp claws into the heron's neck. Seized by sharp pain, the heron cried out, 'Don't squeeze so hard! I'll take you to the lotus pond right this minute! I promise I won't try to eat you!'

"The heron flew to the lotus pond where it intended to let the crab down by the water's edge. But the crab did not release its hold on the heron's neck. Thinking about all the fish and shrimp so cruelly deceived by the heron, the crab dug his claws deeper and deeper into the heron's neck until he cut right through it. The heron dropped down dead and the crab crawled into the water.

"Children, at that time I was the plumeria tree. I witnessed all these events. I learned that if we treat others kindly, we will be treated kindly in return; but if we treat others cruelly, sooner or later, we will suffer the same fate. I vowed that in all my future lives, I would endeavor to help other beings."

The children listened to the Buddha's tale with great interest. They were moved by the plumeria's pain, and they felt pity for the helpless fish and shrimp. They despised the heron's deceit and were impressed by the crab's shrewdness.

King Bimbisara stood up. He joined his palms and bowed. He said, "Master, you have shared an important lesson with young and old alike. I pray that Prince Ajatasattu remembers your words. Our kingdom is blessed to have you among us. I would now like to present you and your sangha with a gift, if you agree."

The Buddha looked at the king, waiting for him to explain. After a moment of silence, the king continued, "About two miles north of Rajagaha, there is a large and beautiful forest known as Venuvana, Bamboo Forest. It is quiet and serene, cool and refreshing. Many gentle squirrels inhabit that forest. I would like to offer you and your sangha Venuvana as a place where you can teach and practice the Way.

O Great Teacher of Compassion, please accept this gift from my heart."

The Buddha reflected for a moment. It was the first time the sangha had been offered land for a monastery. Certainly his bhikkhus did need a place to dwell during the rainy season. The Buddha breathed deeply and smiled, and he nodded his head in acceptance of the king's generous gift. King Bimbisara was overjoyed. He knew that the presence of the monastery would mean that the Buddha would spend more time in Magadha.

Among the many guests at the palace that day were a large number of brahmana religious leaders. Many of them were not pleased with the king's decision but they did not dare to say anything.

The king asked for a golden vase of water. He poured the clear water over the Buddha's hands and solemnly announced, "Master, as the water in this vase pours over your hands, Bamboo Forest is transferred to you and your sangha."

This ritual concluded the offering of Bamboo Forest from the king to the Buddha. The ceremonial feast came to an end, and the Buddha and his 1,250 bhikkhus departed from the palace.

Chapter Thirty-One
I Will Return in the Spring

The very next day, the Buddha visited Bamboo Forest with several of his senior students. It was an ideal location for the sangha, with nearly one hundred acres of healthy bamboo groves. Many kinds of bamboo grew there. At the center of the forest, Kalandaka Lake would be a perfect place for the bhikkhus to bathe, wash their robes, and do walking meditation along the shore. Because the bamboo was so plentiful, it would be easy to build small huts for the older monks to live in. The Buddha's senior students, including Kondanna, Kassapa, and Sariputta, were all delighted with Bamboo Forest. They began planning at once how to best organize a monastery there.

The Buddha said, "The monsoon season is not a good time for travel. The bhikkhus need a place to study and practice together during the rains. Having a place like this will help the community avoid illness from exposure to the elements and also avoid stepping on the many worms and insects that are washed up on the ground during the rainy season. From now on, I would like the bhikkhus to return to a common place at the beginning of every rainy season. We can ask lay disciples of the area to bring food offerings during the three months of retreat. The lay disciples will also benefit from the teachings offered by the bhikkhus." Thus, the tradition of the rainy season retreat began.

Under Moggallana's supervision, the younger bhikkhus built huts from bamboo, thatch, and pounded earth for the Buddha and the older bhikkhus. The Buddha's hut, though small, was quite lovely. Behind it grew a thicket of golden bamboo and to one side grew a thicket of taller green bamboo which provided cool shade. Bhikkhu Nagasamala built a low, wooden platform for the Buddha to sleep upon. He also placed a large earthenware vessel for washing behind the Buddha's hut. Nagasamala was a young bhikkhu who had been Uruvela Kassapa's disciple. He was asked by Kassapa to serve as an attendant to the Buddha when the sangha moved to Bamboo Forest.

Sariputta arranged with a lay disciple from the capital to have a large bell donated to Bamboo Forest Monastery. He hung it from the branch of an ancient tree near Kalandaka Lake. The bell was used to announce times for study and meditation, and became a special part of the practice of mindfulness. The Buddha taught his bhikkhus to pause and observe their breath whenever they heard the bell ring.

Lay disciples assisted in many ways. Kassapa explained to them about the retreat season. "This retreat season will afford all the bhikkhus an opportunity to practice the way of liberation directly under the guidance of the Buddha. They will have time for more intensive study and practice. At the same time, they will avoid accidentally crushing worms and insects on the ground during the rainy season. You can assist the sangha during these three months of retreat by bringing food offerings. If possible, please try to coordinate your efforts to assure that there is the right amount of food each day, neither too much nor too little. Even the poorest of the poor, those who can only offer a chapati or two, will be invited to stay and listen to the Buddha or one of the senior students give a discourse on the Dharma each day. The retreat season will benefit bhikkhus and lay disciples alike."

Kassapa proved to be as talented at organizing the laity as he was at organizing the bhikkhus. He met with lay sponsors of the monastery and helped them organize the food of-

ferings and other forms of assistance. He assured that every
bhikkhu received a robe, begging bowl, meditation cushion,
towel, and water filter for personal use.

The first day of the retreat arrived and the sangha followed the schedule that had been carefully thought out by
the Buddha and his senior students. The wake-up bell rang at
four in the morning. After washing up, the bhikkhus did
walking meditation on their own. They continued to alternate
sessions of sitting and walking meditation until the sun
peeked over the tops of the bamboos. Normally that was the
time to go begging, but since during the retreat food was
brought to them by the laity, the bhikkhus had some extra
time to meet with their individual teachers to study the
Dharma in greater depth and to discuss any difficulties they
were having in their practice. Bhikkhus who served as
teachers were selected according to the depth of progress
they had made on the path. Elders, such as Kondanna, Assaji, Kassapa, Sariputta, Moggallana, Vappa, and Mahanama, each guided fifty or sixty younger bhikkhus. Other
teachers were given responsibility for ten to thirty students.
Every new bhikkhu was assigned a personal teacher who
served as his elder brother in the practice. Kassapa and
Sariputta personally organized this system.

Shortly before midday, the bhikkhus gathered by the
lake and stood in lines holding their begging bowls. Food was
divided and shared equally. When everyone had been
served, they all sat on the grassy shores and ate in silence.
When the meal was completed and the bowls washed, everyone turned towards the Buddha. On some days he directed
his teaching to the bhikkhus but in a way which was also
helpful to the laity. On other days he directed his teaching
to the laity but in a way which also benefited the bhikkhus.
Sometimes his teaching was addressed especially to the
children present. In those Dharma talks, he often told past
life tales.

Sometimes one of the Buddha's senior students gave the
Dharma talk in his place. The Buddha would sit and listen

serenely, offering words of encouragement when he saw that the Dharma was expressed in a correct and clear manner. After the Dharma talks, the lay disciples would return home, and the bhikkhus would rest until the afternoon bell announced the time to resume sitting and walking meditation. The bhikkhus practiced until midnight, before retiring.

The Buddha sat in meditation far into the night. He liked to place his bamboo platform outside his hut and sit on it, enjoying the cool night air, especially on nights with a moon. Before dawn, he liked to do walking meditation around the lake. Ever joyous, peaceful, and relaxed, the Buddha did not require as much sleep as the younger bhikkhus. Kassapa sat in meditation far into the night also.

King Bimbisara visited Bamboo Forest faithfully. He did not bring great numbers of guests as he had the time he visited Palm Forest. Sometimes he was accompanied by Queen Videhi and Prince Ajatasattu. Often he came alone. He would leave his carriage at the edge of the forest and walk on his own to the Buddha's hut. One day after seeing the bhikkhus listening to the Dharma talk in the rain, he asked the Buddha's permission to build a large Dharma hall where the bhikkhus could both eat and listen to the teaching without being drenched by the rain. The Buddha consented, and work on the hall began right away. It was large enough to shelter more than one thousand bhikkhus and one thousand lay disciples. The Dharma hall was a most helpful addition to the monastery.

The Buddha and the king often sat together on the bamboo platform while carrying on conversations. Then Nagasamala built some simple bamboo chairs to enable the Buddha to receive guests more easily. One day as the Buddha and the king sat on two of these chairs, the king confided, "I have another son that you have not yet met. I would like very much for you to meet him and his mother. He is not the child of Queen Videhi. His mother's name is Ambapali and his name is Jivaka. He will soon be sixteen years old. Ambapali lives in Vesali, north of the city Pataliputta. She does not

The Buddha liked to sit in meditation late into the night, enjoying the moon and the cool night air.

like the confined life of the palace, and she is not concerned about titles or prestige. She treasures only her own freedom. I have provided them with several means of support, including a beautiful mango grove. Jivaka is a diligent and intelligent boy who is not at all interested in military or political affairs. He is living near the capital, pursuing medical studies. I love them deeply and hope you will love them too. O Compassionate One, if you would agree to meet Jivaka and his mother, I will ask them to come to Bamboo Forest in the near future."

The Buddha quietly smiled in agreement. The king joined his palms and departed, his heart filled with gratitude.

During that same period, Bamboo Forest Monastery received two very special guests who had come all the way from Kapilavatthu, the Buddha's home. They were the Buddha's old friend, Kaludayi, and Channa, who had driven the Buddha's carriage. Their presence imparted a special warmth to the monastery.

The Buddha had been absent for more than seven years and he was anxious to hear news of home. He asked Kaludayi about the king and queen, Yasodhara, Nanda, Sundari Nanda, his friends, and of course, his son Rahula. Though Kaludayi was still hale and hearty, his face bore the lines of age. Channa looked older too. The Buddha spoke with them for a long time as they sat outside his hut. He learned that Kaludayi now held considerable rank at court and was one of King Suddhodana's most trusted advisors. News that the Buddha had attained the Way and was teaching in Magadha had reached Kapilavatthu two months previously. Everyone rejoiced at the news, especially the king and queen, and Gopa. The king, much to Kaludayi's pleasure, had sent Kaludayi to invite the Buddha to return home. He took three days to prepare for the journey, unable to sleep at night for sheer excitement. Yasodhara suggested he take Channa along. Channa was so happy when Kaludayi agreed that he openly wept. It took the two men nearly a month to reach Bamboo Forest Monastery.

According to Kaludayi, the king's physical health had declined in recent years, though he was still quite alert mentally. The king had several talented advisors to help him run the country. Gotami was as robust as ever. Prince Nanda was now a young man and engaged to a young noblewoman named Kalyani. Nanda was very handsome and liked to dress in fine clothes, but the king was concerned that Nanda still lacked a certain stability and maturity. Sundari Nanda, the Buddha's sister, was now a beautiful and graceful young woman. As for Yasodhara, she had given up wearing all jewelry the day the Buddha departed. She dressed very simply and had sold all her precious possessions in order to give the money to the poor. When she learned that the Buddha ate no more than one meal a day, she began to do the same. She had continued her relief work with the active support of Queen Gotami. Rahula was now a healthy and handsome boy of seven. His black eyes flashed with intelligence and determination. His grandparents dearly cherished him, just as they had cherished Siddhartha as a boy.

Channa confirmed all that Kaludayi told the Buddha. The Buddha's heart was warmed by all the news of home. Finally, Kaludayi asked the Buddha when he might return to Kapilavatthu. The Buddha said, "I will return after the rainy season. I do not want to leave the young bhikkhus here until they are more firmly anchored in their practice. After this period of retreat, I will feel more at ease about leaving them. But Kaludayi! Channa! Why don't you remain here yourselves for a month or so to taste this life? That will still allow you plenty of time to return to Kapilavatthu and inform the king that I will be back after monsoon season."

Kaludayi and Channa were delighted to remain as guests at Bamboo Forest Monastery. They made friends with many of the bhikkhus and were able to taste the joyous and peaceful life of one who leaves home to follow the Way. They learned how practicing the way of awareness in daily life could nourish the mind and heart. Kaludayi spent much time at the Buddha's side and observed him carefully. He was deeply moved by the Buddha's wondrous ease. It was clear that the Buddha had attained a state in which he no longer chased after any desire. The Buddha was like a fish swimming freely, or a cloud floating peacefully in the sky. He dwelled completely in the present moment.

The Buddha's eyes and smile were evidence of the wonderful liberation his spirit enjoyed. Nothing in this world bound him, and yet no one else possessed so great an understanding and love for others as he did. Kaludayi saw that his old friend had left him far behind on the spiritual path. Suddenly, Kaludayi found himself longing for the serene, unfettered life of a bhikkhu. He felt ready to abandon all rank, wealth, and prestige, and all the worries and anxieties that accompanied such a life. After spending just seven days at Bamboo Forest, he confided his wish to be ordained as a bhikkhu to the Buddha. The Buddha looked somewhat surprised, but then he smiled and nodded his head in acceptance.

Channa felt the same desire to become a bhikkhu, but, aware of his duty to the royal family, he reflected that he should not become a bhikkhu without first asking Yasodhara's leave. He resolved to wait until the Buddha returned to Kapilavatthu before making his request.

Chapter Thirty-Two

The Finger Is Not the Moon

One afternoon Sariputta and Moggallana brought a friend, the ascetic Dighanakha, to meet the Buddha. Dighanakha was as well-known as Sanjaya. He also happened to be Sariputta's uncle. When he learned that his nephew had become a disciple of the Buddha, he was curious to learn about the Buddha's teaching. When he asked Sariputta and Moggallana to explain the teaching to him, they suggested he meet directly with the Buddha.

Dighanakha asked the Buddha, "Gautama, what is your teaching? What are your doctrines? For my own part, I dislike all doctrines and theories. I don't subscribe to any at all."

The Buddha smiled and asked, "Do you subscribe to your doctrine of not following any doctrines? Do you believe in your doctrine of not-believing?"

Somewhat taken aback, Dighanakha replied, "Gautama, whether I believe or don't believe is of no importance."

The Buddha spoke gently, "Once a person is caught by belief in a doctrine, he loses all his freedom. When one becomes dogmatic, he believes his doctrine is the only truth and that all other doctrines are heresy. Disputes and conflicts all arise from narrow views. They can extend endlessly, wasting precious time and sometimes even leading to war. Attachment to views is the greatest impediment to the spiritual path.

Bound to narrow views, one becomes so entangled that it is no longer possible to let the door of truth open.

"Let me tell you a story about a young widower who lived with his five-year-old son. He cherished his son more than his own life. One day he left his son at home while he went out on business. When he was gone, brigands came and robbed and burned the entire village. They kidnapped his son. When the man returned home, he found the charred corpse of a young child lying beside his burned house. He took it to be the body of his own son. He wailed in grief and cremated what was left of the corpse. Because he loved his son so dearly, he put the ashes in a bag which he carried with him everywhere he went. Several months later, his son managed to escape from the brigands and make his way home. He arrived in the middle of the night and knocked at the door. At that moment, the father was hugging the bag of ashes and weeping. He refused to open the door even when the child called out that he was the man's son. He believed that his own son was dead and that the child knocking at the door was some neighborhood child mocking his grief. Finally, his son had no choice but to wander off on his own. Thus father and son lost each other forever.

"You see, my friend, if we are attached to some belief and hold it to be the absolute truth, we may one day find ourselves in a similar situation as the young widower. Thinking that we already possess the truth, we will be unable to open our minds to receive the truth, even if truth comes knocking at our door."

Dighanakha asked, "But what of your own teaching? If someone follows your teaching will he become caught in narrow views?"

"My teaching is not a doctrine or a philosophy. It is not the result of discursive thought or mental conjecture like various philosophies which contend that the fundamental essence of the universe is fire, water, earth, wind, or spirit, or that the universe is either finite or infinite, temporal, or eternal. Mental conjecture and discursive thought about truth are like ants crawling around the rim of a bowl—they never get anywhere. My teaching is not a philosophy. It is the result of direct experience. The things I say come from my own experience. You can confirm them all by your own experience. I teach that all things are impermanent and without a separate self. This I have learned from my own direct experience. You too. I teach that all things depend on all other things to arise, develop, and pass away. Nothing is created from a single, original source. I have directly experienced this truth, and you can also. My goal is not to explain the universe, but to help guide others to have a direct experience of reality. Words cannot describe reality. Only direct experience enables us to see the true face of reality."

Dighanakha exclaimed, "Wonderful, wonderful, Gautama! But what would happen if a person did perceive your teaching as a dogma?"

The Buddha was quiet for a moment and then nodded his head. "Dighanakha, that is a very good question. My teaching is not a dogma or a doctrine, but no doubt some people will take it as such. I must state clearly that my teaching is a method to experience reality and not reality itself, just as a finger pointing at the moon is not the moon itself. An intelligent person makes use of the finger to see the moon. A person who only looks at the finger and mistakes it for the moon will never see the real moon. My teaching is a means of practice, not something to hold onto or worship. My teaching is like a raft used to cross the river. Only a fool would carry the raft around after he had already reached the other shore, the shore of liberation."

Dighanakha joined his palms. "Please, Lord Buddha, show me how to be liberated from painful feelings."

The Buddha said, "There are three kinds of feelings—pleasant, unpleasant, and neutral. All three have roots in the perceptions of mind and body. Feelings arise and pass away like any other mental or material phenomena. I teach the method of looking deeply in order to illuminate the nature and source of feelings, whether they are pleasant, unpleasant, or neutral. When you can see the source of your feelings, you will understand their nature. You will see that feelings are impermanent, and gradually you will remain undisturbed by their arising and passing away. Almost all painful feelings have their source in an incorrect way of looking at reality. When you uproot erroneous views, suffering ceases. Erroneous views cause people to consider the impermanent to be permanent. Ignorance is the source of all suffering. We practice the way of awareness in order to overcome ignorance. One must look deeply into things in order to penetrate their true nature. One cannot overcome ignorance through prayers and offerings."

Sariputta, Moggallana, Kaludayi, Nagasamala, and Channa all listened as the Buddha explained these things to Dighanakha. Sariputta was able to grasp the meaning of the Buddha's words the most deeply. He felt his own mind shine like a bright sun. Unable to conceal his joy, he joined his palms and prostrated himself before the Buddha. Moggallana prostrated himself, as well. Then Dighanakha, moved and profoundly impressed by all that the Buddha had said, also prostrated himself before the Buddha. Kaludayi and Channa were deeply touched by this scene. They felt proud to be associated with the Buddha, and their faith and trust in his Way was further strengthened.

A few days after that, Queen Videhi and an attendant visited and made food offerings to the sangha. She also brought a young plumeria sapling and planted it beside the Buddha's hut in remembrance of the story he had told the children in the palace courtyard.

Under the Buddha's guidance, the community made ever greater progress along the path. Sariputta and Moggallana were like shining stars with their keen intelligence, diligence, and leadership abilities. They worked with Kondanna and Kassapa to organize and guide the sangha. However, even as the sangha's reputation was growing, some people began to speak ill of the Buddha and his community. Some of these rumors were spread by members of religious factions who were jealous of the king's support for the sangha. Lay disciples who often visited Bamboo Forest expressed concern over what was being said. Apparently, some people in Rajagaha were distressed that so many young men from wealthy and noble families had become bhikkhus. They feared that soon all the young men would abandon their homes and there would be no more suitable husbands for the noble young women in Rajagaha. Entire family lines could be discontinued, they warned.

Many bhikkhus were not pleased when they heard these things. But when the Buddha was informed, he calmed both the laity and the bhikkhus by saying, "Don't worry about such things. Sooner or later, all such talk will die down." And it did. In less than a month, there was no more talk about such trifling fears.

Chapter Thirty-Three
Beauty That Does Not Fade

Two weeks before the rainy retreat ended, a woman of uncommon beauty paid a visit to the Buddha. She arrived in a white carriage pulled by two white horses, and was accompanied by a youth who appeared to be about sixteen years old. Her manner of dress and her bearing were refined and elegant. She asked a young bhikkhu to show her the way to the Buddha's hut, but when they arrived there, the Buddha had not yet returned from his walking meditation. The bhikkhu invited the woman and the boy to sit on bamboo chairs in front of the hut.

Shortly afterwards the Buddha returned, accompanied by Kaludayi, Sariputta, and Nagasamala. The woman and youth stood and bowed respectfully. The Buddha invited them to sit again as he sat down on a third bamboo chair. He understood that this woman was Ambapali and that the youth was King Bimbisara's son, Jivaka.

Kaludayi had never seen a woman more beautiful in all his life. He had only taken vows as a bhikkhu a month earlier, and he was confused as to whether or not it was proper for a bhikkhu to look at a beautiful woman. Unsure of what to do, he lowered his eyes to the ground. Nagasamala reacted in the same way. Only the Buddha and Sariputta looked directly into the woman's eyes.

Sariputta looked at Ambapali and then at the Buddha. He saw how natural and relaxed the Buddha's gaze was. His face was as serene as a beautiful full moon. The Buddha's eyes were kind and clear. Sariputta felt as though the Buddha's contentment, ease, and joy penetrated Sariputta's own heart in that instant.

Ambapali looked directly into the Buddha's eyes as well. No one had ever looked at her in the way the Buddha was looking at her now. As long as she could remember, men had gazed at her with either embarrassment or desire in their eyes. But the Buddha looked at her as he might look at a cloud, a river, or a flower. She had the impression that he could see deeply into her heart's thoughts. She joined her palms and introduced herself and her son. "I am Ambapali, and this is my son, Jivaka, who is studying to become a doctor. We have heard much about you, and we have both looked forward to this moment."

The Buddha asked Jivaka about his studies and daily life. Jivaka answered politely. The Buddha could see that he was a kind-hearted and intelligent boy. Though he shared the same father as Prince Ajatasattu, it was evident he possessed a character of greater depth than the young prince. Jivaka's heart filled with respect and affection for the Buddha. He told himself that when he finished his medical studies, he would settle near the Buddha at Bamboo Forest.

Before she met him, Ambapali had assumed the Buddha would be like so many other famous teachers she had met. But she had never before met anyone like the Buddha. His gaze was unspeakably tender and kind. She felt as though he could understand all the sufferings locked inside her heart. Much of her pain was soothed just by the way he looked at her. Tears glistened on her eyelashes as she said, "Teacher, my life has been filled with suffering. Though I have never lacked for money or possessions, I have not felt anything to aspire to until now. Today is the happiest day of my life."

Ambapali was an accomplished singer and dancer, but she would not perform for just anyone. If someone's manner or behavior displeased her, she refused to perform no matter how much gold they might offer. When she was sixteen years old,

Ambapali had the impression that the Buddha could see deeply into her heart's thoughts.

she became involved in a love affair that ended in heart-break. Soon afterwards she met the young Prince Bimbisara, and they fell in love. She gave birth to their son, Jivaka. But no one in the palace wanted to accept Ambapali and her son. Some members of the palace household even spread rumors that Jivaka was no more than an abandoned orphan that the prince had rescued from a barrel by the side of the road. Ambapali was hurt by these accusations. She endured humiliation caused by the jealousy and hatred of others in the palace. Soon she saw that her freedom was the only thing worth guarding. She refused to live in the palace and vowed that she would never relinquish her personal freedom to anyone.

The Buddha spoke gently to her, "Beauty arises and passes away like all other phenomena. Fame and fortune are no different. Only the peace, joy, and freedom that are the fruits of meditation bring true happiness. Ambapali, cherish and take good care of all the moments left to you in this life. Do not lose yourself in forgetfulness or idle amusements. This is of utmost importance."

The Buddha told Ambapali how she could arrange her daily life in a new way—breathing, sitting, and working in a spirit of mindfulness, and observing and practicing the five precepts. She was overjoyed to receive these precious teachings. Before departing, she said, "Just outside the city of Vesali, I own a mango grove that is both cool and peaceful. I hope that you and your bhikkhus might consider coming there for a visit. That would be a great honor to me and to my son. Please, Lord Buddha, consider my invitation."

The Buddha smiled his acceptance.

After Ambapali departed, Kaludayi asked permission to sit down beside the Buddha. Nagasamala invited Sariputta to sit on the other chair while he remained standing. A number of other bhikkhus passing by the hut, paused and joined the gathering. Sariputta looked at Kaludayi and smiled. He looked at Nagasamala and smiled too. Then he asked the Buddha, "Master, how should a monk regard a woman's beauty? Is beauty, especially that of a woman, an obstacle to spiritual practice?"

The Buddha smiled. He knew that Sariputta was not asking the question for himself but on behalf of the other bhikkhus. He answered, "Bhikkhus, the true nature of all dharmas transcends beauty and ugliness. Beauty and ugliness are only concepts created by our minds. They are inseparably entwined with the structure of the five aggregates. To the eyes of an artist, anything can appear beautiful and anything can be rendered as ugly. A river, a cloud, a leaf, a flower, a ray of sunshine, or a golden afternoon all possess beauty. The golden bamboo growing nearby us is beautiful. But perhaps no beauty has more capacity to distract a man's concentration than a woman's beauty. If one is obsessed with a woman's beauty, he can lose his way.

"Bhikkhus, when you have seen deeply and have attained the Way, the beautiful may still appear beautiful and the ugly may still appear ugly, but because you have attained liberation, you are not bound by either. When a liberated person looks at beauty, he can see that it is composed of many non-beautiful elements. Such a person understands the impermanent and empty nature of all things, including beauty and ugliness. Thus he is neither mesmerized by beauty nor repulsed by ugliness.

"The only kind of beauty that does not fade and that does not cause suffering is a compassionate and liberated heart. Compassion is the ability to love unconditionally, demanding nothing in return. A liberated heart is unbound by conditions. A compassionate and liberated heart is true beauty. The peace and joy of that beauty is true peace and joy. Bhikkhus, practice diligently and you will realize true beauty."

Kaludayi and the other bhikkhus found the Buddha's words most helpful.

The rainy retreat came to a close. The Buddha summoned Kaludayi and Channa and suggested they leave for Kapilavatthu first in order to announce the Buddha's imminent arrival. Kaludayi and Channa made preparations for their trip without delay. Kaludayi, now a bhikkhu of calm and serene bearing, knew that everyone in the capital would be surprised when they saw him. He looked forward to the happy task of announcing the Buddha's return, but he regretted leaving Bamboo Forest after so brief a stay.

Chapter Thirty-Four
Reunion

Kaludayi told the king, queen, and Yasodhara the news of the Buddha's imminent arrival, and then, taking just his begging bowl, set off alone to meet the Buddha on his way to Kapilavatthu. Kaludayi walked with the serene, slow steps of a bhikkhu. He walked days and rested nights, pausing only briefly in tiny hamlets along the way to beg for food. Wherever he went, he announced that Prince Siddhartha had found the Way and was about to return home. Nine days after he left Kapilavatthu, Kaludayi met the Buddha and three hundred bhikkhus traveling with him. Moggallana, Kondanna, and the Kassapa brothers had remained with the other bhikkhus in Bamboo Forest.

At Kaludayi's suggestion, the Buddha and his bhikkhus rested the night in Nigrodha Park, three miles south of Kapilavatthu. The following morning they entered the city to beg.

The sight of three hundred bhikkhus wearing saffron robes, peacefully and silently holding their bowls to beg, made a deep impression on the city's people. It did not take long for news of their arrival to reach the palace. King Suddhodana ordered a carriage be readied at once to take him out to meet his son. Queen Maha Prajapati and Yasodhara waited anxiously within the palace.

When the king's carriage entered the eastern sector of the city, they encountered the bhikkhus. The carriage driver recognized Siddhartha first. "Your majesty, there he is! He walks ahead of the others and his robe is a bit longer."

Astonished, the king recognized that the bhikkhu clad in a saffron robe was indeed his own son. The Buddha radiated majesty and seemed almost surrounded by a halo of light. He was standing holding his bowl in front of a shabby dwelling. In his serene concentration, it appeared that the act of begging was at that moment the most important thing in his life. The king watched as a woman dressed in tattered clothes came out of the poor hut and placed a small potato in the Buddha's bowl. The Buddha respectfully received it by bowing to the woman. He then moved on to the next house.

The king's carriage was still some distance from where the Buddha stood. The king asked his driver to halt. He stepped out of the carriage and walked towards the Buddha. Just then, the Buddha saw his father approaching. They walked towards each other, the king with hurried steps, the Buddha with calm, relaxed steps.

"Siddhartha!"

"Father!"

Nagasamala came up to the Buddha and took his teacher's bowl, enabling the Buddha to hold the king's hands in his own two hands. Tears streamed down the king's wrinkled cheeks. The Buddha gazed at his father, his eyes filled with loving warmth. The king understood that Siddhartha was no longer the crown prince, but a respected spiritual teacher. He wanted to embrace Siddhartha but felt that might not be proper. Instead he joined his palms and bowed to his son in the manner a king greets a high-ranking spiritual teacher.

The Buddha turned to Sariputta who was nearby and said, "The bhikkhus have completed their begging. Please lead them back to Nigrodha Park. Nagasamala will accompany me to the palace where we can eat our food. We will return to the sangha later in the afternoon."

Sariputta bowed and then turned to lead the others back to the park.

The king looked long and hard at the Buddha before saying, "I thought surely you would come to the palace to see your family first. Who could have guessed you would instead go begging in the city? Why didn't you come to eat at the palace?"

The Buddha smiled at his father. "Father, I am not alone. I have traveled with a large community, the community of bhikkhus. I, too, am a bhikkhu, and like all other bhikkhus, beg for my food."

"But must you beg for food at such poor dwellings as these around here? No one in the history of the Sakya clan has ever done such a thing."

Again the Buddha smiled. "Perhaps no Sakya has ever done so before, but all bhikkhus have. Father, begging is a spiritual practice which helps a bhikkhu develop humility and see that all persons are equal. When I receive a small potato from a poor family, it is no different than when I receive an elegant dish served by a king. A bhikkhu can transcend barriers that discriminate between rich and poor. On my path, all are considered equal. Everyone, no matter how poor he is, can attain liberation and enlightenment. Begging does not demean my own dignity. It recognizes the inherent dignity of all persons."

King Suddhodana listened with his mouth slightly agape. The old prophecies were true. Siddhartha had become a spiritual teacher whose virtue would shine throughout the world. Holding the king's hand, the Buddha walked with him back to the palace. Nagasamala followed them.

Thanks to a palace attendant who spotted the bhikkhus and called out, Queen Gotami, Yasodhara, Sundari Nanda, and young Rahula were able to watch the encounter between the king and the Buddha from a palace balcony. They saw how the king bowed to the Buddha. As the king and the Buddha neared the palace, Yasodhara turned to Rahula. She pointed to the Buddha and said, "Dear son, do you see that monk holding your grandfather's hand, about to enter the palace gates?"

Yasodhara told Rahula, "Dear son, that monk is your own father."

Rahula nodded.

"That monk is your own father. Run down and greet him. He has a very special inheritance to pass on to you. Ask him about it."

Rahula ran downstairs. In a flash he reached the palace courtyard. He ran towards the Buddha. The Buddha knew at once that the little boy running towards him was Rahula. He opened his arms wide and embraced his son. Almost out of breath, Rahula gasped, "Respected monk, mother said I should ask you about my special inheritance. What is it? Can you show it to me?"

The Buddha patted Rahula's cheek and smiled."You want to know about your inheritance? All in good time, I will pass it on to you."

The Buddha took the boy's hand in his, while still holding the king's hand. Together the three of them entered the palace. Queen Gotami, Yasodhara, and Sundari Nanda came downstairs and saw the king, the Buddha, and Rahula entering the royal gardens. The spring sunshine was pleasantly warm. Flowers blossomed everywhere and birds warbled sweet songs. The Buddha sat down with the king and Rahula on a marble bench. He invited Nagasamala to be seated too. At that moment, Queen Gotami, Yasodhara, and Sundari Nanda entered the gardens.

The Buddha immediately stood up and walked towards the three women. Queen Gotami was a picture of good health. She wore a sari the color of cool green bamboo. Gopa was as beautiful as ever, although she appeared somewhat pale. Her sari was as white as fresh-fallen snow. She wore no jewels or ornaments. The Buddha's younger sister, now sixteen years old, wore a gold sari which set off her shining black eyes. The women joined their palms and bowed low to greet the Buddha. The Buddha joined his palms and bowed in return. Then he called out, "Mother! Gopa!"

Hearing his voice call out their names, both women began to weep.

The Buddha took the queen's hand and led her to sit down on a bench. He asked, "And where is my brother, Nanda?"

The queen answered, "He is out practicing martial arts. He should return soon. Do you recognize your younger sister? She has grown much in your absence, wouldn't you say?"

The Buddha gazed at his sister. He had not seen her in more than seven years. "Sundari Nanda, you're a young woman now!"

Then the Buddha approached Yasodhara and gently took her hand. She was so moved, her hand trembled in his. He led her to sit beside Queen Gotami, and then he sat back on his own bench. On the walk back to the palace, the king had asked the Buddha many questions, but now no one spoke, not even Rahula. The Buddha looked at the king and queen, Yasodhara, and Sundari Nanda. The joy of reunion shone in everyone's face. After a long silence, the Buddha spoke, "Father, I have returned. Mother, I have returned. See, Gopa, I came back to you."

Again the two women began to cry. Their tears were tears of joy. The Buddha let them silently weep, and then he asked Rahula to sit beside him. He patted the boy's hair affectionately.

Gotami wiped her tears with the edge of her sari, and, smiling at the Buddha, said, "You were gone a very long time. More than seven years have passed. Do you understand how courageous a woman Gopa has been?"

"I have long understood the depth of her courage, Mother. You and Yasodhara are the two most courageous women I know. Not only have you offered understanding and support to your husbands, but you are models of strength and determination for all. I have been very lucky to have both of you in my life. It has made my task much easier."

Yasodhara smiled but she did not speak.

The king said, "You have told me a bit about your search for the Way up to your ordeals of self-mortification. Could you repeat all you have told me for the others to hear and then continue?"

The Buddha told them about his long search for the Way in brief. He told them about meeting King Bimbisara on the mountain, and about the poor children of Uruvela village. He told them about his five friends who had practiced austerities with him, and about the great reception the bhikkhus received in Rajagaha. Everyone listened intently. Not even Rahula budged.

The Buddha's voice was warm and affectionate. He did not dwell on details and he spoke only sparingly of his period of self-mortification. He used his words to sow helpful seeds of awakening in the hearts of those closest to him.

An attendant came out to the garden and whispered something in Gotami's ear. The queen whispered something back. Soon after, the attendant prepared a table in the garden for the noon meal. Just as the food was being placed upon the table, Nanda arrived. The Buddha greeted him joyfully.

"Nanda! When I left you were only fifteen. Now you're a grown man!"

Nanda smiled. The queen chastised him, "Nanda, greet your elder brother properly. He is a monk now. Join your palms and bow."

Nanda bowed and the Buddha bowed to his younger brother in return.

They all moved to the table. The Buddha asked Nagasamala to sit beside him. A serving maid brought out water for everyone to wash their hands.

The king asked the Buddha, "What did you receive in your begging bowl?"

"I received a potato, but I notice that Nagasamala did not yet receive anything."

King Suddhodana stood up. "Please allow me to offer both of you food from our table." Yasodhara held the platters while the king served the two bhikkhus. He placed fragrant white rice and vegetable curry into their bowls. The Buddha and Nagasamala ate in silent mindfulness and the others followed their example. Birds continued to sing throughout the garden.

When they had finished eating, the queen invited the king and the Buddha to sit again on the marble benches. A servant brought out a platter of tangerines, but Rahula was the only one to eat his. Everyone else was too absorbed in listening to the Buddha recount his experiences. Queen Gotami asked more questions than anyone else. When the king heard about the hut the Buddha lived in at Bamboo Forest, he resolved to have a similar one built at Nigrodha Park for him. He expressed his hope that the Buddha would remain for several months in order to teach them the Way. Queen Gotami, Yasodhara, Nanda, and Sundari Nanda voiced their joyous approval of the king's suggestion.

At last the Buddha said it was time for him to return to his bhikkhus in the park. The king rose and said, "I would like to invite you and all the bhikkhus for a meal offering just as the king of Magadha did. I will invite all the royal family and members of the government at the same time so that they can hear you speak about the Way."

The Buddha said he would be glad to accept the invitation. They arranged for the gathering to take place in seven days. Yasodhara expressed a desire to invite the Buddha and Kaludayi for a private meal in the eastern palace. The Buddha accepted her invitation, as well, but suggested it would be best to wait until a few days after the king's reception.

The king wanted to order a carriage to take the Buddha and Nagasamala back to Nigrodha Park, but the Buddha refused. He explained that he preferred to travel by foot. The entire family accompanied the two bhikkhus to the palace's outer gates. They all joined their palms respectfully and bid the two bhikkhus farewell.

Chapter Thirty-Five
Early Morning Sunshine

News of Siddhartha's return spread quickly throughout the rest of Kapilavatthu, confirmed by the serene presence of the bhikkhus begging every morning in the city. Many families made food offerings and were eager to hear the bhikkhus speak about the teaching.

King Suddhodana asked the people to decorate the city streets with banners and flowers in preparation for the day the Buddha and the bhikkhus were invited to eat at the palace. He also lost no time in having small huts built in Nigrodha Park for the Buddha and his senior students. Many people came to the Park to meet with the Buddha and his bhikkhus. The people were impressed to see the former prince calmly begging in the city. The Buddha's return became the main topic of conversation among all the townspeople.

Gotami and Yasodhara wanted to visit the Buddha at Nigrodha Park, but they were too busy that first week preparing for the reception of the sangha. The king wanted to invite several thousand guests, including all the members of the government, as well as all those in the city who held other political, cultural, and religious positions. He ordered that all dishes for the meal be vegetarian.

Prince Nanda, however, did find the time to visit the Buddha twice that week. He listened as the Buddha explained the Path of Awakening to him. Nanda loved and respected his elder brother, and he felt himself being drawn to the peaceful life of a bhikkhu. He even asked the Buddha whether or not he thought he would make a good bhikkhu, but the Buddha only smiled. He could see that although Nanda was a young man of admirable feelings and good intentions, he did not yet possess a strong sense of purpose or commitment. When he sat with the Buddha, Nanda wanted to become a monk, but when he returned to the palace, he had eyes and thoughts only for his lovely fiancée, Kalyani. Nanda wondered what the Buddha thought about his equivocation.

The day for the reception arrived. The entire city, including the royal palace, was decked with banners and flowers to welcome the Buddha and his sangha. The city bustled with excitement as the entire population formally welcomed home their heroic countryman. Musicians played beautifully as crowds lined the streets. Everyone strained to catch a glimpse of the Buddha. Gotami and Yasodhara personally welcomed all the guests that had been invited by the king. Gopa had even given in to the queen's wishes that she dress in an elegant sari and wear jewels in honor of the occasion.

The Buddha and the bhikkhus walked with slow, calm steps between the crowds. Many people joined their palms and bowed as the Buddha passed. Children were lifted onto their parents' shoulders so they could see. Happy shouts and applause rose from the crowds. The bhikkhus continued to follow their breath mindfully in the midst of the bustling, festive atmosphere.

King Suddhodana greeted the Buddha and his sangha at the outer gates of the palace. He led them to the inner court-yard. All the guests followed the king's example in joining their palms and bowing deeply to the Buddha, even though some of them wondered why it was necessary to show such great respect to a monk so young, even if he was the former prince.

After the Buddha and the bhikkhus were seated, the king motioned to the servants to bring out the food. He himself served the Buddha. Yasodhara and Gotami directed the serving of all the other guests, which included brahmans, ascetics, and hermits. Everyone ate in silence, following the example of the Buddha and his bhikkhus. When all the bhikkhus and all the guests were finished eating and the bhikkhus' bowls had been washed and returned, the king stood and joined his palms. He invited the Buddha to teach the Dharma to all those gathered.

The Buddha sat quietly for a moment in order to gain a sense of those present. He began by briefly recounting his experiences in seeking the Way, as he knew the people were anxious to hear what had happened to him in the past seven years. He spoke to them about the nature of impermanence, the absence of a separate self, and the law of dependent co-arising. He said that practicing awareness in daily life and looking deeply into things led to the cessation of suffering and the realization of peace and joy. He said that offerings and prayers were not effective means to attain liberation.

The Buddha taught the Four Noble Truths: the existence of suffering, the causes of suffering, the cessation of suffering, and the path that leads to the cessation of suffering. He said, "In addition to the sufferings of birth, old age, sickness, and death, human beings endure other sufferings which they themselves create. Out of ignorance and false views, people say and do things that create suffering for themselves and others. Anger, hatred, suspicion, jealousy, and frustration cause suffering. All these arise from lack of awareness. People are caught in their suffering as if they were caught in a house on fire, and most of our suffering we create ourselves. You cannot find freedom by praying to some god. You must look deeply into your own mind and situation in order to uproot the false views which are the root of suffering. You must find the source of your suffering in order to understand the nature of suffering. Once you understand the nature of suffering, it can no longer bind you.

"If someone is angry at you, you can get angry back at him, but that only creates more suffering. If you follow the Way of

Awareness, you will not react with anger. Instead, you will quiet your mind in order to discover why that person is angry at you. By looking deeply, you can uncover the causes that led to the person's anger. If you see that you bear responsibility for angering the person, you will not become angry, but you will accept that your own misconduct has contributed towards creating his anger. If you are without blame, you can try to see why the person has misunderstood you. Then you can find a way to help him understand your true intentions. In this way, you will avoid causing more suffering to both yourself and the other person.

"Your majesty and honored guests! All suffering can be overcome by looking deeply into things. On the Path of Awareness, we learn to follow our breath to maintain mindfulness. We follow the precepts in order to build concentration and attain understanding. The precepts are principles of living which foster peace and joy. Practicing the precepts, our ability to concentrate develops, and we are able to live with greater awareness and mindfulness. Mindfulness nurtures the capacity to illuminate the true nature of our mind and our environment. With that illumination comes understanding.

"Only with understanding can we love. All suffering is overcome when we attain understanding. The path of true liberation is the path of understanding. Understanding is *prajña*. Such understanding can only come from looking deeply into the true nature of things. The path of precepts, concentration, and understanding is the path which leads to liberation."

The Buddha paused for a moment and then smiled before continuing to speak. "But suffering is only one face of life. Life has another face, the face of wonder. If we can see that face of life, we will have happiness, peace, and joy. When our hearts are unfettered, we can make direct contact with the wonders of life. When we have truly grasped the truths of impermanence, emptiness of self, and dependent co-arising, we see how wondrous our own hearts and minds are. We see how wonderful our bodies, the branches of violet bamboo, the golden chrysanthemums, the clear stream, and the radiant moon are.

"Because we imprison ourselves in our suffering, we lose the ability to experience the wonders of life. When we can break through ignorance, we discover the vast realm of peace, joy, liberation, and *nirvana*. Nirvana is the uprooting of ignorance, greed, and anger. It is the appearance of peace, joy, and freedom. Honored guests, take time to look at a clear stream or a ray of early morning sunshine. Can you experience peace, joy, and freedom? If you are still locked in the prison of sorrow and anxiety, you will be unable to experience the wonders of the universe which include your own breath, body, and mind. The path I have discovered leads to transcending sorrow and anxiety by looking deeply into their true nature. I have shared this path with many others and they, too, have succeeded in discovering it for themselves."

Everyone was deeply touched by the Buddha's Dharma talk. The king's heart welled with happiness as did Queen Gotami's and Yasodhara's. They all wanted to learn more about the methods of looking deeply into the nature of things in order to attain liberation and enlightenment. After the Dharma talk, the king escorted the Buddha and the bhikkhus to the outer gates. The guests all congratulated the king on his son's great attainment.

Nigrodha Park was soon transformed into a monastery. The ancient fig trees that grew there provided cool shade. Many new bhikkhus were ordained, and many laypersons, including a number of young people of the Sakya clan, took the five precepts.

Yasodhara made frequent visits to the Buddha at Nigrodha Park, accompanied by the queen and young Rahula. She listened to his Dharma talks and in private asked him about the relation between practicing the Way and performing social service. The Buddha showed her how to observe her breath and practice meditation in order to nourish peace and joy in her own heart. She understood that without peace and joy, she could not truly help others. She learned that by developing deeper understanding, she could deepen her capacity to love. She was happy to discover that she could practice the way of awareness in the very midst of her efforts to serve others. Peace and joy were possible right in the very moments she was working. Means and ends were not two different things.

Queen Gotami was also making great progress in the practice.

Chapter Thirty-Six
Lotus Vow

Princess Yasodhara invited the Buddha, Kaludayi, Nagasa-mala, and the queen to share a meal in her palace. After they finished eating, she invited them to accompany her to a poor hamlet where she worked with children. Rahula joined them also. Yasodhara led them to the old rose-apple tree where the Buddha had his first experience of meditation as a young child. The Buddha marvelled how it seemed like only yesterday when in fact twenty-seven years had passed. The tree had grown much bigger over the years.

At Yasodhara's request, many poor children gathered by the tree. Yasodhara told the Buddha that the children he had met there so many years ago were now married with families of their own. The children beneath the tree were between the ages of seven and twelve. When they saw the Buddha arrive, they stopped playing and formed two rows for the Buddha to walk between. Yasodhara had showed them beforehand how to greet the Buddha. They placed a special bamboo chair beneath the tree for the Buddha and spread a mat for Gotami, Yasodhara, and the two bhikkhus to sit upon.

The Buddha felt happy to sit there. He thought about the days he had spent with the poor children of Uruvela village. He told the children about the buffalo boy, Svasti, and the young girl, Sujata, who gave him milk. He spoke about nourishing a heart of love by deepening one's understanding, and he told them the story about rescuing the swan after his cousin had shot it down. The children listened to all he said with great interest.

The Buddha motioned Rahula to sit down in front of him. Then he told all the children a past life story.

"Long ago, at the foot of the Himalayas, lived a young man named Megha. He was kind and industrious. Though he was without money, he confidently set out for the capital where he hoped to study. He took no more than his walking stick, a hat, a water jug, the clothes he was wearing, and a coat. Along the way, he stopped and worked on farms for rice and sometimes money. By the time he reached the capital of Divapati, he had accumulated five hundred rupees.

"When he entered the city, the people seemed to be preparing for an important celebration. Wondering what the occasion was, he looked around for someone to ask. At that moment, a beautiful young woman walked by him. She was holding a bouquet of half-opened lotus flowers.

"Megha asked her, 'What is the celebration today?'

"The young woman answered, 'You must be a stranger to Divapati or you would surely know that today the enlightened Master Dipankara is arriving. He is said to be like a torch lighting the path for all beings. He is the son of King Arcimat who left in search of the True Path and has found it. His path brightens all the world and so the people have organized this celebration in honor of him.'

"Megha was overjoyed to hear about the presence of an enlightened teacher. He wanted very much to offer something to the teacher and request to become his student. He asked the young woman, 'How much did you pay for those lotus flowers?'

"She looked at Megha and could easily see he was a bright and considerate young man. She answered, 'I only paid for five. The other two I picked from the pond at my own house.'

"Megha asked, 'How much did you pay for the five?'

"'Five hundred rupees.'

"Megha asked to buy the five lotuses for his five hundred rupees in order to offer the flowers to Dipankara. But the woman refused, saying, 'I bought these to offer to him myself. I had no intention of selling them to someone else.'

"Megha tried to persuade her. 'But you can still offer the two you picked from your own pond. Please let me buy the other five. I want to offer something to the Master. It is a rare and precious opportunity to encounter such a teacher in this life. I want to meet him and even ask to become his student. If you agree to let me buy your five lotus flowers, I will be grateful to you for the rest of my life.'

"The woman looked at the ground and did not answer.

"Megha implored her. 'If you let me buy those five flowers, I will do anything you ask.'

"The young woman appeared embarrassed. She did not lift her eyes from the ground for a long moment. Finally, she said, 'I do not know what connection we have shared in a past life, but I fell in love with you the moment I saw you. I have met many young men, but my heart has never trembled in this way before. I will give you these flowers to offer to the Enlightened One, but only if you promise me that in this life and all our future lives, I may be your wife.'

"She said these words hurriedly and was almost out of breath when she finished. Megha did not know what to say. After a moment of silence, he said, 'You are very special and most honest. When I saw you, I also felt something special inside. But I am seeking the path of liberation. If I married, I would not be free to follow the path when the right opportunity presented itself.'

"The young woman answered, 'Promise that I will be your wife and I vow that when the time comes for you to seek your path, I will not prevent you from going. On the contrary, I will do everything I can to help you fully achieve your quest.'

"Megha happily accepted her proposal, and together they went to find Master Dipankara. The crowds were so dense that they could barely see him up ahead. But even just

Megha asked the beautiful, young woman if he could buy her five lotuses to offer to Master Dipankara.

catching a glimpse of his face was enough for Megha to know that he was a truly enlightened one. Megha felt a great joy and vowed that he, too, would one day attain such enlightenment. He wanted to get closer to be able to offer Dipankara the flowers, but it was impossible to move through the throngs of people. Not knowing what else to do, he tossed his flowers into the air in the direction of Dipankara. Miraculously, they landed right in the arms of the Master. Megha was ecstatic to see how the sincerity of his heart had made itself known. The young woman asked Megha to throw her flowers to the Master, too. Her two flowers also landed in the Master's arms. Dipankara called out, asking the persons who had offered the lotus flowers to present themselves. The crowds parted for Megha and the young woman to pass. Megha clasped the young woman's hand. Together they bowed before Dipankara. The Master looked at Megha and said, 'I understand the sincerity of your heart. I can see you have great resolve to follow the spiritual path to attain total enlightenment and to save all beings. Take comfort. One day in a future life, you will attain your vow.'

"Then Dipankara looked at the young woman kneeling by Megha's side, and he spoke to her. 'You shall be Megha's closest friend in this life and in many lives to come. Remember to keep your promise. You will help your husband to realize his vow.'

"Megha and the young woman were deeply moved by the Master's words. They devoted themselves to studying the path of liberation taught by the Enlightened One, Dipankara.

"Children, in that life and in many lives thereafter, Megha and the young woman lived as husband and wife. When the husband needed to leave in order to pursue his spiritual path, his wife helped him in every way she could. She never tried to prevent him. Because of that, he felt the deepest gratitude towards her. At last, he realized his great vow and became a truly enlightened one himself, just as Dipankara had predicted so many lifetimes ago.

"Children, money and fame are not the most precious things in life. Money and fame can fade very quickly. Understanding and love are the most precious things in life. If you have understanding and love, you will know happiness. Megha and his wife shared happiness for many lives, thanks to their understanding and love. With understanding and love, there is nothing you cannot accomplish."

Yasodhara joined her palms and bowed to the Buddha. She was moved to tears. She knew that although he told the story to the children, he meant it especially for her. It was his way of thanking her. Queen Prajapati looked at her. She too understood why the Buddha had recounted this story. She placed her hand on her daughter-in-law's shoulder and said to the children, "Do you know who Megha is in this life? He is the Buddha. In this very life he has become an enlightened one. And do you know who Megha's wife is in this life? She is none other than your own Yasodhara. Thanks to her understanding, Prince Siddhartha was able to follow his path and attain awakening. We should offer thanks to Yasodhara."

The children had long loved Yasodhara. They now turned towards her and bowed to her to express all the love in their hearts. The Buddha was deeply touched. Then he stood up and walked slowly back to the monastery with the bhikkhus Kaludayi and Nagasamala.

Chapter Thirty-Seven
A New Faith

Two weeks later, King Suddhodana invited the Buddha to a private family meal at the palace. Sariputta was also invited. Queen Gotami, Yasodhara, Nanda, Sundari Nanda, and Rahula were all present. In the close-knit atmosphere of his family, the Buddha showed them how to follow their breath, how to look deeply into their feelings, and how to do walking and sitting meditation. He emphasized how they could transcend the worries, frustrations, and irritations of daily life by practicing mindfulness in daily life.

Rahula sat next to Sariputta and placed his small hand in the elder monk's hand. Rahula was very fond of Sariputta.

When the time came for the Buddha and Sariputta to return to the monastery, everyone walked with them to the gate. Nanda held the Buddha's bowl as the Buddha joined his palms and bowed farewell to each person. To Nanda's surprise, the Buddha did not take his bowl back. Not knowing what to do, Nanda followed the Buddha back to the monastery waiting for the right moment to return the bowl. When they arrived at the monastery, the Buddha asked Nanda if he would like to spend a week at the monastery to enjoy a deeper taste of the life of a bhikkhu. Nanda loved and respected his elder brother, and so he agreed. It was also true that Nanda felt drawn to the calm and relaxed life of the bhikkhus he saw around him. When the Buddha asked him at the end of the week if he would like to be ordained and live a bhikkhu's life for several months under the Buddha's guidance, Nanda was most willing. The Buddha asked Sariputta to give Nanda basic instruction and to ordain him as a bhikkhu.

The Buddha had first consulted with his father, the king, about allowing Nanda to live as a bhikkhu for a period of time. The king agreed with the Buddha that while Nanda was a well-meaning young man, he lacked the strength of character and determination required of a future king. The Buddha said he could provide Nanda with training that would help Nanda build clarity and resolve. The king was in agreement.

Less than a month passed, however, when Nanda began to pine away for his fiancée, the beautiful Janapada Kalyani. He tried to conceal his longing, but the Buddha saw clearly into his feelings. One day the Buddha said to Nanda, "If you want to realize your goal, you must first overcome clinging to ordinary emotions. Devote your whole self to your practice and train your mind. Only then can you become an effective leader who can serve others well."

The Buddha also asked Sariputta to see that Nanda was no longer sent to do his begging in Kalyani's neighborhood. When Nanda learned of this, he felt a mixture of both resentment and gratitude to the Buddha. He understood that the Buddha could see into his deepest thoughts and needs.

Rahula envied his young uncle for being able to live at the monastery. He wanted to be allowed to do the same. But when he asked his mother, she patted his head and said that he must first grow much bigger before he could become a monk. Rahula asked how he could grow faster. She told him to eat well and exercise each day.

One day when she saw the bhikkhus begging close to the palace, Yasodhara turned to Rahula and said, "Why don't you run down and greet the Buddha? Ask him again about your inheritance."

Rahula ran downstairs. He loved his mother dearly, but he also loved his father. He had spent all his days with his mother, but had never spent even one whole day with his father. He wished he could be like Nanda and live by the Buddha's side. He ran quickly across the courtyard and out the south gate until he caught up with the Buddha. The Buddha smiled and extended his hand. Though the spring sun was already growing hot, Rahula felt protected by his father's shadow and love. He looked up at his father and said, "It is very cool and refreshing by your side."

Yasodhara watched them from the palace balcony. She knew that the Buddha had given Rahula permission to return with him to the monastery for the day.

Rahula asked the Buddha, "What is my inheritance?"

The Buddha answered, "Come to the monastery, and I will transmit it to you."

When they returned to the monastery, Sariputta shared his food with Rahula. Rahula ate in silence as he sat between the Buddha and Sariputta. He was glad to see his young uncle, Nanda. The Buddha told Rahula that he could sleep the night in Sariputta's hut. All the bhikkhus were fond of Rahula and treated him so warmly, Rahula wished he could live at the monastery forever. But Sariputta explained to him that if he wanted to stay at the monastery, he would have to become a monk. Rahula clasped Sariputta's hand and asked if he could ask the Buddha to ordain him. The Buddha nodded yes when Rahula asked him, and he instructed Sariputta to ordain the young boy.

At first Sariputta thought the Buddha was jesting, but when he saw how serious the Buddha was, he asked, "But, Master, how can one so young become a bhikkhu?"

The Buddha answered, "We will allow him to practice in preparation for full vows in the future. Let him take the vows of a novice for now. He can be given the task of chasing away the crows that disturb the bhikkhus during sitting meditation."

Sariputta shaved Rahula's head and gave him the three refuges. He taught Rahula four precepts: do not kill, do not steal, do not speak falsehoods, and do not drink alcohol. He took one of his own robes and cut it down to size for Rahula. He showed Rahula how to wear it and how to hold the bowl for begging. Rahula looked just like a miniature bhikkhu. He slept in Sariputta's hut and went begging with him each day in the small hamlets that bordered the monastery. Although the older bhikkhus ate only one meal a day, Sariputta feared Rahula would lack adequate nutrition for his growing body, and so he let the boy eat an evening meal, too. Lay disciples remembered to bring milk and extra food for the little monk.

When the news that Rahula had shaved his head and put on a bhikkhu's robe reached the palace, it caused King Suddhodana to become very upset. Both the king and queen missed Rahula terribly. They had expected him to visit the monastery for just a few days and then return to the palace. They hadn't dreamed he might remain in the monastery as a novice. They were lonely without their grandson. Yasodhara felt a mixture of sadness and happiness. Though she missed her son intensely, she was comforted to know he was now close to his father after not seeing him for so many years.

One afternoon, the king mounted his royal carriage with Queen Gotami and Yasodhara, and paid a visit to the monastery. They were met by the Buddha. Nanda and Rahula came out to greet them too. In his excitement, Rahula ran to his mother, and Yasodhara embraced her son warmly. Then Rahula hugged both his grandparents.

The king bowed to the Buddha and then said rather reproachfully, "I suffered unbelievably when you abandoned home to become a monk. Not long ago, Nanda left me as well. It is too much to bear to lose Rahula. For a family man like myself, the bonds between father and son and grandfather and grandson are very important. The pain I felt when you left was like a knife cutting into my skin. After cutting into my skin, the knife cut into my flesh. After cutting into my flesh, the knife has cut clear to the bone. I beseech you to consider your actions. In the future, you should not allow a child to be ordained unless he has received prior approval by his parents."

The Buddha tried to comfort the king by speaking about the truths of impermanence and the absence of a separate self. He reminded him that the daily practice of mindfulness was the only gate by which suffering could be overcome. Nanda and Rahula now had a chance to deeply live such a life. The Buddha encouraged his father to appreciate their good fortune and to continue to practice the way of awareness in daily life in order to find true happiness.

The king felt his pain lighten. Gotami and Yasodhara were also comforted and reassured by the Buddha's words.

Later that day, the Buddha said to Sariputta, "From now on, we will not receive children into the community of bhikkhus without the approval of their parents. Please note that in our monastic code."

Time passed quickly. The Buddha and his sangha had rested in the kingdom of Sakya for more than six months. New ordinations had increased the number of bhikkhus to more than five hundred. The number of lay disciples was too great to be counted. King Suddhodana also gave the sangha another place to build a monastery—the former summer palace of Prince Siddhartha, north of the capital, with its cool and spacious gardens. Venerable Sariputta organized a large number of bhikkhus to set up monastic living there. The presence of this new monastery helped assure a firm foundation for the practice of the Way in the Sakya kingdom.

The Buddha wished to return to Bamboo Forest in time for the rainy season retreat, as he had promised King Bimbisara and the bhikkhus who had remained there. King Suddhodana invited the Buddha for a last meal before his departure and asked him to give a discourse on the Dharma for the royal family and all members of the Sakya clan.

The Buddha used this occasion to speak about applying the Way to political life. He said the Way could illuminate the realm of politics, assisting those involved in governing the kingdom to bring about social equality and justice. He said, "If you practice the Way, you will increase your understanding and compassion and better serve the people. You will find ways to bring about peace and happiness without depending on violence at all. You do not need to kill, torture, or imprison people, or confiscate property. This is not an impossible ideal, but something which can be actually realized.

"When a politician possesses enough understanding and love, he sees the truth about poverty, misery, and oppression. Such a person can find the means to reform the government in order to reduce the gap between rich and poor and cease the use of force against others.

"My friends, political leaders and rulers must set an example. Don't live in the lap of luxury because wealth only creates a greater barrier between you and the people. Live a simple, wholesome life, using your time to serve the people, rather than pursuing idle pleasures. A leader cannot earn the trust and respect of his people if he does not set a good example. If you love and respect the people, they will love and respect you in return. Rule by virtue differs from rule by law and order. Rule by virtue does not depend on punishment. According to the Way of Awakening, true happiness can only be attained by the path of virtue."

King Suddhodana and all those present listened intently to the Buddha. Prince Dronodanaraja, the Buddha's uncle and the father of Devadatta and Ananda, said, "Rule by virtue, as you have described it, is truly beautiful. But I believe that you alone possess the character and virtue needed to realize such a path. Why don't you stay in Kapilavatthu and help create a new form of government right here in Sakya kingdom which will bring peace, joy, and happiness to all the people?"

King Suddhodana added, "I am old. If you agree to remain, I will gladly abdicate the throne in your favor. With your virtue, integrity, and intelligence, I am sure all the people will stand behind you. Before long our country would prosper as it never has before."

The Buddha smiled and did not speak right away. Looking kindly at his father, he said, "Father, I am no longer the son of one family, one clan, or even one country. My family is now all beings, my home is the Earth, and my position is that of a monk who depends on the generosity of others. I have chosen this path, not the path of politics. I believe I can best serve all beings in this way."

Although Queen Gotami and Yasodhara did not think it befitting to express their own views during this gathering, they were both moved to tears by the Buddha's words. They knew what he said was correct.

The Buddha continued speaking to the king and all those present about the five precepts and how to apply them in family life and society. The five precepts were the foundation of a happy family and a peaceful society. He explained each precept carefully, and concluded by saying, "If you want the people to be united, you must first obtain their faith and trust. If political leaders practice the five precepts, the people's faith and trust will grow. With that faith and trust, there is nothing the country can't accomplish. Peace, happiness, and social equality will be assured. Create a life based on awareness.. The dogmas of the past do not build faith and trust nor do they encourage equality among the people. Let the Way of Awakening offer a new path and a new faith."

The Buddha assured them that although he would soon be departing for Magadha, he would return to Kapilavatthu in the future. The king and all those present were glad to hear that.

Chapter Thirty-Eight
O, Happiness!

From the country of Sakya, the Buddha entered the northern region of Kosala. He was accompanied by one hundred twenty bhikkhus, including many young men from noble families. They rested in a park near the city of Anupiya, which was home to the Malla people. Venerable Sariputta was traveling with the Buddha, as were Kaludayi, Nanda, and the novice Rahula.

Less than a month after the Buddha departed from Kapilavatthu, two young men of the Sakya clan from a very wealthy family also considered leaving home to be ordained as bhikkhus. Their names were Mahanama and Anuruddha. Their family owned three magnificent residences, one for each season. Mahanama wanted to follow several of his friends who had become bhikkhus, but when he learned that his brother had similar thoughts, he changed his mind. There were only two sons in their family. He felt it would be a pity if both became monks. And so Mahanama yielded to his younger brother's desire and granted him the privilege of asking to be ordained.

But when Anuruddha asked his mother for her permission, she protested, "My sons are my only happiness in this life. If you become a monk, I could not bear it."

Anuruddha reminded her of the many other nobles who had already become bhikkhus. He told her how practicing the Way could bring peace and happiness not only to the

monk but to his family and society. Because Anuruddha listened to many of the Dharma talks the Buddha had given at
Nigrodha Park, he was able to speak eloquently about the
teaching to his mother. Finally she said, "Very well, I will
let you go, but only on the condition that your good friend,
Baddhiya, decides to become a bhikkhu as well."

She was certain that Baddhiya would never consider becoming a bhikkhu. He was also a member of the imperial
clan and commanded a high post. His vast responsibilities
and his esteemed reputation would be difficult to abandon for
the simple life of a monk. But Anuruddha lost no time in
seeking out his friend. Baddhiya was the governor of the
northern provinces. He had many soldiers under his command.
Even his own palace was flanked day and night by armed
guards. All day his quarters bustled with the comings and go-
ings of important dignitaries.

Baddhiya received Anuruddha as an honored guest.

Anuruddha told him. "I want to leave home and become a
bhikkhu under the Buddha's guidance, but I cannot, and you
are the reason why."

Baddhiya laughed, "What do you mean? How have I ever
prevented you from becoming a bhikkhu? Why, I would do
anything I could to help you fulfill your wish."

Anuruddha explained his predicament. He concluded by
saying, "You have just said you would do anything you could
to help me become a bhikkhu. But the only way is for you to
become a bhikkhu yourself."

Baddhiya felt caught. It wasn't that he did not also feel
drawn to the Buddha and the Path of Awakening. In fact, he
had secretly intended to become a bhikkhu at a later date,
though certainly not at present. He said, "In seven more
years, I will become a bhikkhu. Wait until then."

"Seven years is too long to wait. Who knows if I will even
be alive then?"

Baddhiya laughed. "What are you so pessimistic about?
But very well, give me three years, and I will become a
bhikkhu."

"Even three years is too long."

"Very well, seven months. I need to settle all my household arrangements and hand over my governing duties."

"Why should one about to abandon home to follow the Way require so much time to settle his affairs? A bhikkhu freely leaves all behind in order to follow the path of freedom and liberation. If you take too long, you might change your mind."

"Alright, alright, my friend. Give me seven days and I will join you."

Ecstatic, Anuruddha went home to inform his mother. She had not dreamed that Governor Baddhiya would so easily abandon his prestigious position. Suddenly she sensed the power of the path of liberation and she felt better about letting her son leave home.

Anuruddha persuaded a number of other friends to join him. They were Bhagu, Kimbila, Devadatta, and Ananda. They were all princes of the imperial clan. On the appointed day, they gathered at Devadatta's house and set off in search of the Buddha. They were all of age except Ananda who was still eighteen. But Ananda had received his father's permission to follow his elder brother, Devadatta. The six princes traveled by carriage until they reached a small town close to the Kosala border. They had heard that the Buddha was staying near Anupiya.

Anuruddha suggested they get rid of their jewels and ornaments before they crossed the border. They all removed their necklaces, rings, and bangles and wrapped them in a cloak. They agreed to find some poor person to give them to. They noticed a tiny barber shop by the side of the road which was run by a young man about their own age. He was an attractive fellow but shabbily dressed. Anuruddha entered his shop and asked him his name.

The young barber replied, "Upali."

Anuruddha asked Upali if he could direct them across the border. Upali gladly led them there himself. Before they left him, they handed him the cloak containing the precious jewels and ornaments. Anuruddha said, "Upali, we intend to follow the Buddha and live as bhikkhus. We have no more use of these jewels. We would like to give them to you. With these, you will have enough to live in leisure the rest of your days."

The princes bid Upali farewell and crossed the border. When the young barber opened up the cloak, the glint of gems and gold dazzled his eyes. He belonged to the lowest caste in society. No one in his family had ever owned so much as an ounce of gold or even a single ring. Now he had an entire cloakful of precious gems. But instead of being happy, he was suddenly seized with panic. He clasped the bundle tightly in his arms. All his former feelings of well-being disappeared. He knew there were many people who would kill to get at the contents of the cloak.

Upali reflected. The young noblemen who had enjoyed great wealth and power were giving it all up in order to become monks. No doubt they had come to see the dangers and burdens that wealth and fame can bring. Suddenly, he too wanted to cast the bundle aside and follow the princes in pursuit of true peace, joy, and liberation. Without a moment's hesitation, he hung the bundle on a nearby branch for the first passerby to claim, and then he too crossed the border. Before long, he caught up with the young nobles.

Surprised to see Upali running after them, Devadatta asked, "Upali, why are you running after us? Where's the bundle of gems we gave you?"

Upali caught his breath and explained how he had tied the bundle to a tree to be claimed by the first passerby. He said he didn't feel at ease with such riches and wanted to join them in becoming a bhikkhu under the guidance of the Buddha.

Devadatta laughed. "You want to become a bhikkhu? But you're a—"

Anuruddha cut Devadatta off, "Wonderful! Wonderful! We would be pleased if you would join us. The Buddha teaches that the sangha is like a great sea and the bhikkhus are like many rivers that flow into that sea becoming one with it. Though we may be born into different castes, once we join the sangha, we are all brothers with no distinctions dividing us."

Baddhiya extended his hand to shake Upali's. He introduced himself as the former governor of the north provinces of Sakya. He introduced the other princes to Upali who bowed deeply to each one. Together the seven young men continued on their way.

They reached Anupiya the next day and were told that the Buddha was staying in a forest two miles northeast of the city. They made their way to the forest and there met the Buddha. Baddhiya spoke on behalf of the group. The Buddha nodded his acceptance of their request to be ordained. Baddhiya also said, "We would like to ask that Upali be ordained first. We will then bow to Upali as our elder brother in the Dharma, releasing any vestiges of false pride and discrimination that may remain in us."

The Buddha ordained Upali first. Because Ananda was only eighteen he took the vows of a novice to prepare for full ordination when he reached twenty years of age. Ananda was now the youngest member of the sangha next to Rahula. Rahula was delighted to see Ananda.

Three days after their ordination, they departed with the Buddha and the other bhikkhus and headed towards Vesali, where they rested three days in Mahavana Park. After that, it took them ten days to reach Bamboo Forest Monastery in Rajagaha.

Venerables Kassapa, Moggallana, and Kondanna were happy to see the Buddha again, as were all six hundred bhikkhus living at Bamboo Forest. King Bimbisara lost no time in paying the Buddha a visit as soon as he learned of his arrival. The atmosphere at Bamboo Forest was happy and warm. The rainy season was fast approaching and Venerables Kondanna and Kassapa were well prepared. This was the third rainy season since the Buddha's Awakening. He spent the first at the Deer Park and the second at Bamboo Forest.

Before Baddhiya accepted the governor's post, he had wholeheartedly studied spiritual matters. Now, under Venerable Kassapa's guidance at Bamboo Forest, he devoted heart and mind to his practice, spending almost all his time meditating. He preferred sleeping beneath the trees to sleeping in a hut. One night while sitting in meditation beneath a tree, he experienced a happiness greater than any he had ever known. He exclaimed, "O, happiness! O, happiness!"

Another bhikkhu sitting nearby heard Baddhiya call out. The next morning this same bhikkhu reported to the Buddha, "Lord, late last night while I was sitting in meditation, I heard bhikkhu Baddhiya suddenly call, 'O, happiness! O, happiness!' It appears he misses the wealth and fame he left behind. I thought it best to tell you."

The Buddha only nodded.

After the noon meal, the Buddha gave a Dharma talk. When he was finished, he asked bhikkhu Baddhiya to come forward before the community, which also included many lay disciples. The Buddha asked him, "Baddhiya, late last night while sitting in meditation, did you call out, 'O, happiness! O, happiness!'"

Baddhiya joined his palms and answered, "Teacher, last night I did indeed call out those very words."

"Can you tell us why?"

"Lord, when I was the governor, I lived a life of fame, power, and wealth. Everywhere I went I was flanked by four soldiers for protection. My palace was never without armed guards, day and night. Even so, there was never a moment I felt safe. I was almost constantly filled with fear and anxiety. But now I can walk and sit alone in the deep forest. I know no fear or anxiety. Instead I feel ease, peace, and joy such as I never felt before. Teacher, living the life of a bhikkhu brings me such great happiness and contentment, I am no longer afraid of anyone or of losing anything. I am as happy as a deer living freely in the forest. Last night during my meditation, this became so clear to me that I exclaimed, 'O, happiness! O, happiness!' Please forgive me for any disturbance it caused you and the other bhikkhus."

The Buddha praised Baddhiya before the entire community. "It is wonderful, Baddhiya. You have made great strides on the path of self-contentment and detachment. The peace and joy you feel is the peace and joy to which even the gods aspire."

During the rainy season retreat, the Buddha ordained many new bhikkhus, including a talented young man named Mahakassapa. Mahakassapa was the son of the richest man in Magadha. His father's wealth was exceeded only by the national treasury. Mahakassapa was married to a woman from Vesali named Bhadra Kapilani. They had lived as husband and wife for twelve years, but both longed to follow the spiritual path.

Early one morning, Mahakassapa awoke before his wife. Suddenly he noticed a poisonous snake creeping beside his wife's arm that was hanging over the side of the bed. Mahakassapa did not dare breathe for fear of startling the snake. It slowly crept past Kapilani's arm and out of the room. Mahakassapa woke his wife up and told her what had just taken place. Together they reflected on the uncertainty and transiency of life. Kapilani urged Mahakassapa to seek a teacher without delay in order to study the Way. Because he had heard about the Buddha, he went at once to Bamboo Forest. The moment he saw the Buddha, he understood that the Buddha was his true teacher. The Buddha could easily see that Mahakassapa was a man of rare depth, and he ordained him. Mahakassapa told the Buddha of his wife's longing to become a nun and follow the Way, but the Buddha answered that the time was not yet ripe to admit women into the sangha and that she would need to wait a little longer.

Chapter Thirty-Nine
Waiting for Daybreak

Three days after the rainy season ended, a young man named Sudatta paid a visit to the Buddha to ask if he would come teach the Way of Awakening in Kosala. Sudatta was an extremely wealthy merchant. He lived in the capital city, Savatthi, in the kingdom of Kosala which was ruled by King Pasenadi. Sudatta was known to his countrypeople as a philanthropist who always set aside a generous portion of his income to share with orphans and the destitute. His charitable efforts gave him much satisfaction and happiness. His people called him "Anathapindika," which means "the one who cares for the poor and abandoned."

Sudatta traveled frequently to Magadha to buy and sell goods. When in Rajagaha, he stayed with his wife's elder brother, who was also a merchant. His brother-in-law always treated him with the greatest affection, assuring that every detail of his stay was pleasant. He was staying with his brother-in-law at the end of the rainy season.

Unlike usual, his brother-in-law did not cater to many of his needs. Instead, he busily directed family members and servants in preparation for some great feast. Sudatta was surprised to arrive and find the household in the midst of so much activity. He asked if they were preparing to hold a wedding or death anniversary observance.

The brother-in-law answered, "Tomorrow I have invited the Buddha and his bhikkhus for a meal."

Sudatta asked, with some surprise, "Doesn't 'Buddha' mean 'one who is awake?'"

"That is right. The Buddha is an awakened person. He is an enlightened master. He is wondrous and radiant. Tomorrow you will have a chance to meet this wonderful person."

He could not explain why, but just hearing the name Buddha filled Sudatta with happiness and inspiration. He sat his brother-in-law down and asked to hear more about this enlightened teacher. The brother-in-law explained how after watching the serene bhikkhus beg in the city, he had gone to hear the Buddha at Bamboo Forest Monastery. He had become one of the Buddha's lay disciples and had even built a number of thatched huts at the monastery as an offering, in order to protect the bhikkhus from the sun and rain. He had overseen the building of sixty huts in a single day.

Perhaps, Sudatta marvelled, it was from a past life connection, but he felt great love and respect for the Buddha well within his heart. He could not wait until the following noon to meet the Buddha. He spent a restless night, anxiously waiting for daybreak so that he could pay a morning visit to Bamboo Forest Monastery. Three times he arose from his bed to see if it was dawn yet, but each time the sky was still dark. Unable to sleep anymore, he got up anyway. He dressed, slipped into his shoes, and walked out the door. The air was cold and misty. He passed through Sivaka Gate and made his way to Bamboo Forest. By the time he arrived, the first rays of morning sunlight were shining on the bamboo leaves. Though he wanted nothing more than to meet the Buddha, he felt somewhat nervous. To calm himself, he whispered, "Sudatta, do not worry."

At that very moment, the Buddha, who was doing walking meditation, passed Sudatta. He stopped and said softly, "Sudatta."

Sudatta joined his palms and bowed before the Buddha. They walked to the Buddha's hut, and Sudatta asked the Buddha if he had slept well. The Buddha replied he had. Sudatta told the Buddha how restless a night he had spent, so anxious was he to come and meet the Buddha. He asked the Buddha to teach him the Way. The Buddha spoke to Sudatta about understanding and love.

Sudatta was filled with great happiness. He prostrated before the Buddha and asked to become a lay disciple. The Buddha accepted him. Sudatta also invited the Buddha and all his bhikkhus to come have a meal the following day at the home of his brother-in-law.

The Buddha laughed gently. "My bhikkhus and I have already been invited to eat there today. There is no reason we should expect to eat there tomorrow, too."

Sudatta said, "Today my brother-in-law will host you. Tomorrow shall be my offering. I regret I do not have a house of my own in Rajagaha. I entreat you to accept my invitation."

The Buddha smiled his acceptance. Overjoyed, Sudatta bowed again and then quickly returned home to assist his brother-in-law with preparations for that day's meal offering.

When Sudatta heard more of the Buddha's teaching at his brother-in-law's home, his happiness knew no bounds. He accompanied the Buddha and the bhikkhus to the gate when the teaching was finished, and at once began to prepare for the following day's meal offering. His brother-in-law joined his efforts with enthusiasm and even said, "Sudatta, you are still my guest. Why don't you let me take care of all the preparations."

But Sudatta would not hear of it. He insisted on taking care of all the expenses himself, only agreeing to let the family help ready the home and cook some of the dishes.

When Sudatta heard more of the Buddha's teaching the next day, his heart opened like a flower. He knelt down and said, "Lord Buddha, the people of Kosala have not yet had an opportunity to welcome you and your sangha and to learn the Way of Awakening. Please consider my invitation for you to come to Kosala and spend a period of time. Please show compassion to the people of Kosala."

The Buddha agreed to discuss the idea with his senior disciples. He promised to give Sudatta a response within a few days.

A few days later Sudatta visited Bamboo Forest Monastery and received the happy news that the Buddha had decided to accept his invitation. The Buddha asked him if there would be some suitable place near Savatthi where a large community of bhikkhus could dwell. Sudatta assured him that he would find a place and would provide for all the sangha's needs while they were there. Sudatta also suggested that the Buddha allow Venerable Sariputta to come to Kosala with him first in order to assist in preparations for the Buddha's arrival. The Buddha asked Sariputta whether or not he would like that, and Sariputta replied he would be happy to go.

A week later Sudatta came to Bamboo Forest where he met Sariputta. They set off together, crossing the Ganga and traveling to Vesali, where they were met by Ambapali, and they rested the night in her mango grove. Sariputta told her that she could expect the Buddha and a large number of bhikkhus to pass through Vesali on their way to Kosala in another six months. Ambapali said she would be most happy to offer them food and a place to sleep. She told Sariputta and Sudatta that she was most honored to receive them as guests. She commended the young merchant on his many charitable works and encouraged him in his efforts to have the Buddha bring the teaching to Kosala.

After bidding farewell to Ambapali, they headed northwest along the banks of the Aciravati River. Sudatta had never walked such distances before, having always used a carriage in the past. Everywhere they stopped, he announced to people that the Buddha and his sangha would be traveling through the land, and he asked the people to welcome him.

"The Buddha is an awakened master. Prepare to welcome him and his sangha with jubilation."

Kosala was a large and prosperous kingdom, no less powerful than Magadha. Its southern border was marked by the Ganga and its northern border brushed the feet of the Himalayas. Sudatta or "Anathapindika," was known to everyone wherever he went. The people trusted what he told them, and they all looked forward to meeting the Buddha and his sangha. Every morning when Venerable Sariputta went begging, Sudatta accompanied him to speak to as many people as he could about the Buddha.

They reached Savatthi after a month. Sudatta invited Sariputta to his home for a meal and introduced him to his parents and wife. He asked Sariputta to speak about the Dharma, after which his parents and wife asked to take the three refuges and five precepts. Sudatta's wife was a lovely and graceful woman. Her name was Punnalakkhana. They had four children—three girls and a boy. The daughters were named Subhadra Elder, Subhadra Younger, and Sumagadha. Their son, the youngest child, was named Kala.

Sariputta begged every morning in the city and slept in the forest by the banks of the river at night. Sudatta lost no time in searching for a place to host the Buddha and the bhikkhus.

Chapter Forty

Cover the Land in Gold

Of all the places Sudatta visited, none was more beautiful and peaceful than the park which belonged to Prince Jeta. Sudatta felt sure that if he could acquire this park it would serve as the perfect place from which the Buddha's Way of Awakening could be spread to all corners of the kingdom. Sudatta went to see Prince Jeta and found him entertaining a palace official. Sudatta respectfully greeted them both and then expressed directly his hope that the prince would sell him the park to provide a practice center for the Buddha. Prince Jeta was only twenty years old. The park had been a gift the previous year from his father, King Pasenadi. The prince looked at the palace official and then at Sudatta, and replied, "My royal father gave me the park. I am very attached to it. I would only part with it if you agreed to cover every square inch of it in gold coins."

Prince Jeta was speaking in jest. He certainly wasn't prepared for the young merchant to take him seriously. But Sudatta responded, "Agreed, I will meet your price. Tomorrow I will have the gold brought to the park."

Prince Jeta was startled. "But I was only joking. I do not want to sell my park. Don't bother bringing the gold."

Sudatta answered with resolve, "Honorable Prince, you are a member of the royal family. You must carry out the words you have spoken."

Sudatta looked at the palace official drinking tea for support. "Is that not so, Your Excellency?"

The official nodded. He turned to the prince and said, "The merchant Anathapindika speaks the truth. If you hadn't actually quoted a price, it would be different. But you cannot withdraw your offer now."

Prince Jeta submitted, but he secretly hoped Sudatta would not be able to meet his price. Sudatta bowed and departed. Early the next morning, Sudatta sent great carts of gold coins and had his servants spread it over the entire park.

Prince Jeta was astounded when he saw the great mounds of gold. He understood that this had been no ordinary business agreement. He asked himself why anyone would give so much gold for one park? This Buddha and his sangha must be truly extraordinary for the young merchant to go to such lengths. The prince asked Sudatta to tell him about the Buddha. Sudatta's eyes shone as he spoke about his Teacher, the Dharma, and the Sangha. He promised that he would bring Venerable Sariputta to meet the prince the following day. Prince Jeta found himself moved by the things Sudatta told him about the Buddha. He looked up to see that Sudatta's men had already spread gold coins over two thirds of the forest. Just as a fourth cart was arriving, he held out his hand and stopped them.

He said to Sudatta, "That is enough gold. Let the remaining land be my gift. I want to contribute to this beautiful project of yours."

Sudatta was pleased to hear this. When he brought Sariputta to meet the prince, the prince was impressed by the bhikkhu's peaceful bearing. Together they went to visit the park, which Sudatta had decided to call "Jetavana," or "Jeta Grove," in honor of the prince. Sudatta suggested to Sariputta that he live at Jetavana to help direct the building of the monastery. He said his family could bring food offerings to Sariputta each day. Together Sudatta, Sariputta, and the prince discussed building huts, a Dharma hall, a meditation hall, and bathrooms. Sudatta expressed a wish to build a three-tiered gate at the forest's entrance. Sariputta contributed a number of helpful suggestions regarding setting up the monastery, as he was now well experienced in such matters. They selected an especially cool and tranquil spot to build the Buddha's thatched hut. They oversaw the making of pathways and the digging of wells.

The city people soon heard how Sudatta had paved the forest in gold in order to purchase it from the prince. They learned that a monastery was being built to welcome the Buddha and his sangha, who would soon arrive from Magadha. Sariputta began to give Dharma talks at Jetavana and the number of people who attended grew daily. Though none of the people had yet met the Buddha, they all felt drawn to his teaching.

Four months later the monastery was nearly completed. Sariputta set off for Rajagaha in order to lead the Buddha and the bhikkhus back to Jetavana. He met them in the streets of Vesali. Several hundred bhikkhus, clad in saffron robes, were begging in the streets. He learned that the Buddha and the bhikkhus had arrived in Vesali only a few days previously and were dwelling nearby at Great Forest. The Buddha asked about preparations in Savatthi, and Sariputta recounted how well things were going.

The Buddha told Sariputta that he had left Kondanna and Uruvela Kassapa in charge of the community at Bamboo Forest. Of the five hundred bhikkhus presently with the Buddha in Vesali, two hundred would remain to practice in the vicinity. The remaining three hundred would accompany him on the journey to Kosala. The Buddha told Sariputta that Ambapali had invited the entire sangha for a meal offering the next day. The day after that they would depart for Savatthi.

Ambapali was happy for the chance to offer the Buddha and his bhikkhus a meal in her mango grove. She only regretted that her son, Jivaka, was unable to attend because of his medical studies. A curious thing happened the day before she was to serve the Buddha and his bhikkhus a meal. On her way home from visiting the Buddha, her carriage was stopped by several princes of the Licchavi clan. They were the most powerful and wealthiest lords in Vesali and traveled in handsome, elegant carriages. They asked her where she was going, and she replied she was on her way home to prepare to receive the Buddha and his bhikkhus the following day. The young nobles suggested she forget about the Buddha and invite them instead.

The princes said, "Invite us and we will pay for the meal with one hundred thousand pieces of gold." They were certain that hosting a monk could not possibly be as amusing or profitable as entertaining themselves.

Ambapali was not interested. She replied, "It is clear you do not know the Buddha or you would not speak in such a manner. I have already made arrangements to invite the Buddha and his sangha. Even if you offered me the entire city of Vesali and all the land surrounding it, I would refuse. Now if you please, let me pass. I have much to do to prepare for tomorrow."

Taken aback, the Licchavi nobles let her pass. Little did Ambapali know that after their encounter with her, they decided to go and see this teacher who was so highly respected by Ambapali. They left their carriages at the entrance to Great Forest and walked in.

The Buddha could tell that these young men possessed many seeds of compassion and wisdom. He invited them to be seated and he told them about his own life and search for the Way. He told them about the path to overcome suffering and realize liberation. He knew they belonged to the same warrior caste he had belonged to and looking at them, he could see himself as a young man. He spoke to them with warm understanding.

Their hearts were opened by the Buddha's words. They felt they could see themselves for the first time. They understood that wealth and power were not enough to bring them true happiness. They knew they had found a path for their lives. They all asked to be accepted as lay disciples. They also asked if they could offer the Buddha and his sangha a meal the next day.

The Buddha said, "We have already been invited by Ambapali for tomorrow."

The young nobles smiled, remembering their encounter with Ambapali.

"Then allow us to offer you a meal on the following day."

The Buddha smiled his acceptance.

Ambapali invited all her relations and friends to the mango grove the next day. She invited the Licchavi nobles, as well, to hear the Buddha offer teaching.

The day after, the Buddha and a hundred bhikkhus ate in the princes' palace. They were served elegant and refined vegetarian dishes that had been prepared with the utmost skill and care. The princes also offered the bhikkhus jackfruit, mangos, bananas, and rose-apples freshly picked from their own orchards. When the meal was finished, the Buddha spoke about dependent co-arising and the Noble Eightfold Path. He touched everyone's heart with the teaching. Twelve young nobles asked to be ordained as bhikkhus. The Buddha happily accepted them. They included Otthaddha and Sunakhatta, two princes who wielded great influence in the Licchavi clan.

When the meal and teaching were completed, the Licchavi nobles entreated the Buddha to come dwell in Vesali the following year. They promised to build a monastery in Great Forest where several hundred bhikkhus could dwell. The Buddha accepted their proposal.

Ambapali visited the Buddha early the next morning. She expressed her desire to offer the mango grove to the Buddha and his sangha. The Buddha accepted her gift. Shortly afterwards, the Buddha, Sariputta, and three hundred bhikkhus headed north for Savatthi.

Chapter Forty-One
Has Anyone Seen My Mother?

The road to Savatthi was now familiar to Sariputta. Because he and Anathapindika had nourished people's interest in the Buddha and the sangha, they were greeted warmly wherever they went. At nights the bhikkhus rested in the cool forests along the banks of the Aciravati River. They traveled in three groups. The Buddha and Sariputta led the first group. The second group was headed by Assaji. The third group was under the guidance of Moggallana. The bhikkhus maintained peaceful serenity as they walked. Sometimes local people gathered in the forests or along the riverbanks to listen to the Buddha's teaching.

The day they arrived in Savatthi, they were greeted by Sudatta and Prince Jeta who took them to the new monastery. Seeing how well planned Jetavana was, the Buddha praised Sudatta. Sudatta responded by saying it was all thanks to the ideas and labor of Venerable Sariputta and Prince Jeta.

Novice Rahula was now twelve years old. Though he had been assigned to study under Sariputta's guidance, Sariputta had been gone for six months, and so Moggallana had taken his place. At Jetavana, Rahula could resume his studies with Sariputta.

Prince Jeta and Sudatta arranged a reception immediately after the Buddha's arrival. Prince Jeta had come to deeply admire the Buddha through his contacts with Venerable Sariputta. They invited all the local people to come to hear the Buddha speak on the Dharma. Many came, including Price Jeta's mother, Queen Mallika, and his sixteen-year-old sister, Princess Vajiri. After hearing about the Buddha for months, everyone was most anxious to see him in person. The Buddha spoke about the Four Noble Truths and the Noble Eightfold Path.

After hearing the Dharma talk, the queen and princess felt their hearts open. They both wanted to become lay disciples, but did not dare to ask. The queen wanted to first seek the approval of her husband, King Pasenadi. She was sure that in the near future the king would meet the Buddha and share her feelings. Pasenadi's own sister, who was King Bimbisara's wife, had already taken the three refuges with the Buddha three years before.

Many important religious leaders in Savatthi also attended the Buddha's discourse that day. Most came out of curiosity rather than a desire to learn anything. But several of them felt their hearts suddenly illuminated when they heard the Buddha speak. Others saw in him a worthy opponent who challenged their own beliefs. Everyone agreed that his presence in Savatthi was a significant event in the spiritual life of Kosala.

When the reception and Dharma talk were over, Sudatta respectfully knelt before the Buddha and said, "My family and I, together with all our friends and relations, offer Jetavana monastery to you and your sangha."

The Buddha said, "Sudatta, your merit is great. Thanks to you, the sangha will be protected from sun and rain, wild animals, snakes, and mosquitoes. This monastery will draw bhikkhus from all four directions, now and in the future. You have supported the Dharma with all your heart. I hope you will continue to devote yourself to practicing the Way."

The next morning the Buddha and the bhikkhus went into the city to beg. Sariputta divided the bhikkhus into twelve groups, each numbering fifteen. The presence of the saffron-robed monks further aroused the people's interest in the new

Jetavana Monastery. The people admired the calm and quiet manner of the bhikkhus.

Once a week the Buddha gave a Dharma talk at Jetavana. Great numbers of people attended. Thus, it was not long before King Pasenadi was well aware of the impact of the Buddha's presence. He was too busy with political affairs to visit the Buddha himself, but he listened to many members of his court speak about the new monastery and the bhikkhus from Magadha. During a family meal, the king brought up the subject of the Buddha. Queen Mallika informed him of Prince Jeta's contributions to the monastery. The king asked the prince to tell him about the Buddha and the prince recounted all he had seen and heard. The prince said that if the king granted permission, he wished to become a lay disciple of the Buddha.

King Pasenadi had a hard time believing that a monk as young as the Buddha could have achieved true enlightenment. According to the prince, the Buddha was thirty-nine years old, the same age as the king. The king speculated that there was no way the Buddha could have attained a higher state than such elderly spiritual teachers as Puruna Kassapa, Makkhali Gosala, Nigantha Nathaputta, and Sanjaya Belatthiputta. Although the king would have liked to believe his son, he had his doubts. He decided that when an occasion arose he would go and meet the Buddha himself.

The rainy season was approaching and the Buddha decided to spend it at Jetavana. Thanks to the experience gained during previous rainy seasons at Bamboo Forest, the Buddha's senior disciples organized the retreat with ease. Sixty new bhikkhus joined the community in Savatthi. Sudatta also introduced many friends who became lay disciples and enthusiastically supported the activities of the monastery.

One afternoon, the Buddha received a young man whose face was lined with grief and misery. The Buddha learned that the man had recently lost his only son and for several days had stood in the cemetery crying out loud, "My son, my son, where have you gone?" The man was unable to eat, drink, or sleep.

The Buddha told him, "In love there is suffering."

The man objected, "You are wrong. Love doesn't cause suffering. Love brings only happiness and joy."

The bereaved man abruptly left before the Buddha could explain what he had meant. The man wandered aimlessly about until he stopped to chat with a group of men gambling in the street. He told them of his encounter with the Buddha. The men agreed with him that the Buddha was mistaken.

"How can love cause suffering? Love brings only happiness and joy! You're right. That monk Gautama was wrong."

Before long, news of this story spread throughout Savatthi and became a subject for heated debate. Many spiritual leaders contended that the Buddha was wrong about love. This matter reached the ears of King Pasenadi and that evening during the family meal, he said to the queen, "The monk the people call 'Buddha' may not be as great a teacher as the people seem to think he is."

The queen asked, "What makes you say that? Has someone said something bad about Teacher Gautama?"

"This morning, I heard some palace officials discussing Gautama. They said that according to him, the more you love the more you suffer."

The queen said, "If Gautama said that, it is undoubtedly true."

The king retorted impatiently, "You shouldn't speak like that. Examine things for yourself. Don't be like some small child who believes everything the teacher says."

The queen said no more. She knew that the king had not yet met the Buddha. The next morning she asked a close friend, the brahman Nalijangha, to visit the Buddha and ask him whether or not he had said that love was the source of suffering, and if he had to explain why. She asked her friend to note carefully everything the Buddha said and report back to her.

Nalijangha went to see the Buddha and asked him the queen's question. The Buddha responded, "Recently I heard that a woman in Savatthi lost her mother. She was so grief-stricken that she lost her mind and has been wandering the streets asking everyone, 'Have you seen my mother? Have you seen my mother?' I also heard about two young lovers who committed suicide together because the girl's parents were forcing her to marry someone else. These two stories alone demonstrate that love can cause suffering."

Nalijangha repeated the Buddha's words to Queen Mallika. One day soon after that she caught the king in a moment of leisure, and she asked him, "My husband, do you not love and cherish Princess Vajiri?"

"Indeed I do," answered the king, surprised by the question.

"If some misfortune befell her, would you suffer?"

The king was startled. Suddenly he saw clearly that the seeds of suffering existed within love. His sense of well-being was replaced with worry. The Buddha's words contained a cruel truth which greatly disturbed the king. He said, "I will go visit this monk Gautama as soon as I have a chance."

The queen was happy for she was confident that once the king met the Buddha, he would understand how extraordinary the Buddha's teaching was.

Chapter Forty-Two
Love Is Understanding

King Pasenadi came all alone to visit the Buddha, unaccompanied by even a guard. He left his carriage and driver at the monastery gate. He was greeted by the Buddha in front of the Buddha's thatched hut. After exchanging formal greetings, the king spoke to the Buddha most frankly, "Teacher Gautama, people praise you as the Buddha, one who has attained perfect enlightenment. But I have been asking myself how could one as young as yourself have attained enlightenment. Even the great masters such as Purana Kassapa, Makkhali Gosala, Nigantha Nathaputta, and Sanjaya Belatthiputta, who are all advanced in years, do not claim to have attained total enlightenment. Not even Pakudha Kaccayana and Ajita Kesakambali. Do you know of these masters?"

The Buddha responded, "Your majesty, I have heard of all those masters and have met a number of them. Spiritual realization does not depend on age. Months and years do not guarantee the presence of enlightenment. There are some things which should never be disdained—a young prince, a small snake, a spark of fire, and a young monk. A prince may be young but he possesses the characteristics and destiny of a king. A small poisonous snake can kill a grown man in an instant. One spark of fire can cause an entire forest or a large city to burn to ash. And a young monk can attain total enlightenment! Your majesty, a wise person never disdains a young prince, a small snake, a spark of fire, or a young monk."

King Pasenadi looked at the Buddha. He was impressed. The Buddha had spoken in a calm and quiet voice and what he had said was at once simple and profound. The king felt he could trust the Buddha. He then asked the question that was burning within him.

"Teacher Gautama, there are people who say you advise people not to love. They say you have said that the more a person loves, the more he will suffer and despair. I can see some truth in that statement, but I am unable to find peace with it. Without love, life would seem empty of meaning. Please help me resolve this."

The Buddha looked at the king warmly. "Your majesty, your question is a very good one, and many people can benefit from it. There are many kinds of love. We should examine closely the nature of each kind of love. Life has a great need of the presence of love, but not the sort of love that is based on lust, passion, attachment, discrimination, and prejudice. Majesty, there is another kind of love, sorely needed, which consists of loving kindness and compassion, or *maitri* and *karuna*.

"Usually when people speak of love they are referring only to the love that exists between parents and children, husbands and wives, family members, or the members of one's caste or country. Because the nature of such love depends on the concepts of 'me' and 'mine', it remains entangled in attachment and discrimination. People want only to love their parents, spouse, children, grandchildren, their own relatives and countrymen. Because they are caught in attachment, they worry about accidents that could befall their loved ones even before such things actually take place. When such accidents do occur, they suffer terribly. Love that is based on discrimination breeds prejudice. People become indifferent or even hostile to those outside their own circle of love. Attachment and discrimination are sources of suffering for ourselves and others. Majesty, the love for which all beings truly hunger is loving kindness and compassion. Maitri is the love that has the capacity to bring happiness to another. Karuna is the love which has the capacity to remove another's suffering. Maitri and karuna do not demand anything in return. Loving kindness and compassion are not limited to one's parents, spouse, children, relatives, caste members, and countrymen. They extend to all people and all beings. In maitri and karuna there is no discrimination, no 'mine' or 'not mine.' And because there is no discrimination, there is no attachment. Maitri and karuna bring happiness and ease suffering. They do not cause suffering and despair. Without them, life would be empty of meaning, as you said. With loving kindness and compassion, life is filled with peace, joy, and contentment. Majesty, you are the ruler of an entire country. All your people would benefit by your practice of loving kindness and compassion."

The king bent his head in thought. He looked up and asked the Buddha, "I have a family to care for and a country to rule. If I don't love my own family and people, how can I care for them? Please help clarify this for me."

"Naturally, you should love your own family and people. But your love can also extend beyond your own family and people. You love and care for the prince and princess, but that doesn't prevent you from loving and caring for the other young people in the kingdom. If you can love all the young people, your now limited love will become an all embracing love, and all the young people of the kingdom will be as your children. That is what is meant by having a heart of compassion. It is not just some ideal. It is something which can actually be realized, especially by someone like you who has so many means at his disposal."

"But what about the young people of other kingdoms?"

"Nothing prevents you from loving the young people of other kingdoms as your sons and daughters, even though they do not dwell under your rule. Just because one loves one's own people is no reason not to love the peoples of other kingdoms."

"But how can I show my love for them when they are not under my jurisdiction?"

The Buddha looked at the king. "The prosperity and security of one nation should not depend on the poverty and insecurity of other nations. Majesty, lasting peace and prosperity are only possible when nations join together in a common commitment to seek the welfare of all. If you truly want Kosala to enjoy peace and to prevent the young men of your kingdom from losing their lives on the battlefield, you must help other kingdoms find peace. Foreign and economic policies must follow the way of compassion for true peace to be possible. At the same time as you love and care for your own kingdom, you can love and care for other kingdoms such as Magadha, Kasi, Videha, Sakya, and Koliya.

"Majesty, last year I visited my family in the kingdom of Sakya. I rested several days in Arannakutika at the foot of the Himalayas. There I spent much time reflecting on a politics based on nonviolence. I saw that nations can indeed enjoy peace and security without having to resort to violent measures such as imprisonment and execution. I spoke of these things with my father, King Suddhodana. Now I take this opportunity to share these same ideas with you. A ruler who nourishes his compassion does not need to depend on violent means."

The king exclaimed, "Wondrous! Truly wondrous! Your words are most inspiring! You truly are the enlightened one! I promise to reflect on all you have said today. I will penetrate your words, which contain so much wisdom. But for now, please allow me to ask one more simple question. Ordinarily, love does contain elements of discrimination, desire, and attachment. According to you, that kind of love creates worry, suffering, and despair. How can one love without desire and attachment? How can I avoid creating worry and suffering in the love I hold for my own children?"

The Buddha replied, "We need to look at the nature of our love. Our love should bring peace and happiness to the ones we love. If our love is based on a selfish desire to possess others, we will not be able to bring them peace and happiness. On the contrary, our love will make them feel trapped. Such a love is no more than a prison. If the persons we love are unable to be happy because of our love, they will find a way to free themselves. They will not accept the prison of our love. Gradually the love between us will turn to anger and hatred.

"Majesty, did you hear of the tragedy that took place ten days ago in Savatthi because of selfish love? A mother felt she had been abandoned by her son when he fell in love and married. Rather than feeling as if she had gained a daughter, she only felt that she had lost her son, and she felt betrayed by him. Because of that, her love turned to hatred, and she put poison in the young couple's food, killing them both.

"Majesty! According to the Way of Enlightenment, love cannot exist without understanding. Love *is* Understanding. If you cannot understand, you cannot love. Husbands and wives who do not understand each other cannot love each other. Brothers and sisters who do not understand each other cannot love each other. Parents and children who do not understand each other cannot love each other. If you want your loved ones to be happy, you must learn to understand their sufferings and their aspirations. When you understand, you will know how to relieve their sufferings and how to help them fulfill their aspirations. That is true love. If you only want your loved ones to follow your own ideas and you remain ignorant of their needs, it is not truly love. It is only a desire to possess another and attempt to fulfill your own needs, which cannot be fulfilled in that way.

"Majesty! The people of Kosala have sufferings and aspirations. If you can understand their sufferings and aspirations, you will be able to truly love them. All the officials in your court have sufferings and aspirations. Understand those sufferings and aspirations, and you will know how to bring them happiness. Thanks to that, they will remain loyal to you all their lives. The queen, prince, and princess have their own sufferings and aspirations. If you can understand those sufferings and aspirations, you will be able to bring them happiness. When every person enjoys happiness, peace, and joy, you yourself will know happiness, peace, and joy. That is the meaning of love according to the Way of Awakening."

King Pasenadi was deeply moved. No other spiritual teacher or brahmana priest had ever opened the door to his heart and allowed him to understand things so deeply. The presence of this teacher, he thought to himself, was of great value to his country. He wanted to be the Buddha's student. After a moment of silence, he looked up at the Buddha and said, "I thank you for shedding so much light on these matters for me. But there remains one thing that still bothers me. You said that love based on desire and attachment creates suffering and despair, while love based on compassion brings only peace and happiness. But while I see that love based on the way of compassion is not selfish or self-serving, it still can bring pain and suffering. I love my people. When they suffer from some natural disaster like a typhoon or flood, I suffer, too. I am sure it is the same for you. Surely you suffer when you see someone who is sick or dying."

"Your question is very good. Thanks to this question, you will be able to understand more deeply the nature of compassion. First of all, you should know that the suffering caused by a love based on desire and attachment is a thousand times greater than the suffering that results from compassion. It is necessary to distinguish between the two kinds of suffering— one which is entirely useless and serves only to disturb our minds and bodies and the other which nourishes caring and responsibility. Love based on compassion can provide the energy needed to respond to the suffering of others. Love based on attachment and desire only creates anxiety and more suffering. Compassion provides fuel for the most helpful actions and service. Great King! Compassion is most necessary. Pain that results from compassion can be a helpful pain. If you cannot feel another person's pain, you are not truly human.

"Compassion is the fruit of understanding. Practicing the Way of Awareness is to realize the true face of life. That true face is impermanence. Everything is impermanent and without a separate self. Everything must one day pass away. One day your own body will pass away. When a person sees into the impermanent nature of all things, his way of looking becomes calm and serene. The presence of impermanence does not disturb his heart and mind. And thus the feelings of pain that result from compassion do not carry the bitter and heavy nature that other kinds of suffering do. On the contrary, compassion gives a person greater strength. Great King! Today you have heard some of the basic tenets of the Way of Liberation. On another day, I would like to share more of the teachings with you."

King Pasenadi's heart was filled with gratitude. He stood up and bowed to the Buddha. He knew that one day soon he would ask to be accepted as a lay disciple of the Buddha. He knew that Queen Mallika, Prince Jeta, and Princess Vajiri already felt a special bond with the Buddha. He wanted the entire family to receive the refuges together. He knew that his younger sister, Kosaladevi, and her husband, King Bimbisara, had already received them.

That evening, Queen Mallika and Princess Vajiri noticed a marked difference in the king. He seemed unusually calm and content. They knew it was the result of his encounter with the Buddha. They wanted very much to ask the king about his meeting with the Buddha, but they knew that they should wait and let the king tell them about it in his own time.

Chapter Forty-Three
Everyone's Tears Are Salty

King Pasenadi's visit to Jetavana stirred interest among the people and added to the stature of the Buddha's sangha. Palace officials noticed how King Pasenadi did not miss a single weekly Dharma talk, and many of them began to join him. Some did so out of admiration for the Buddha's teaching, while others went only in hopes of pleasing the king. The number of intellectuals and young people visiting Jetavana also mounted daily. During the three months of retreat, more than a hundred fifty young men were ordained by Sariputta. Religious leaders of other sects that had long enjoyed the king's patronage began to feel threatened, and some of them began to regard Jetavana Monastery with less than sympathetic eyes. The retreat season concluded with a large service at which the king offered new robes to every bhikkhu and distributed food and other basic necessities to poor families. At this ceremony, the king and his family formally took the three refuges.

After the retreat, the Buddha and other bhikkhus traveled to neighboring regions in order to spread the Dharma to more and more people. One day, as the Buddha and bhikkhus were begging in a village near the banks of the Ganga, the Buddha spotted a man carrying nightsoil. The man was an untouchable named Sunita. Sunita had heard about the Buddha and bhikkhus, but this was the first time he had ever seen them. He was alarmed, knowing how dirty his clothes were and how foul he smelled from carrying nightsoil. He quickly moved off the path and made his way down to the river. But the Buddha was determined to share the Way with Sunita. When Sunita veered from the path, the Buddha did the same. Understanding the Buddha's intent, Sariputta and Meghiya, the Buddha's attendant at the time, followed him. The rows of other bhikkhus came to a halt and they quietly watched.

Sunita was panic-stricken. He hastily put the buckets of nightsoil down and looked for a place to hide. Above him stood the bhikkhus in their saffron robes, while before him approached the Buddha and two other bhikkhus. Not knowing what else to do, Sunita waded up to his knees in water and stood with his palms joined.

Curious villagers came out of their homes and lined the shore to watch what was happening. Sunita had veered off the path because he was afraid he would pollute the bhikkhus. He could not have guessed the Buddha would follow him. Sunita knew that the sangha included many men from noble castes. He was sure that polluting a bhikkhu was an unforgivable act. He hoped the Buddha and bhikkhus would leave him and return to the road. But the Buddha did not leave. He walked right up to the water's edge and said, "My friend, please come closer so we may talk."

Sunita, his palms still joined, protested, "Lord, I don't dare!"

"Why not?" asked the Buddha.

"I am an untouchable. I don't want to pollute you and your monks."

The Buddha replied, "On our path, we no longer distinguish between castes. You are a human being like the rest of us. We are not afraid we will be polluted. Only greed, hatred, and delusion can pollute us. A person as pleasant as yourself brings us nothing but happiness. What is your name?"

"Lord, my name is Sunita."

Sunita protested, "Lord, I do not dare come closer. I am an untouchable."

"Sunita, would you like to become a bhikkhu like the rest of us?"

"I couldn't!"

"Why not?"

"I'm an untouchable!"

"Sunita, I have already explained that on our path there is no caste. In the Way of Awakening, caste no longer exists. It is like the Ganga, Yamuno, Aciravati, Sarabhu, Mahi, and Rohini rivers. Once they empty into the sea, they no longer retain their separate identities. A person who leaves home to follow the Way leaves caste behind whether he was born a brahman, kshatriya, vaishya, shudra, or untouchable. Sunita, if you like, you can become a bhikkhu like the rest of us."

Sunita could hardly believe his ears. He placed his joined palms before his forehead and said, "No one has ever spoken so kindly to me before. This is the happiest day of my life. If you accept me as your disciple, I vow to devote all my being to practicing your teaching."

The Buddha handed his bowl to Meghiya and reached his hand out to Sunita. He said, "Sariputta! Help me bathe Sunita. We will ordain him a bhikkhu right here on the bank of the river."

Venerable Sariputta smiled. He placed his own bowl on the ground and came forward to assist the Buddha. Sunita felt awkward and uncomfortable as Sariputta and the Buddha scrubbed him clean, but he didn't dare protest. The Buddha asked Meghiya to go up and ask Ananda for an extra robe. After Sunita was ordained, the Buddha assigned him to Sariputta's care. Sariputta led him back to Jetavana while the Buddha and the rest of the bhikkhus calmly continued their begging.

The local people had witnessed all this take place. News quickly spread that the Buddha had accepted an untouchable into his sangha. This caused a furor among higher castes in the capital. Never in the history of Kosala had an untouchable been accepted into a spiritual community. Many condemned the Buddha for violating sacred tradition. Others went so far as to suggest that the Buddha was plotting to overthrow the existing order and wreak havoc in the country.

The echoes of all these accusations reached the monastery through lay disciples as well as from bhikkhus who heard people saying such things in the city. Senior disciples Sariputta, Mahakassapa, Mahamoggallana, and Anuruddha met to discuss the people's reactions with the Buddha.

The Buddha said, "Accepting untouchables into the sangha was simply a question of time. Our way is a way of equality. We do not recognize caste. Though we may encounter difficulties over Sunita's ordination now, we will have opened a door for the first time in history that future generations will thank us for. We must have courage."

Moggallana said, "We do not lack courage or endurance. But how can we help reduce the hostility of public opinion to make it easier for the bhikkhus to practice?"

Sariputta said, "The important thing is to remain trusting of our practice. I will strive to assist Sunita in making progress on the path. His success will be the strongest argument in our favor. We can also seek ways to explain our belief in equality to the people. What do you think, Master?"

The Buddha placed his hand on Sariputta's shoulder. "You have just spoken my own thoughts," he said.

Before long, the uproar over Sunita's ordination reached the ears of King Pasenadi. A group of religious leaders requested a private audience with him and expressed their grave concerns over the matter. Their convincing arguments disturbed the king, and although he was a devoted follower of the Buddha, he promised the leaders that he would look into the matter. Some days later he paid a visit to Jetavana.

He climbed down from his carriage and walked into the monastery grounds alone. Bhikkhus passed him on the path beneath the cool shade of trees. The king followed the path that led to the Buddha's hut. He bowed to each bhikkhu he passed. As always, the serene and composed manner of the bhikkhus reinforced his faith in the Buddha. Halfway to the hut, he encountered a bhikkhu sitting on a large rock beneath a great pine tree teaching a small group of bhikkhus and lay disciples. It was a most appealing sight. The bhikkhu offering the teaching looked less than forty years old, yet his face radiated great peace and wisdom. His listeners were clearly absorbed by what he had to say. The king paused to listen and was moved by what he heard. But suddenly he remembered the purpose of his visit, and he continued on his way. He hoped to return later to listen to the bhikkhu's teaching.

The Buddha welcomed the king outside his hut, inviting him to sit on a bamboo chair. After they exchanged formal greetings, the king asked the Buddha who the bhikkhu sitting on the rock was. The Buddha smiled and answered, "That is Bhikkhu Sunita. He was once an untouchable who carried nightsoil. What do you think of his teaching?"

The king felt embarrassed. The bhikkhu with so radiant a bearing was none other than the nightsoil carrier Sunita! He would never have guessed such was possible. Before he knew how to respond, the Buddha said, "Bhikkhu Sunita has devoted himself wholeheartedly to his practice from the day of his ordination. He is a man of great sincerity, intelligence, and resolve. Though he was ordained only three months ago, he has already earned a reputation for great virtue and purity of heart. Would you like to meet him and make an offering to this most worthy bhikkhu?"

The king replied with frankness, "I would indeed like to meet Bhikkhu Sunita and make an offering to him. Master, your teaching is deep and wondrous! I have never met any other spiritual teacher with so open a heart and mind. I do not think there is a person, animal, or plant that does not benefit from the presence of your understanding. I must tell you that I came here today with the intention of asking how you could accept an untouchable into your sangha. But I have seen, heard, and understood why. I no longer dare ask such a question. Instead, allow me to prostrate myself before you."

The king stood up intending to prostrate himself, but the Buddha stood up, as well, and took the king's hand. He asked the king to be seated again. When they were both seated, the Buddha looked at the king and said, "Majesty, in the Way of Liberation, there is no caste. To the eyes of an enlightened person, all people are equal. Every person's blood is red. Every person's tears are salty. We are all human beings. We must find a way for all people to be able to realize their full dignity and potential. That is why I welcomed Sunita into the sangha of bhikkhus."

The king joined his palms. "I understand now. I also know that the path you have chosen will be filled with obstacles and difficulties. But I know you possess the strength and courage needed to overcome all such obstacles. For my own part, I will do everything in my power to support the true teaching."

The king took his leave of the Buddha and returned to the pine tree in hopes of listening to Bhikkhu Sunita's teaching. But Bhikkhu Sunita and his listeners had disappeared. The king saw no more than a few bhikkhus walking slowly and mindfully down the path.

Chapter Forty-Four
The Elements Will Recombine

One day Meghiya spoke to the Buddha about Nanda's unhappiness as a monk. Nanda had confided to Meghiya how much he missed his fiancée in Kapilavatthu. Nanda said, "I still remember the day I carried the Buddha's bowl back to Nigrodha Park. As I was leaving, Janapada Kalyani looked into my eyes and said, 'Hurry back. I will be waiting for you.' I can so clearly recall the sheen of her black hair as it brushes her slender shoulders. Her image often arises during my sitting meditation. Every time I see her in my mind, I am filled with longing. I am not happy being a monk."

The next afternoon, the Buddha invited Nanda to go for a walk with him. They left Jetavana and headed towards a distant hamlet located by a lake. They sat on a large boulder that overlooked the crystal clear water. A family of ducks swam by leisurely. Birds sang in the overhanging branches of trees.

The Buddha said, "Some of our brothers have told me that you are not happy living the life of a bhikkhu. Is that true?"

Nanda was silent. After a moment, the Buddha asked, "Do you feel ready to return to Kapilavatthu to prepare to take over the throne?"

Nanda replied hastily, "No, no. I have already told everyone that I do not like politics. I know I don't have the ability to rule a kingdom. I do not wish to become the next king."

"Then why are you unhappy being a bhikkhu?"

Again Nanda was silent.

"Do you miss Kalyani?"

Nanda blushed but he did not speak.

The Buddha said, "Nanda, there are many young women here in Kosala as beautiful as your Kalyani. Do you remember the reception we attended at King Pasenadi's palace? Did you notice any women there as pretty as Kalyani?"

Nanda admitted, "Perhaps there are young women here as pretty as she is. But I care only for Kalyani. In this life there is only one Kalyani."

"Nanda, attachment can be a great barrier to spiritual practice. The physical beauty of a woman fades as surely as the beauty of a rose. You know that all things are impermanent. You must learn to penetrate the impermanent nature of things. Look." The Buddha pointed to an old woman leaning on a cane and hobbling across the bamboo bridge. Her face was covered with wrinkles.

"That old woman was surely once a beauty. Kalyani's beauty will also fade with the years. During that same time your search for enlightenment could bring peace and joy for this life and lives to come. Nanda, look at the two monkeys playing over on that branch. You might not find the female attractive with her long, pointed snout and red bottom, but to the male she is the most beautiful monkey on earth. To him she is unique and he would sacrifice his very life to protect her. Can you see that—"

Nanda interrupted the Buddha. "Please don't say anything more. I understand what you are trying to say. I will devote myself more wholeheartedly to my practice."

The Buddha smiled at his younger brother. "Pay special attention to observing your breath. Meditate on your body, feelings, mental formations, consciousness, and objects of your consciousness. Look deeply in order to see the process of birth, growth, and fading of every phenomenon, from your own body, emotions, mind, and objects of your mind. If there is anything you don't understand, come and ask me or Sariputta. Nanda, remember that the happiness liberation brings is true, unconditional happiness. It can never be destroyed. Aspire to that happiness."

The sky was growing dark. The Buddha and Nanda stood and walked back to the monastery.

Jetavana now hosted a strong and stable monastic life. The number of bhikkhus living there had risen to five hundred. The following year the Buddha returned to Vesali for the retreat season. The Licchavi princes had transformed Great Forest into a monastery. They had built a two-story Dharma hall with a roof, which they named Kutagara. A number of smaller buildings were scattered throughout the forest of sal trees. The princes were the sponsors of the retreat season with generous contributions from Ambapali.

Bhikkhus throughout Magadha and as far away as Sakya gathered to spend the retreat season there with the Buddha. They numbered six hundred in all. Lay disciples traveled to spend the rainy season there, as well, in order to receive the Buddha's teaching. They brought daily food offerings and attended all the Dharma talks.

One morning in early autumn just after the retreat came to a close, the Buddha received news that King Suddhodana was on his deathbed in Kapilavatthu. The king had sent Prince Mahanama, his nephew, as a messenger to summon the Buddha in hopes of seeing his son one last time. At Mahanama's special request, the Buddha agreed to travel in the carriage in order to save time. Anuruddha, Nanda, Ananda, and Rahula accompanied him. They left so quickly that even the Licchavi princes and Ambapali were unable to see them off. After the carriage departed, two hundred bhikkhus, including all the former princes of the Sakya clan, began to walk towards Kapilavatthu. They wanted to be with the Buddha at his father's funeral.

The royal family met the Buddha at the palace gates. Mahapajapati led him at once into the king's chambers. The king's face, pale and wan, brightened when he saw the Buddha. The Buddha sat down by the bed and took the king's hand in his own. The king, now eighty-two years old, was thin and frail.

The Buddha said, "Father, please breathe gently and slowly. Smile. Nothing is more important than your breath at this moment. Nanda, Ananda, Rahula, Anuruddha, and I will breathe together with you."

The king looked at each one of them. He smiled and began to follow his breath. No one dared cry. After a moment, the king looked at the Buddha and said, "I have seen clearly the impermanence of life and how if a person wants happiness he should not lose himself in a life of desires. Happiness is obtained by living a life of simplicity and freedom."

Queen Gotami told the Buddha, "These past months, the king has lived very simply. He has truly followed your teaching. Your teaching has transformed the lives of every one of us here."

Still holding the king's hand, the Buddha said, "Father, take a deep look at me, at Nanda and Rahula. Look at the green leaves on the branches outside your window. Life continues. As life continues, so do you. You will continue to live in me and in Nanda and Rahula, and in all beings. The temporal body arises from the four elements which dissolve only to endlessly recombine again. Father, don't think that because the body passes away, life and death can bind us. Rahula's body is also your body."

The Buddha motioned to Rahula to come and hold the king's other hand. A lovely smile arose on the face of the dying king. He understood the Buddha's words and he no longer feared death.

The king's advisors and ministers were all present. He motioned for them to approach and in a feeble voice said, "During my reign, I have doubtlessly upset and wronged you. Before I die, I ask your forgiveness."

The advisors and ministers could not hold back their tears. Prince Mahanama knelt by the bed and said, "Your majesty, you have been the most virtuous and just of kings. No one here has any reason to fault you."

Mahanama continued, "I humbly wish to suggest that Prince Nanda now leave monastic life and return to Kapilavatthu to ascend the throne. The people would all be happy to see your own son as king. I pledge to assist and support him with all my being."

Nanda looked at the Buddha as if to plead for rescue. Queen Gotami also looked the Buddha's way. Quietly, the Buddha spoke, "Father, Ministers, please allow me to share my insight in this matter. Nanda does not yet possess the inclination or ability to serve as a political ruler. He needs more years of spiritual practice to be ready for such a task. Rahula is only fifteen years old and too young to become king. I believe Prince Mahanama is the best qualified to be king. He is a man of great intelligence and talent, as well as a man of compassion and understanding. Furthermore, he has served as the king's chief advisor these past six years. On behalf of the royal family, on behalf of the people, I ask Prince Mahanama to accept this difficult responsibility."

Mahanama joined his palms and protested, "I fear my talent falls far short of what is required of a king. Please, your Majesty, Lord Buddha, and Ministers, choose someone more worthy than myself."

The other ministers voiced their approval of the Buddha's suggestion. The king nodded his approval, as well, and called Mahanama to his side. He took Mahanama's hand and said, "Everyone places his trust in you. The Buddha himself has faith in you. You are my nephew and I would be honored and happy to pass the throne onto you. You will continue our line for a hundred generations."

Mahanama bowed, submitting to the king's wishes.

The king was overjoyed. "Now I can close my eyes in peace. I am happy to have seen the Buddha before I left this world. My heart is now without any cares whatsoever. I have no regrets or bitterness. I hope that the Buddha will rest in Kapilavatthu for a time in order to assist Mahanama in the first days of his reign. Your virtue, Lord Buddha, will assure our country a hundred generations of peace." The king's voice faded to barely a whisper.

The Buddha said, "I will remain here for whatever time is needed to help Mahanama."

The king smiled weakly, but his eyes radiated peace. He closed his eyes and passed from this life. Queen Gotami and Yasodhara began to cry. The ministers sobbed in grief. The Buddha folded the king's hands on his chest and then motioned for everyone to stop crying. He told them to follow their breathing. After several moments, he suggested they meet in the outer chamber to discuss arrangements for the funeral.

The funeral took place seven days later. More than a thousand brahmans attended the ceremony. But King Suddhodana's funeral was made unique by the presence of five hundred saffron-robed bhikkhus who represented the Way of the Buddha. In addition to the traditional brahmana prayers and recitations, sutras of the Way were chanted. The bhikkhus chanted the Four Noble Truths, the Sutra on Impermanence, the Sutra on Fire, the Sutra on Dependent Co-arising, and the Three Refuges. They chanted in the tongue of Magadhi, which was spoken by all the peoples east of the Ganga.

The Buddha slowly circled the funeral pyre three times. Before he lit the funeral pyre, he said, "Birth, old age, sickness, and death occur in the life of all persons. We should reflect on birth, old age, sickness, and death every day in order to prevent ourselves from becoming lost in desires and in order to be able to create a life filled with peace, joy, and contentment. A person who has attained the Way looks on birth, old age, sickness, and death with equanimity. The true nature of all dharmas is that there is neither birth nor death, neither production nor destruction, neither increasing nor decreasing."

Once lit, flames consumed the pyre. The sound of gongs and drums intertwined with chanting. The people of Kapilavatthu attended in great numbers to see the Buddha light the king's funeral pyre.

After Mahanama's coronation, the Buddha remained in Kapilavatthu for three months. One day Mahapajapati Gotami visited him at Nigrodha Park. She offered a number of robes and also requested to be ordained as a nun. She said, "If you will allow women to be ordained, many will benefit. Among our clan, many princes have left home to become your disciples. Many of them had wives. Now their wives desire to study the Dharma as nuns. I want to be ordained myself. It would bring me great joy. This has been my sole desire since the king died."

The Buddha was silent for a long moment before he said, "It is not possible."

Lady Pajapati pleaded, "I know this is a difficult issue for you. If you accept women into the sangha you will be met with protest and resistance from society. But I do not believe you are afraid of such reactions."

Again the Buddha was silent. He said, "In Rajagaha, there are also a number of women who want to be ordained, but I don't believe it is the right time yet. Conditions are not yet ripe to accept women in the sangha."

Gotami pleaded three times with him, but his answer remained the same. Deeply disappointed, she departed. When she returned to the palace she told Yasodhara of the Buddha's response.

A few days later, the Buddha returned to Vesali. After his departure, Gotami gathered all the women who wished to be ordained. They included a number of young women who had never been married. All the women belonged to the Sakya clan. She told them, "I know beyond a doubt that in the Way of Awakening, all people are equal. Everyone has the capacity to be enlightened and liberated. The Buddha has said so himself. He has accepted untouchables into the sangha. There is no reason he should not accept women. We are full persons too. We can attain enlightenment and liberation. There is no reason to regard women as inferior.

"I suggest we shave our heads, get rid of our fine clothes and jewels, put on the yellow robes of bhikkhus, and walk barefoot to Vesali where we will ask to be ordained. In this way we will prove to the Buddha and everyone else that we are capable of living simply and practicing the Way. We will walk hundreds of miles and beg for our food. This is the only hope we have to be accepted into the sangha."

All the women agreed with Gotami. They saw in her a true leader. Yasodhara smiled. She had long appreciated Gotami's strong will. Gotami was not one to be stopped by any obstacle, as proved by her years of working on behalf of the poor with Yasodhara. The women agreed on a day to put their plan into action.

Gotami said to Yasodhara, "Gopa, it would be best if you didn't come with us this time. Things may go more smoothly. When we have succeeded, there will be plenty of time for you to follow."

Yasodhara smiled in understanding.

Chapter Forty-Five
Opening the Door

Early one morning on his way to the lake to get some water, Ananda met Gotami and fifty other women standing not far from the Buddha's hut. Every woman had shaved her head and was wearing a yellow robe. Their feet were swollen and bloody. At first glance, Ananda thought it was a delegation of monks, but suddenly he recognized Lady Gotami. Hardly able to believe his eyes, he blurted, "Good heavens, Lady Gotami! Where have you come from? Why are your feet so bloody? Why have you and all the ladies come here like this?"

Gotami answered, "Venerable Ananda, we have shaved our heads and given away all our fine clothes and jewels. We no longer have any possessions in this world. We left Kapilavatthu and have walked for fifteen days, sleeping by the roadsides and begging for our food in small villages along the way. We wish to show that we are capable of living like bhikkhus. I beseech you, Ananda. Please speak to the Buddha on our behalf. We wish to be ordained as nuns."

Ananda said, "Wait here. I will speak to the Buddha at once. I promise to do all I can."

Ananda entered the Buddha's hut just as the Buddha was putting on his robe. Nagita, the Buddha's assistant at that time, was also present. Ananda told the Buddha all he had just seen and heard. The Buddha did not say anything.

Ananda then asked, "Lord, is it possible for a woman to attain the Fruits of Stream Enterer, Once-Returner, Never-Returner, and Arhatship?"

The Buddha answered, "Beyond a doubt."

"Then why won't you accept women into the sangha? Lady Gotami nurtured and cared for you from the time you were an infant. She has loved you like a son. Now she has shaved her head and renounced all her possessions. She has walked all the way from Kapilavatthu to prove that women can endure anything that men can. Please have compassion and allow her to be ordained."

The Buddha was silent for a long moment. He then asked Nagita to summon Venerables Sariputta, Moggallana, Anuruddha, Bhaddiya, Kimbila, and Mahakassapa. When they arrived, he discussed the situation with them at length. He explained that it was not discrimination against women which made him hesitant to ordain them. He was unsure how to open the sangha to women without creating harmful conflict both within and outside of the sangha.

After a lengthy exchange of ideas, Sariputta said, "It would be wise to create statutes which define the roles of nuns within the sangha. Such statutes would diminish public opposition which is certain to erupt, since there has been discrimination against women for thousands of years. Please consider the following eight rules:

"First, a nun, or bhikkhuni, will always defer to a bhikkhu, even if she is older or has practiced longer than he has.

"Second, all bhikkhunis must spend the retreat season at a center within reach of a center of bhikkhus in order to receive spiritual support and further study.

"Third, twice a month, the bhikkhunis should delegate someone to invite the bhikkhus to decide on a date for *uposatha*, the special day of observance. A bhikkhu should visit the nuns, teach them, and encourage them in their practice.

"Fourth, after the rainy season retreat, nuns must attend the Pavarana ceremony and present an account of their practice, not only before other nuns, but before the monks.

"Fifth, whenever a bhikkhuni breaks a precept, she must confess before both the bhikkhunis and the bhikkhus.

"Sixth, after a period of practice as a novice, a bhikkhuni will take full vows before the communities of both monks and nuns.

"Seventh, a bhikkhuni should not criticize or censure a bhikkhu.

"Eighth, a bhikkhuni will not give Dharma instruction to a community of bhikkhus."

Moggallana laughed. "These eight rules are clearly discriminatory. How can you pretend otherwise?"

Sariputta replied, "The purpose of these rules is to open the door for women to join the sangha. They are not intended to discriminate but to help end discrimination. Don't you see?"

Moggallana nodded, acknowledging the merit of Sariputta's statement.

Bhaddiya said, "These eight rules are necessary. Lady Gotami has commanded much authority. She is the Lord's mother. Without rules such as these, it would be difficult for anyone except the Buddha himself to guide her in her practice."

The Buddha turned to Ananda, "Ananda, please go and tell Lady Mahapajapati that if she is willing to accept these Eight Special Rules, she and the other women may be ordained."

The sun had already climbed high into the sky, but Ananda found Lady Gotami and the other women patiently waiting. After hearing the Eight Rules, Gotami was overjoyed. She replied, "Venerable Ananda, please tell the Buddha that just as a young girl gladly accepts a garland of lotus flowers or roses to adorn her hair after washing it with perfumed water, I happily accept the Eight Rules. I will follow them all my life if I am granted permission to be ordained."

Ananda returned to the Buddha's hut and informed him of Lady Gotami's response.

The other women looked at Gotami with concern in their eyes, but she smiled and reassured them, "Don't worry, my sisters. The important thing is that we have earned the right to be ordained. These Eight Rules will not be barriers to our practice. They are the door by which we may enter the sangha."

All fifty-one women were ordained that same day. Venerable Sariputta arranged for them to live temporarily at Ambapali's mango grove. The Buddha also asked Sariputta to teach the nuns the basic practice.

Eight days later, Bhikkhuni Mahapajapati paid a visit to the Buddha. She said, "Lord, please show compassion, and explain how I may best make quick progress on the path of liberation."

The Buddha answered, "Bhikkhuni Mahapajapati, the most important thing is to take hold of your own mind. Practice observing the breath and meditate on the body, feelings, mind, and objects of mind. Practicing like that, each day you will experience a deepening of humility, ease, detachment, peace, and joy. When those qualities arise, you can be sure you are on the correct path, the path of awakening and enlightenment."

Bhikkhuni Mahapajapati wanted to build a convent in Vesali in order to enable the nuns to dwell close to the Buddha and his senior disciples. She also wanted later to return to Kapilavatthu to open a convent in her homeland. She sent a messenger to Yasodhara to announce the good news of the women's ordination. Bhikkhuni Gotami knew that the acceptance of women into the sangha would create an uproar. Bitter opposition would undoubtedly result, and many people would condemn the Buddha and his sangha. She knew the Buddha would have to face many difficulties. She was grateful, and understood that the Eight Rules were temporarily necessary to protect the sangha from harmful conflict. She was sure that later on, once the ordination of women was an established fact, the Eight Rules would no longer be necessary.

The Buddha's community now had four streams—the bhikkhus, bhikkhunis, *upasakas* (male lay disciples), and *upasikas* (female lay disciples).

Bhikkhuni Mahapajapati gave careful thought as to how the bhikkhunis should dress. Her suggestions were all accepted by the Buddha. The bhikkhus wore three garments— the *antaravasaka* or pants, the *uttarasanga* or inner robe, and the *sanghati* or outer robe. In addition to these three garments, the bhikkhunis added a cloth wrapped around the chest called a *samkakshika*, and a skirt called a *kusulaka*. In addition to their robes and begging bowl, each monk and nun also had the right to own a fan, a water filter, a needle and thread to mend their robes, a pick to clean their teeth, and a razor to shave their heads twice a month.

Chapter Forty-Six
A Handful of Simsapa Leaves

Venuvana monastery in Rajagaha, Kutagarasala monastery in Vesali, and Jetavana monastery in Savatthi, had become thriving centers for the practice and teaching of the Way. Other monastic centers had been founded throughout Magadha, Kosala, and neighboring kingdoms. Everywhere, the sight of saffron-robed bhikkhus had become familiar. The Way of Awakening had spread far and wide in the first six years after the Buddha's Enlightenment.

The Buddha spent his sixth rainy season retreat on Mankula mountain and the seventh season on Samkassa mountain upstream from the Ganga. He spent the eighth season at Sumsumaragira in Bhagga and the ninth near Kosambi. Kosambi was a large town in the kingdom of Vamsa situated along the Jamuna River. An important monastery had been built there in a large forest called Ghosita, named after the lay disciple who donated the forest. Senior disciples such as Mahakassapa, Mahamoggallana, Sariputta, and Mahakaccana were not with the Buddha during the ninth rainy season retreat at Ghosita, but Ananda was. Rahula remained with Sariputta.

Ghosita was filled with simsapa trees under which the Buddha liked to meditate during hot afternoons. One day after his meditation, he returned to the community holding a handful of simsapa leaves. He held them up and asked the bhikkhus, "Bhikkhus, which is greater—the number of leaves in my hand or the number of leaves in the forest?"

The bhikkhus answered, "The number of leaves in the forest."

The Buddha answered, "Just so, what I see is much greater than what I teach. Why? Because I teach only those things that are truly necessary and helpful in attaining the Way."

The Buddha said this because at Ghosita there were many bhikkhus who tended to lose themselves in philosophical speculation. Bhikkhu Malunkyaputta had been especially advised by the Buddha not to entangle himself in esoteric questions that were not essential for the practice. This was because Malunkyaputta had a habit of asking the Buddha such questions as whether the universe was finite or infinite, temporal or eternal. The Buddha always refused to answer such questions. One day Malunkyaputta felt he could no longer endure the Buddha's silence. He resolved that he would ask the Buddha his questions one last time and if the Buddha still refused to answer him, he would ask to be relieved of his vows as a bhikkhu.

He found the Buddha and said, "Teacher, if you will agree to answer my questions, I will continue to follow you. If you refuse, I will abandon the sangha. Tell me if you know whether or not the universe is finite or infinite. If you don't know the answer, just say so."

The Buddha looked at Malunkyaputta and said, "When you asked to be ordained, did I promise to answer such questions? Did I say, 'Malunkyaputta, become a bhikkhu, and I will solve your metaphysical problems?'"

"No, Lord, you did not."

"Then why do you insist that I do so now? Malunkyaputta, you are like a person shot with a poisoned arrow whose family summons the doctor to have the arrow removed. The man is given an antidote, but he refuses to let the doctor do anything before certain questions can be answered. The wounded man wants to know who shot the arrow, what his caste and job is, and why he shot him. He wants to know what kind of bow the man used and how he acquired the ingredients used in preparing the poison. Malunkyaputta, such a man will die before getting the answers to his questions. It is no different for one who follows the Way. I teach only those things necessary to realize the Way. Things which are not helpful or necessary, I do not teach.

"Malunkyaputta, whether the universe is finite or infinite, temporal or eternal, there is one truth you must accept, and that is the presence of suffering. Suffering has causes which can be illuminated in order to be removed. The things I teach will help you attain detachment, equanimity, peace, and liberation. I refuse to speak about all those things which are not helpful in realizing the Way."

Feeling ashamed, Malunkyaputta asked the Buddha to forgive him for making such a foolish demand. The Buddha encouraged all the bhikkhus to focus on their practice and avoid useless philosophical speculation and debate.

Ghosita, the lay disciple who donated the forest, also sponsored the building of two other monasteries—Kukkuta and Pavarikambavana. A fourth monastery was also built in the region and called Badarika.

At Ghosita, as at all the other monasteries, certain bhikkhus were assigned the task of memorizing the teachings of the Buddha. They were called sutra masters, as the words of the Buddha were called sutras. One was the *Sutra on Turning the Wheel of Dharma,* the discourse given to the Buddha's five first disciples in the Deer Park. A few sutras, such as the *Sutra on the Nature of the Non-Self,* the *Sutra on Dependent Co-arising,* and the *Sutra on the Noble Eightfold Path,* were memorized and recited twice monthly by the entire community of bhikkhus.

In addition to sutra masters, there were precept masters, who were experts in the different precepts for novices and ordained bhikkhus. Rahula and the other novices who had not yet reached twenty years of age followed what were called the *samanera* precepts.

That year at Ghosita, a conflict arose between a sutra master and a precept master. Their argument stemmed from a small event, but ended up creating a sharp division in the sangha. A sutra master forgot to clean out the wash basin he had used and was charged with a violation of a lesser precept by a precept master. The sutra master was a proud person and contended that since he had not intentionally left the basin dirty, he was not to blame. Students of each bhikkhu took the side of their own teacher, and the argument escalated. One side accused the other of slander, while the other side accused their opponents of acting foolishly. Finally, the precept master publicly announced the sutra master's transgression and forbade him from attending the biweekly precepts recitation ceremony until he formally confessed before the sangha.

The situation grew more and more intense. Both sides spoke ill of each other. Their words flew like poisoned arrows. Most of the other bhikkhus took sides, although naturally there were some who refused to take either side. They said, "This is terrible! This will only create harmful division in the sangha."

Though the Buddha was residing not far from the monastery, he was unaware of the conflict until a delegation of concerned bhikkhus visited him, told him of it, and asked him to intervene. The Buddha went to meet directly with the precept master and said, "We should not become too attached to our own viewpoint. We should listen carefully in order to understand the other's viewpoint. We should seek all means to prevent the community from breaking." Then he went to the sutra master and said the same things. Returning to his hut, he was hopeful the two men would reconcile.

But the Buddha's intervention did not have the desired effect. Too many ill words had already been spoken. Many wounds had been inflicted. The bhikkhus who remained impartial did not possess enough influence to bring the two sides together. The conflict reached the ears of the lay disciples, and before long, even other religious sects had heard of the trouble in the Buddha's sangha. It was a serious blow to the integrity of the sangha. Nagita, the Buddha's attendant, was unable to endure the situation anymore. He discussed the matter again with the Buddha, beseeching him to intervene once more.

The Buddha put on his outer robe and went at once to the monastery's meeting hall. Nagita rang the bell to summon the community. When all were present, the Buddha said, "Please cease your arguing. It is only creating division in the community. Please return to your practice. If we truly follow our practice, we will not become victims of pride and anger."

One bhikkhu stood up and said, "Master, please don't involve yourself in this matter. Return and dwell peacefully in your meditation. This matter does not concern you. We are adults and capable of resolving this on our own."

Dead silence followed the bhikkhu's words. The Buddha stood up and left the meeting hall. He returned to his hut, picked up his bowl, and walked down into Kosambi to beg. When he was finished begging, he entered the forest to eat alone. Then he stood up and walked out of Kosambi. He headed for the river. He did not tell anyone of his departure, not even his attendant, Nagita, or Venerable Ananda.

The Buddha walked until he reached the town of Balaka-lonakaragama. There he met his disciple, the Venerable Bhagu. Bhagu invited him into the forest where he dwelled alone. He offered the Buddha a towel and wash basin to wash his face and hands. The Buddha asked Bhagu how his practice was going. Bhagu replied that he found great ease and joy in the practice, even though he was presently dwelling all alone. The Buddha remarked, "Sometimes it is more pleasant to live alone than with many people."

After bidding Bhagu farewell, the Buddha headed for Eastern Bamboo Forest, which was not far way. As he was about to enter the forest, the groundskeeper stopped him and said, "Monk, don't go in there or you may disturb the monks already practicing in there."

Before the Buddha could think of a response, Venerable Anuruddha appeared. He happily greeted the Buddha and said to the groundskeeper, "This is my own teacher. Please allow him to enter."

Anuruddha led the Buddha into the forest where he lived with two other bhikkhus, Nandiya and Kimbila. They were very happy to see the Buddha. Nandiya took the Buddha's bowl and Kimbila took his outer robe. They cleared a place for him to sit by a thicket of gold bamboo. They brought a towel and wash basin. The three bhikkhus joined their palms and bowed to the Buddha. The Buddha asked them to be seated and he asked, "Are you content here? How is your practice going? Do you encounter any difficulties in begging or sharing the teaching in this region?"

Anuruddha answered, "Lord, we are very content here. It is calm and peaceful. We receive ample food offerings and are able to share the Dharma. We are all making progress in our practice."

The Buddha asked, "Do you live in harmony with one another?"

Anuruddha said, "Lord, we care deeply for each other. We live in harmony like milk mixes with water. I consider living with Nandiya and Kimbila a great blessing. I treasure their friendship. Before I say or do anything, whether they are present or not, I stop and ask myself what their reaction would be. Would my words or actions disappoint my brothers in any way? If I feel any doubts, I refrain from the words or actions intended. Lord, although we are three persons, we are also one."

The Buddha nodded his approval. He looked at the other two bhikkhus. Kimbila said, "Anuruddha speaks the truth. We live in harmony and care deeply for each other."

Nandiya added, "We share all things, from our food to our insight and experience."

The Buddha praised them, "Excellent! I am most pleased to see how you live in harmony. A sangha is only a true sangha when such harmony exists. You have experienced real

awakening and that is why you have realized such harmony."

The Buddha spent one month with the three bhikkhus. He
observed how they went begging every morning after meditation. Whichever bhikkhu returned first from begging always
prepared a place for the others to sit, gathered water for
washing, and set out an empty bowl. Before he ate anything
himself, he would place some of his food into the empty bowl
in case one of his brothers had not received any food. After
they had all finished eating, they placed any leftover food
on the ground or in the stream, careful not to harm any creatures that lived there. Then they washed their bowls together.

Whoever saw that the toilet needed scrubbing did it at
once. They joined together to do any tasks that required more
than one person. They sat down regularly to share insights
and experiences.

Before the Buddha left the three bhikkhus, he spoke to
them, "Bhikkhus, the very nature of a sangha is harmony. I
believe harmony can be realized by following these principles:

"1. Sharing a common space such as a forest or home.

"2. Sharing the essentials of daily life together.

"3. Observing the precepts together.

"4. Using only words that contribute to harmony, avoiding
all words that can cause the community to break.

"5. Sharing insights and understanding together.

"6. Respecting others' viewpoints and not forcing another
to follow your own viewpoint.

"A sangha that follows these principles will have happiness and harmony. Bhikkhus, let us always observe these six
principles."

The bhikkhus were happy to receive this teaching from
the Buddha. The Buddha bid them farewell and walked until he reached Rakkhita Forest, near Parileyyaka. After sitting in meditation beneath a lush sal tree, he decided to
spend the approaching rainy season alone in the forest.

Chapter Forty-Seven
Follow the Dharma

Beneath the sal tree, the Buddha enjoyed ease, peace, and joy. It was a lovely forest of green hills, clear springs, and a lake. The Buddha enjoyed the solitude. He thought of the bhikkhus in Kosambi living in conflict. Even the lay disciples had been disturbed. He felt sad that the bhikkhus were unwilling to listen to his guidance, but he understood that their minds were clouded by anger.

The Buddha encountered many animals in Rakkhita Forest, including a family of elephants. The eldest female, the matriarch queen, often led the younger elephants to the lake to bathe. She taught them how to drink the cool water and eat water lilies. The Buddha watched how she grasped a bunch of lilies with her trunk and rinsed them in the water in order to shake off any mud still clinging to them. The little elephants imitated her.

The elephants grew fond of the Buddha and became his friends. Sometimes the queen picked fruit and offered it to the Buddha. The Buddha liked to pat the heads of the elephant calves, and he often walked with them down to the lake. He liked to listen to the queen's majestic call. It sounded like a great trumpet. He practiced until he could imitate her call perfectly. Once when the queen called out, he also gave a great trumpeting call. She gazed at him and then came and knelt before him as if to bow. The Buddha gently stroked her head.

Sometimes the elephant queen picked fruit and offered it to the Buddha.

It was the tenth retreat season since the Buddha's Enlightenment, but only the second one he had spent alone. He stayed in that cool forest the entire retreat season, leaving only briefly in the mornings to beg. When the rainy season came to an end, the Buddha departed from his elephant friends and headed northeast. After two weeks of walking, he reached Jetavana Monastery in Savatthi. Sariputta was most happy to see him, as was Rahula. Several senior disciples were also there including Mahamoggallana, Mahakassapa, Mahakaccana, Upali, Mahakotthita, Mahakappina, Mahacunda, Revata, and Devadatta. Anuruddha, Kimbila, and Nandiya had also traveled to Jetavana from their bamboo grove in Karagama. Even Bhikkhuni Gotami was in Savatthi. Everyone rejoiced to see the Buddha.

When he entered his hut at Jetavana, the Buddha found Ananda tidying up and sweeping the floor. A year and four months had passed since the Buddha had last been there. Ananda put down his broom and bowed. The Buddha asked him about the situation in Kosambi, and Ananda replied, "After your departure, a number of brothers came to me and said, 'Brother, the Master has left. He is all alone. Why don't you follow him and act as his assistant? If you won't go, we will go ourselves.' But I told them, 'If the Buddha has departed without telling anyone, it is because he wants to be alone. We should not bother him.' Six months later, the same brothers came to me and said, 'Brother, it has been a long time since we received any direct teaching from the Buddha. We want to search for him.' This time I agreed, and we set out looking for you, but without success. No one knew where you were. At last we made our way to Savatthi, but you were not here, either. We decided to wait here, knowing that eventually you would come. We were confident you would not abandon your disciples."

"When you left Kosambi, what was the situation like? Were the bhikkhus still divided?"

"Lord, the conflict became even worse. Neither side would have anything to do with the other. The atmosphere was tense and uncomfortable. Lay disciples expressed their dismay to the rest of us when we went begging in the city. We explained that many of us refused to take sides. Little by little, the lay disciples decided to take matters more into their own hands. They came to the monastery and spoke to the bhikkhus involved in the conflict. They said things like, 'You made the Buddha so sad he left. You bear a grave responsibility. You have caused many lay disciples to lose trust in the sangha. Please reconsider your actions.' At first the bhikkhus involved in the conflict did not pay attention to the lay disciples. But then the lay disciples decided not to offer food to any bhikkhu involved in the conflict. They said, 'You are not worthy of the Buddha because you are unable to live in harmony. If you listened to the Buddha's teaching, you would reconcile with one another and then go find the Buddha and make a confession. Only by doing so can you regain our trust.' Lord, the lay disciples stood their ground. The day I left Kosambi, the two sides had agreed to meet together. I am sure that before long they will come here to make a formal confession."

The Buddha picked up the broom which Ananda had set down. "Let me do that. Please find Sariputta and tell him I would like to speak with him."

The Buddha leisurely swept the hut and then sat on one of his bamboo chairs outside. Jetavana was truly beautiful. The trees were covered with new leaves. Birds sang throughout the forest. Sariputta appeared and sat silently beside the Buddha for a long, peaceful moment.

The Buddha told Sariputta what was on his mind. "We should do everything we can to prevent useless conflicts from arising in this beautiful monastery."

They spoke on this matter for a long time.

One afternoon soon after, Venerable Sariputta received news that the bhikkhus from Kosambi were on their way to the monastery, having already arrived in Savatthi. Sariputta went to the Buddha and asked him, "The brothers from Kosambi will soon arrive. How should we handle the situation?"

The Buddha replied, "Handle it according to the Dharma."

"Can you explain what you mean more clearly?"

"You, Sariputta, can still ask such a question?"

Sariputta fell silent. Just then Moggallana, Kassapa, Kaccana, Kotthita, Kappina, and Anuruddha appeared. They, too, asked, "How should we handle the arrival of the brothers from Kosambi?"

They all looked at Sariputta but he only smiled. The Buddha looked at his senior disciples and said, "Listen carefully to both sides without prejudice. Carefully consider everything you hear to determine which things are in accord with the teaching and which things are not. Things in accord with the teaching lead to peace, joy, and liberation. They are the things I myself practice. Things I have cautioned against and which I do not practice are not in accord with the teaching. When you understand what things are in accord with the teaching and what things are not, you will know how to help both sides find reconciliation."

At that moment, a number of lay patrons led by Anathapindika arrived at the Buddha's hut. They said, "Lord, the bhikkhus from Kosambi have arrived. How should we receive them? Should we give both sides food offerings?"

The Buddha smiled. "Offer food to both sides. Express your support of the sangha. Offer your praise when any of them say things in accord with the Dharma."

Ananda returned and announced to Sariputta that the bhikkhus from Kosambi were already at the monastery gates. Sariputta turned to the Buddha and asked, "Shall we let them enter now?"

The Buddha said, "Open the gates and welcome them."

Sariputta said, "I will arrange places for them all to sleep."

"Let the two sides dwell in separate locations for the time being."

"We may have difficulty finding adequate places for everyone to sleep."

"We can endure crowded conditions for now. But don't make any of the elders sleep outdoors. Distribute food and medicine equally to all."

Sariputta issued orders for the gates to be opened. The Kosambi bhikkhus were given places to sleep and provided with basic necessities.

The following morning, the newly arrived bhikkhus were told to go out begging as usual. Sariputta divided them into groups and sent them to different locales as the Buddha had counselled. That evening the bhikkhus asked Sariputta to arrange a meeting with the Buddha in order for them to make a confession. Sariputta said, "Making a confession to the Buddha is not the most important thing. You must first achieve true reconciliation. Only if reconciliation has taken place will the ceremony of confession have meaning."

That night the sutra master, responsible for starting the conflict by his refusal to be corrected, went to the precept master. He joined his palms and bowed. Then he knelt in front of the precept master and said, "Venerable, I accept that I violated a precept. It was proper for you to correct me. I am ready to make confession before the sangha."

The sutra master knew that the only way to resolve the conflict was to swallow his pride. The precept master responded by kneeling before the sutra master and saying, "I confess that I, too, lacked humility and tact. Please accept my sincere apologies."

Late that night a confession ceremony was held for the sutra master. Everyone gave a sigh of relief, especially the Kosambi bhikkhus who had remained impartial throughout the conflict. It was after midnight when Sariputta informed the Buddha that reconciliation had finally taken place. The Buddha nodded silently. The conflict was ended, but he knew that it would take time for all the wounds to heal.

Chapter Forty-Eight
Covering Mud with Straw

Venerable Moggallana suggested that a meeting take place between the Buddha's senior disciples at Jetavana and the principal instigators of the Kosambi conflict. The goal of the meeting was to learn from the experience in order to come up with ways to prevent such conflicts from taking place again. Venerable Mahakassapa presided over the meeting.

To begin the meeting, Mahakassapa asked Anuruddha to repeat the six principles of harmonious living that the Buddha had expounded during his stay at Eastern Bamboo Forest. After hearing Anuruddha explain the six principles, Moggallana suggested that bhikkhus and bhikkhunis in all monastic centers be asked to memorize them.

After four days of discussion, the bhikkhus in the meeting formulated seven practices of reconciliation to be used to settle disputes within the sangha. They named these seven methods *Saptadhikarana-shamatha*:

The first practice is *sammukha-vinaya* or Face-to-Face Sitting. According to this practice, the dispute must be stated before the entire convocation of bhikkhus, with both sides of the conflict present. This is to avoid private conversations about the conflict which inevitably influence people against one side or the other, creating further discord and tension.

The second practice is smriti-vinaya or Remembrance. In the convocation, both parties involved try to remember from the beginning everything that led up to the conflict. Details should be presented with as much clarity as possible. Witnesses and evidence should be provided, if available. The community listens quietly and patiently to both sides in order to obtain adequate information to examine the dispute.

The third practice is *amudha-vinaya* or Non-stubbornness. The monks in question are expected to resolve the conflict. The community expects both parties to demonstrate their willingness to reach reconciliation. Stubbornness is to be considered negative and counterproductive. In case a party claims he violated a precept because of ignorance or an unsettled state of mind, without actually intending to violate it, the community should take that into account in order to find a solution that is agreeable to both sides.

The fourth practice is *tatsvabhavaishiya-vinaya* or Voluntary Confession. Each party is encouraged to admit his own transgressions and shortcomings without having to be prodded by the other party or the community. The community should allow each party ample time to confess his own failings, no matter how minor they may seem. Admitting one's own faults begins a process of reconciliation and encourages the other party to do likewise. This leads to the possibility of full reconciliation.

The fifth practice is *pratijñakaraka-vinaya* or Accepting the Verdict. When the verdict is reached, *jñapticaturthamkarmavacana*, it will be read aloud three times. If no one in the community voices disagreement with it, it is considered final. Neither party in dispute has the right to challenge the verdict. They have agreed to place their trust in the community's decision and carry out whatever verdict the community reaches.

The sixth practice is *yadbhuyasikiya-vinaya* or Decision by Consensus. After hearing both sides and being assured of the wholehearted efforts by both sides to reach a settlement, the community reaches a verdict by consensus.

The seventh practice is *trinaprastaraka-vinaya* or Covering Mud with Straw. During the convocation, a venerable elder monk is appointed to represent each side in the conflict. These are high monks who are deeply respected and listened to by others in the sangha. They sit and listen intently, saying little. But when they do speak, their words carry special weight. Their words have the capacity to soothe and heal wounds, to call forth reconciliation and forgiveness, just as straw covers mud, enabling someone to cross it without dirtying his clothes. Thanks to the presence of these elder bhikkhus, the disputing parties find it easier to release petty concerns. Bitterness is eased and the community is able to reach a verdict agreeable to both sides.

The Buddha's senior disciples submitted the Seven Practices of Reconciliation for his approval. He praised their work and agreed that the practices should become part of the formal precepts.

The Buddha remained at Jetavana for six months before returning to Rajagaha. He stopped to visit the bodhi tree on the way and entered Uruvela to visit Svasti's family. Svasti was twenty-one years old. The Buddha had returned to fulfill his promise to welcome Svasti into the sangha when he was old enough. Svasti was ordained and fast became Rahula's closest friend.

Chapter Forty-Nine
Earth's Lessons

Svasti listened with great interest to all that Assaji and
Ananda recounted about the Buddha's efforts to spread the
Dharma. Bhikkhuni Gotami and Rahula listened intently
too. Ananda's memory was truly phenomenal. He filled in
many details that Assaji forgot to mention. Svasti was grateful to both bhikkhus, and to Bhikkhuni Gotami and novice
Rahula. Thanks to them he learned much about the Buddha's
life he could never have learned otherwise. Svasti hoped
that he would always be able to live close by the Buddha in
order to witness his life and receive his teachings directly.

Thanks to Sujata, even though Svasti was an untouchable
buffalo boy, he had learned the basics of a young man's edu-
cation. But his lessons with her had ended several years ago
when she left Uruvela to marry a man in the village of
Nadika. Svasti knew that he could learn a great deal from
Rahula. He found Rahula's bearing full of gentle dignity.
Not only was Rahula from a noble caste, but he had spent
the past eight years living in the serene and concentrated
atmosphere of the sangha. Compared to Rahula, Svasti felt
rough and awkward. But his feelings caused him to devote
great efforts to his practice. Sariputta asked Rahula to show
Svasti basic practices such as putting on the robe, holding the
begging bowl, walking, standing, lying down, sitting, eating,
washing, listening to Dharma talks, all in mindfulness. A
bhikkhu memorized and paid diligent attention to forty-five

practices, all of which helped to deepen his focus and serenity.

In principle, Rahula was still only a novice, a samanera. He had to wait until he was twenty years old to take full vows. A samanera had ten precepts—do not kill, do not steal, do not engage in sexual relations, do not speak falsehoods, do not drink alcohol, do not wear jewelry, flowers, or perfume, do not sit or lie down on any wide, high, or fancy bed, do not participate in secular dancing and singing parties, do not handle money, and do not eat past the noon hour. The forty-five practices were followed by ordained bhikkhus, but Rahula was expected to study and observe them in preparation for his full vows. A bhikkhu observed one hundred twenty precepts, which included the forty-five practices. Rahula told Svasti that additional precepts would probably be added, and that he had heard they might well number two hundred or more in time.

Rahula explained to Svasti that in the first years of the sangha, there were no precepts. Ordination was simple. A person had only to kneel at the feet of the Buddha or another bhikkhu and recite the three refuges three times. It became necessary to create and enforce precepts as the sangha grew, because in so large a community, there were bhikkhus who needed rules and guidelines in order to better discipline themselves.

Rahula told Svasti that the first person to violate the spirit of the sangha was a bhikkhu named Sudinna. It was because of Sudinna that the Buddha created the first precepts. Before he was ordained, Sudinna was married and lived in the village Kalanda on the outskirts of Vesali. When he heard the Buddha teach, he asked to be ordained. Shortly after that, he had a chance to return to Kalanda. His family invited him for a meal in their home and he consented. His family implored him to return to secular life and help run the family business. He refused. His parents complained because Sudinna was their only child, and they had no one to inherit the business. They feared that the family's wealth would fall into someone else's hands. Seeing Sudinna's determination to remain a bhikkhu, his mother suggested that the least he could do was to leave a child as an heir. Persuaded by his mother's pleas, and without precepts to guide him, he agreed to meet with his former wife in Mahavana Forest. His wife conceived and gave birth to a boy they named Bijaka, which means "seed." Sudinna's friends taunted him by calling him "Seed's father." The reputation of the sangha was tarnished. The Buddha called the bhikkhus together and chastised Sudinna. Because of this incident, formal precepts were instituted. It was decided that whenever a bhikkhu violated the spirit of the Way of Enlightenment and Liberation, a convocation would be called and a new precept added. The precepts were called *Patimokkha*.

Four precepts were considered cardinal. The violation of any one of these four resulted in being expelled from the community. All the other precepts could be forgiven by making confession. The four cardinal precepts were—do not engage in sexual relations, do not steal, do not kill, and do not claim to have attained insight that you have not actually attained. These four precepts were called *parajika*.

Rahula also told Svasti that the Buddha had never treated him with special favors even though his father dearly loved him. He recalled how, at the age of eleven, he told a fib to Sariputta because he was afraid of being scolded for running off and playing when he had other duties. He ended up having to tell four fibs in a row for fear that Sariputta would uncover the truth. But as is almost always the case, the truth came out. The Buddha used this occasion to teach Rahula how important it was always to tell the truth.

At that time Sariputta and Rahula dwelled in Ambalatthika Park, not far from Bamboo Forest, where the Buddha was staying. One day the Buddha paid them a visit. Rahula set out a chair for him and brought him a basin of water to wash his hands and feet. When the Buddha was finished washing, he poured out most of the water in the basin. He

Rahula set out a chair for the Buddha and brought him a basin of water to wash his feet.

looked at Rahula and asked, "Rahula, is there a little or a lot of water in this basin?"

Rahula answered, "There is very little left."

The Buddha said, "You should know, Rahula, that a person who does not tell the truth has as little integrity left as the water in this basin."

Rahula was silent. The Buddha poured out the remaining water and asked his son, "Rahula, do you see how I have emptied all the water out?"

"Yes, I see."

"Those who continue to tell untruths lose all their integrity just as this basin has lost all its water."

The Buddha turned the basin upside down and asked Rahula, "Do you see how this basin is turned upside down?"

"Yes, I see. "

"If we don't practice correct speech, our integrity is turned upside down just like this basin. Don't tell fibs even in jest. Rahula, do you know why one uses a mirror?"

"Yes, a mirror is used to look at one's reflection."

"Just so, Rahula. Regard your own actions, thoughts, and words just as a person looks into a mirror."

Rahula's story made Svasti more deeply aware of the importance of right speech. He could recall times he had fibbed to his parents, and even once to Sujata. He was thankful he had never lied to the Buddha. Actually, it seemed impossible to lie to the Buddha. Even if someone did, the Buddha would surely be able to tell. Svasti thought to himself, "I will resolve always to speak the truth to everyone I meet, even the smallest child. This will be the way I can show my gratitude to the Buddha for all he has done for me. I will observe the precepts diligently."

Twice a month, on new moon and full moon days, the bhikkhus gathered to recite the precepts. Each precept was read aloud and then the community was asked if anyone had failed to keep that precept. If no one spoke, the next precept was read. If someone had violated the precept, he stood and made a confession to the community. With the exception of the four parajika, confession was enough to make amends.

On many days, Svasti was asked to join the Buddha's group for begging, joined by Sariputta and Rahula. That retreat season they dwelled in the hills near the town of Ekanala, south of Rajagaha. One afternoon as the bhikkhus passed by rice fields near Ekanala, they were stopped by a wealthy farmer from a noble caste named Bharadvaja. He owned several thousand acres. It was the season for plowing, and he was out directing the efforts of hundreds of laborers. When he saw the Buddha pass by, he stood directly in his way and said with some contempt, "We are farmers. We plow, sow seeds, fertilize, tend, and harvest crops in order to eat. You do nothing. You produce nothing, yet you still eat. You are useless. You don't plow, sow, fertilize, tend, or harvest."

The Buddha responded, "Oh, but we do. We plow, sow, fertilize, tend, and harvest."

"Then where are your plows, your buffaloes, and your seeds? What crops do you tend? What crops do you harvest?"

The Buddha answered, "We sow the seeds of faith in the earth of a true heart. Our plow is mindfulness and our buffalo is diligent practice. Our harvest is love and understanding. Sir, without faith, understanding, and love, life would be nothing but suffering."

Bharadvaja found himself unexpectedly moved by the Buddha's words. He asked an attendant to bring the Buddha fragrant rice simmered in milk, but the Buddha refused by saying, "I have not shared these things with you in order to be given food. If you would like to make an offering, please do so at another time."

The landowner was so impressed by this that he prostrated himself before the Buddha and asked to be accepted as a lay disciple. Svasti witnessed this take place firsthand. He understood how much he could learn by remaining close to the Buddha's side. He knew that of the several thousand bhikkhus in the Buddha's sangha, few had the good fortune to be as close to the Buddha as he himself was.

After the retreat season, the Buddha traveled northwest to spread the Dharma. He returned to Savatthi at the end of autumn. One morning when they were out begging, Rahula strayed from mindfulness. Although he continued to walk in file, his mind was elsewhere. He gazed at the Buddha ahead of him and wondered what the Buddha would have become if he had not followed the spiritual path. If he had become a mighty emperor, what would Rahula himself be now? Thinking such thoughts, Rahula forgot to observe his breathing and steps. Even though the Buddha could not see Rahula, he knew his son had lost his mindfulness. The Buddha stopped and turned around. The other bhikkhus came to a halt. The Buddha looked at Rahula and said, "Rahula, are you observing your breath and maintaining mindfulness?"

Rahula lowered his head.

The Buddha said, "To dwell in mindfulness, you must continue to observe your breath. We practice meditation even as we beg. Continue to meditate on the impermanent and non-self nature of the aggregates which comprise all beings. The five aggregates are the body, feelings, perceptions, mental formations, and consciousness. Observe your breath and thoughts, and your mind will not become dispersed."

The Buddha turned back around and continued to walk. His words served as a reminder to all the bhikkhus to maintain their mindfulness. But a few steps after that, Rahula abandoned the line of bhikkhus and entered the forest where he sat alone beneath a tree. Svasti followed him, but Rahula looked up at him and said, "Please go begging with the others. I don't have the heart to go begging right now. The Buddha corrected me before the entire community. I feel so ashamed, I'd rather sit here alone and meditate." Seeing he was unable to help his friend, Svasti rejoined the other bhikkhus.

On the walk back to the monastery, Venerable Sariputta and Svasti stopped in the forest to invite Rahula to walk back with them. At the monastery, Svasti shared half of his food with Rahula, and when they finished eating, Sariputta told Rahula that the Buddha wished to see him. Svasti was permitted to accompany him.

The Buddha understood that Rahula was ripe to receive certain teachings. He said, "Rahula, learn from the earth. Whether people spread pure and fragrant flowers, perfume, or fresh milk on it, or discard filthy and foul-smelling feces, urine, blood, mucus, and spit on it, the earth receives it all equally without clinging or aversion. When pleasant or unpleasant thoughts arise, don't let them entangle or enslave you.

"Learn from the water, Rahula. When people wash dirty things in it, the water is not sad or disdainful. Learn from fire. Fire burns all things without discrimination. It is not ashamed to burn impure substances. Learn from the air. The air carries all fragrances whether sweet or foul.

"Rahula, practice loving kindness to overcome anger. Loving kindness has the capacity to bring happiness to others without demanding anything in return. Practice compassion to overcome cruelty. Compassion has the capacity to remove the suffering of others without expecting anything in return. Practice sympathetic joy to overcome hatred. Sympathetic joy arises when one rejoices over the happiness of others and wishes others well-being and success. Practice non-attachment to overcome prejudice. Non-attachment is the way of looking at all things openly and equally. This is because that is. That is because this is. Myself and other are not separate. Do not reject one thing only to chase after another.

"Rahula, loving kindness, compassion, sympathetic joy, and non-attachment are beautiful and profound states of mind. I call them the Four Immeasurables. Practice them and you will become a refreshing source of vitality and happiness for others.

"Rahula, meditate on impermanence in order to break through the illusion of self. Meditate on the nature of the body's birth, development, and death in order to free yourself from desires. Practice observing your breath. Mindfulness of the breath brings great joy."

Svasti was happy to be sitting next to Rahula, listening to all the Buddha had to say. Though Svasti had memorized sutras such as *Turning the Wheel of Dharma* and the *Nature of Non-Self*, he felt that he had never tasted the subtle flavor of the Dharma as deeply as today. Perhaps it was because he had not heard the other sutras spoken directly by the Buddha. The first sutra he had heard directly was the *Sutra on Tending Water Buffaloes*. But at that time he was not yet ripe enough to grasp many of its deeper meanings. He promised himself that during his free time he would recite all the sutras using his newly gained insight.

That day, the Buddha also spent time teaching the two young men various methods of observing the breath. Though Svasti and Rahula had received similar instruction before, this was the first time they received it directly from the Buddha. The Buddha told them that the first fruit of mindfully observing the breath was overcoming dispersion and forgetfulness.

"Breathing in, you are aware that you are breathing in. Breathing out, you are aware that you are breathing out. During such moments of breathing practice, focus your mind on nothing but your breath. Useless and scattered thoughts will cease, allowing your mind to dwell in mindfulness. When you are aware of your breathing, you dwell in mindfulness. Dwelling in mindfulness, you cannot be led astray by any thoughts. With just one breath, you can attain awakening. That awakening is the Buddha-nature that exists in all beings.

"Breathing in a short breath, you know that you are breathing in a short breath. Breathing out a long breath, you know that you are breathing out a long breath. Be totally aware of each breath. Mindfully observing your breathing will help you build concentration. With concentration, you will be able to look deeply into the nature of your body, feelings, mind, and the objects of mind which are called *sarva-dharma*."

The Buddha had taught them wholeheartedly. His words were simple but profound. Svasti was confident that, thanks to this special session with the Buddha, he would find it easier to maintain mindfulness of breathing and therefore would be able to make greater progress in his practice. After bowing to the Buddha, Svasti and Rahula walked to the lake together. They repeated to each other all the things the Buddha had taught them in order to remember them well.

Chapter Fifty
A Handful of Bran

The following year the Buddha spent the retreat season in Veranja with five hundred bhikkhus. Sariputta and Moggallana served as his assistants. Halfway into the retreat season, drought hit the area, and the heat was almost unbearable. The Buddha spent most of each day beneath the refreshing shade of a nimba tree. He ate, gave Dharma talks, meditated, and slept beneath this same tree.

By the beginning of the third month of retreat, the bhikkhus were receiving fewer and smaller food offerings. Food was scarce because of the drought, and even the food reserves maintained by the government for difficult times had dwindled to almost nothing. Many monks returned to the monastery with empty bowls. The Buddha himself often returned from begging with an empty bowl, and he filled his stomach with water to ease the hunger. The bhikkhus grew thin and wan. Venerable Moggallana suggested they all move south to Uttarakuru for the remaining days of the retreat, where food would be easier to find, but the Buddha refused, saying, "Moggallana, we are not the only ones suffering. All the local people, with the exception of a few wealthy households, are suffering from hunger. We should not abandon the people now. We have a chance to share and understand their suffering. We should remain here until the end of the retreat season."

The wealthy merchant, Agnidatta, had invited the Buddha and his bhikkhus for the retreat season in Veranja, after he heard the Buddha teach. But he was away on business and had no idea of the situation back home.

One day Moggallana pointed to a glade of healthy green trees and grasses growing near the monastery and said to the Buddha, "Teacher, I believe those plants have remained fresh and strong thanks to the rich nutrients in the soil. We could dig up some of that rich humus and mix it with water to make a nutritious food for the bhikkhus."

The Buddha said, "It would not be correct to do so, Moggallana. In fact, I tried doing just that during my days of self-mortification on Dangsiri mountain, but I noticed no nutritional benefits. Many living beings live in the soil protected from the heat of the sun. If we dig up the ground, many of those creatures will die, and plants will be killed also." Moggallana said no more.

It had long been monastic custom for bhikkhus to place a portion of the food offerings they received into an empty receptacle set out to provide food for bhikkhus who did not receive adequate food offerings. Svasti noticed that in the past ten days, the receptacle had remained empty of even a grain of rice or piece of chappati. Rahula privately confided in Svasti that although none of the bhikkhus were receiving adequate food, the people tended to offer food first to the elder bhikkhus. Younger bhikkhus received little or nothing. Svasti had noticed the same. He said, "Even on days when I receive a little food, I still feel hungry after I eat it. Is it the same for you?"

Rahula nodded. He found it difficult to sleep at night because of his hunger.

One day after returning from begging, Venerable Ananda placed an earthenware pot on a three-legged outdoor stove. He gathered some pieces of wood and began to build a fire. Svasti came to see what he was doing and offered to tend the fire. Svasti was more skilled at such matters, anyway. In no time at all, he had a fine fire blazing. Ananda lifted his

begging bowl and poured something that looked like saw-
dust into the pot. He said, "This is bran. We can roast it
until it is fragrant and then offer it to the Buddha."

Svasti stirred the bran with two small sticks while Ananda
told him how he met a horse merchant who had recently arrived in Veranja with five hundred horses. Because the merchant saw the plight of the bhikkhus, he told Ananda that
anytime the bhikkhus were unable to receive food offerings,
they could come to his stables and he would offer each
bhikkhu a handful of the bran he used to feed his horses.
That day he offered two handfuls to Ananda, one was meant
for the Buddha. Ananda promised he would announce the
merchant's generous offer to the other bhikkhus.

The bran was soon toasted and fragrant. Ananda scooped
it back into the begging bowl and invited Svasti to accompany him on the walk to the nimba tree. Ananda offered the
bran to the Buddha. The Buddha asked Svasti if he had received any food offerings, and Svasti showed him the sweet
potato he had been lucky enough to receive. The Buddha invited them to sit down and eat with him. He lifted his bowl
with great reverence. Svasti held his potato mindfully in his
hand. As he watched the Buddha scoop up the bran and eat
it with grateful appreciation, he felt like weeping.

After the Dharma talk that day, Venerable Ananda told the
community about the horse merchant's offer. Ananda asked
them to visit the stables only when they had received no
food offerings at all, as the bran was meant for the horses
and he didn't want them to go hungry.

That night beneath the moon, Sariputta paid a visit to the
Buddha who sitting beneath the nimba tree. He said, "Lord,
the Way of Awakening is so wondrous! It has the capacity to
transform everyone who hears, understands, and practices it.
Lord, how can we assure that the Way will continue to be
transmitted after you are gone?"

"Sariputta, if the bhikkhus grasp the true meaning of sutras and practice what the sutras teach, if they sincerely fol-

low the precepts, the Way of Liberation will continue for centuries."

"Lord, great numbers of bhikkhus diligently memorize and recite the sutras. If future generations of monks continue to study and recite the teachings, your loving kindness and your insight will surely extend far into the future."

"Sariputta, transmitting the sutras is not enough. It is necessary to practice what is contained in the sutras. It is especially important to observe the precepts. Without that, the Dharma cannot last long. Without the precepts, the true Dharma would quickly fade."

"Is there a way of putting the precepts into a form that can be preserved for thousands of lives to come?"

"That is not yet possible, Sariputta. A finished set of precepts cannot be created in one day or by one person. In the first years of the sangha, we didn't have any precepts. Gradually, because of shortcomings and errors committed by brothers, we have created precepts. Now we have one hundred twenty precepts. That number will increase over time. The precepts are not yet complete, Sariputta. I believe the number may rise to two hundred or more."

The final day of the retreat arrived. The merchant Agnidatta returned from his travels and was shocked to learn how much the bhikkhus had suffered from hunger. He felt ashamed and organized a meal offering at his home. He also offered each bhikkhu a new robe. After the Buddha delivered his final talk of the season, the bhikkhus headed south.

It was a lovely journey. The bhikkhus walked without haste. They rested nights and begged in the mornings. After their meal and a rest in the cool forests, they continued to walk each day. Sometimes they remained several days in a village where the people were especially delighted to receive the teaching. At night, the monks studied and recited the sutras before meditation and sleep.

One afternoon, Svasti came across a group of young buffalo boys leading their buffaloes home. He stopped and talked to them, reminiscing about his own youth. Suddenly he was seized with a longing to see his family. He missed Rupak and Bala, and most of all, Bhima. He still wondered if it was proper for a bhikkhu to think about the family he had left. Of course, Rahula told him that he had missed his family too.

Svasti was twenty-two years old. He preferred the company of younger people, feeling more at ease with them. He enjoyed time spent with Rahula the most. They often shared their innermost thoughts. Svasti told Rahula about his life as a buffalo boy. Rahula had never had an occasion to sit on a water buffalo's back. He had a hard time believing that so large a creature could be as docile as Svasti claimed. Svasti assured him that water buffaloes were the gentlest of animals. He told Rahula of the countless times he had lain on a buffalo's back as they walked home along the banks of the river. He would look up at the blue sky and drifting clouds, enjoying moments of peaceful leisure on the warm, smooth back of the buffalo. Svasti also told Rahula about the games he played with other buffalo boys. Rahula loved to hear these stories. It was a life he had never known, since he had been raised in a palace. Rahula said he wished he could experience riding on a buffalo's back, and Svasti promised him that he would somehow arrange it.

Svasti wondered how he could arrange a buffalo ride for Rahula. They were both ordained monks! He decided that when they traveled in the vicinity of his home village, he would ask the Buddha's permission to go and see his family. He would ask if Rahula could join him. Then, when no one else was around, he would ask Rupak to let Rahula climb on the back of one of the buffaloes Rupak tended. Rahula could ride along the banks of the Neranjara River. Svasti planned to take off his monk's robe and ride on a buffalo too, just like in the old days.

The next year, the Buddha spent the retreat season on the stony mountain Calika. It was the thirteenth retreat season since the Buddha's Enlightenment. Meghiya was serving as the Buddha's assistant. One day Meghiya confided to the

Buddha that when he sat alone in the forest, he was disturbed by thoughts of desire and passion. He was concerned because the Buddha encouraged the bhikkhus to spend time alone in order to meditate, but whenever he meditated in solitude, he was confronted by mental obstacles.

The Buddha told him that practicing in solitude did not mean to live without the support of friends. Wasting time in idle chatter and useless gossip with others was not beneficial to the spiritual life, but receiving the support of friends in one's practice was most important. Bhikkhus needed to live in communities to support and encourage each other. That was the meaning of taking refuge in the sangha.

The Buddha also told him, "A bhikkhu requires five things. The first is understanding and virtuous friends who share the path. The second is precepts to help the bhikkhu maintain mindfulness. The third is ample opportunity to study the teaching. The fourth is diligence. And the fifth is understanding. The last four conditions are closely linked to and depend upon the presence of the first condition—having friends to practice with.

"Meghiya, practice the contemplations on death, compassion, impermanence, and the full awareness of breathing:

"To overcome desire, practice the contemplation on a corpse, looking deeply at the nine stages of the body's decay from the time the breathing ceases to the time the bones turn to dust.

"To overcome anger and hatred, practice the contemplation on compassion. It illuminates the causes of anger and hatred within our own minds and in the minds of those who have precipitated it.

"To overcome craving, practice the contemplation on impermanence, illuminating the birth and death of all things.

"To overcome confusion and dispersion, practice the contemplation on the full awareness of breathing.

"If you regularly practice these four contemplations, you will attain liberation and enlightenment."

Chapter Fifty-One

The Treasure of Insight

W hen the thirteenth retreat season ended, the Buddha returned to Savatthi. Svasti and Rahula followed him. It was the first time Svasti had been to Jetavana Monastery. He was delighted to discover how beautiful and inviting a place it was to practice. Jetavana was cool, refreshing, and friendly. Everyone smiled warmly at Svasti. They knew that the *Sutra on Tending Water Buffaloes* had been inspired by him. Svasti was confident that in so supportive an environment he would make great progress in his practice. He was beginning to understand why the Sangha was as important as the Buddha and the Dharma. Sangha was the community of persons practicing the Way of Awareness. It provided support and guidance. It was necessary to take refuge in the sangha.

Rahula turned twenty years old, and Sariputta performed his ordination ceremony. He was now a fully ordained bhikkhu and all the community rejoiced. Venerable Sariputta devoted several days prior to the ordination to give Rahula special teaching. Svasti accompanied him during these sessions and so benefited from Sariputta's teaching as well.

After Rahula's ordination, the Buddha also spent time to teach him different methods of contemplation. Svasti was invited to these sessions, too. The Buddha taught them the contemplation on the six sense organs: eyes, ears, nose, tongue, body, and mind; on the six sense objects: forms, sounds, smells, tastes, tactile objects, and objects of mind; and the six sense consciousnesses: eye-consciousness, ear-consciousness, nose-consciousness, taste-consciousness, body-consciousness, and mind-consciousness. The Buddha showed them how to look deeply into the impermanent nature of these eighteen domains of sense, called the eighteen *dhatus,* which comprised the six sense organs, the six sense objects, and the six sense consciousnesses or internal objects of sense. Perceptions arose because of contact between a sense organ and a sense object. All the domains of sense depended on each other for existence; they were all impermanent and interdependent. If one could understand that, one could penetrate the truth of the emptiness of self and transcend birth and death.

The Buddha gave Rahula the teaching on the emptiness of self in great detail. He said, "Rahula, among the five *skandhas*—body, feelings, perceptions, mental formations, and consciousness—there is nothing that can be considered to be permanent and nothing that can be called a 'self.' This body is not the self. This body is not something that belongs to the self either. The self cannot be found in the body, and the body cannot be found in the self.

"There are three kinds of views of self. The first is that this body is the self, or these feelings, perceptions, mental formations, or consciousness are the self. This is 'the belief in skandha as self,' and it is the first wrong view. But when one says, 'The skandhas are not the self,' one may fall into the second wrong view and believe that the self is something that exists independently from the skandhas and that the skandhas are its possessions. This second wrong view is called 'skandha is different from the self.' The third wrong view consists in the belief that there is a presence of the self in the skandhas, and there is the presence of the skandhas in the self. This is called 'the belief in the presence of skandhas and self in each other.'

"Rahula, practicing deeply the meditation on the emptiness of the self means looking into the five skandhas in order to see that they are neither self, belonging to self, nor interbeing with self. Once we overcome these three wrong views, we can experience the true nature of 'emptiness of all dhar-mas.'"

Svasti noticed how a bhikkhu at Jetavana named Thera never spoke to anyone else. He always walked alone. Vener-able Thera did not disturb anyone nor did he violate any pre-cepts, and yet it seemed to Svasti that he did not live in gen-uine harmony with the rest of the community. Once Svasti tried to speak with him, but he walked away without re-sponding. The other bhikkhus nicknamed him "the one who lives alone." Svasti had often heard the Buddha encourage the bhikkhus to avoid idle talk, meditate more, and develop self-sufficiency. But Svasti felt that Venerable Thera was not living the kind of self-sufficiency the Buddha intended. Con-fused, Svasti decided to ask the Buddha about it.

The next day, during his Dharma talk, the Buddha sum-moned the elder Thera. He asked him, "Is it true that you prefer to keep to yourself and that you do all things alone, avoiding contact with other bhikkhus?"

The bhikkhu answered, "Yes, Lord, that is true. You have told us to be self-sufficient and to practice being alone."

The Buddha turned to the community and said, "Bhikkhus, I will explain what true self-sufficiency is and what is the better way to live alone. A self-sufficient person is a person who dwells in mindfulness. He is aware of what is going on in the present moment, what is going on in his body, feelings, mind, and objects of mind. He knows how to look deeply at things in the present moment. He does not pur-sue the past nor lose himself in the future, because the past no longer is and the future has not yet come. Life can only take place in the present moment. If we lose the present mo-ment, we lose life. This is the better way to live alone.

"Bhikkhus, what is meant by 'pursuing the past'? To pur-sue the past means to lose yourself in thoughts about what you looked like in the past, what your feelings were then, what rank and position you held, what happiness or suffer-ing you experienced then. Giving rise to such thoughts entan-gles you in the past.

"Bhikkhus, what is meant by 'losing yourself in the future'? To lose yourself in the future means to lose yourself in thoughts about the future. You imagine, hope, fear, or worry about the future, wondering what you will look like, what your feelings will be, whether you will have happiness or suffering. Giving rise to such thoughts entangles you in the future.

"Bhikkhus, return to the present moment in order to be in direct contact with life and to see life deeply. If you cannot make direct contact with life, you cannot see deeply. Mindfulness enables you to return to the present moment. But if you are enslaved by desires and anxieties over what is happening in the present, you will lose your mindfulness and you will not be truly present to life.

"Bhikkhus, one who really knows how to be alone dwells in the present moment, even if he is sitting in the midst of a crowd. If a person sitting alone in the middle of a forest is not mindful, if he is haunted by the past and future, he is not truly alone."

The Buddha then recited a gatha to summarize his teaching:

> "Do not pursue the past.
> Do not lose yourself in the future.
> The past no longer is.
> The future has not yet come.
> Looking deeply at life as it is
> in the very here and now,
> the practitioner dwells
> in stability and freedom.
> We must be diligent today.
> To wait until tomorrow is too late.
> Death comes unexpectedly.
> How can we bargain with it?
> The sage calls a person who knows
> how to dwell in mindfulness
> night and day

'one who knows
the better way to live alone.'"

After reading the gatha, the Buddha thanked Thera and invited him to be seated again. The Buddha had neither praised nor criticized Thera, but it was clear that the bhikkhu now had a better grasp of what the Buddha meant by being self-sufficient or being alone.

During the Dharma discussion that took place later that evening, Svasti listened to the senior disciples say how important the Buddha's words had been that morning. Venerable Ananda repeated the Buddha's discourse, including the gatha, word for word. Svasti was always amazed at Ananda's memory. Ananda even spoke with the same stress on words as the Buddha. When Ananda was finished, Mahakaccana stood up and said, "I would like to suggest that we make a formal sutra of the Buddha's teaching this morning. I further suggest that we name it the *Bhaddekaratta Sutta*, the *Sutra on Knowing the Better Way to Live Alone*. Every bhikkhu should memorize this sutra and put it into practice."

Mahakassapa stood up and voiced his support for Mahakaccana's idea.

The next morning when the bhikkhus were out begging, they encountered a group of children playing by the rice paddies. The children had caught a crab which one boy held down with his forefinger. With his other hand, he ripped one of the crab's claws off. The other children clapped their hands and squealed. Pleased with their reaction, the boy ripped the other claw off. Then he tore all of the crab's legs off, one by one. He tossed the crab back into the paddy and caught another one.

When the children saw the Buddha and bhikkhus arrive, they bowed their heads and then returned to tormenting the next crab. The Buddha told the children to stop. He said, "Children, if someone ripped off your arm or leg, would it hurt?"

"Yes, Teacher," the children answered.

"Did you know that crabs feel pain just as you do?"

The children did not answer.

The Buddha continued, "The crab eats and drinks just like you. It has parents, brothers, and sisters. When you make it suffer, you make its family suffer as well. Think about what you are doing."

The children appeared sorry for what they had done. Seeing that other villagers had gathered around to see what he and the children were talking about, the Buddha used the occasion to offer a teaching about compassion.

He said, "Every living being deserves to enjoy a sense of security and well-being. We should protect life and bring happiness to others. All living beings, whether large or small, whether two-legged or four-legged, whether swimmers or fliers, have a right to live. We should not harm or kill other living beings. We should protect life.

"Children, just as a mother loves and protects her only child at the risk of her own life, we should open our hearts to protect all living beings. Our love should encompass every living being on, below, within, outside, and around us. Day and night, whether standing or walking, sitting or lying down, we should dwell in that love."

The Buddha asked the children to release the crab they had caught. Then he told everyone, "Meditating on love in this way brings happiness first to the one who practices it. You sleep better and wake up more at ease; you do not have nightmares; you are neither sorrowful nor anxious; and you are protected by everyone and everything around you. Those people and beings you bring into your mind of love and compassion bring you great joy, and, slowly, their suffering leaves them."

Svasti knew that the Buddha was committed to sharing the teaching with children. To help with that, he and Rahula organized special classes for children at Jetavana. With the assistance of young laypersons, especially Sudatta's four children, the young people gathered for special teaching once a month. Sudatta's son, Kala, was not very enthusiastic at first about attending. He only did so because he was fond of Svasti. But little by little his interest grew. Princess Vajiri, the king's daughter, also lent her support to these classes.

One full moon day, she asked the children to bring flowers to offer to the Buddha. The children arrived with flowers picked from their own gardens and from fields along the way to the monastery. Princess Vajiri brought an armful of lotus flowers she had gathered from the palace's lotus pool. When she and the children went to find the Buddha at his hut, they learned he was in the Dharma hall preparing to give a discourse to both bhikkhus and laypersons. The princess led the children quietly into the hall. All the adults moved to make a pathway for the children. They placed their flowers on the small table in front of the Buddha and then bowed. The Buddha smiled and bowed in return. He invited the children to sit right in front of him.

The Buddha's Dharma talk that day was most special. He waited for the children to be seated quietly, and then he slowly stood up. He picked up one of the lotus flowers and held it up before the community. He did not say anything. Everyone sat perfectly still. The Buddha continued to hold up the flower without saying anything for a long time. People were perplexed and wondered what he meant by doing that. Then the Buddha looked out over the community and smiled.

He said, "I have the eyes of true Dharma, the treasure of wondrous insight, and I have just transmitted it to Mahakassapa."

Everyone turned to look at Venerable Kassapa and saw that he was smiling. His eyes had not wavered from the Buddha and the lotus he held. When the people looked back at the Buddha, they saw that he too was looking at the lotus and smiling.

Though Svasti felt perplexed, he knew that the most important thing was to maintain mindfulness. He began to observe his breath as he looked at the Buddha. The white lotus in the Buddha's hand had newly blossomed. The Buddha

The Buddha's Dharma talk that day was most special.

held it in a most gentle, noble gesture. His thumb and forefinger held the stem of the flower which trailed the shape of his hand. His hand was as beautiful as the lotus itself, pure and wondrous. Suddenly, Svasti truly saw the pure and noble beauty of the flower. There was nothing to think about. Quite naturally, a smile arose on his face.

The Buddha began to speak. "Friends, this flower is a wondrous reality. As I hold the flower before you, you all have a chance to experience it. Making contact with a flower is to make contact with a wondrous reality. It is making contact with life itself.

"Mahakassapa smiled before anyone else because he was able to make contact with the flower. As long as obstacles remain in your minds, you will not be able to make contact with the flower. Some of you asked yourselves, 'Why is Gautama holding that flower up? What is the meaning of his gesture?' If your minds are occupied with such thoughts, you cannot truly experience the flower.

"Friends, being lost in thoughts is one of the things that prevents us from making true contact with life. If you are ruled by worry, frustration, anxiety, anger, or jealousy, you will lose the chance to make real contact with all the wonders of life.

"Friends, the lotus in my hand is only real to those of you who dwell mindfully in the present moment. If you do not return to the present moment, the flower does not truly exist. There are people who can pass through a forest of sandalwood trees without ever really seeing one tree. Life is filled with suffering, but it also contains many wonders. Be aware in order to see both the suffering and the wonders in life.

"Being in touch with suffering does not mean to become lost in it. Being in touch with the wonders of life does not mean to lose ourselves in them either. Being in touch is to truly encounter life, to see it deeply. If we directly encounter life, we will understand its interdependent and impermanent nature. Thanks to that, we will no longer lose ourselves in desire, anger, and craving. We will dwell in freedom and liberation."

Svasti felt happy. He was glad he had smiled and understood before the Buddha spoke. Venerable Mahakassapa had smiled first. He was one of Svasti's teachers and a senior disciple who had traveled far on the path. Svasti knew he could not compare himself to Mahakassapa and the other elders like Sariputta, Moggallana, and Assaji. After all, he was still only twenty-four years old!

Chapter Fifty-Two
Fields of Merit

The following year Svasti spent the retreat season at Nigrodha monastery in Kapilavatthu. The Buddha had returned to his homeland prior to the retreat after hearing about the conflict and unrest between the kingdoms of Sakya and Koliya. Koliya was his mother's native land. Princess Yasodhara was also from Koliya.

The two kingdoms were separated by the Rohini River. In fact, the dispute concerned the rights to the river's water. Because of a drought, neither kingdom had enough water to irrigate its fields. Both kingdoms wanted to build a dam in the Rohini in order to have what little water there was. At first the conflict began as no more than angry words hurled back and forth across the river by farmers, but soon passions escalated and farmers began to throw rocks at each other. Police were sent in to protect citizens, and finally, soldiers were lined up on either side of the river. It looked as if the conflict could erupt into a war at any moment.

The Buddha wanted, first of all, to understand the causes of the dispute. He asked the Sakya generals by the river, and they accused the citizens of Koliya of threatening the lives and property of Sakya citizens. Then he asked the generals on the Koliya side, and they accused the Sakya citizens of threatening the lives and property of the citizens of Koliya. Only when the Buddha spoke directly to the local farmers did he learn that the real source of the conflict was the lack of water.

Thanks to his close ties with both the Sakya and Koliya dynasties, the Buddha was able to bring about a meeting between King Mahanama and King Suppabuddha. He asked them to negotiate a quick solution to the crisis, because both sides would lose in a war, whether the loss was greater or smaller. He said, "Your Majesties, which is more precious, water or human lives?"

The kings agreed that human lives were infinitely more precious.

The Buddha said, "Your Majesties, the need for adequate irrigation water has caused this conflict. If pride and anger had not flared up, this conflict could have been easily resolved. There is no need for war! Examine your hearts. Do not waste the blood of your people because of pride and anger. Once pride and anger are released, the tensions that lead to war will disappear. Sit down and negotiate how the river water can be shared equally with both sides in this time of drought. Both sides must be assured of an equal amount of water."

Thanks to the Buddha's counsel, the two sides quickly reached an agreement. Warm and cordial relations were re-established. King Mahanama asked the Buddha to remain and spend the retreat season in Sakya. It was the fifteenth retreat season since the Buddha attained Enlightenment.

After the retreat, the Buddha returned south. He spent the sixteenth retreat season in Alavi, the seventeenth at Bamboo Forest, the eighteenth in Koliya, and the nineteenth in Rajagaha.

Whenever he stayed in Rajagaha, the Buddha preferred dwelling on Gijjhakuta Mountain. Because the peak resembled a vulture, it was called Vulture Peak. King Bimbisara frequently visited the Buddha on Vulture Peak for Dharma instruction. He even had steps built into the mountainside that led all the way to the Buddha's hut. He also had small bridges built over the tumbling waterfalls and springs. He liked to leave his carriage at the foot of the mountain and climb up the stone steps. Close by the Buddha's hut was a rock as large as several houses, and a clear stream where he could wash his robes and dry them on a smooth rock. The Buddha's hut was constructed of stones gathered on the mountain. The view from the Buddha's hut was magnificent. He especially enjoyed watching the sunsets. Senior disciples such as Sariputta, Uruvela Kassapa, Moggallana, Upali, Devadatta, and Ananda, also had huts on Vulture Peak.

The Buddha's sangha now had eighteen practice centers in and near Rajagaha. In addition to Bamboo Forest (Venuvana) and Vulture Peak, some of the centers were Vaibharavana, Sarpasundika-pragbhara, Saptaparnaguha, and Indrashaila-guha. The last two were located in enormous caves.

Jivaka, the son of Ambapali and King Bimbisara, was now a physician, and he lived in a hut close by Vulture Peak, having become one of the Buddha's closest lay disciples. He was already renowned for his skill in curing fatal diseases. He served as King Bimbisara's personal physician.

Jivaka looked after the health of the Buddha and bhikkhus on Vulture Peak and at Bamboo Forest. Every winter, he arranged for friends to bring extra robes for the bhikkhus to use as blankets for warmth at night. He offered a robe to the Buddha himself. Jivaka was interested in the prevention of diseases as well as their cure. He suggested a number of basic sanitary measures to the bhikkhus. He suggested that before drinking the water taken from ponds and lakes, it should be boiled, that the bhikkhus wash their robes at least once every seven days, and that more toilets be provided on the monastery grounds. He cautioned the bhikkhus not to eat food left over from the night before. The Buddha accepted all of Jivaka's suggestions.

Robe offering became a very popular practice among the laypeople. One day the Buddha spotted a bhikkhu returning to the monastery with a pile of robes heaped on his shoulder.

The Buddha washed the robe that Jivaka had given him.

The Buddha asked him, "How many robes do you have there?"

The bhikkhu answered, "Lord, I have eight."

"Do you think you need that many?"

"No, Lord, I do not. I only accepted them because the people offered them to me."

"How many robes do you think a bhikkhu actually needs?"

"Lord, according to my way of thinking, three robes are adequate. Three are plenty to keep warm on cold nights."

"I share your thoughts. I find three robes sufficient on cold nights. From now on let us announce that each bhikkhu will own only one begging bowl and no more than three robes. If more than that are offered, the bhikkhu will decline them."

The bhikkhu bowed to the Buddha and then walked back to his own hut.

One day while standing on a high hill, the Buddha looked out over the fields of rice paddies. He turned to Ananda and said, "Ananda, how beautiful are the golden patches of rice that stretch to the horizon! Wouldn't it be nice to sew our robes in the same checkered pattern?"

Ananda said, "Lord, it is a wonderful idea. Sewing bhikkhus' robes in the same pattern as rice fields would be lovely. You have said that a bhikkhu who practices the Way is like a fertile field in which seeds of virtue and merit have been sown to benefit both the present and future generations. When one makes offerings to such a bhikkhu or studies and practices with him, it is like sowing seeds of virtue and merit. I will tell the rest of the community to sew future robes in the pattern of rice fields. We can call our robes 'fields of merit.'"

The Buddha smiled his approval.

The following year the Buddha returned to Jetavana for the retreat season, after Sudatta came to Rajagaha and reminded the Buddha how long it had been since he had spent a retreat at Jetavana. It was the twentieth retreat season since the Buddha attained Enlightenment. The Buddha was now fifty-five years old. King Pasenadi rejoiced when he heard of the Buddha's return, and he visited the Buddha with all the royal family, including his second wife, Vrishab-hakshatriya, and their two children, Prince Vidudabha and Princess Vajna. His second wife was of the Sakya clan. After King Pasenadi had become the Buddha's disciple years ago, he sent a delegation to Sakya to request the hand of a Sakya princess. King Mahanama sent his own daughter, the beautiful Vrishabhakshatriya.

King Pasenadi did not miss a single Dharma talk given by the Buddha during the retreat season. More and more people came to hear the Buddha teach. One of the most supportive new lay disciples was Lady Visakha who offered the bhikkhus her large and verdant forest east of Savatthi. Though it was somewhat smaller in size, it was no less beautiful than Jetavana. With the help of many of her friends, Lady Visakha had a meditation hall, Dharma hall, and huts built in the forest. At Venerable Sariputta's suggestion they named this new monastery Eastern Park, or Purvarama. The Dharma hall located in the center of the forest was named Visakha Hall.

Lady Visakha was born in the city of Bhaddiya in the kingdom of Anga. She was the daughter of an extremely wealthy man named Dhananjaya. Her husband, a wealthy man from Savatthi, and her son had been disciples of Nigantha Nataputta and neither had felt drawn to the Buddha initially. However, inspired by Lady Visakha's devotion to the Dharma, they slowly began to be interested and finally asked to became lay disciples. Lady Visakha and her friend Lady Suppiya visited the Buddha's monasteries frequently, offering medicine, robes, and towels to any bhikkhus and bhikkhunis who needed them. She also pledged to support Sister Mahapajapati's efforts in building a spiritual center for the bhikkhunis along the right bank of the Ganga. Lady Visakha was an ardent supporter of the nuns, both in material and spiritual matters. Her compassionate wisdom was helpful on more than one occasion in helping to resolve minor conflicts among the bhikkhunis.

Two important decisions were made during a Dharma meeting that took place in Visakha's Hall. The first was that Ananda should be the Buddha's permanent assistant. The second one was that the Buddha should return every year to Savatthi for the rainy retreat season.

The first suggestion was proposed by Sariputta who said, "Brother Ananda has the finest memory among us. No one else possesses his uncanny ability to remember every word the Buddha speaks. He can repeat the Buddha's discourses without leaving out one word. If Ananda serves as the Buddha's attendant, he will be present to hear all that the Buddha teaches, whether it is a Dharma talk delivered to a large crowd or a private conversation with a lay disciple. The Buddha's teaching is infinitely precious. We should make every effort to preserve and protect it. Through our negligence in the past twenty years, we have lost many things the Buddha has uttered. Brother Ananda, on behalf of all of us and on behalf of future generations, please accept the task of being the Buddha's attendant."

All the bhikkhus voiced their support for Venerable Sariputta's proposal. Venerable Ananda, however, expressed reluctance. He said, "I see a number of problems. To begin with, it is not certain that the Buddha will agree to have me as his attendant. The Buddha has always been careful not to treat members of the Sakya clan with special favors. He is even strict and reserved with Bhikkhuni Mahapajapati, his own stepmother. Rahula has never slept in the Buddha's hut or shared a private meal with him. The Buddha has never afforded me any special privileges. I am afraid that if I am chosen as his attendant, some brothers will accuse me of using my position to attain special favors. Other brothers may accuse me of pointing out their faults to the Buddha should the Buddha happen to correct them."

Ananda looked at Sariputta, and then continued, "The Buddha has especially high regard for our brother Sariputta, the most talented and intelligent brother among us. Sariputta has been instrumental in teaching and organizing the sangha, and it is only natural that the Buddha places a great deal of trust in him. Even so, Sariputta has earned the jealousy of many brothers. Although the Buddha always confers with several people before making a major decision, some brothers complain that Sariputta makes the decisions, as if the Buddha were incapable of making his own decisions. These accusations are ridiculous, but it is because of this sort of misunderstanding that I wish to decline becoming the Buddha's attendant."

Venerable Sariputta smiled. "I am not afraid of another brother's jealousy that may arise from his temporary misunderstanding. I believe that each of us should do what we see to be correct and beneficial, regardless of what others may say. Ananda, we know that you are careful and attentive in all your actions. Please accept this position. If you don't, the Dharma will suffer in this generation and for generations to come."

Venerable Ananda sat silently. After a long hesitation, he finally said, "I will accept this position if the Buddha will agree to these requests: First, the Buddha will never give me any of his own robes. Second, the Buddha will not share his food offerings with me. Third, the Buddha will not allow me to dwell in the same hut with him. Fourth, the Buddha will not ask me to accompany him to a lay disciple's home for a meal. Fifth, if I am invited to a lay disciple's home for a meal, the Buddha can go as well. Sixth, the Buddha will allow me to use my discretion in admitting or refusing people who come to request an audience with him. Seventh, the Buddha will let me ask him to repeat things he says that I have not fully grasped. And eighth, the Buddha will repeat the essence of any Dharma talks he gives that I have been unable to attend."

Venerable Upali stood to speak, "Ananda's conditions seem most reasonable. I am sure the Buddha will agree to them. However, I cannot agree with the fourth request. If our brother Ananda does not accompany the Buddha to the homes of lay disciples, how will he be able to record things the

Buddha says to laymen and women which may be of benefit to future generations and all of us? I suggest that whenever the Buddha is invited for a meal at a layperson's home, he take another bhikkhu in addition to Ananda. That way, no one can accuse Ananda of receiving special favors."

Ananda said, "Brother, I do not think that is such a good suggestion. What if the lay disciple only has the means to offer food to two bhikkhus?"

Upali retorted, "Then the Buddha and you two bhikkhus will have to be content eating less!"

The rest of the bhikkhus burst into hearty laughter. They knew the problem of finding the best attendant for the Buddha had been solved. They next considered the proposal that the Buddha hold every rainy season retreat in Savatthi. Savatthi was a good location because Jetavana, Eastern Park, and the bhikkhunis' convent were all nearby. It would serve well as the sangha's main center. With the Buddha in the same location every year, many people could plan to attend the retreat and receive the Buddha's teaching directly. Lay patrons such as Anathapindika and Lady Visakha had already pledged to provide food, medicine, robes, and lodging for any bhikkhus and bhikkhunis traveling to Savatthi for the retreat season.

The bhikkhus concluded their meeting by agreeing to hold every rainy retreat in Savatthi, and they went directly to the Buddha's hut to present their ideas. The Buddha happily accepted both proposals.

Chapter Fifty-Three
Dwelling in the Present Moment

In the spring of the following year, the Buddha delivered the *Satipatthana Sutta*, the *Sutra on the Four Establishments of Mindfulness*, to a gathering of more than three hundred bhikkhus in Kammassadhamma, which was the capital of Kuru. This was a sutra fundamental for the practice of meditation. The Buddha referred to it as the path which could help every person attain peace of body and mind, overcome all sorrows and lamentations, destroy suffering and grief, and attain highest understanding and total emancipation. Later, Venerable Sariputta told the community that this was one of the most important sutras the Buddha had ever given. He encouraged every bhikkhu and bhikkhuni to study, memorize, and practice it.

Venerable Ananda repeated every word of the sutra later that night. *Sati* means "to dwell in mindfulness," that is, the practitioner remains aware of everything taking place in his body, feelings, mind, and objects of mind—the four establishments of mindfulness, or awareness.

First the practitioner observes his body—his breath; the four bodily postures of walking, standing, lying, and sitting; bodily actions such as going forward and backward, looking, putting on robes, eating, drinking, using the toilet, speaking, and washing robes; the parts of the body such as hair, teeth, sinews, bones, internal organs, marrow, intestines, saliva, and sweat; the elements which compose the body such as water, air, and heat; and the stages of a body's decay from the time it dies to when the bones turn to dust.

While observing the body, the practitioner is aware of all details concerning the body. For example, while breathing in, the practitioner knows he is breathing in; breathing out, he knows he is breathing out; breathing in and making his whole body calm and at peace, the practitioner knows he is breathing in and making his whole body calm and at peace. Walking, the practitioner knows he is walking. Sitting, the practitioner knows he is sitting. Performing movements such as putting on robes or drinking water, the practitioner knows he is putting on robes or drinking water. The contemplation of the body is not realized only during the moments of sitting meditation, but throughout the entire day, including the moments one is begging, eating, and washing one's bowl.

In the contemplation of feelings, the practitioner contemplates feelings as they arise, develop, and fade, feelings which are pleasant, unpleasant, or neutral. Feelings can have as their source either the body or the mind. When he feels pain from a toothache, the practitioner is aware that he feels pain from a toothache; when he is happy because he has received praise, the practitioner is aware that he is happy because he has received praise. The practitioner looks deeply in order to calm and quiet every feeling in order to clearly see the sources which give rise to feelings. The contemplation of feelings does not take place only during the moments of sitting meditation. It is practiced throughout the day.

In the contemplation of mind, the practitioner contemplates the presence of his mental states. Craving, he knows he is craving; not craving, he knows he is not craving. Angry or drowsy, he knows he is angry or drowsy; not angry or drowsy, he knows he is not angry or drowsy. Centered or distracted, he knows he is centered or distracted. Whether he is open-minded, close-minded, blocked, concentrated, or enlightened, the practitioner knows at once. And if he is not experiencing any of those states, the practitioner also knows at once. The practitioner recognizes and is aware of every mental state which arises within him in the present moment.

In the contemplation of the objects of mind, the practitioner contemplates the five hindrances to liberation (sense-desire, ill-will, drowsiness, agitation, and doubt) whenever they are present; the five skandhas which comprise a person (body, feelings, perceptions, mental formations, and consciousness); the six sense organs and the six sense objects; the Seven Factors of Awakening (full attention, investigating dharmas, energy, joy, ease, concentration, and letting-go); and the Four Noble Truths (the existence of suffering, the causes of suffering, liberation from suffering, and the path that leads to liberation from suffering). These are all objects of the mind, and they contain all dharmas.

The Buddha carefully explained each of the four establishments. He said that whoever practiced these four establishments for seven years would attain emancipation. He added that anyone who practiced them for seven months could also attain emancipation. He said that even after practicing these four contemplations for seven days, one could attain emancipation.

During a Dharma discussion, Venerable Assaji reminded the community that this was not the first time the Buddha had taught the Four Establishments of Mindfulness. He had, in fact, spoken about them on several occasions, but this was the first time he had compiled all of his previous teaching on the subject in so complete and thorough a way. Assaji agreed with Sariputta that this sutra should be memorized, recited, and practiced by every bhikkhu and bhikkhuni.

When the Buddha returned to Jetavana towards the end of spring that year, he met and transformed a notorious murderer named Angulimala. One morning when the Buddha entered Savatthi, it seemed like a ghost town. All doors were bolted shut. No one was on the streets. The Buddha stood in front of a home where he normally received food offerings. The door opened a crack and seeing it was the Buddha, the owner hastily ran out and invited him to enter. Once inside, the owner latched the door and invited the Buddha to sit. He suggested the Buddha remain to eat his meal inside the house. He said, "Lord, it is very dangerous to go outdoors today. The murderer Angulimala has been seen in these parts. They say he has killed many people in other cities. Every time he kills someone, he cuts off one of their fingers and adds it to a string he wears around his neck. They say that once he has killed a hundred people and has a talisman of a hundred fingers hanging around his neck, he will gain even more terrible, evil powers. It is strange—he never steals anything from the people he murders. King Pasenadi has organized a brigade of soldiers and police to hunt him down."

The Buddha asked, "Why must the king enlist the aid of an entire brigade of soldiers to hunt down just one man?"

"Respected Gautama, Angulimala is very dangerous. He possesses phenomenal fighting skills. Once he overcame forty men who surrounded him on a street. He killed most of them. The survivors had to flee for their lives. Angulimala is said to hide out in Jalini Forest. No one dares pass by there anymore. Not long ago, twenty armed police entered the forest to try to capture him. Only two came out alive. Now that Angulimala has been spotted in the city, no one dares go out to work or shop."

The Buddha thanked the man for telling him about Angulimala and then stood up to take his leave. The man implored the Buddha to remain safely inside, but the Buddha refused. He said that he could only preserve the trust of the people by continuing to do his begging as usual.

As the Buddha walked slowly and mindfully down the street, he suddenly heard the sound of steps running behind him in the distance. He knew it was Angulimala, but he felt no fear. He continued to take slow steps, aware of everything taking place within and outside of himself.

Angulimala shouted, "Stop, monk! Stop!"

The Buddha continued taking slow, stable steps. He knew from the sound of Angulimala's footsteps that he had slowed down to a brisk walk and was not far behind. Although the

Buddha was now fifty-six-years old, his sight and hearing were keener than ever. He held nothing but his begging bowl. He smiled as he recollected how quick and agile he had been in martial arts as a young prince. The other young men were never able to deliver him a blow. The Buddha knew that Angulimala was very close now and was surely carrying a weapon. The Buddha continued to walk with ease.

When Angulimala caught up to the Buddha, he walked alongside him and said, "I told you to stop, monk. Why don't you stop?"

The Buddha continued to walk as he said, "Angulimala, I stopped a long time ago. It is you who have not stopped."

Angulimala was startled by the Buddha's unusual reply. He blocked the Buddha's path, forcing the Buddha to stop. The Buddha looked into Angulimala's eyes. Again, Angulimala was startled. The Buddha's eyes shone like two stars. Angulimala had never encountered someone who radiated such serenity and ease. Everyone else always ran away from him in terror. Why didn't this monk show any fear? The Buddha was looking at him as if he were a friend or brother. The Buddha had said Angulimala's name, so it was clear that he knew who Angulimala was. Surely he knew about his treacherous deeds. How could he remain so calm and relaxed when faced with a murderer? Suddenly Angulimala felt he could no longer bear the Buddha's kind and gentle gaze. He said, "Monk, you said you stopped a long time ago. But you were still walking. You said I was the one who has not stopped. What did you mean by that?"

The Buddha replied, "Angulimala, I stopped committing acts that cause suffering to other living beings a long time ago. I have learned to protect life, the lives of all beings, not just humans. Angulimala, all living beings want to live. All fear death. We must nurture a heart of compassion and protect the lives of all beings. "

"Human beings do not love each other. Why should I love other people? Humans are cruel and deceptive. I will not rest until I have killed them all."

The Buddha spoke gently, "Angulimala, I know you have suffered deeply at the hands of other humans. Sometimes humans can be most cruel. Such cruelty is the result of ignorance, hatred, desire, and jealousy. But humans can also be understanding and compassionate. Have you ever met a bhikkhu before? Bhikkhus vow to protect the lives of all other beings. They vow to overcome desire, hatred, and ignorance. There are many people, not just bhikkhus, whose lives are based on understanding and love. Angulimala, there may be cruel people in this world, but there are also many kind people. Do not be blinded. My path can transform cruelty into kindness. Hatred is the path you are on now. You should stop. Choose the path of forgiveness, understanding, and love instead."

Angulimala was moved by the monk's words. Yet his mind was thrown into confusion, as well, and suddenly he felt as if he had been cut open and salt thrown on the open wound. He could see that the Buddha spoke from love. There was no hatred in the Buddha, no aversion. The monk looked at Angulimala as if he considered him a whole person worthy of respect. Could this monk be the very Gautama he had heard people praise, the one they called "the Buddha"? Angulimala asked, "Are you the monk Gautama?"

The Buddha nodded.

Angulimala said, "It is a great pity I did not meet you sooner. I have gone too far already on my path of destruction. It is no longer possible to turn back."

The Buddha said, "No, Angulimala, it is never too late to do a good act."

"What good act could I possibly do?"

"Stop traveling the road of hatred and violence. That would be the greatest act of all. Angulimala, though the sea of suffering is immense, look back and you will see the shore."

"Gautama, even if I wanted to, I could not turn back now. No one would let me live in peace after all I have done."

The Buddha grasped Angulimala's hand and said, "Angulimala, I will protect you if you vow to abandon your mind of hatred and devote yourself to the study and practice of the Way. Take the vow to begin anew and serve others. It is easy to see you are a man of intelligence. I have no doubt you could succeed on the path of realization."

Angulimala knelt before the Buddha. He removed the sword strapped to his back, placed it on the earth, and prostrated himself at the Buddha's feet. He covered his face in his hands and began to sob. After a long time, he looked up and said, "I vow to abandon my evil ways. I will follow you and learn compassion from you. I beg you to accept me as your disciple."

At that moment, Venerables Sariputta, Ananda, Upali, Kimbila, and several other bhikkhus arrived on the scene. They surrounded the Buddha and Angulimala. Seeing the Buddha safe and Angulimala preparing to take the refuges, their hearts rejoiced. The Buddha asked Ananda to give him an extra set of robes. He told Sariputta to ask the next house if they could borrow a razor for Upali to shave Angulimala's head. Angulimala was ordained right then and there. He knelt down, recited the three refuges, and was given the precepts by Upali. Afterwards, they returned to Jetavana together.

Over the next ten days, Upali and Sariputta taught Angulimala about the practice of the precepts, the practice of meditation, and the way of begging. Angulimala made a greater effort than any other bhikkhu before him. Even the Buddha was astonished at his transformation when he visited Angulimala two weeks after his ordination. Angulimala radiated serenity and stability, and so rare a gentleness that the other bhikkhus called him "Ahimsaka" which means "Nonviolent One." It had, in fact, been his name at birth. Svasti found it a most fitting name for him, for outside of the

Angulimala prostrated himself at the Buddha's feet.

Buddha, there was no other bhikkhu whose gaze was more filled with kindness.

One morning, the Buddha entered Savatthi to beg, accompanied by fifty other bhikkhus, including bhikkhu Ahimsaka. As they reached the city gates, they met King Pasenadi mounted on a steed leading a battalion of soldiers. The king and his generals were dressed in full fighting gear. When the king saw the Buddha, he dismounted and bowed.

The Buddha asked, "Majesty, has something happened? Has another kingdom invaded your borders?"

The king replied, "Lord, no one has invaded Kosala. I have gathered these soldiers to capture the murderer Angulimala. He is extremely dangerous. No one has yet been able to bring him to justice. He was seen in the city just two weeks ago. My people are still living in constant fear."

The Buddha asked, "Are you sure Angulimala is really that dangerous?"

The king said, "Lord, Angulimala is a danger to every man, woman, and child. I cannot rest until he is found and killed."

The Buddha asked, "If Angulimala repented his ways and vowed never to kill again, if he took the vows of a bhikkhu and respected all living beings, would you still need to capture and kill him?"

"Lord, if Angulimala became your disciple and followed the precept against killing, if he lived the pure and harmless life of a bhikkhu, my happiness would know no bounds! Not only would I spare his life and grant him freedom, I would offer him robes, food, and medicine. But I hardly think such a thing will come to pass!"

The Buddha pointed to Ahimsaka standing behind him and said, "Your majesty, this monk is none other than Angulimala. He has taken the precepts of a bhikkhu. He has become a new man in these past two weeks."

King Pasenadi was horrified when he realized he was standing so close to the notorious killer.

The Buddha said, "There is no need to fear him, your majesty. Bhikkhu Angulimala is gentler than a handful of earth. We call him Ahimsaka now."

The king stared long and hard at Ahimsaka and then bowed to him. He asked, "Respected monk, what family were you born into? What was your father's name?"

"Your majesty, my father's name was Gagga. My mother was Mantani."

"Bhikkhu Gagga Mantaniputta, allow me to offer you robes, food, and medicine."

Ahimsaka answered, "Thank you, your majesty, but I have three robes already. I receive my food each day by begging, and I have no need for medicine at present. Please accept my heartfelt gratitude for your offer."

The king bowed again to the new bhikkhu and then turned to the Buddha. "Enlightened Master, your virtue is truly wondrous! You bring peace and well-being to situations no one else can. What others fail to resolve by force and violence, you resolve by your great virtue. Let me express my profound gratitude."

The king departed after informing his generals they could disband the troops and everyone could return to their regular duties.

Chapter Fifty-Four
Dwell in Mindfulness

News about Angulimala's ordination spread quickly throughout the city. Everyone sighed with relief. Even neighboring kingdoms soon learned of the murderer's transformation, and the people held the Buddha and his sangha in ever greater esteem.

The sangha continued to attract many bright and able young men who abandoned other sects to follow the teaching of the Buddha. The story of how lay disciple Upali left the Nigantha sect became a heated topic of conversation among religious circles in Magadha and Kosala. Upali was a wealthy and talented young man who lived in northern Magadha. He was one of the chief patrons of the Nigantha sect, led by a teacher named Nataputta. The ascetics of Nigantha lived most frugally, shunning even clothes, and they were highly regarded by the people.

That spring, the Buddha was dwelling in Pavarika Mango Grove in Nalanda. He received a visit from one of Nataputta's senior students, the ascetic Digha Tappasi, who stopped by one day after begging in Nalanda. The Buddha learned from Tappasi that the followers of Nigantha did not speak of karma (*karmani*), but only of sins (*dandani*). Tappasi explained that there were three kinds of sin: sins committed by the body, sins caused by wrong speech, and sinful thoughts. When the Buddha asked him which form of sin was the most serious, the ascetic answered, "Sins committed by the body are the most serious."

The Buddha told him that according to the Way of Awakening, unwholesome thought was considered more serious because the mind was more fundamental. Ascetic Tappasi had the Buddha repeat this three times so that he could recant it later. He then took his leave and returned to Nataputta who burst out laughing when Tappasi told him what the Buddha had said.

Nataputta said, "That monk Gautama has made a grave error. Sinful thought and speech are not the greatest sins. Sins committed by the body are the most serious and have the longest lasting consequences. Ascetic Tappasi, you have grasped the essentials of my teaching."

A number of other disciples were present during this exchange, including the merchant Upali who was visiting with several of his friends from Balaka. Upali expressed an interest in visiting the Buddha himself to challenge the Buddha's view on this matter. Nataputta encouraged Upali to go, but Tappasi expressed reservations. He was worried that the Buddha might be able to convince Upali and perhaps even convert him.

Nataputta had great faith in Upali and said, "There is no need to fear that Upali will leave us to become a disciple of Gautama's. Who can say, perhaps Gautama will become a disciple of Upali's!"

Tappasi still tried to discourage Upali from going, but Upali's mind was set. When Upali met the Buddha, he was immediately impressed by the Buddha's lively and stimulating way of speaking. By using seven examples, the Buddha showed Upali why unwholesome thought was more fundamental than unwholesome speech or action. The Buddha knew that disciples of the Nigantha sect observed the precept not to kill. He knew how careful they were not to step on insects for fear they would crush them, and he praised them for this. Then he asked Upali, "If you do not intentionally step on an insect, but do so accidentally, have you committed a sin?"

Upali responded, "Master Nataputta says that if you did not intend to kill, you have not committed a sin."

The Buddha smiled and said, "Then Master Nataputta agrees that thought is what is fundamental. How then can he maintain that sinful action is more serious?"

Upali was impressed with the Buddha's clarity and wisdom. He later confessed to the Buddha that the first example was sufficiently convincing, and he had only pressed the Buddha to provide more examples in order to have a chance to listen to more of the Buddha's teaching. When the Buddha finished explaining the seventh example, Upali prostrated before him and asked to be accepted as a disciple.

The Buddha said, "Upali, you should consider such a request carefully. A man of your intelligence and stature should not make a hasty decision. Reflect until you are sure."

The Buddha's words made Upali respect him all the more. He could see that the Buddha was not interested in converting others in order to add to his own prestige. No other spiritual teacher had ever told Upali to reflect carefully before supporting his community. Upali answered, "Lord, I have reflected enough. Please allow me to take refuge in the Buddha, the Dharma, and the Sangha. I am most grateful and happy to have discovered the true and correct path."

The Buddha said, "Disciple Upali, you have long been a major patron of the Nigantha sect. Even though you take refuge with me, please do not cease making offerings to your former sect."

Upali said, "Lord, you are truly noble. You are open and generous, unlike any teacher I have ever known."

When Tappasi delivered the news to Nataputta that Upali had become one of the Buddha's disciples, Nataputta couldn't believe it. He went with Tappasi to Upali's house where Upali confirmed the truth.

More and more people throughout the kingdoms of Magadha and Kosala accepted the Path of Awakening. Many bhikkhus announced this happy news to the Buddha when they visited him in Savatthi.

The Buddha told them, "Whether the increase in numbers of people accepting the Path as their own is good news or not depends on how diligent the bhikkhus are in their practice. We should not cling to concepts of success or failure. We should look at both fortune and misfortune with equanimity."

One morning as the Buddha and the bhikkhus prepared to leave the monastery to go begging, several police entered Jetavana with orders to search for the body of a woman. The bhikkhus were dismayed, not understanding why the police expected to find a woman's corpse on the monastery grounds. Venerable Bhaddiya asked who the woman was and was told she was a young woman named Sundari who belonged to a large religious sect in Savatthi. The bhikkhus recognized the name as belonging to an attractive young woman who in recent months had attended several Dharma talks at the monastery. The bhikkhus told the police there was no chance her body would be found at Jetavana, but the police insisted on looking anyway. To everyone's surprise, they found the body buried in a shallow grave not too distant from the Buddha's hut. No one could understand how she had died and why she had been buried there. After the police departed with the body, the Buddha told the bhikkhus to go out begging as usual.

"Dwell in mindfulness," he told them.

Later that same day, members of Sundari's sect carried her body throughout the city, wailing in loud voices. They stopped at intervals and cried out to the people, "This is the body of Sundari! Her broken body was discovered in a shallow grave at Jetavana Monastery. Those monks who claim to come from the noble line of Sakya, who claim to live chaste, pure lives—they raped Sundari, killed her, and then tried to hide her body! Their talk of loving kindness, compassion, joy, and equanimity is nothing but a sham! See for yourselves!"

The citizens of Savatthi were disturbed. Even some of the most solid disciples of the Buddha felt their faith waver.

Others were convinced that the whole affair had been orchestrated to harm the Buddha's reputation, and they suffered deeply. Other spiritual sects which felt threatened by the Buddha seized the opportunity to openly condemn and malign the sangha. The bhikkhus were interrogated and heckled wherever they went. They did their best to maintain their serenity and to dwell in mindfulness, but it was difficult, especially for bhikkhus still new to the practice. Many young bhikkhus felt shamed and no longer wanted to beg in the city.

The Buddha gathered the bhikkhus together one afternoon and spoke to them. "Unjust accusations can occur anywhere at any time. There is no need for you to feel ashamed. The only cause for shame would be if you ceased your efforts to live your pure life of practice. This false accusation will spread and then it will pass away. Tomorrow when you go begging, if anyone asks you about this affair, simply answer, 'Whoever is responsible will reap the fruits.'"

The bhikkhus were much comforted by the Buddha's words.

Meanwhile, Lady Visakha, who was greatly disturbed over the affair, went to see Sudatta. Together they discussed the matter at some length. They agreed to secretly hire someone to make an investigation in order to uncover the real culprits. They shared their plan with Prince Jeta who agreed to help them.

Within seven days, the secret investigator discovered who the actual killers were. The two men responsible became drunk and began to argue over their spoils. In their angry, drunken state, they let the truth slip out. Royal police were summoned and the men were arrested. They made a confession and told the police how they were hired by the leaders of Sundari's sect to kill her and bury her near the Buddha's hut.

King Pasenadi visited Jetavana at once to share the news that the killers had been found. He expressed his unwavering faith in the sangha and his joy that the truth would now be known to all the people. The Buddha asked the king to forgive those responsible for the crime. He also said that similar crimes could happen again unless people learned to overcome their hatred and jealousy.

The people of Savatthi once again regarded the bhikkhus with great admiration and respect.

Chapter Fifty-Five
Appearance of the Morning Star

One day the Buddha and Ananda visited a small monastery located just outside the city. They arrived when most of the bhikkhus were out begging. As they strolled around the monastery grounds, they suddenly heard a pitiful groan coming from one of the huts. The Buddha entered the hut and found an emaciated bhikkhu curled up in one corner. A terrible stench filled the air. The Buddha knelt beside him and asked, "Brother, are you ill?"

The bhikkhu answered, "Lord, I have dysentery."

"Isn't anyone looking after you?"

"Lord, the other brothers have gone out begging. There is no one here but me. When I first fell ill, several of the brothers did try to care for me, but when I saw I was of no use to anyone, I told them not to bother with me anymore."

The Buddha told Ananda, "Go fetch some water. We will bathe our brother."

Ananda brought a bucket of water and helped the Buddha bathe the sick bhikkhu. They changed his robe and lifted him back onto his bed. The Buddha and Ananda then scrubbed the floor and washed the bhikkhu's soiled robes. They were hanging the robes out to dry when the other bhikkhus returned. Venerable Ananda asked them to boil some water and prepare medicine for their brother.

The community invited the Buddha and Ananda to eat with them. After the meal, the Buddha asked them, "From what illness is the bhikkhu in that hut suffering?"

"Lord Buddha, he has dysentery."

"Has anyone been caring for him?"

"Lord Buddha, at first we tried to look after him but then he asked us not to."

"Bhikkhus, when we leave our homes to follow the Way, we leave parents and family behind. If we don't look after each other when we are sick, who will? We must care for one another. Whether the ill person is a teacher, a student, or a friend, we must tend to him until he has regained his health. Bhikkhus, if I were sick, would you tend to my needs?"

"Yes, certainly, Lord Buddha."

"Then you must tend to the needs of any bhikkhu who falls ill. Caring for any bhikkhu is the same as caring for the Buddha."

The bhikkhus joined their palms and bowed.

The next summer the Buddha stayed at Eastern Park in Savatthi at the same time that Bhikkhuni Mahapajapati was teaching a large community of nuns in Savatthi. She was assisted by Bhikkhuni Khema, who once had been one of King Bimbisara's wives. She had become a disciple of the Buddha twenty years earlier. At that time her profound natural insight was somewhat marred by her arrogance, but after receiving instruction from the Buddha, she learned humility. After only four years of practice as a lay disciple, she asked to be ordained. She was most diligent in her practice and was now an important teacher and leader among the nuns. Lady Visakha regularly visited her and the other bhikkhunis. One day she invited Sudatta—also known as Anathapindika, the philanthropist who had purchased the Jeta Grove for the sangha—to accompany her. She introduced him to Sisters Khema, Dhammadinna, Uppalavanna, and Patacara. Lady Visakha later told him that she knew them before they became nuns.

Another day Sudatta visited the bhikkhunis' center with
a male friend also named Visakha, who was a relative of
Bhikkhuni Dhammadinna, a well-known teacher among the
nuns. The two men listened to Bhikkhuni Dhammadinna give
a Dharma talk on the five skandhas and the Noble Eightfold Path. Visakha was astonished by her profound grasp of
subtle truths. When he returned to Jetavana, he told the
Buddha everything Bhikkhuni Dhammadinna had said.

The Buddha replied, "If you asked me about the same subjects, I would have said the very same things as Sister
Dhammadinna. She has truly grasped the teaching of emancipation and enlightenment."

The Buddha turned to Ananda and said, "Ananda, please
remember Sister Dhammadinna's discourse and repeat it to
the entire community of monks. Her discourse is an important
one."

Bhikkhuni Bhadda Kapilani was also renowned for her
grasp of the Dharma. Like Sister Dhammadinna, she was often invited to travel to offer teaching.

The story of Bhikkhuni Patacara was heart-wrenching.
She was the only daughter of a wealthy family in Savatthi.
Her parents were overly protective of her and never allowed
her to leave the house. All day long she was required to stay
inside. Thus, she never had a chance to meet many people.
When she reached an age suitable for marriage, she fell in
love, without her parents' knowledge, with a young servant
in their household. When her parents arranged for her to
marry the son of another wealthy family, Patacara urged her
secret lover to run away with her. Early on the morning she
was to be married, she disguised herself as a servant girl and
pretended to go outside to fetch water. As soon as she was
outside, she met her lover and they fled to a distant village
where they were married.

Three years later Patacara became pregnant. When she
neared her time, she asked her husband to take her to her
parents' house to give birth there, as was the custom. Her
husband was reluctant but because she insisted, he agreed.

But halfway there, Patacara went into labor and delivered a son. As there was no longer any need to return to her parents' home, they went back to their own village.

Two years later, Patacara was again with child. Again she insisted her husband take her to her parents' house. This time they met with tragedy. Along the way, a storm broke, just as she was going into labor. Her husband asked her to wait by the side of the road while he entered the forest to cut some branches to make a shelter. Patacara waited for a long time, but her husband did not return. In the middle of the night, surrounded by rain and wind, she gave birth to a second son. At dawn, she lifted her newborn son in one arm and held her other son's hand, and entered the forest to look for her husband. She found him dead from a poisonous snake bite. She wept bitterly for a long time. Then she stood up and headed with her two sons towards her old home in Savatthi. At last she reached the river. The waters were swollen from the rain, making the water too deep for her first son to wade across. She told him to wait on the bank while she carried the baby safely to the other side first. She held the infant over her head as she walked through the deep waters. When she was halfway across, a mighty eagle swept down and grabbed the baby in its talons. She screamed at the bird to release her child, but it flew away. When her other son heard her cries, he thought she was calling him to join her. When Patacara turned around, she saw him stepping into the rushing waters. She shouted at him to wait, but it was too late. The strong currents swept him away, and she was unable to save him.

At last, Patacara crossed to the other shore, and collapsed on the banks. When she came to, she stood up and walked for several days until she reached Savatthi. When she finally arrived, she learned that her parents' home had been destroyed in the storm and both her parents killed when a wall collapsed on them. Patacara had returned on the same day her parents' bodies were being cremated.

Patacara collapsed by the side of the road. She no longer wanted to live. Some people took pity on her and took her to see the Buddha. He listened to her tell her story, and he told her in a gentle voice, "Patacara, you have suffered terribly. But life is not only suffering and misfortune. Be brave! Practice the Way of Enlightenment, and one day you will be able to smile even at your most painful sufferings. You will learn how to create new peace and joy in the present and for the future."

Patacara bowed and asked to take the refuges. The Buddha entrusted her to Sister Mahapajapati's care. Soon afterwards Patacara was ordained as a bhikkhuni. She was deeply loved by Sister Mahapajapati and the other bhikkhunis. After several years of practice, she learned to smile again. One day, while washing her feet, she watched the streams of water disappear back into the earth, and she had sudden insight into the nature of impermanence. She held that image in her mind during her meditation for several days and nights, and one dawn, she broke through the problem of birth and death. Spontaneously, she wrote a poem:

The other day, while washing my feet,
I watched the streams of water flow
back into the heart of the earth.
I asked, "To where does the water return?"

Contemplating in serene silence,
mind and body held in mindfulness,
I looked into the nature of the six sense objects
with the spirit of a strong, quick horse.

Staring at the oil lamp wick,
I concentrated my mind.
Time passed quickly.
The oil lamp still shone.

I took a needle
and pushed the wick down.
The light was instantly extinguished,
submerging all in darkness.

The flame was extinguished,
but suddenly my soul was bright.
My mind was released from all bondage
as the morning star appeared.

When Patacara presented her poem to Sister Mahapajapati, the abbess gave it her deepest praises.

Sister Uppalavanna was another bhikkhuni who came to
the Dharma after great suffering, thanks to the efforts of
Venerable Moggallana. She was a woman of uncommon
beauty, even with her head shaved. She was most diligent in
her practice and one of Abbess Pajapati's finest assistants.

Venerable Moggallana met Sister Uppalavanna one day
while he was walking past a city park. She was standing
there, a flower of the night. She was known to men as Beautiful Lotus. Indeed, her beauty surpassed that of even the
most lovely lotus flower. But Venerable Moggallana saw the
suffering in her eyes. He knew she hid many sorrows in her
heart. He stopped and said, "You are indeed beautiful and
dressed in the finest garments, but I can see that you are
filled with suffering and confusion. Your burden is heavy, and
yet you continue to pursue a path that leads to even more
darkness."

Uppalavanna was taken aback by Moggallana's ability to
read her innermost thoughts. But she pretended to be non-
plussed and retorted, "Perhaps what you say is true, but this
is the only path I have."

Moggallana said, "Why be so pessimistic? No matter
what your past has been like, you can transform yourself and
create a better future. Soiled clothes can be washed. A heart
burdened by confusion and weariness can be purified by the

waters of enlightenment. The Buddha teaches that everyone has the capacity to awaken and find peace and joy."

Uppalavanna began to weep. "But my life is filled with sinful deeds and injustices. I'm afraid that even the Buddha cannot help me."

Moggallana comforted her. "Don't worry. Please share your story with me."

Uppalavanna told Venerable Moggallana that she was the daughter of a wealthy family. She was married at sixteen. Soon after her husband's father died, her mother-in-law began sleeping with her own son, Uppalavanna's husband. Uppalavanna gave birth to a daughter, but unable to endure the incestuous relationship of her husband and mother-in-law, she ran away, leaving her daughter behind. Some years later, she met and married a merchant. When she learned he was secretly keeping a concubine, she investigated until she uncovered the horrible truth that his concubine was the very daughter she had abandoned years earlier.

Her pain and bitterness were so great that she began to hate all the world. She no longer loved or trusted anyone. She became a courtesan and sought money, jewels, and material pleasures for solace. She confessed she had even been thinking of trying to seduce Moggallana when he passed by as a means to expose humanity's false virtue.

Beautiful Lotus covered her face and sobbed. Moggallana let her cry to ease her pain. Then he spoke to her about the Dharma and took her to meet the Buddha. The Buddha spoke words of comfort to her and asked if she would like to study with the bhikkhunis under the guidance of Abbess Gotami. She was ordained and after only four years of diligent practice was considered by all as an exceptional example for everyone.

BOOK THREE

BOOK THREE

Chapter Fifty-Six
Full Awareness of Breathing

Sometimes the Buddha or one of his senior disciples gave a Dharma talk at the bhikkhunis' monastery. Once a month, the bhikkhunis also attended Dharma discourses at Jetavana or Eastern Park. One year, thanks to a suggestion made by Venerable Sariputta, the Buddha extended the retreat season an extra month. Sariputta knew that by extending the retreat one month, many bhikkhus and bhikkhunis from distant centers would be able to travel to Savatthi for direct teaching from the Buddha after they had concluded the retreats at their own centers. And indeed, many came. Lay patrons Sudatta, Visakha, and Mallika used all the means at their disposal to provide food and dwelling for nearly three thousand monks and nuns. The Pavarana ceremony, held at the end of each rainy-season retreat, fell on the full moon day of the month of Kattika that year, rather than Assayuja.

When the full moon day of Kattika arrived, kumudi flowers were blossoming everywhere. Because the kumudi, a white lotus, always blossomed at the same time each year, the full moon day of Kattika was called Kumudi Day. That evening the Buddha and his three thousand disciples sat beneath the radiant full moon. The delicate fragrance of lotus flowers drifted up from the lake. The bhikkhus and bhikkhunis sat silently as the Buddha looked out over the community, and praised them for their diligence. The Bud-

That evening under the full moon, the Buddha delivered the Su-
tra on the Full Awareness of Breathing *to 3,000 disciples.*

dha used this special occasion to deliver the *Sutra on the Full Awareness of Breathing*.

Of course, every bhikkhu and bhikkhuni present had been taught the method on the awareness of breathing. But this was the first time that most of them had an opportunity to hear this teaching directly from the Buddha. This was also the first time the Buddha compiled and summarized all his previous teachings on the awareness of breathing. Venerable Ananda listened intently, knowing that this sutra would be an important one to transmit to all the sangha's centers.

Bhikkhuni Yasodhara, Rahula's mother, and his sister Bhikkhuni Sundari Nanda were among those assembled. They both had been ordained several years earlier under the guidance of Bhikkhuni Gotami. They practiced in a monastery north of Kapilavatthu founded by Bhikkhuni Gotami. Yasodhara had requested to be ordained just six months after her mother-in-law, and after one year of practice she became one of Bhikkhuni Gotami's chief assistants.

The bhikkhunis did their best to attend all the retreat seasons in Savatthi in order to receive direct teaching from the Buddha and his senior disciples. Queen Mallika and Lady Visakha were wholehearted supporters of the nuns. For two years the nuns were given a place in the Imperial Gardens to stay, but by the third year they had their own nunnery, thanks to the generous patronage of the Queen and Lady Visakha. Because she was growing old, Bhikkhuni Gotami devoted careful attention to training new leaders among the bhikkhunis, including Bhikkhunis Yasodhara, Sela, Vimala, Soma, Mutta, and Nanduttara. All of them were present that evening in Eastern Park. Venerable Svasti was introduced to Sister Yasodhara and Sister Sundari Nanda by Venerable Rahula. He was deeply moved to meet them at last.

The Buddha delivered the sutra:

"Bhikkhus and bhikkhunis, the method of the Full Awareness of Breathing, if developed and practiced continuously, will bring great rewards and advantages. It will lead to success in practicing the Four Establishments of Mindfulness and the Seven Factors of Awakening, which will give rise to Understanding and Liberation.

"One practices as follows:

"The first breath: 'Breathing in a long breath, I know I am breathing in a long breath. Breathing out a long breath, I know I am breathing out a long breath.'

"The second breath: 'Breathing in a short breath, I know I am breathing in a short breath. Breathing out a short breath, I know I am breathing out a short breath.'

"These two breaths enable you to cut through forgetfulness and unnecessary thinking, at the same time giving rise to mindfulness and enabling you to encounter life in the present moment. Forgetfulness is the absence of mindfulness. Breathing with awareness enables us to return to ourselves and to life.

"The third breath: 'Breathing in, I am aware of my whole body. Breathing out, I am aware of my whole body.'

"This breath enables you to contemplate the body and be in direct contact with your own body. Awareness of the whole body and awareness of every part of the body allows you to see the wondrous presence of your body and the process of birth and death unfolding in your body.

"The fourth breath: 'I am breathing in and making my whole body calm and at peace. I am breathing out and making my whole body calm and at peace.'

"This breath helps you realize calmness and peace in the body and arrive at a state in which mind, body, and breath are one harmonious reality.

"The fifth breath: 'I am breathing in and feeling joyful. I am breathing out and feeling joyful.'

"The sixth breath: 'I am breathing in and feeling happy. I am breathing out and feeling happy.'

"With these two breaths, you cross into the domain of feelings. These two breaths create peace and joy that can nourish mind and body. Thanks to the cessation of dispersion and forgetfulness, you return to yourself, aware of the present moment. Happiness and joy arise within you.

"You dwell in the wonders of life, able to taste the peace and joy mindfulness brings. Thanks to this encounter with the wonders of life, you are able to transform neutral feelings into pleasant feelings. These two breaths thus lead to pleasant feelings.

"The seventh breath: 'I am breathing in and am aware of the activities of the mind in me. I am breathing out and am aware of the activities of the mind in me.'

"The eighth breath: 'I am breathing in and making the activities of the mind in me calm and at peace. I am breathing out and making the activities of the mind in me calm and at peace.'

"These two breaths enable you to look deeply at all the feelings arising within you, whether they are pleasant, unpleasant, or neutral, and enable you to make those feelings calm and at peace. The 'activities of the mind' mean, in this case, the feelings. When you are aware of your feelings and can see deeply into their roots and nature, you can control them and make them calm and at peace, even though they may be unpleasant thoughts which arise from desire, anger, and jealousy.

"The ninth breath: 'I am breathing in and am aware of my mind. I am breathing out and am aware of my mind.'

"The tenth breath: 'I am breathing in and making my mind happy and at peace. I am breathing out and making my mind happy and at peace.'

"The eleventh breath: 'I am breathing in and concentrating my mind. I am breathing out and concentrating my mind.'

"The twelfth breath: 'I am breathing in and liberating my mind. I am breathing out and liberating my mind.'

"With these four breaths you cross into the third domain, which is the mind. The ninth breath enables you to recognize all the states of the mind, such as perceptions, thinking, discrimination, happiness, sadness, and doubt. You observe and recognize these states in order to see deeply into the mind's activities. When the mind's activities are observed and recognized, you are able to concentrate your mind, making it quiet and at peace. This is brought about by the tenth and eleventh breaths. The twelfth breath enables you to release all obstacles of the mind. Thanks to illuminating your mind, you can see the roots of all mental formations, and thus overcome all obstacles.

"The thirteenth breath: 'I am breathing in and observing the impermanent nature of all dharmas. I am breathing out and observing the impermanent nature of all dharmas.'

"The fourteenth breath: 'I am breathing in and observing the fading of all dharmas. I am breathing out and observing the fading of all dharmas.'

"The fifteenth breath: 'I am breathing in and contemplating liberation. I am breathing out and contemplating liberation.'

"The sixteenth breath: 'I am breathing in and contemplating letting go. I am breathing out and contemplating letting go.'

"With these four breaths, the practitioner passes into the domain of objects of the mind, and concentrates the mind in order to observe the true nature of all dharmas. First is the observation of the impermanent nature of all dharmas. Because all dharmas are impermanent, they must all fade. When you clearly understand the impermanent and fading nature of all dharmas, you are no longer bound by the endless cycle of birth and death. Thanks to that, you can let go and attain liberation. Letting go does not mean to disdain or run away from life. Letting go means letting go of craving and clinging so you do not suffer from the endless cycle of birth and death to which all dharmas are subject. Once you have let go and attained liberation, you can live in peace and joy in the very midst of life. There is no longer anything which can bind you."

So taught the Buddha how to observe deeply the body, feelings, mind, and objects of mind through the sixteen methods of conscious breathing. He also applied the sixteen exercises to the practice of the Seven Factors of Awakening, which are full attention, investigating dharmas, energy, joy, ease, concentration, and letting go.

Venerable Svasti had already heard the *Sutra on the Four Establishments of Mindfulness*. He now felt that, thanks to this *Sutra on the Full Awareness of Breathing*, he could more deeply penetrate the Four Establishments. He saw how these two sutras complemented one another and how fundamental they both were to the practice of meditation.

Three thousand bhikkhus and bhikkhunis joyously received the Buddha's teaching that night beneath the light of the full moon. Svasti's heart filled with gratitude to Venerable Sariputta for having made this night possible.

One day Venerable Ahimsaka returned from begging covered with blood and barely able to walk. Svasti ran to help him. Ahimsaka asked to be taken to the Buddha. He explained that while he was out begging in the city, some people recognized him as the former Angulimala. They cornered him and began to beat him. Ahimsaka did not resist their blows, but joined his hands to form a lotus bud while allowing them to vent their anger and hatred. They battered him until he was vomiting blood.

When the Buddha saw that Ahimsaka was hurt, he called to Ananda to get a basin of water and a towel to wash away the blood. He asked Svasti to gather medicinal leaves to make into poultices to place on Ahimsaka's wounds.

Although he was in great pain, Venerable Ahimsaka did not cry out. The Buddha said, "Your sufferings today can rinse away all the sufferings of the past. Enduring suffering in love and awareness can erase the bitter hatred of a thousand lifetimes. Ahimsaka, your robe has been torn to shreds. Where is your bowl?"

"Lord, they shattered it."

"I will ask Ananda to find you a new robe and bowl."

As Svasti applied poultices to Ahimsaka's wounds, he realized what an example of nonviolence Ahimsaka was. Venerable Ahimsaka told Svasti a story that had taken place only the day before when he was out begging.

Beneath a tree in the forest, Ahimsaka encountered a woman in labor. She was in extreme pain and unable to give birth to the child. Ahimsaka cried out, "Such terrible pain!" and ran to ask the Buddha what could be done.

The Buddha said, "Run back to her and tell her, 'Madam, from the day I was born I have never intentionally harmed any living being. By that merit, may you and your child be peaceful and safe.'"

Ahimsaka protested, "I would be lying if I said such a thing! The truth is I have harmed a great many living beings."

The Buddha said, "Then go and tell her, 'Madam, since the day I was born in the noble Dharma, I have never intentionally harmed any living being. By that merit, may you and your child be peaceful and safe.'"

Ahimsaka ran back to the forest and spoke those words. Within a few minutes, the woman safely gave birth to her child.

Venerable Ahimsaka had traveled far along the path, earning the Buddha's highest praises.

Chapter Fifty-Seven
The Raft Is Not the Shore

That winter the Buddha stayed in Vesali. One day while he was meditating not far from Kutagarasala Dharma Hall, several bhikkhus committed suicide in another part of the monastery. When the Buddha was informed, he asked what led them to kill themselves. He was told that after meditating on the impermanent and fading nature of the body, these bhikkhus expressed aversion for the body and no longer wished to live. The Buddha was saddened to hear this. He called all the remaining bhikkhus together.

He said, "Bhikkhus, we meditate on impermanence and fading in order to see into the true nature of all dharmas so that we will not be bound by them. Enlightenment and freedom cannot be attained by escaping the world. They can only be attained when one sees deeply into the true nature of all dharmas. These brothers did not understand and so they foolishly sought to escape. By doing so, they violated the precept against killing.

"Bhikkhus, a liberated person neither clings to dharmas nor feels aversion to them. Clinging and aversion are both ropes that bind. A free person transcends both in order to dwell in peace and happiness. Such a happiness cannot be measured. A free person does not cling to narrow views about permanence and a separate self nor does he cling to narrow views about impermanence and non-self. Bhikkhus, study and practice the teaching intelligently in a spirit of non-attachment." And the Buddha taught the bhikkhus the practice of conscious breathing to help them refresh themselves.

When he returned to Savatthi, the Buddha gave further teaching on breaking through attachment in response to a bhikkhu named Arittha, who was bound to narrow views because he also misunderstood the teaching. Sitting before the bhikkhus at Jetavana, the Buddha said, "Bhikkhus, if the teaching is misunderstood, it is possible to become caught in narrow views which will create suffering for oneself and others. You must listen to, understand, and apply the teaching in an intelligent manner. Someone who understands snakes uses a forked stick to pin down a snake's neck before trying to pick it up. If he picks the snake up by the tail or body, the snake can easily bite him. Just as you would use your intelligence in catching a snake, you should use it to study the teaching.

"Bhikkhus, the teaching is merely a vehicle to describe the truth. Don't mistake it for the truth itself. A finger pointing at the moon is not the moon. The finger is needed to know where to look for the moon, but if you mistake the finger for the moon itself, you will never know the real moon.

"The teaching is like a raft that carries you to the other shore. The raft is needed, but the raft is not the other shore. An intelligent person would not carry the raft around on his head after making it across to the other shore. Bhikkhus, my teaching is the raft which can help you cross to the other shore beyond birth and death. Use the raft to cross to the other shore, but don't hang onto it as your property. Do not become caught in the teaching. You must be able to let it go.

"Bhikkhus, all the teaching I have given you, such as the Four Noble Truths, the Noble Eightfold Path, the Four Establishments of Mindfulness, the Seven Factors of Awakening, Impermanence, Non-self, Suffering, Emptiness, Signlessness, and Aimlessness, should be studied in an intelligent, open manner. Use the teachings to help you reach liberation. Do not become attached to them."

The monastery for bhikkhunis housed five hundred nuns. They frequently invited the Buddha and other Venerables from Jetavana to come and give them Dharma talks. Venerable Ananda was asked by the Buddha to be in charge of selecting which monks should go to deliver Dharma talks to the bhikkhunis. One day he assigned Venerable Bhanda to go. Venerable Bhanda had attained deep fruits in his practice, but he was not noted for his speaking talent. The following day, after begging and eating his meal alone in the forest, he went to the bhikkhunis' center. The sisters warmly received him and Bhikkhuni Gotami invited him to sit on the pedestal to give his Dharma talk.

After settling on his cushion, he recited a short poem:
"Dwelling in tranquility,
seeing the Dharma, returning to the source
without hatred or violence,
joy and peace overflow.
Mindfulness is held perfectly;
True peace and ease are realized.
Transcending all desires
is the greatest happiness."
The venerable said no more, but proceeded to enter into a state of deep concentration. Though his words had been few, his presence radiated peace and happiness, which most of the sisters found greatly encouraging. Some of the younger sisters, however, were disappointed by how short his talk was. They urged Bhikkhuni Gotami to ask if he might say something more. Bhikkhuni Gotami bowed to Venerable Bhanda and expressed the wish of the younger sisters. But Venerable Bhanda simply repeated the same poem again and then stepped down from the pedestal.

Some days later, the Buddha was told about Venerable Bhanda's Dharma talk. It was suggested to the Buddha that, in the future, monks more talented at speaking should give the Dharma talks. But the Buddha replied that a person's presence was more important than his words.

One morning after returning from his begging, the Buddha was unable to find Ananda. Venerable Rahula and others said they had not seen him. Then one bhikkhu reported that he had seen Ananda go begging in a nearby village of untouchables. The Buddha asked that bhikkhu to go to the village and look for Ananda. The bhikkhu found Ananda and returned with him to the monastery. He also brought back two women, a mother and her daughter, whose name was Prakriti.

The Buddha listened to Ananda explain how he had been delayed that day. One day several weeks before, on his way back to the monastery after begging, Ananda suddenly felt thirsty. He stopped by the well in the untouchable village for a drink. There he found Prakriti lifting a bucket of water from the well. She was a beautiful young woman. Ananda asked her for a drink of water but she refused. She told him she was an untouchable and did not dare pollute a monk by offering him water.

Ananda told her, "I do not need high rank or caste. I only need a drink of water. I would be happy to receive it from you. Please don't be afraid of polluting me."

Prakriti offered him water at once. She felt drawn to this kind and handsome monk who spoke so gently. She was smitten with love. At night she could not sleep. All her thoughts were of Ananda. She waited by the well every day after that in hopes of catching a glimpse of him. She persuaded her mother to invite him to share a meal in their home. He accepted twice, but sensing that the young woman had fallen in love with him, he refused additional invitations.

Prakriti was lovesick. She grew thin and pale. Finally she confessed her feelings to her mother. She said she wanted Ananda to renounce his vows and marry her. Her shocked mother shouted at her and told her it was a foolish and impossible love. But Prakriti said she would sooner die than give up Ananda. Fearing for her daughter's health, Prakriti's mother prepared an aphrodisiac in hopes she might get Ananda to respond to her daughter's passion. She was from the Matanga clan and knew a number of shamanistic potions.

Prakriti offered Ananda a drink of water from the well.

That morning, Prakriti met Ananda on the street and implored him to accept one last invitation to eat at their home.
Ananda was confident he could offer Prakriti and her mother
teaching that would enable Prakriti to let go of her desire for
him. But he had no chance to teach anything before he drank
the tainted tea. His head began to swim and his limbs went
weak. He realized at once what had happened, and he
turned to his breathing to counteract the effects of the herbs.
The bhikkhu sent by the Buddha found him in Prakriti's hut,
sitting perfectly still in the lotus position.

The Buddha gently asked Prakriti, "You love Bhikkhu
Ananda deeply, don't you?"

Prakriti answered, "I love him with all my heart."

"What is it you love about him? Is it his eyes, his nose, or
perhaps his mouth?"

"I love everything about him—his eyes, his nose, his
mouth, his voice, the way he walks. Master, I love everything about him."

"Besides his eyes, nose, mouth, voice, and walk, Bhikkhu
Ananda possesses many beautiful qualities which you do not
know yet."

"What qualities are those?" asked Prakriti.

The Buddha answered, "His heart of love is one. Do you
know what Bhikkhu Ananda loves?"

"Sir, I do not know what he loves. I only know that he
doesn't love me."

"You are mistaken. Bhikkhu Ananda does love you, but not
in the way you desire. Bhikkhu Ananda loves the path of
liberation, freedom, peace, and joy. Thanks to the liberation
and freedom he experiences, Bhikkhu Ananda often smiles.
He loves all other beings. He wants to bring the path of liberation to all others so that they too may enjoy freedom,
peace, and joy. Prakriti, Bhikkhu Ananda's love comes from
understanding and liberation. He does not suffer or feel hopeless because of his love, unlike the way your love makes you
feel. If you truly love Bhikkhu Ananda, you will understand
his love and you will allow him to continue living the life of

liberation he has chosen. If you knew how to love in the way Bhikkhu Ananda does, you would no longer suffer and feel hopeless. Your suffering and hopelessness result from your wanting Bhikkhu Ananda all to yourself. That is a selfish kind of love."

Prakriti looked at the Buddha and asked, "But how can I love in the way that Bhikkhu Ananda loves?"

"Love in a way that will preserve the happiness of Bhikkhu Ananda as well as your own happiness. Bhikkhu Ananda is like a fresh breeze. If you catch a breeze and trap it in a prison of love, the breeze will soon die and no one will be able to benefit from its coolness, including yourself. Love Ananda as you would a refreshing breeze. Prakriti, if you could love like that, you could become a cool, refreshing breeze yourself. You would relieve your own pains and burdens and those of many others as well."

"Please, Master, teach me how to love in such a way."

"You can choose the same path as Bhikkhu Ananda. You can live a life of liberation, peace, and joy, bringing happiness to others just as Bhikkhu Ananda does. You could be ordained just as he is."

"But I am an untouchable! How can I be ordained?"

"We have no caste in our sangha. Several untouchable men have already been ordained as bhikkhus. Venerable Sunita, so highly regarded by King Pasenadi, was an untouchable. If you wanted to become a bhikkhuni, you would be the first nun to come from the untouchables. If you want, I will ask Sister Khema to perform an ordination ceremony for you."

Overcome with joy, Prakriti prostrated herself before the Buddha and asked to be ordained. The Buddha gave Prakriti into Sister Khema's care. After the nun and young woman departed, the Buddha looked at Ananda and then spoke to the entire community.

"Bhikkhus, Ananda's vows are still intact, but I want all of you to be more careful in your outside relations. If you dwell continuously in mindfulness, you will see what is taking place both within and without you. Detecting something

early on will enable you to deal effectively with it. By practicing mindfulness every moment of your daily life, you will
be able to develop the concentration needed to avoid situations such as this. When your concentration is strong and
stable, your vision will be clear and your actions timely. Concentration and Understanding go hand and hand with each
other. Each contains the other. They are one.

"Bhikkhus, regard women older than yourself as your
mother or elder sister. Regard women younger than yourself
as your younger sister or daughter. Do not let your attractions
create difficulties for your practice. If necessary, until your
concentration is stronger, limit your contacts with women.
Speak only words which relate to the study and practice of
the Way."

The bhikkhus were happy to receive the Buddha's guidance.

A Handful of Precious Earth

One day while out begging in a poor hamlet, the Buddha met some children playing on a dirt path. They were building a city from dirt and sand, complete with a city wall, storehouse, dwellings, and even a river. When the children saw the Buddha and bhikkhus approaching, one child said to the others, "The Buddha and bhikkhus are traveling past our city. It is only proper for us to make an offering to them."

The other children liked the idea, but said, "What do we have to offer the Buddha? We're only children."

The first child answered, "Listen, my friends, there are great reserves of harvested rice in the storehouse of our city of dirt and sand. We can offer some of it to the Buddha."

The other children clapped their hands in delight. They dug out a handful of dirt from their storehouse and, pretending it was rice, placed it on a leaf. The first child lifted the leaf in his two hands and respectfully knelt before the Buddha. The other children knelt beside him. He said, "The people of our city respectfully offer this rice from our storehouse. We pray you will accept it."

The Buddha smiled. He patted the boy on the head and said, "Thank you, children, for offering this precious rice to us. You are most thoughtful."

The Buddha turned to Ananda and said, "Ananda, please take this offering and as soon as we return to the monastery, we can mix it with water and daub it on the earthen bricks of my hut."

Ananda took the handful of earth. The children invited the Buddha to sit with them on a large rock beneath a nearby banyan tree. Ananda and the other bhikkhus gathered around too.

The Buddha told the children a story:

"Many lives ago, there lived a prince named Visvantara. He was a very generous and kind-hearted man. He always shared with the poor and needy, never hesitating to part with anything he owned. His wife, Madri, was equally generous. She knew how much pleasure it gave her husband to help others, and she never expressed any regret about the things he gave away. They had a son named Jalin and a daughter named Krishnajina.

"During a famine, Prince Visvantara asked his father's permission to distribute rice and cloth from the imperial stores to the poor. The king consented. So great was the people's need that the stores were nearly exhausted. This caused alarm to a number of imperial advisors. They wanted to devise a scheme that would prevent the prince from giving any more away. First they told the king that the prince's indiscriminate giving would be the ruin of the kingdom. They revealed that the prince had given away one of the treasured imperial elephants. At this, even the king grew alarmed. He allowed his ministers to talk him into banishing his only son to the remote mountains of Jayatura, where the prince would experience firsthand the hardships of a simple life. Thus, Visvantara, Madri, and the two children were sent into exile.

"On their journey to the mountains, they met a poor beggar. The prince removed his fine jacket and gave it to the man. When they encountered more poor people, Madri removed her own fine jacket and gave it to them. Before long, Jalin and Krishnajina had given away their jackets, as well. The family also gave away their jewels and ornaments to needy people along the route. Before they reached the mountains, they had given away everything they owned that could be traded for food. At last, the prince gave away even their carriage and two horses. The prince carried Jalin, and Madri lifted Krishnajina into her arms. Without regrets, they walked until they reached Jayatura. They walked and sang as though they didn't have a care in the world. Their hearts felt light and free.

It was a long trek, and Visvantara and Madri's feet were swollen and bloody by the time they made it to the remote mountains. They were lucky to find an abandoned hut on the mountain slope. The hut had once belonged to a hermit. They swept and tidied the hut and gathered leafy branches to make beds. In the forest, they found an ample supply of wild fruits and greens to eat. The children learned how to gather food, wash clothes in a mountain spring, sow seeds, and tend a garden. The prince and his wife taught the children how to read and write using large leaves for paper and thorns for pens.

"Though their life was difficult, they were content. For three years they lived in peace. But then one day when Prince Visvantara and Madri were out gathering fruit deep in the forest, a stranger came and kidnapped the children. The prince and his wife searched for many days throughout the forest and in nearby villages, but they could not find a trace of their beloved children.

"Finally, exhausted and discouraged, they returned to their hut, hoping against hope that the children might have returned there on their own. Instead, they were surprised to meet one of the king's messengers waiting for them. They were greatly relieved when he informed them that Jalin and Krishnajina were safe at the palace with the king. When they asked how the children came to be there, the messenger explained, 'Several days ago, one of the palace ladies saw the children being sold at a market in the capital. She recognized them as your children, and she quickly returned to the palace to inform her husband, a royal advisor. He ran to the market and told the merchant to take the children to the palace where he could be assured of receiving a handsome price for them. The king recognized his grandchildren even with their tattered clothes and soiled faces. He realized how deeply he missed you and your family.'

"The king asked, 'Where did you find these children? How much are you selling them for?'

"Before the merchant could respond, the royal advisor spoke, 'Your majesty, the girl is being sold for one thousand pounds of gold and one thousand cattle. The price for the boy is one hundred pounds of gold and one hundred cattle.'

"Everyone, including the merchant and children, were surprised to hear these words. The king asked, 'Why is the girl so much more than the boy?'

"The royal advisor replied, 'You clearly value girls more than boys. You never scold or punish the princesses for any indulgences. Even the palace servant girls are treated with kindness and respect by you. You have only one son and yet you exiled him to a remote mountain region where tigers and leopards roam and where there is nothing but wild fruit to eat. Surely, you value girls more than boys.'

"The king was moved to tears. 'Please say no more. I understand your meaning.'

"The king learned from the merchant that he had bought the children from another man in the mountains. The king paid the merchant and then ordered him to lead the imperial police to the kidnapper. The king embraced his two grandchildren and asked them about their life in the mountains. He issued orders for his son and daughter-in-law to be allowed to return to the capital. From then on, the king cherished his son and generously assisted in the son's efforts to relieve the suffering of the poor."

The children liked the Buddha's story very much. The Buddha smiled at them and said, "Prince Visvantara was happy to share all he owned with others. Today, you shared a handful of precious earth from your city's storehouse with me. You have made me very happy. You can make others happy by offering them some small gift each day. It doesn't have to be something you buy. When you pick a flower by the rice fields and offer it to your parents, you make them happy. A word of thanks or love can also be a precious gift. A kind look or a small gesture of caring brings happiness to others. Offer such gifts every day to your family and friends. The bhikkhus and I must go now, but we will always remember the fine offering you made today."

The children promised they would invite more friends and go visit the Buddha and bhikkhus at Jetavana. They wanted to hear more stories.

The next summer the Buddha returned to Rajagaha to teach. Afterwards he went to Vulture Peak. Jivaka paid him a visit and invited him to spend a few days at the mango grove. The Buddha accepted the invitation, and Ananda joined him. The physician's mango grove was cool and refreshing. The trees were in their eighth year of bearing fruit. Jivaka readied a small hut for the Buddha and prepared vegetarian dishes for him every day. He suggested that the Buddha rest from begging for a few days in order to rebuild his strength. He also prepared an herbal tonic for the Buddha, made from roots, leaves, and fruits.

One day as they sat together, Jivaka said, "Lord, some people say you let the bhikkhus eat meat. They claim that Gautama tolerates the killing of animals to feed himself and his students. Some even make wild accusations that Gautama requires people to offer meat to the sangha. I know these things are not true, but I would appreciate your thoughts on these matters."

The Buddha replied, "Jivaka, people do not speak the truth when they say I allow animals to be killed to provide food for myself and the bhikkhus. I have, in fact, spoken on this matter a number of times. If a bhikkhu sees someone killing an animal for the purpose of offering it as food to the bhikkhu, the bhikkhu must refuse it. Even if he doesn't actually see the animal being killed, but is told it was killed on his behalf, he must refuse it. Furthermore, if he merely suspects it may have been killed on his behalf, he must refuse it. Jivaka, according to the practice of begging, a bhikkhu accepts whatever is offered unless an animal has been killed on the bhikkhu's behalf. People who understand the bhikkhus' vows of compassion offer only vegetarian food to the monks. But sometimes a person only has food that has been prepared with meat. Also, persons who have not had previous contact with the Buddha, the Dharma, and the Sangha do not know that the bhikkhus prefer vegetarian food. In such situations, the bhikkhu accepts whatever is offered to avoid offending the giver and to create an opportunity for contact so that the person may learn about the Path of Liberation.

"Jivaka, some day all the people will understand that bhikkhus do not want animals to be killed. At that time, no one will offer meat to the bhikkhus, and the bhikkhus will be able to eat only vegetarian food."

Jivaka said, "I believe that a vegetarian diet promotes better health. One feels lighter and is less prone to illness. I have been a vegetarian for ten years now. It is good for the health and for nurturing a heart of compassion. I am happy, Lord, for receiving your clear teaching about this."

Jivaka also commended the sangha's practice of being careful not to eat food left over from the previous day. Food kept overnight could spoil and cause illness. The Buddha thanked Jivaka and invited him to come to the monastery to speak to the monks again about basic sanitary practices.

Chapter Fifty-Nine
The Net of Theories

Jivaka's mango grove was tranquil and spacious. Scattered throughout the orchard were small huts for the bhikkhunis. One evening, a young bhikkhuni named Subha came to discuss a problem with the Buddha. She had completed her begging and was returning to the mango grove by way of a deserted street, when suddenly a young man appeared and stood in her way. She sensed his dishonorable intentions, and began to observe her breath in order to remain calm and clear-headed. She looked directly into his eyes and said, "Sir, I am a nun who follows the Way of the Buddha. Please move out of my way so that I may return to my nunnery."

The man said, "You are still young and very pretty. Why waste your life by shaving your head and wearing yellow robes? Why live like an ascetic? Listen, Miss, your lovely body should be clad in a silk sari from Kasi. Why, I've never seen a woman as pretty as you. Let me show you the pleasures of the body. Come with me."

Subha remained calm. "Don't speak foolishly. I seek my happiness in a life of liberation and enlightenment. The five categories of desire only lead to suffering. Allow me to pass. I will be grateful for your understanding."

But the man refused. "Your eyes are so beautiful. I've never seen such beautiful eyes. Don't think I'm foolish enough to let you go. You will come with me."

He reached out to grab her but Subha stepped out of reach and said, "Sir, do not touch me. You must not violate a nun. Because I was weary of a life burdened with craving and hatred, I chose the life of spiritual practice. You say my eyes are beautiful. Very well, I will pluck them out and give them to you. Better to be blind than violated by you."

Subha's voice was full of determination. The man flinched. He knew she was capable of doing what she said. He stepped back. Subha continued, "Don't let your desires cause you to commit crimes. Don't you know that King Bimbisara has issued a decree that anyone who harms a member of the Buddha's sangha will be dealt with severely? If you do not behave properly, if you threaten my chastity or my life, you will be arrested and punished."

Suddenly the young man came to his senses. He saw how blind passion can lead to suffering. He stepped out of the nun's way to let her pass. He called after her, "Please forgive me, Sister. I hope you attain your goal on the spiritual path."

Subha walked on without looking back.

The Buddha praised the young nun for her courage and clarity. He said, "It is dangerous for nuns to walk alone on deserted paths. That is one of the reasons I hesitated initially to ordain women. Subha, from now on, no bhikkhuni should travel alone. Whether crossing a river, entering a village to beg, or walking through a forest or a field, no bhikkhuni should walk alone. No bhikkhuni should sleep alone, either. Whether she sleeps in a nunnery, a small hut, or beneath a tree, no bhikkhuni should sleep by herself. She should always travel and sleep with at least one other bhikkhuni so they can watch out for each other and protect each other."

The Buddha turned to Ananda and instructed him, "Ananda, please make careful note of this new rule. Request all the bhikkhuni elders to place this rule in their precepts."

When the Buddha departed from Jivaka's mango grove, he went to Nalanda, accompanied by a large number of bhikkhus. They all walked slowly and mindfully. Each bhikkhu observed his breath. Behind the bhikkhus traveled two ascetics, Suppiyo and his disciple, Brahmadatta. They spoke in loud voices about the Buddha and his teaching. Suppiyo criticized and ridiculed the Buddha. Oddly enough, his disciple countered his statements by commending the Buddha and his teaching. The disciple spoke eloquently and convincingly to his teacher, moving the bhikkhus who could not help but hear the conversation going on behind them.

That evening the bhikkhus stopped to rest in Ambalatthika, a lush forest that belonged to the royal family. King Bimbisara allowed all spiritual seekers from all sects to stop at Ambalatthika whenever they needed rest. Suppiyo and Brahmadatta stopped the night there.

The next morning, the bhikkhus discussed among themselves the conversation between the two ascetics. The Buddha heard them and said, "Bhikkhus, whenever you hear someone criticize or ridicule me or the Dharma, do not give rise to feelings of anger, irritation, or indignation. Such feelings can only harm yourselves. Whenever you hear someone praise me or the Dharma, do not give rise to feelings of happiness, pleasure, or satisfaction. That too will only harm yourselves. The correct attitude is to examine the criticism to see what parts may be true and what parts are not true. Only by doing that will you have a chance to further your studies and make real progress.

"Bhikkhus, most people who praise the Buddha, Dharma, and Sangha possess only superficial understanding. They appreciate how the bhikkhus lead chaste, simple, and serene lives, but they do not see beyond that. Those who have grasped the most subtle and profound depths of the Dharma speak few words of praise. They understand the true wisdom of enlightenment. Such wisdom is profound, sublime, and marvelous. It transcends all ordinary thoughts and words.

"Bhikkhus, there are countless philosophies, doctrines, and theories in this world. People criticize each other and argue endlessly over their theories. According to my investigation, there are sixty-two main theories which underlie the thousands of philosophies and religions current in our world. Looked at from the Way of Enlightenment and Emancipation, all sixty-two of these theories contain errors and create obstacles."

The Buddha proceeded to explain the sixty-two theories and expose their errors. He spoke on the eighteen theories concerning the past—four theories of eternalism, four theories of partial eternalism, four theories on the finitude and infinity of the world, four theories of endless equivocation, and two theories that claim that causality does not exist. He spoke about the forty-four theories that concern the future— sixteen that allege the soul lives on after death, eight that say there is no soul after death, eight that posit there is neither a soul that continues after death nor ceases to continue after death, seven annihilistic theories, and five theories that say that the present is already Nirvana. After exposing all the errors contained in these theories, the Buddha said, "A good fisherman places his net in the water and catches all the shrimp and fish he can. As he watches the creatures try to leap out of the net, he tells them, 'No matter how high you jump, you will only land in the net again.' He is correct. The thousands of beliefs flourishing at present can all be found in the net of these sixty-two theories. Bhikkhus, don't fall into that bewitching net. You will only waste time and lose your chance to practice the Way of Enlightenment. Don't fall into the net of mere speculation.

"Bhikkhus, all these beliefs and doctrines have arisen because people have been led astray by their perceptions and feelings. When mindfulness is not practiced, it is impossible to see the true nature of perceptions and feelings. When you can penetrate the roots and see into the true nature of your perceptions and feelings, you will see the impermanent and interdependent nature of all dharmas. You will no longer be caught in the net of desire, anxiety, and fear, or the net of the sixty-two false theories."

After the Dharma talk, Venerable Ananda took a walk and focused his attention on recalling every word the Buddha spoke. He thought, "This is an important sutra. I will call it the *Brahmajala Sutra*, the *Sutra of the Great Net*. This net collects all the false theories and dogmas of this world."

Chapter Sixty
Lady Visakha's Grief

After Ambalatthika, the Buddha went to teach in Nalanda, and then to Campa, a large city in the state of Anga. Anga was a populous and fertile region under the jurisdiction of King Bimbisara. There the Buddha dwelled in a cool forest by Gaggara Lake, where many fragrant lotus flowers grew.

People came in great numbers to listen to the Buddha teach. A young, wealthy brahman named Sonadanda also came to meet the Buddha. Sonadanda was known and admired in the region for his astute intelligence. Several of his friends discouraged him from paying a visit to the Buddha. They felt a visit by Sonadanda would grant too much prestige to the monk Gautama. Sonadanda smiled and said that he did not want to pass up an opportunity to meet a man like the Buddha, who was known to possess uncommon insight. Such a chance only presented itself once in a thousand years, he said.

"I must go to deepen my own knowledge," said Sonadanda. "I want to see in which areas Monk Gautama exceeds me and in which areas I exceed Monk Gautama."

Several hundred brahmans decided to join Sonadanda. They walked to Gaggara Lake, placing their faith in Sonadanda. They were sure he would show the teaching of their caste to be superior to that of the Buddha. They knew Sonadanda would not bring shame to the brahmans.

When Sonadanda stood before the Buddha, who was already surrounded by dense crowds, he faltered for a moment, not knowing how to begin. The Buddha assisted him by speaking first. He said, "Sonadanda, can you tell us what characteristics are essential to be a true brahman? If necessary, please cite the *Vedas* as evidence."

Sonadanda was pleased. The Vedas were his particular field of specialty. He said, "Monk Gautama, an authentic brahman possesses five characteristics—an attractive appearance, skill in chanting and performing rituals, purity of blood that can be traced back seven generations, virtuous action, and wisdom."

The Buddha asked, "Of those five characteristics, which are the most essential? Can one still be a true brahman if any of the characteristics are absent?"

Sonadanda reflected and responded that the last two characteristics were the only ones truly indispensable. Physical beauty, skill in chanting and performing rituals, and purity of blood were not absolutely essential. Hearing Sonadanda say this disturbed the five hundred brahmans that had accompanied him. They all stood and shook their arms to challenge Sonadanda's statements. They felt he had been swayed by the Buddha's questioning and that his responses were an embarrassment to their caste.

The Buddha turned to them and said, "Honored guests! If you have faith in Sonadanda, please be quiet and allow him to continue speaking with me. If you no longer have faith in him, ask him to sit down, and I will speak with any one of you instead."

Everyone fell silent. Sonadanda looked at the Buddha and said, "Monk Gautama, please allow me to address a few words to my friends."

Sonadanda turned to his fellows and pointed to a young man sitting in the front row of their ranks. He said, "Do you see my cousin Angaka here? Angaka is a handsome and elegant youth. His demeanor is refined and noble. Few, except Monk Gautama, can compete with his handsome looks. Angaka is also well versed in the *Vedas*. He possesses skill in chanting and performing rituals. He can claim purity of blood traced back seven generations on both sides of his family. No one can deny that he possesses these three characteristics. But let us suppose that Angaka was a drunkard who murdered, robbed, raped, and lied. Of what value would his attractive looks, chanting skills, and purity of blood be then? Dear friends, we must admit that virtuous action and wisdom are the only two characteristics truly essential to be a true brahman. This is a truth for all, not just a private truth for Monk Gautama."

The crowds applauded with approval. When the applause died down, the Buddha asked Sonadanda, "Of these two characteristics, virtuous action and wisdom, is one more essential than the other?"

Sonadanda answered, "Monk Gautama, virtuous action develops from wisdom, and wisdom increases thanks to virtuous action. They cannot be separated. It is like using one hand to wash the other, or using one foot to scratch the other. Virtuous action and wisdom assist and nurture each other. Virtuous action enables wisdom to shine forth. Wisdom enables action to grow ever more virtuous. These two qualities are the most precious things in life."

The Buddha responded, "Excellent, Sonadanda! You speak the truth. Virtuous action and wisdom are the two most precious things in life. Can you tell us more? How can one develop virtuous action and wisdom to the highest degree?"

Sonadanda smiled and joined his palms. He bowed to the Buddha and said, "Master, please guide us. We know the principles, but you are the one who has actually attained the true path. Please tell us how to develop virtuous action and wisdom to the highest degree."

The Buddha spoke to them about the Path of Liberation. He told them of the Three Steps to Enlightenment—Precepts, Concentration, and Understanding. Observing the precepts develops concentration. Concentration leads to understanding. Understanding enables one to practice the precepts more deeply. The more deeply the precepts are observed, the greater one's concentration grows. The greater one's concentration, the deeper one's understanding. The Buddha also spoke about meditating on dependent co-arising in order to break through false concepts of permanence and a separate self. Meditating on dependent co-arising enables one to cut the bonds of greed, anger, and ignorance, in order to attain liberation, peace, and joy.

Sonadanda listened spellbound. When the Buddha was finished, Sonadanda stood up and joined his palms. He said, "Master Gautama, please accept my gratitude. You have opened my eyes today. You have led me out of the darkness. Please allow me to take refuge in the Buddha, the Dharma, and the Sangha. I would also like to invite you and all the bhikkhus to my home tomorrow for a meal offering."

The enthusiastic exchange that took place that day between the Buddha and young Sonadanda sent waves throughout all levels of society in the region. A large number of brahmana intellectuals became disciples of the Buddha in the village of Icchanankala, including a well-known brahman named Ambattha and his teacher Pokkharasadi. As more and more young brahmans became disciples of the Buddha, it became difficult to quell the jealousy and resentment of certain brahmana leaders and leaders of other religious sects.

While they were still staying in Ambalatthika, Svasti asked Venerable Moggallana about the different religious movements of the times. Moggallana summarized the main tenets of each sect for him.

First of all, there was the sect of Purana Kassapa. His followers were skeptical about morals and ethics, maintaining that good and evil were only concepts that resulted from habit and convention.

The followers of Makkhali Gosala were fatalists. They believed that one's lot in life was predetermined and beyond any individual's power to change. If one attained liberation after five hundred or a thousand years of reincarnation, it was due to one's predetermined fate and not to any special efforts.

Ajita Kesakambali taught the doctrine of hedonism. He maintained that humans were comprised of the four elements, earth, water, fire, and air. When one died, nothing remained. According to this sect, one should experience as much pleasure as possible while still alive.

The sect headed by Pakudha Kaccayana took the opposite view. They believed that one's true soul and body could never be destroyed. They claimed that humans were comprised of seven elements—earth, water, fire, air, suffering, happiness, and life energy. Birth and death were merely outward forms that resulted from the temporary combination and dissolution of the seven elements, while one's true essence was immortal and beyond destruction.

Venerables Sariputta and Moggallana had belonged to the sect founded by Sanjaya Belatthiputta. Sanjaya taught a doctrine of relativity. He believed that truth changed according to circumstances, time, and place. What was true for one situation might not be true for another. A person's awareness was the measuring rod of all things.

Nigantha Nataputta led a sect of ascetics who practiced austerities. They did not wear clothes and they strictly observed the precept against killing other living beings. Nigantha taught a kind of dualistic fatalism. He believed that two forces, *jiva* and *ajiva*, or life and non-life, were the basis of the universe. His sect commanded great respect and influence in the society of the times. The bhikkhus frequently came into contact with Nataputta's ascetics. Both communities shared a common respect for life. But there were many differences between the two communities, and some of Nigantha's followers bitterly opposed the bhikkhus. Venerable Moggallana found the views of the ascetics too extreme and he did not hesitate to express his opinion. Because of that, many of the ascetics were particularly hostile to Venerable Moggallana.

The Buddha returned to Savatthi and stayed in Eastern Park. There was a constant stream of visitors. One morning Lady Visakha came to see him. Her hair and clothes were drenched with rain. The Buddha asked her, "Visakha, where have you been? Why are your clothes and hair so wet?"

Lady Visakha wept. "Lord, my little grandson just died. I wanted to come see you, but in my grief I forgot to take my hat or parasol to protect me from the rain."

"How old was your grandson, Visakha? How did he die?"

"Lord, he was only three years old. He died of typhoid fever."

"The poor little one. Visakha, how many children and grandchildren do you have?"

"Lord, I have sixteen children. Nine are married. I had eight grandchildren. Now there are only seven."

"Visakha, you like having a lot of grandchildren, don't you?"

"Oh yes, Lord. The more the better. Nothing would make me happier than to have as many children and grandchildren as there are people in Savatthi."

"Visakha, do you know how many people die each day in Savatthi?"

"Lord, sometimes nine or ten, but at least one person dies every day in Savatthi. There is no day without a death in Savatthi."

"Visakha, if your children and grandchildren were as numerous as the people of Savatthi, your hair and clothes would be as soaked as they are today every day."

Visakha joined her palms. "I understand! I really don't want as many children and grandchildren as there are people in Savatthi. The more attachments one has, the more one suffers. You have often taught me this, but I always seem to forget."

The Buddha smiled gently.

Visakha told him, "Lord, you usually return from your travels only just before the rainy season begins. Your disciples miss you greatly the rest of the year. We come to the monastery but it seems empty without you. We walk around your hut a few times and then return home, not knowing what else to do."

The Buddha said, "Visakha, diligent practice of the teaching is more important than paying visits. When you come to the monastery, you have a chance to listen to other Venerables teach the Dharma. You can ask them questions to assist you in your practice. The teaching and the teacher are one. Please don't neglect your practice simply because I am not here."

Venerable Ananda, who was standing nearby, proposed an idea. "It would be nice to plant a bodhi tree here at the monastery. That way, whenever disciples come to visit and you are gone, they could visit the bodhi tree in your place. They could even bow to it as though bowing to you. We could place a stone altar beneath the tree where disciples could offer flowers. They could walk slowly around the tree while practicing the contemplation of the Buddha."

Lady Visakha said, "That is a wonderful idea! But where will you find a bodhi tree?"

Ananda answered, "I can ask for a seed from the bodhi tree in Uruvela where the Buddha attained Awakening. Don't worry. I will acquire the seed, sprout it, and tend the tree."

Lady Visakha felt lighter and comforted. She bowed to the Buddha and to Venerable Ananda and then returned home.

Chapter Sixty-One

The Lion's Roar

That same retreat season, Ananda asked a question about dependent co-arising, and so the Buddha taught the bhikkhus about the twelve links in the chain of existence.

He explained, "The teaching on dependent co-arising is most profound and subtle. Do not think it can be grasped through words and discourse. Bhikkhus, thanks to hearing the teaching on dependent co-arising, Venerable Uruvela Kassapa entered the path of true Dharma. Venerable Sariputta, another of our most respected brothers, entered the path thanks to hearing a gatha concerning dependent co-arising. Contemplate the nature of dependent co-arising during every moment. When you look at a leaf or a raindrop, meditate on all the conditions, near and distant, that have contributed to the presence of that leaf or raindrop. Know that the world is woven of interconnected threads. This is, because that is. This is not, because that is not. This is born, because that is born. This dies, because that dies.

"The birth and death of any dharma are connected to the birth and death of all other dharmas. The one contains the many and the many contains the one. Without the one, there cannot be the many. Without the many, there cannot be the one. This is the marvelous truth of the teaching on dependent co-arising. If you look deeply into the nature of all dharmas, you will be able to transcend all anxiety concerning birth and death. You will break through the circle of birth and death.

"Bhikkhus, the interconnected links consist of many layers and levels, but four realms can be distinguished—chief causes, contributory causes, the immediately-preceding-moment as cause, and objects as cause.

"A chief cause is the first condition necessary to give rise to a phenomenon. For example, a grain of rice is the chief cause necessary to give rise to a rice plant. Contributory causes are supportive conditions. In the case of a grain of rice, these include sun, rain, and earth which enable the seed to grow into a rice plant.

"The immediately-preceding-moment as cause is an uninterrupted process and serves as an underlying cause. Without this continual process, the rice plant's growth would be interrupted before reaching fruition. Objects as cause refer to objects of consciousness. A grain of rice and all the near and distant conditions that make the presence of the rice plant possible are objects of consciousness. They cannot be separated from consciousness. Mind is a basic condition for the existence of all dharmas.

"Bhikkhus, suffering exists because of the presence of birth and death. What gives rise to birth and death? Ignorance. Birth and death are first of all mental notions. They are the product of ignorance. If you look deeply and penetrate the causes of all things, you will overcome ignorance. Once you have overcome ignorance, you will transcend all thoughts of birth and death. Transcending all thoughts of birth and death, you will overcome all anxieties and sorrows.

"Bhikkhus, there is the concept of death because there is the concept of birth. These wrong views are based on a false view of the self. There is a false view of the self because there is grasping. There is grasping because there is desire. There is desire because one does not see into the true nature of feelings. One does not see into the true nature of feelings because one is caught up in the contact that takes place between the sense organs and their objects. One is caught up in the contact that takes place between the sense organs and their objects because one's mind is not clear and calm. One's mind is not clear and calm because there are drives and impulses. These drives and impulses are due to ignorance. These twelve links of the chain of existence are connected to each other. In each link, you can see the other eleven links. If one link is missing, the other eleven will be missing. These twelve links are Death, Birth, Becoming, Grasping, Craving, Feelings, Contact, the Six Sense Organs, Name and Form, Consciousness, Drives and Impulses, and Ignorance.

"Bhikkhus, ignorance underlies all twelve links of the chain of existence. Thanks to the contemplation on the nature of dependent co-arising, we can dispel ignorance in order to transcend all anxieties and sorrows. An enlightened person walks over the waves of birth and death and does not drown in them. An enlightened person uses the twelve links of the chain of existence like the wheels of a carriage. An enlightened person lives in the very midst of the world but is never submerged by it. Bhikkhus, do not try to run away from birth and death. You need only rise above them. Transcending birth and death is the attainment of Great Beings."

In a Dharma discussion several days later, Venerable Mahakassapa reminded the community that the Buddha had given the teaching on dependent co-arising many times in the past, and that this teaching could be considered the heart of the Way of Awakening. He reminded the community that the Buddha had once used a bunch of reeds to illustrate the teaching on dependent co-arising. The Lord had said that things do not need a creator, that they arise from one another. Ignorance causes drives and impulses, and drives and impulses cause ignorance, just as reeds lean on one another to stand, and if one reed falls, the other reeds also fall. This is true of all things in the universe—the one creates the many, and the many the one. If we look deeply, we can see the one in the many and the many in the one.

During that same retreat season, several brahmans conspired to falsely accuse the Buddha of sleeping with a woman and making her pregnant. They found an attractive, young brahmana woman named Cinca and told her that the

Buddha had caused a rapid decline in the faith of their ancestors by luring many young men to become his disciples. Anxious to protect her faith, Cinca agreed to the plan.

Every day she went to Jetavana dressed in a beautiful sari and carrying a fresh bouquet of flowers. She did not arrive in time for the Dharma talks, but waited outside the Dharma hall as people left to return home. At first, whenever anyone asked her where she was going or what she was doing, she only smiled. After several days, she answered coyly, "I'm going where I'm going." After several weeks of such vague comments, she began to answer, "I'm going to visit Monk Gautama." And finally, she was heard to exclaim, "Sleeping at Jetavana is delightful!"

Such words burned the ears of many people. Some laypeople began to feel doubts and suspicions, but no one said anything. One day, Cinca came to one of the Buddha's Dharma talks. Her belly was noticeably round. In the middle of the Buddha's discourse, she stood up and loudly said, "Teacher Gautama! You speak eloquently about the Dharma. You are held in high esteem. But you care nothing for this poor woman made pregnant by you. The child I carry is your own. Are you going to take responsibility for your own child?"

A wave of shock passed through the community. Everyone looked up at the Buddha. The Buddha only smiled calmly and replied, "Miss, only you and I can know whether or not your claims are true."

The Buddha's calm smile made Cinca feel uneasy, but she retorted, "That's right, only you and I know whether my claims are true."

The community could no longer suppress their astonishment. Several people stood up in anger. Cinca suddenly felt afraid the people would beat her. She looked for a way to escape, but in her panic, she ran into a post and stumbled. As she strained to stand back up, a large round block of wood fell from where it was tied onto her abdomen, and landed on her foot. She cried out in pain and grabbed her crushed toes. Her stomach was now perfectly flat.

A sigh of relief rose from the crowd. Several people began laughing and others derided Cinca. Bhikkhuni Khema stood up and gently assisted Cinca out of the hall. When the two women were gone, the Buddha resumed his Dharma talk as if nothing had happened.

The Buddha spoke, "Community, the Way of Enlightenment can tear down the walls of ignorance, just as light can disperse the shadows. The Four Noble Truths, Impermanence, Non-self, Dependent Co-arising, the Four Establishments of Mindfulness, the Seven Factors of Awakening, the Three Gates, and the Noble Eightfold Path have all been proclaimed to the world like a lion's roar, dispelling countless false doctrines and narrow views. The lion is king of the beasts. When he leaves his den, he stretches and gazes out over all the directions. Before seeking his prey, he lets forth a mighty roar that causes the other creatures to tremble and flee. Birds fly high, crocodiles dive beneath the water, foxes slip into their holes. Even village elephants, decked in fancy belts and ornaments and shaded by golden parasols, run away at the sound of that roar.

"Community, the proclamation of the Way of Enlightenment is like that lion's roar! False doctrines fear and tremble. When Impermanence, Non-self, and Dependent Co-arising are proclaimed, all those who have long sought false security in ignorance and forgetfulness must awaken, celestial beings as well as human beings. When a person sees the dazzling truth, he exclaims, 'We embraced dangerous views for so long, taking the impermanent to be permanent, and believing in the existence of a separate self. We took suffering to be pleasure and look at the temporary as if it were eternal. We mistook the false for the true. Now the time has come to tear down all the walls of forgetfulness and false views.'

"Community, the Way of Enlightenment allows humanity to remove the thick veil of false views. When an enlightened person appears, the Way echoes like the majestic sound of the rising tide. When the tide rises, all false views are swept away.

"Community, people are easily caught by four traps. The first is attachment to sensual desires. The second is attachment to narrow views. The third is doubt and suspicion. The fourth is false view of self. The Way of Enlightenment helps people overcome the four great traps.

"Community, the teaching on dependent co-arising will enable you to overcome every obstacle and trap. Contemplate the nature of interdependence in your daily life—in your body, feelings, mind, and objects of mind."

The next day in the main hall, Ananda repeated the Buddha's Dharma talk. He named it *Sutra of the Lion's Roar*.

That retreat season, many bhikkhus fell ill with malaria. Many grew thin and pale and no longer had the strength to go out begging for themselves. Other bhikkhus readily shared their food with them, but much of the food contained rice and curry, which was too harsh on the stomachs of the sick. The Buddha gave permission to lay disciples to prepare special dishes for the sick bhikkhus. They cooked food that was easily digested, such as rice porridge with wholesome ingredients like honey, milk, cane sugar, and oil. Thanks to these foods, the bhikkhus slowly regained their health.

One day after sitting meditation, the Buddha heard the squawking of a great number of crows. When he went to investigate, he found a number of bhikkhus tossing the special foods prepared for the sick bhikkhus to the crows. They explained that a number of brothers had felt too ill to eat that morning. The hour of noon had passed and the bhikkhus were not to partake of food after noon. When the Buddha asked why they didn't save the special foods for the following day, he was reminded that food was not to be kept overnight. The Buddha told them that sick bhikkhus could be relieved of the precept not to eat anything after the noon hour, and if certain foods would keep, they could be saved overnight.

Not long after, a physician from the capital paid a visit to the Venerable Sariputta. He suggested that sick bhikkhus be served a dish of special herbs and ingredients. Thanks to that, the bhikkhus regained their health more quickly.

Chapter Sixty-Two
Sariputta's Roar

W hen the retreat season ended, Venerable Sariputta bid farewell to the Buddha before traveling to spread the Dharma. The Buddha wished him a calm and safe journey, and a body and mind free of all cares. He said he hoped Sariputta's efforts to spread the Dharma would not meet with too many obstacles. Venerable Sariputta thanked the Lord and then departed.

That noon a bhikkhu came to the Buddha and complained of being mistreated by Sariputta. He said, "I asked Venerable Sariputta where he was going. He refused to answer me, and in fact, pushed me out of his way so hard that I was knocked to the ground. He made no apology but continued on his way."

The Buddha turned to Ananda and said, "I do not think Sariputta will have traveled too far yet. Send one of the novices after him. Tonight we will hold a community meeting in Jeta Dharma Hall."

Ananda did as the Buddha asked, and by late afternoon Venerable Sariputta had returned to the monastery with the novice. The Buddha told him, "Sariputta, tonight the entire community will meet in the Dharma hall. A bhikkhu has accused you of knocking him to the ground without apologizing."

That afternoon Venerables Moggallana and Ananda visited all corners of the monastery to announce the evening meeting. They said, "You are invited to attend a meeting in the Dharma hall tonight. Tonight Brother Sariputta will have a chance to offer his lion's roar."

Not one bhikkhu was absent from the hall that evening. Everyone wanted to see how Sariputta would respond to those who had for so long begrudged his position in the sangha. Venerable Sariputta was one of the Buddha's most trusted disciples, and because of that he was the object of much misunderstanding and jealousy. Some of the bhikkhus felt the Buddha placed too much trust in Sariputta. They felt Sariputta wielded too great an influence. When some bhikkhus were corrected by the Buddha, they mistakenly blamed Sariputta for pointing out their errors to the Buddha. Some bhikkhus felt almost a hatred for Sariputta. They were unable to forget that some years before, the Buddha had invited Sariputta to share his seat.

Venerable Ananda recalled one monk named Kokalika, who had lived at Jetavana eight years earlier. Kokalika hated Sariputta and Moggallana so much that not even the Buddha himself could persuade him otherwise. Kokalika said that Sariputta and Moggallana were both hypocrites whose actions were motivated by ambition. The Buddha met privately with him and said that these two elders were sincere and that their actions arose from loving kindness. But Kokalika's mind was filled with jealousy and hatred, and finally, he left the monastery, joined the Venerable Devadatta in Rajagaha, and became one of Devadatta's closest associates.

It was because of these kinds of problems that Ananda had been reluctant to accept the responsibility of becoming the Buddha's attendant. Without the conditions he had suggested, such as not sleeping in the same room or sharing the same food with the Buddha, Ananda knew that many brothers would resent him also. Some brothers felt they did not receive enough of the Buddha's attention. Ananda knew that such feelings could lead to anger and hatred, and could even lead some to abandon the Buddha, their teacher.

Ananda also recalled a woman in Kalmashadamya Village in Kosambi named Magandika, who grew to hate the Buddha when she did not receive special attention from him. She was a beautiful brahmana woman. The Buddha was forty-four years old when she met him. She was immediately attracted to him and as her feelings grew stronger, she longed to know if the Buddha felt any special regard for her. Magandika did everything she could think of to receive his special attention, but the Buddha treated her as he did everyone else. In the end, her affections turned to hatred. When she later became the wife of King Udena of Vatsa, she used her position and influence to spread rumors and insults about the Buddha. She even pressured the authorities into forbidding the Buddha to give public Dharma talks. When Samavati, a beloved concubine of King Udena, became a disciple of the Buddha, Magandika found ways to make her suffer. Disturbed by all of this, Ananda suggested to the Buddha that they leave Kosambi to spread the Dharma in a more hospitable place. The Buddha asked him, "If we go somewhere else and meet with insult and difficulty there too, what should we do?"

Ananda replied, "Move on to some other place."

The Buddha disagreed. "That would not be correct, Ananda. We must not become discouraged every time we meet with difficulty. Solutions should be sought in the very midst of hardship. Ananda, if we practice equanimity, we will not be bothered by insults and slander. The people who slander us cannot harm us. They only harm themselves. When a man spits at the sky, the sky is not sullied. The spit falls back in the face of the one who spat."

Ananda had no worries about Sariputta's ability to deal with the present situation. Venerable Sariputta was rightfully trusted by the Buddha. He was a truly virtuous and worthy elder of the sangha. Because of his deep insight, the Buddha depended on his help in guiding the sangha. He was the author of several sutras, including the *Hatthipadopama Sutta*—the *Sutra on the Elephant's Footprints*—in which he spoke about the relation of the four elements to the five aggregates in an original way, based on the fruits of his own practice.

When the Buddha entered the Dharma hall, all the bhikkhus rose to their feet. He motioned for them to be seated again and then sat down himself. He motioned to Venerable Sariputta to sit on a low chair placed next to him. The Buddha spoke to Sariputta, "A bhikkhu has accused you of knocking him down and not apologizing. Do you have anything to say about this?"

Venerable Sariputta stood and joined his palms. He bowed first to the Buddha and then to the community. He said, "Lord, a monk who does not practice, who does not contemplate the body in the body, who is not mindful of the actions of the body, such a monk could knock down a fellow monk and leave him there without apologizing.

"Lord, I still remember the lesson you gave fourteen years ago to Bhikkhu Rahula. He was only eighteen years old at the time. You taught him to contemplate the nature of earth, water, fire, and air in order to nourish and develop the four virtues of loving kindness, compassion, joy, and equanimity. Although your teaching was directed at Rahula, I learned from it also. I have made efforts to observe that teaching throughout the past fourteen years and I have often thanked you inwardly.

"Lord, I have practiced to be more like earth. Earth is wide and open, and has the capacity to receive and transform. Whether people toss pure and fragrant substances such as flowers, perfume, or fresh milk upon the earth, or toss unclean and foul-smelling substances such as excrement, urine, blood, mucus, and spit upon it, the earth receives it all equally with neither grasping nor aversion.

"Lord, I have contemplated to make my mind and body more like the earth. A monk who does not contemplate the body in the body, who is not mindful of the actions of the body, such a monk could knock down a brother monk and leave him without apologizing. Such is not my way.

"Lord, I have practiced to be more like water. Whether someone pours fragrant substances or defiled substances into water, the water receives them both without grasping or aversion. Water is immense and flowing and has the capacity to transform and purify. Respected Buddha, I have contemplated to make my body and mind more like water. A monk who does not contemplate the body in the body, who is not mindful of the actions of the body, such a monk could knock down a brother monk and leave him without apologizing. Such is not my way.

"Lord, I have practiced to be more like fire. Fire burns all things, the beautiful as well as the impure, without grasping or aversion. Fire has the ability to burn, purify, and transform. Respected Buddha, I have contemplated to make my body and mind more like fire. A monk who does not contemplate the body in the body, who is not mindful of the actions of the body, such a monk could knock down a brother monk and leave him without apologizing. Such is not my way.

"Lord, I have practiced to be more like air. The air carries all manner of smells, good and bad, without grasping or aversion. Air has the capacity to transform, purify, and release. Respected Buddha, I have contemplated to make my body and mind become more like the air. A monk who does not contemplate the body in the body, who is not mindful of the actions of the body, such a monk could knock down a brother monk and leave him without apologizing. Such is not my way.

"Lord, like a small untouchable child with tattered clothes who clasps a bowl and begs in the street for scraps of food, I practice to hold no false pride or arrogance. I have tried to make my heart like the heart of an untouchable child's heart. I have tried to practice humility, not daring to place myself higher than others. Respected Buddha, a monk who does not contemplate the body in the body, who is not mindful of the actions of the body, such a monk could knock down a brother monk and leave him without apologizing. Such is not my way."

Venerable Sariputta was prepared to continue speaking, but his accuser could bear no more. He stood up and draped a corner of his sanghati robe over his shoulder, and then bowed to the Buddha. With his palms joined, he confessed, "Lord Buddha, I have violated the precepts. I have born false witness against Venerable Sariputta. I confess my transgression before you and the entire community. I vow to observe my precepts in the future."

The Buddha said, "It is good that you have confessed your transgression before the community. We accept your confession."

Venerable Sariputta joined his palms and said, "I bear no grudge against my brother, and I ask him to forgive anything I may have done to upset him in the past."

The bhikkhu bowed to Sariputta with his palms joined. Sariputta returned his bow. Happiness filled the Dharma hall. Venerable Ananda stood up and said, "Brother Sariputta, please stay with us for a few more days. Your brothers would welcome a chance to spend more time with you."

Venerable Sariputta smiled his acceptance.

With the retreat season over, the Buddha traveled to many villages in the countryside. One day he spoke in Kesaputta, a village which belonged to the Kalama clan. Many young people gathered to hear him. They had all heard about the Monk Gautama but this was the first opportunity they had to meet him in person.

One young man joined his palms and spoke, "Teacher, for a long time, many brahmana priests have come to Kesaputta in order to teach their various doctrines. Each priest claims that his doctrine is superior to others' doctrines. This has confused us. We do not know which path to follow. In fact, we have lost faith in all the doctrines. We have heard that you are an enlightened Master. Can you tell us whom we should believe and whom we should not? Who speaks the truth and who is merely spreading false doctrines?"

The Buddha answered, "I can understand why you have given rise to doubts. Friends, do not be hasty to believe a thing even if everyone repeats it, or even if it is written in holy scripture or spoken by a teacher revered by the people. Accept only those things which accord with your own reason, things which the wise and virtuous support, things which in practice bring benefit and happiness. Abandon those things which do not accord with your own reason, which are not supported by the wise and virtuous, and which in practice do not bring benefit and happiness."

The Kalamas asked the Buddha to tell them more. He said, "Friends, suppose there is a person ruled by greed, anger, and ignorance. Will his greed, anger, and ignorance bring him happiness or suffering?"

The people answered, "Master, greed, anger, and ignorance will cause such a person to commit acts that bring suffering to himself and others."

"Is living by greed, anger, and ignorance supported by the wise and virtuous?"

"No, Master."

The Buddha continued, "Take the example of someone who lives according to loving kindness, compassion, sympathetic joy, and equanimity, who makes others happy by relieving their suffering, who rejoices over the good fortune of others, and who treats others without discrimination. Will such qualities bring that person happiness or suffering?"

"Teacher, such qualities will bring happiness to the person and to all those around him."

"Are loving kindness, compassion, joy, and equanimity supported and encouraged by the wise and virtuous?"

"Yes, Master."

"My friends, you are already qualified to discern which things to accept and which things to discard. Believe and accept only those things which accord with your own reason, those things which are supported by the wise and virtuous, and those things which in practice bring benefit and happiness to yourselves and others. Discard things which oppose these principles."

The Kalama youth were encouraged by the Buddha's words. They saw that his teaching did not require unconditional faith. The Buddha's way truly respected freedom of thought. Many of the Kalamas asked to be accepted by the Buddha as disciples that day.

Chapter Sixty-Three
All the Way to the Sea

During his travels, the Buddha stopped in the village of Alavi. The Buddha and eight bhikkhus were offered a meal in a public building there, while all the local people were served food as well. Following the meal, the Buddha was about to begin a Dharma talk, when an elderly farmer, almost out of breath, entered the hall. He was late because he'd had to search for a lost water buffalo. The Buddha could see that the old farmer had not eaten all day, and he asked that rice and curry be served to the old man before he would begin the Dharma talk. Many people felt impatient. They did not understand why one man should be allowed to hold up the Buddha's discourse.

When the farmer was finished eating, the Buddha said, "Respected Friends, if I delivered a Dharma talk while our brother was still hungry, he would not be able to concentrate. That would be a pity. There is no greater suffering than hunger. Hunger wastes our bodies and destroys our well-being, peace, and joy. We should never forget those who are hungry. It is a discomfort to miss one meal, but think of the suffering of those who have not had a proper meal in days or even weeks. We must find ways to assure that no one in this world is forced to go hungry."

After Alavi, the Buddha followed the Ganga northwest towards Kosambi. He paused to watch a piece of driftwood being carried downstream. He called to the other bhikkhus, pointed to the piece of wood, and said, "Bhikkhus! If that piece of driftwood does not become lodged against the riverbank, if it does not sink, if it does not become moored on a sandbar, if it isn't lifted out of the water, if it isn't caught in a whirlpool, or rot from the inside out, it will float all the way to the sea. It is the same for you on the path. If you don't become lodged against the riverbank, if you don't sink, if you don't become moored on a sandbar, if you are not lifted out of the water, if you do not become caught in a whirlpool, or rot from the inside out, you are certain to reach the great sea of enlightenment and emancipation."

The bhikkhus said, "Please, Lord, explain this more fully. What does it mean to become lodged against the riverbank, to sink, or to be moored on a sandbar?"

The Buddha answered, "To become lodged against the riverbank is to become entangled by the six senses and their objects. If you practice diligently, you will not become entangled in feelings which result from contact between the senses and their objects. To sink means to become enslaved by desire and greed, which rob you of the strength needed to persevere in your practice. To become moored on a sandbar means to worry about serving only your own desires, forever seeking advantages and prestige for yourself while forgetting the goal of enlightenment. To be lifted from the water means to lose yourself in dispersion, loitering with people of poor character instead of pursuing the practice. To be caught in a whirlpool means to be bound by the five categories of desire—being caught by good food, sex, money, fame, or sleep. To rot from the inside out means to live a life of false virtue, deceiving the sangha while using the Dharma to serve your own desires.

"Bhikkhus, if you practice diligently and avoid these six traps, you will certainly attain the fruit of enlightenment, just as that piece of driftwood will make it to the sea if it overcomes all obstacles."

As the Buddha spoke these words to the bhikkhus, a youth tending water buffaloes nearby stopped to listen. His name was Nanda. He was so moved by the Buddha's words, that he approached the bhikkhus and asked to be accepted as a disciple. He said, "Teacher, I want to be a bhikkhu like these brothers. I want to follow the spiritual path. I promise to devote myself to studying the Way. I will avoid becoming caught against the riverbank, sinking, becoming moored on a sandbar, being lifted from the water, becoming caught in a whirlpool, and rotting from the inside out. Please accept me as a disciple."

The Buddha was pleased by the young man's bright countenance. He knew the young man was capable and diligent, although he had probably had little or no schooling. The Buddha nodded his acceptance and asked, "How old are you?"

Nanda answered, "Master, I am sixteen."

"Are your parents living?"

"No, Master, they are both dead. I have no other family. I take care of a rich man's water buffaloes in exchange for shelter."

The Buddha asked, "Can you live on just one meal a day?"

"I have been doing that already for a long time."

The Buddha said, "In principle, you should be twenty years old before being accepted into the sangha. Most young men are not mature enough to live the life of a homeless monk until they are at least twenty. But you are clearly special. I will ask the community to waive the usual requirement in your case. You can practice as a samanera novice for four years before taking the full precepts. Return the water buffaloes and ask your master's permission to leave his employment. We will wait here for you."

The youth replied, "Master, I do not think that will be necessary. These buffaloes are very obedient. They will return to the stable on their own even without my assistance."

The Buddha said, "No, you must lead them back yourself and speak to your master before you can join us."

"But what if you are gone by the time I return?"

The Buddha smiled. "Do not worry. You have my word that we will wait here for you."

While Nanda led the buffaloes back to their stable, the Buddha spoke with Svasti. "Svasti, I will place this young man under your care. I believe you understand best how to guide and support him."

Svasti joined his palms and smiled. Venerable Svasti was thirty-nine years old now. He knew why the Buddha wanted him to be young Nanda's instructor. Long ago, the Buddha delivered the *Sutra on Tending Water Buffaloes*, after being inspired by his friendship with Svasti when Svasti was a buffalo boy like Nanda. Svasti knew he could guide Nanda well on the path. He knew that his closest friend, Venerable Rahula, would assist him also. Rahula was now thirty-six.

Svasti's siblings were all grown with families of their own. The hut they once shared had long since perished. Svasti recalled with a smile the visit he made to Uruvela one year with Rahula. It was after Rupak had married and moved to another village. At that time Bhima and Bala still lived together and supported themselves by making and selling cakes. Bhikkhus Svasti and Rahula walked to the Neranjara River. Svasti had not forgotten his promise to give Rahula the experience of riding on a water buffalo, and so he called to some young buffalo boys who were grazing their buffaloes near the riverbanks. He asked them to help Bhikkhu Rahula climb onto the back of one of the great beasts. At first Rahula hesitated, but then he removed his sanghati and handed it to Svasti. Rahula was touched by how gentle the mighty beast was. He shared his impressions of the leisurely ride with Svasti, and he wondered aloud what the Buddha would think if he could see him. Svasti smiled. He knew that if Rahula had remained in the Sakya palace to one day become king, he would never have enjoyed this water buffalo ride.

Svasti returned to the present moment just as young Nanda arrived. That night he shaved Nanda's hair and showed him how to wear the robe, carry the begging bowl, walk, stand, lie down, and sit as a mindful bhikkhu. Nanda was mature and diligent, and Svasti enjoyed helping him.

Bhikkhu Rahula handed his robe to Svasti, so that he could ride on the back of the water buffalo.

He recalled how some years ago, seventeen young people had been accepted into the sangha at Bamboo Forest. The oldest boy, Upali, was seventeen and the youngest only twelve. They were all from wealthy families. When Upali asked his parents to allow him to become a bhikkhu and they agreed, sixteen of his friends implored their parents to let them do the same. Once they joined the sangha, they were expected to follow the life of a bhikkhu, including eating only one meal before noon. The first night, several of the youngest boys cried from hunger. When the Buddha asked the next morning why he heard children crying in the night, he was told about the boys being accepted into the community. The Buddha said, "Henceforth, we will accept only young men who are at least twenty years of age into the sangha. Children cannot be expected to live the life of a homeless monk."

The boys were allowed to stay, but the Buddha asked that those fifteen years old and younger be given an additional meal in the evening. All the boys remained bhikkhus. The youngest one, Svasti realized, was already twenty now.

Chapter Sixty-Four
The Round of Birth and Death

One day while sitting in Bhesakala Park in Sumsumaragiri, the Buddha spoke to the bhikkhus, "Bhikkhus, I want to tell you about the Eight Realizations of Great Beings. Venerable Anuruddha has spoken about these eight realizations before. They are the realizations taught by Great Beings to help others overcome forgetfulness and attain enlightenment.

"The first realization is the awareness that all dharmas are impermanent and without a separate self. By contemplating on the impermanent and non-self nature of all dharmas, you can escape suffering and attain enlightenment, peace, and joy.

"The second realization is the awareness that more desire brings more suffering. All hardships in life arise from greed and desire."

"The third realization is the awareness that living simply, having few desires, leads to peace, joy, and serenity. Living simply allows for more time and concentration to practice the Way and to help others.

"The fourth realization is the awareness that only diligent effort leads to enlightenment. Laziness and indulging in sensual desires are obstacles to the practice.

"The fifth realization is the awareness that ignorance is the cause of the endless round of birth and death. You must always remember to listen and learn in order to develop your understanding and eloquence.

"The sixth realization is the awareness that poverty creates hatred and anger, which in turn create a vicious cycle of negative thoughts and actions. Followers of the Way, when practicing generosity, should consider everyone, friends and enemies alike, as equal, not condemning anyone's past wrongdoings or hating those who are presently causing harm.

"The seventh realization is the awareness that although we dwell in the world to teach and assist others, we should not become caught up in worldly matters. One who leaves home to follow the Way possesses only three robes and a bowl. He always lives simply and looks at all beings with the eyes of compassion.

"The eighth realization is the awareness that we do not practice for our individual enlightenment alone, but devote our whole being to guiding all others to the gates of enlightenment.

"Bhikkhus, these are the Eight Realizations of the Great Beings. All Great Beings, thanks to these eight realizations, have attained enlightenment. Wherever they go in life, they use these eight realizations to open minds and educate others, so that everyone may discover the path that leads to enlightenment and emancipation."

When he returned to Bamboo Forest in Rajagaha, the Buddha was informed that Bhikkhu Vakkali was gravely ill and hoped to see the Buddha before he died. Vakkali's attendant came to see the Buddha. After bowing three times, he said, "Lord, my teacher is very ill. He is staying in the home of a lay disciple who is a potter. He asked me to come bow before you in his place."

The Buddha turned to Ananda and said, "We will go at once to visit Venerable Vakkali."

When he saw the Buddha enter the room, Bhikkhu Vakkali made a great effort to sit up.

"Please, Vakkali," said the Buddha, "don't try to sit up. Ananda and I will sit close by the bed on these chairs."

After he and Ananda were seated, the Buddha said, "Vakkali, I hope your strength is improving and that the pains in your body are easing."

"Lord, my strength is rapidly declining. I am most uncomfortable. The pains are growing more severe."

"I hope then that you do not suffer from any worries or regrets."

"Lord, I do suffer from worries and regrets."

"I hope your regrets are not about violating your precepts."

"No, Lord, I have observed my precepts fully and feel no shame."

"What then do you worry about and regret?"

"I regret that, due to my illness, it has been a long time since I have been able to visit you."

The Buddha gently scolded, "Vakkali, do not worry about such things. You have lived a blameless life. That is what keeps teacher and student close. Do you think you need to see my face in order to see the Buddha? This body is not important. Only the teaching is important. If you can see the teaching, you can see the Buddha. If you can see this body but not the teaching, it is of no value at all."

After a moment of silence, the Buddha asked, "Vakkali, do you understand how impermanent the body is, mine as well as yours?"

"Lord, I see that most clearly. The body is constantly being born, dying, and transforming. I see how feelings are also impermanent, constantly being born, dying, and transforming. Perceptions, mental formations, and consciousness follow the same law of birth and death. All are impermanent. Before your visit today, I contemplated deeply on the impermanent nature of the five skandhas. I have seen that there is nothing in the five rivers of form, feelings, perceptions, mental formations, or consciousness that contains a separate self."

"Wonderful, Vakkali! I have faith in you. Nothing in the five skandhas contains a separate self. Open your eyes and look. Where is Vakkali not present? What is not Vakkali? The wonder of life is everywhere. Vakkali, birth and death cannot touch you. Smile at your body comprised of the four elements. Smile even at the pain rising and falling in your body."

Tears glistened in Vakkali's eyes and he smiled. The Buddha stood up and took his leave. When the Buddha and Ananda were gone, Vakkali asked his friends to carry him on his bed to Isigili mountain. He said, "How can someone like me die in a room? I want to die on the mountainside beneath the spacious skies."

His friends carried him to Isigili. That night the Buddha meditated deep into the night. In the early hours of the morning, he told a number of bhikkhus he met near his hut, "Go visit Vakkali and tell him there is nothing to fear. His death will be peaceful and blameless. Tell him to put his heart at rest. I have great faith in him."

When the bhikkhus found Venerable Vakkali at Isigili, they told him they carried a message from the Buddha. Vakkali said, "Please, friends, lift me off this bed and place me on the earth. How can I lie on a high bed while receiving the Lord Buddha's words?"

They did as he asked and then repeated the Buddha's words. Vakkali joined his palms and said, "Please, brothers, when you return to the monastery, bow three times to the Buddha on my behalf and tell him that Bhikkhu Vakkali is deathly ill and in terrible pain. Vakkali sees clearly that the five skandhas are impermanent and without a separate self. Vakkali is no longer bound by the five skandhas. In his last moments, Vakkali has released all fears and worries."

The bhikkhus said, "Brother, ease your heart. We will return and bow three times to the Buddha and speak your last words to him."

The bhikkhus were no sooner out of sight than Bhikkhu Vakkali passed away.

That afternoon the Buddha climbed Isigili with several bhikkhus. The blue sky was cloudless. Only a thin strand of smoke curled up into the sky from a hut at the foot of the mountain. It drifted for a moment and then vanished. Looking at the vast round sky, the Buddha said, "Vakkali has been liberated. No delusion or phantom can disturb him now."

The Buddha again traveled, this time to Nalanda and Vesali. One day, at the Kutagara monastery in the Great Woods, the Buddha told the bhikkhus, "As living beings, people have to suffer, more or less. However, those who devote themselves to the study and practice of the Dharma suffer much less than others, because they possess understanding, the fruit of their practice."

That day it was still very hot, but the Buddha was seated with his bhikkhus in the shade of many beautiful sala trees. He picked up a small piece of earth, held it between his thumb and forefinger, and asked, "Bhikkhus, if we compare this piece of earth with Gayasisa mountain, which is larger?"

"Of course, Gayasisa is much larger, Lord."

"It is like that, O Bhikkhus. For those who have arrived at Understanding thanks to their study and practice of the Dharma, their suffering is almost nothing compared with the suffering of those who are submerged in ignorance. Ignorance magnifies suffering by millions of times.

"Bhikkhus, suppose someone is struck by an arrow. He will feel pain. But if a second arrow strikes him at the very same spot, the pain will be much more than just doubled. And if a third arrow strikes him at that same spot again, the pain will be a thousand times more intense. Bhikkhus, ignorance is the second and the third arrow. It intensifies the pain.

"Thanks to understanding, a practitioner can prevent the pain in himself and others from being intensified. When an unpleasant feeling, physical or mental, arises in him, the wise man does not worry, complain, weep, pound his chest, pull his hair, torture his body and mind, or faint. He calmly observes his feeling and is aware that it is only a feeling. He knows that he is not the feeling, and he is not caught by the feeling. Therefore, the pain cannot bind him. When he has a painful physical feeling, he knows that there is a painful physical feeling. He does not lose his calmness, does not worry, does not fear, and does not complain. Thus the feeling remains a painful physical feeling, and it is not able to grow and ravage his whole being.

"Bhikkhus, be diligent in your practice of looking deeply so that the fruit of Understanding may arise and you will no longer be bound by pain. Birth, sickness, old age, and death will also stop bothering you.

"When a bhikkhu is about to pass away, he should dwell in the contemplation of the body, the feelings, the mind, and the objects of mind. Every position and every act of the body should be placed under mindfulness. Every feeling should also be placed under mindfulness. The bhikkhu contemplates the nature of impermanence and the nature of interdependence of the body and of the feelings, so that he will not be bound by the body and the feelings, even pleasant ones.

"If he needs all his strength to bear the pain, he should only observe, 'This is a kind of pain that needs all my strength to bear. This pain is not me. I am not this pain. I am not caught by this pain. The body and the feelings are, at this moment, like a lamp whose oil and wick are running out. It is by conditions that the light manifests or ceases to manifest. I am not bound by conditions.' If a monk practices in this way, calmness and release will come."

When the first rains began to relieve the summer heat, he returned to Jetavana for the retreat season. He taught the bhikkhus and bhikkhunis more about the law of dependent co-arising. One bhikkhu stood up and asked, "Lord, you have taught that consciousness is the basis of name and form. Does it then follow that the existence of all dharmas arises from consciousness?"

The Buddha answered, "That is correct. Form is an object of consciousness. The subject and the object of consciousness are two faces of one reality. There can be no consciousness without the object of consciousness. Consciousness and the object of consciousness cannot exist independently of each other. Because the subject and object of consciousness cannot be separated, they are both said to arise from mind."

"Lord, if form arises from consciousness, consciousness can be said to be the source of the universe. Is it possible to know how consciousness or mind came to be? When did mind begin? Can one speak of the beginning of mind?"

"Bhikkhus, the concepts of beginning and end are only mental constructs created by the mind. In truth, there is no beginning or end. We only think about beginnings and endings when we are trapped in ignorance. It is because of ignorance that people are caught in an endless round of birth and death."

"If the round of birth and death has no beginning and no end, how can one escape it?"

"Birth and death are only concepts created out of ignorance. To transcend the thoughts of birth-and-death and beginning-and-end is to transcend the endless round. Bhikkhus, that is all I wish to say today. Practice looking deeply into all things. We will speak again about this subject another day."

Chapter Sixty-Five

Neither Full nor Empty

After the Dharma talk, Venerable Svasti noticed how pensive many of the monks looked. He also felt that he had not grasped what the Buddha taught. He resolved to listen carefully to the elder disciples during their Dharma discussions.

At the next Dharma talk, Venerable Ananda was asked by the monks to ask questions to the Buddha in front of the entire assembly. His first question was, "Lord, what is meant by 'the world' and 'the dharmas'?"

The Buddha said, "Ananda, the world *(loka)* is the collective whole of all things subject to change and dissolution. All dharmas are contained in the eighteen realms: the six sense organs, the six sense objects, and the six sense consciousnesses. The six sense organs, as you know, are eye-consciousness, ear-consciousness, nose-consciousness, tongue-consciousness, body-consciousness, and mind-consciousness. The six sense objects are form, sound, smell, taste, touch, and objects of mind. The six sense consciousnesses are seeing, hearing, smelling, tasting, touching, and perceiving. There are no dharmas apart from the eighteen realms. All eighteen realms are subject to birth and death, to change and dissolution. That is why I have said that the world is the collective whole of all things which possess the nature of change and dissolution."

Ananda then asked, "Lord, you have often said that all dharmas are empty. What is meant by that?"

The Buddha said, "Ananda, I have said that all dharmas are empty because all dharmas are without a separate self. None of the six sense organs, six sense objects, or six sense consciousnesses, possess a separate, individual self."

Ananda said, "Lord, you have said that the Three Gates of Liberation are emptiness, signlessness, and aimlessness. You have said that all dharmas are empty. Is it because all dharmas are subject to change and dissolution that they are also empty?"

"Ananda, I have spoken often about emptiness and the contemplation on emptiness. The contemplation on emptiness is a wondrous meditation which can help people transcend suffering, birth, and death. Today I will speak more on this contemplation.

"Ananda, we are all sitting together in the Dharma hall. There are no markets, buffaloes, or villages inside the Dharma hall. There are only bhikkhus, sitting and listening to the Dharma. We can say that the hall is empty of all that is not here, and that it contains what is actually here. The Dharma hall is empty of markets, buffaloes, and villages, but contains bhikkhus. Do you agree that that is correct?"

"Yes, Lord."

"After the Dharma talk, we will all leave the Dharma hall and there will no longer be any bhikkhus here. At that moment, the Dharma hall will be empty of markets, buffaloes, villages, and bhikkhus. Do you agree that that is so?"

"Yes, Lord, at that moment the Dharma hall will be empty of all those things."

"Ananda, full always means full of something, and empty always means empty of something. The words full and empty have no meaning on their own."

"Please, Lord, could you explain that more."

"Consider this—empty is always empty of something, such as empty of markets, buffaloes, villages, and bhikkhus. We cannot say that emptiness is something which exists independently. Fullness is the same. Full is always full of something, such as full of markets, buffaloes, villages, or bhikkhus. Fullness is not something which exists independently. At the present moment, we can say that the Dharma hall is empty of markets, buffaloes, and villages. As for all dharmas, if we say that all dharmas are full, what are they full of? If we say that all dharmas are empty, what are they empty of?

"Bhikkhus, the emptiness of all dharmas refers to the fact that all dharmas are empty of a permanent and unchanging self. That is the meaning of the emptiness of all dharmas. You know that all dharmas are subject to change and dissolution. Because of that, they cannot be said to possess a separate, independent self. Bhikkhus, empty means empty of self.

"Bhikkhus, there is no aggregate among the five aggregates that possesses a permanent, unchanging nature. All the aggregates of body, feelings, perceptions, mental formations, and consciousness, are without a separate self. They do not possess a permanent and unchanging nature. A permanent and unchanging nature would be an essential self. Contemplating in order to see the absence of such an independent, separate self is contemplating emptiness."

Ananda said, "All dharmas are without a self. This we understand. But then, Lord, do the dharmas actually exist?"

The Buddha quietly looked down at the small table before him on which was placed a bowl of water. He pointed to the bowl and asked Ananda, "Ananda, would you say this bowl is full or empty?"

"Lord, the bowl is full of water."

"Ananda, take this bowl outside and empty all the water out of it."

Venerable Ananda did as the Buddha instructed. When he returned, he placed the empty bowl back on the table. The Buddha lifted the bowl and turned it upside down. He asked, "Ananda, is this bowl now full or empty."

"Lord, it is no longer full. It is empty."

"Ananda, are you sure the bowl is empty?"

"Yes, Lord, I am sure the bowl is empty."

"Ananda, this bowl is no longer full of water, but it is full of air. You have forgotten already! Empty means empty of something and full means full of something. In this case, the bowl is empty of water but full of air."

"I understand now."

"Good. Ananda, this bowl can be either empty or full. Of course, whether there is emptiness or fullness depends on the presence of the bowl. Without a bowl, there would be no emptiness or fullness. It is just like the Dharma hall. In order for it to be full or empty, it must first be there."

"Ah!" the bhikkhus suddenly exclaimed with one voice.

Venerable Ananda joined his palms. "Lord, then the dharmas do exist. The dharmas are real."

The Buddha smiled. "Ananda, don't be caught by words. If the dharmas are phenomena empty of self, their existence is not the existence of ordinary perception. Their existence has the same meaning as 'emptiness.'"

Ananda joined his palms. "Please, Lord, can you explain that further."

"Ananda, we have spoken about an empty and a full bowl. We have also spoken about an empty and a full Dharma hall. I have briefly spoken about emptiness. Let me speak more about fullness.

"Although we have agreed that the bowl on the table is empty of water, if we look deeply, we will see that is not entirely true."

The Buddha lifted the bowl and then looked at Ananda. "Ananda, among the interwoven elements that have given rise to the bowl, do you see water?"

"Yes, Lord. Without water, the potter would not have been able to mix the clay he used to fashion the bowl."

"Just so, Ananda. Looking deeply, we can see the presence of water in the bowl, even though we earlier stated that it is empty of water. The presence of the bowl depends on the presence of water. Ananda, can you see the fire element in this bowl?" ·

"Yes, Lord. Fire was necessary to complete the bowl. Looking deeply, I can see the presence of heat and fire in the bowl."

"What else can you see?"

"I see the air. Without air, the fire could not have burned and the potter could not have lived. I see the potter and his skillful hands. I see his consciousness. I see the kiln and the wood stacked in the kiln. I see the trees the wood came from. I see the rain, sun, and earth which enabled the trees to grow. Lord, I can see thousands of interpenetrating elements which gave rise to this bowl."

"Excellent, Ananda! Contemplating the bowl, it is possible to see the interdependent elements which gave rise to the bowl. Ananda, these elements are present within and without the bowl. Your own awareness is one of the elements. If you took away heat and returned it to the sun, if you returned the clay to the earth and the water to the river, if you returned the potter to his parents and the wood to the forest trees, could the bowl still exist?"

"Lord, the bowl could no longer exist. If you returned the interdependent elements which gave rise to the bowl to their sources, the bowl could no longer be present."

"Ananda, contemplating the law of dependent co-arising, we see that the bowl cannot exist independently. It can only exist in interdependent relation with all other dharmas. All dharmas depend on each other for birth, existence, and death. The presence of one dharma implies the presence of all other dharmas. The presence of all dharmas is implied by the presence of just one dharma. Ananda, this is the principle of interpenetration and interbeing.

"Ananda, interpenetration means that within this, that is, and within that, this is. For example, when we look at this bowl we can see the potter, and when we look at the potter we can see the bowl. Interbeing means that 'this is that' and 'that is this.' For example, waves are water, and water is waves. Ananda, at present there are no markets, buffaloes, or villages in the Dharma hall. But that is only from one

viewpoint. In reality, without the presence of markets, buffaloes, and villages, this Dharma hall could not exist. Thus,
Ananda, when you look at the empty Dharma hall, you
should be able to see the presence of markets, buffaloes, and
villages. Without this, that is not. The basic meaning of
emptiness *(sunnata)* is 'this is because that is.'"

The bhikkhus listened in perfect silence. The Buddha's
words made a deep impression on them. After a brief pause,
the Buddha lifted the empty bowl again and said,
"Bhikkhus, this bowl cannot exist independently. It is here
thanks to all the things we consider non-bowl entities such as
earth, water, fire, air, potter, and so forth. It is the same for
all dharmas. Every dharma exists in interdependent relation
to all other dharmas. All dharmas exist by the principles of
interpenetration and interbeing.

"Bhikkhus, look deeply at this bowl, and you can see the
entire universe. This bowl contains the entire universe. There
is only one thing the bowl is empty of and that is a separate,
individual self. What is a separate, individual self? It is a
self which exists completely on its own, independent of all
other elements. No dharma can exist independently from
other dharmas. No dharma possesses a separate, essential
self. That is the meaning of emptiness. Empty means empty of
self.

"Bhikkhus, the five aggregates are the basic elements of a
person. Form does not contain a self, because form cannot exist
independently. Within form exist feelings, perceptions, mental formations, and consciousness. It is the same for feelings.
Feelings do not possess a self because feelings cannot exist independently. Within feelings are form, perceptions, mental
formations, and consciousness. The same is true for the other
three aggregates. No aggregate possesses a separate identity.
The five aggregates depend on each other in order to exist.
Thus the five aggregates are all empty.

"Bhikkhus, the six sense organs, the six sense objects, and
the six sense consciousnesses are all empty. Every sense organ,
every sense object, and every sense consciousness depends on

all other sense organs, sense objects, and sense consciousnesses in order to exist. No sense organ, sense object, or sense consciousness possesses an independent, separate nature.

"Bhikkhus, let me repeat this so that it will be easy for you to remember. This is, therefore that is. All dharmas depend on each other in order to exist. Thus all dharmas are empty. Empty here means empty of an independent, separate self."

Venerable Ananda said, "Lord, some brahmana scholars and leaders of other religious sects claim that the Monk Gautama teaches annihilism. They say that you lead people to negate all of life. Do they misunderstand you because you say that all dharmas are empty?"

The Buddha answered, "Ananda, the brahmana scholars and leaders of other religious sects do not speak correctly about this. I have never taught the doctrine of annihilism. I have never led others to deny life. Ananda, among false views there are two which entangle people the most—views of being and views of non-being. The first view regards all things as having a separate and permanent self-nature. The second regards all things as illusions. If you are caught in either view, you cannot see the truth.

"Ananda, once Bhikkhu Kaccayana asked me, 'Lord, what is false view and what is right view?' I answered that false view is to be caught in either the notion of being or the notion of non-being. When we see into the true nature of reality, we are no longer bound by either of these views. A person with right view understands the process of birth and death in all dharmas. Because of that, he is not disturbed by thoughts of existence or non-existence. When suffering arises, the person with right view knows that suffering is arising. When suffering fades, the person with right view knows that suffering is fading. The arising and fading of all dharmas does not disturb the person with right view. The two false views of permanence and illusion are too extreme. Dependent co-arising transcends both extremes and dwells in the middle.

"Ananda, being and non-being are concepts which do not accord with reality. Reality transcends the boundaries of such concepts. An enlightened person is one who has transcended the concepts of being and non-being.

"Ananda, not only are being and non-being empty, but birth and death are also empty. They are also merely concepts."

Venerable Ananda asked, "Lord, if birth and death are empty, why have you often said that all dharmas are impermanent, constantly being born and dying?"

"Ananda, at the relative, conceptual level, we speak of dharmas being born and passing away. But from the point of view of the absolute, all dharmas are by nature birthless and deathless."

"Please, Lord, explain this."

"Ananda, take the example of the bodhi tree you planted in front of the Dharma hall. When was it born?"

"Lord, it was born four years ago at the very moment the seed put forth roots."

"Ananda! Before that did the bodhi tree exist?"

"No, Lord, before that there was no bodhi tree."

"Do you mean to say that the bodhi tree arose from nothing? Can any dharma come into being from nothing?"

Venerable Ananda fell silent.

The Buddha continued, "Ananda, there is no dharma in all the universe which can come into being from nothing. Without the seed there could be no bodhi tree. The bodhi tree owes its existence to the seed. The tree is the continuation of the seed. Before the seed penetrated roots into the earth, the bodhi tree was already present in the seed. If a dharma is already present, how can it be born? The bodhi tree's nature is without birth."

The Buddha asked Ananda, "After the seed penetrated roots into the earth, did the seed die?"

"Yes, Lord, the seed died in order to give birth to the tree."

"Ananda, the seed did not die. To die means to pass from existence to non-existence. Is there any dharma in all the universe which can pass from existence to non-existence? A leaf, a mote of dust, a trail of incense smoke—none of these can pass from existence to non-existence. All these dharmas transform into different dharmas, that is all. The bodhi seed is the same. The seed did not die. It transformed into a tree. The seed and the tree are both birthless and deathless. Ananda, the seed and the tree, you, me, the bhikkhus, the Dharma hall, the leaf, a dust mote, a trail of incense smoke—all are without birth and death.

"Ananda, all dharmas are without birth and death. Birth and death are only mental concepts. All dharmas are neither full nor empty, neither created nor destroyed, neither defiled nor immaculate, neither increasing nor decreasing, neither coming nor going, neither one nor many. All these are merely concepts. Thanks to the contemplation on the empty nature of all dharmas, it is possible to transcend all discriminating concepts in order to realize the true nature of all things.

"Ananda, the true nature of all things is that there is neither full nor empty, birth nor death, becoming nor dissolving. It is based on that true nature that the world of birth and death, fullness and emptiness, becoming and dissolving arises. If not, how could there be a way out of birth and death, fullness and emptiness, becoming and dissolving?

"Ananda, have you ever stood on the seashore and watched the waves rise and fall on the surface of the sea? Birthlessness and deathlessness are like the water. Birth and death are like the waves. Ananda, there are long waves and short waves, high waves and low waves. Waves rise and fall, but the water remains. Without water, there could be no waves. The waves return to water. Waves are water, water is waves. Though the waves may rise and pass away, if they understand that they themselves are the water, they will transcend notions of birth and death. They will not worry, fear, or suffer because of birth and death.

"Bhikkhus, the contemplation on the empty nature of all dharmas is wondrous. It leads to liberation from all fear, worry, and suffering. It will help you transcend the world of birth and death. Practice this contemplation with all your being."

The Buddha was finished speaking.

Venerable Svasti had never heard the Buddha speak more profoundly or wondrously. The eyes and smiles of the Buddha's senior disciples radiated happiness. Svasti felt he understood the Buddha's words, but had not penetrated their deepest meaning. He knew that Ananda would repeat the entire Dharma talk in the coming days. He would then have an opportunity to learn more by listening to the senior disciples discuss what the Buddha had said.

Four Mountains

Early one morning, Venerable Moggallana came to the Buddha, his eyes filled with tears. The Buddha asked him what was the matter, and Moggallana answered, "Lord, last night during my meditation, my thoughts turned to my mother. I contemplated on my feelings for her. I know when I was young I sometimes caused her sorrow, but that is not the source of my pain. My pain arises from the knowledge that I was unable to help my mother while she was still alive, nor can I help her in death. Lord, my mother's karma is heavy. She committed many crimes during her life, and I am sure that her bad karma follows her and continues to make her suffer. During my meditation, I saw my mother, thin as a ghoul, in a dark, foul place. There was a bowl of rice nearby, and I offered it to her. But when she placed the rice in her mouth, it turned into live coals, and she had to spit it out in pain. Lord, this image will not leave me. I don't know how I can lighten her bad karma and help her to find release."

The Buddha asked, "What crimes did she commit when she was alive?"

Moggallana answered, "Lord, she did not practice respect for life. Her work required her to kill many creatures. She did not practice right speech. Her words were often sources of suffering to others. She was like someone who rips up living trees and plants dead ones in their place. I dare not recount all her transgressions. It is enough to say that she violated all five of the wonderful precepts. Lord, I would endure any suffering to reverse my mother's karma. Please, Lord, in your compassion, tell me what I might do."

The Buddha said, "Moggallana, I am deeply moved by your love for your mother. The debt of gratitude we owe our parents is as wide as the sky and as deep as the sea. A child should never forget that debt of gratitude day and night. In times when there are no Buddhas or holy persons, parents should serve as Buddhas and holy persons. Moggallana, you did your best to help your mother while she was still living. Your concern continues now that she has died. This shows how deep your love is. I am happy to see that.

"Moggallana, the most important way to offer tribute to one's parents is by living a life of happiness and virtue. That is the best way to repay our debt of gratitude and to fulfill our parents' aspirations for us. Your life, Moggallana, is such a life. Your life of peace and joy, happiness and virtue, serves as a model to others. You have helped many people find the path. Offer your life and good merit on behalf of your mother and her karma can be transformed.

"Moggallana, I have a suggestion to help your mother. On Pavarana Day, the last day of the retreat season, ask the entire community to join you in a transformation ceremony for your mother to pray and transfer our merits to her. Many monks in our sangha possess deep concentration and virtue. Their energy of transformation and their prayers joined with yours will be most powerful. Thanks to that, your mother's bad karma will dissolve, and she will have a chance to enter the path of true Dharma.

"I am sure there are others in our sangha with similar situations. We should organize this ceremony on behalf of everyone's parents. Arrange with Sariputta to hold a special transformation ceremony on Pavarana Day on behalf of all parents, those who have died and those who are still living. This will also provide a good occasion to teach young people about the gratitude we owe our parents and ancestors.

"Moggallana, most people only appreciate their parents after they have already died. Having parents is a great happiness. Parents can be a source of great joy for their children. Children should cherish their parents while they are still alive, truly seeing them and finding ways to make them happy. Whether parents are alive or have passed away, loving actions can bring them happiness and share good merit with them. Helping the poor and infirm, visiting the lonely, freeing prisoners, releasing animals destined for the butcher, planting trees, these are all compassionate actions which can transform the present situation and bring happiness to our parents. On Pavarana Day, we will encourage everyone to perform these kinds of acts."

Deeply comforted, Moggallana bowed to the Buddha.

That afternoon after his walking meditation, the Buddha met King Pasenadi at the monastery gates. As they exchanged greetings, seven ascetics from the Nigantha sect passed by. Ascetics in their sect wore no clothes, practiced austerities, did not shave their beards or cut their hair, and did not cut their nails. The king excused himself from the Buddha and approached the ascetics. He bowed respectfully and said, "Respected monks of high virtue, I am Pasenadi, King of Kosala." He bowed to them two more times, repeating the same words, before he returned to the Buddha's side. After they were out of sight, he asked the Buddha, "Lord, according to you, have any of those ascetics yet attained Arhatship? Are any of them close to attaining such fruits?"

The Buddha answered, "Your majesty, you live the life of a ruler and thus are more accustomed to men of government and politics. It is only natural that you would find it difficult to ascertain which monks have attained certain levels of spiritual practice. But in fact, it is difficult for anyone to know whether or not someone is enlightened after merely meeting them once or twice. It is necessary to live close to them, observing them carefully to see how they respond to difficult circumstances, to see how they converse with others, and to understand the depth of their wisdom, virtue, and attainment."

The king understood. He said, "Lord, it is similar to when I send spies to investigate situations in other places. They disguise themselves so they will not be recognized. Often when they return to the palace, even I do not recognize them until they have discarded their disguises and washed their faces. Yes, I see you are correct. Unless you know someone in depth, you cannot understand the depth of their virtue, wisdom, and attainment."

The Buddha invited the king to walk with him to his hut. When they arrived, the Buddha asked Ananda to put out chairs.

The king confided to the Buddha, "Lord, I am now seventy years old. I want to devote more time to spiritual studies. I feel I should do more sitting and walking meditation than I have in the past. But Lord, palace affairs are most time-consuming and demanding. Sometimes when I come to your Dharma talks, I am so tired I cannot keep my eyes open. I feel so ashamed. Lord, I am also guilty of overindulgence in food. One day I came to the monastery after eating entirely too much. It made me sleepy, and I went for a walk in hopes that walking meditation would clear my mind. But I grew more and more sleepy. I did not even notice you were standing on the same path, and I bumped right into you. Do you remember?"

The Buddha laughed. "Yes, I remember, your Majesty. Majesty, simply eat less. Doing so will make your mind and body feel lighter, which will improve your ability to perform both your work of governing and your spiritual practice. You might ask Queen Mallika or Princess Vajiri to help you by supervising your daily meals. They could serve you smaller quantities, still paying attention to the quality of nutrition."

The king joined his palms to accept the Buddha's suggestion.

The Buddha continued, "It is good to devote more time to looking after your health and pursuing your spiritual practice. Not much time remains you in this life. Majesty, suppose a trusted messenger brought you news that a mighty mountain, high as the sky, was approaching from the East, crushing every living thing in its path. Just as you begin to worry about this situation, another trusted messenger brings news that a mighty mountain is advancing from the West, also crushing everything in its path. Then messengers from the North and South arrive bearing similar messages. Four mountains are advancing towards the capital, crushing every being in their paths. You know that you cannot escape. There is nothing you can do to prevent the mountains from coming. Your time is short. What would your Majesty do?"

The king pondered for a moment and then said, "Lord, I believe there is only one thing I could do. That would be to live my remaining hours in as worthy and serene a way as possible, following the true teaching."

The Buddha praised the king. "Yes, your Majesty! Those four mountains are the mountains of birth, old age, sickness, and death. Old age and death are closing in on us, and we can never escape."

The king joined his palms. "Lord, remembering that old age and death are approaching, I understand that the best thing I can do is to live my remaining days and months according to your teaching, living serenely, mindfully, and benefiting others, including the future generations."

The king stood up and bowed to the Buddha before taking his leave.

That rainy season, many brahmans and members of different religious sects gathered in Savatthi. They organized sermons, lectures, and debates throughout the region, inviting people from the city to attend. At the debates, different sects were given a chance to expound their doctrines. Several of the Buddha's lay disciples attended some of these debates. They told the Buddha and the bhikkhus what they had seen and heard. They said that every metaphysical problem imaginable was presented and that every speaker considered his doctrine the only correct one. The debates began cordially but often ended in angry shouting matches.

The Buddha told his disciples the following fable:

"Once upon a time, a clever king invited several people blind from birth to visit the palace. He brought out an elephant and asked them to touch it and then describe what the elephant was like. The blind man who rubbed its legs said that the elephant was like the pillars of a house. The man who stroked its tail said the elephant was like a feather duster. The person who touched its ears said it was like a winnowing basket, and the man who touched its stomach said it was like a round barrel. The person who rubbed its head said the elephant was like a large earthenware jar, and the person who touched its tusk said the elephant was like a stick. When they sat down to discuss what the elephant was like, no one could agree with anyone else, and a very heated argument arose.

"Bhikkhus, what you see and hear comprises only a small part of reality. If you take it to be the whole of reality, you will end up having a distorted picture. A person on the path must keep a humble, open heart, acknowledging that his understanding is incomplete. We should devote constant effort to study more deeply in order to make progress on the path. A follower of the Way must remain open-minded, understanding that attachment to present views as if they were absolute truth will only prevent us from realizing the truth. Humility and open-mindedness are the two conditions necessary for making progress on the path."

Chapter Sixty-Seven
Ocean Poet

At the end of the retreat season, many monks bid farewell to the Buddha and then took to the road to spread the Dharma. Venerable Punna, one of the Buddha's most capable and respected bhikkhus, told the Buddha of his plans to return to his native region in order to teach the Dharma. He was from the island Sunaparanta located in the Eastern Sea.

The Buddha said, "I have heard that your native land is still largely uncivilized and that many of the people there are known for their fierce nature and violent conflicts. I'm not sure whether it is a good idea for you to go there to teach."

Venerable Punna responded, "Lord, it is precisely because the people are still fierce and uncivilized that I wish to go teach there. I can show them the way of compassion and non-violence. I believe I will be successful."

"Punna, what if they scream and curse at you?"

"Respected Buddha, that is nothing. At least they won't be throwing rocks and garbage at me."

"What if they do throw rocks and garbage at you?"

"Respected Buddha, that would still be nothing. At least they won't be beating me with sticks and clubs."

"What if they do beat you with sticks and clubs?"

Venerable Punna laughed. "I would still consider them gentle. After all, they won't be killing me."

"Punna, what if they do kill you?"

"I doubt very much that will come to pass, Lord. But if it does, I would consider dying on behalf of the way of compassion and nonviolence a meaningful death that may even help demonstrate the teaching. Everyone must die. I would not regret dying for the Way."

The Buddha praised him, "You are wonderful, Punna! You possess the courage to spread the Dharma in Sunaparanta. Actually, I only asked all these questions for the benefit of the other bhikkhus standing here. I have no doubts about your abilities and your practice of nonviolence."

Venerable Punna had formerly been a merchant. He and his brother-in-law traded local products from Sunaparanta with merchants in Savatthi. They traveled by boat and ox cart. One day while waiting for a shipment of goods to arrive in Savatthi, Punna met a group of bhikkhus out begging. He was deeply impressed by their serene demeanor, so he went to Jetavana to hear the Buddha give a Dharma talk. By the end of the Dharma talk, Punna no longer desired to be a merchant; he wanted to become a bhikkhu. He gave the rest of his goods and money to his brother-in-law and was ordained in the Buddha's sangha. He made quick progress in his practice and was soon a capable teacher himself. He traveled throughout Kosala and Magadha spreading the Dharma. All the bhikkhus were confident he would succeed in his native land.

The next spring, the Buddha returned east. He stopped in Vesali and Campa. He followed the river to the sea where he taught along the coast. One day as they stood at the sea's edge, Ananda said to him, "Lord, listening to the sound of the tide and looking out over the waves, I follow my breath and dwell in the present moment. My mind and body find perfect ease. I find that the ocean renews me." The Buddha nodded.

Another day the bhikkhus stopped to talk with a fisherman. Venerable Ananda asked him his feelings about the sea. The man was tall and handsome, his skin bronzed by the sun. He told Ananda, "I love many things about the ocean. First, the sandy shores gently slope downwards into the water which makes it easier for us to drag our boats and nets. Second, the ocean stays in the same place. You always know where to find it. Third, the ocean never holds on to a corpse but thrusts it back onto the shore. Fourth, all rivers—Ganga, Yamuna, Aciravati, Sarabhu, Mahi—empty into the ocean and leave their own names behind. The sea receives them all. Fifth, even though rivers empty into the sea, day and night, the ocean remains at the same level. Sixth, sea water is always salty. Seventh, the ocean contains beautiful coral, mother-of-pearl, and precious stones. Eighth, the ocean gives refuge to thousands of living beings, from enormous creatures that measure hundreds of feet in length to creatures no bigger than the eye of a needle or a speck of dust. I think you can see, Venerable, how much I love the ocean."

Ananda looked at the fisherman with admiration. Though he was a simple fisherman, he spoke like a poet. Ananda turned to the Buddha and said, "How eloquently this man has praised the sea! He loves it in the way I love the Way of Enlightenment. May we hear more of your teaching?"

The Buddha smiled and pointed to some large rocks. He said, "Let's go sit on those rocks while I speak to you of the special characteristics of the Way of Enlightenment."

They all followed the Buddha, including the fisherman. When everyone was seated, the Buddha began, "Our brother fisherman has described eight wonderful characteristics of the sea. I will now describe eight wonderful characteristics of the true path. First, the Dharma is not unlike the ocean whose shores slope gently downwards enabling the fishermen to more easily pull their boats and nets into the sea. In the teaching, every person can progress from the easy to the difficult, from the low to the high, from the superficial to the profound. The Dharma is broad enough to accommodate every temperament. Anyone can enter the path, whether young or old, educated or unschooled. Every person can find methods suitable to his or her individual needs.

"Second, as the ocean stays in the same place, so does the Dharma. The principles of the teaching never change. The precepts have been clearly transmitted. The true Dharma dwells wherever people study and practice the principles and precepts. The Dharma cannot be lost or misplaced.

"Third, as the ocean never holds onto a corpse, the Dharma does not tolerate ignorance, laziness, or violation of the precepts. Any person who does not maintain the practice will find himself eventually thrust from the community.

"Fourth, as the ocean receives all rivers equally, the Dharma receives persons from all castes equally. And just as rivers that empty into the sea leave their own names behind, those who enter the path leave their caste, lineage, and former positions behind in order to take the name of bhikkhu.

"Fifth, just as the level of the sea remains constant, the Dharma remains constant no matter how many or how few people follow it. The Dharma cannot be measured by numbers.

"Sixth, as seawater is always salty, the Dharma, though it be revealed in countless ways and though there be countless methods of practice, has only one taste. That is the taste of liberation. If the teaching does not lead to liberation, it is not true teaching.

"Seventh, as the ocean contains coral, mother-of-pearl, and precious stones, the Dharma contains sublime and precious teachings like the Four Noble Truths, the Four Right Efforts, the Five Faculties, the Five Powers, the Seven Factors of Awakening, and the Noble Eightfold Path.

"Eighth, as the ocean provides a safe refuge to thousands of living beings, whether they are as tiny as a grain of sand or several hundred feet in length, the Dharma provides refuge to all, whether they are unschooled children or Great Beings like the Bodhisattvas. There are countless students of the Dharma who have attained the fruits of Stream Enterer, Once Returner, Never Returner, or Arhat.

"Like the ocean, the Dharma is a source of inspiration and an immeasurable treasure."

Venerable Ananda joined his palms and looked at the Buddha. He said, "Lord, you are a spiritual Master, and you are also a poet."

Chapter Sixty-Eight
Three Wondrous Gates

After leaving the coast, the Buddha visited Pataliputta and Vesali, and then headed towards his homeland. Upon reaching the town of Samagama in Sakya, he learned that Nathaputta, leader of the Nigantha sect, had died and that his followers had divided into two bitter camps. Each side denounced the other for false interpretation of doctrine, and each vied for the laity's support. The people were dismayed and confused, and did not know which side to follow.

The novice Cunda, Sariputta's attendant, explained the Nigantha dispute to Ananda. He was aware of all the details because he had lived for a time in Pava where Nathaputta taught. Ananda told the Buddha about the conflict, and then added in a worried tone of voice, "Lord, I hope there will be no split in the sangha after you pass away."

The Buddha patted Ananda on the shoulder and said, "Ananda, do any of the bhikkhus presently argue over the contents of the teaching? Do they argue about the Four Establishments of Mindfulness, the Four Right Efforts, the Five Faculties, the Five Powers, the Seven Factors of Awakening, or the Noble Eightfold Path?"

"No, I have never seen any bhikkhus arguing with each other over the teaching. But you are still among us. We take refuge in your virtue. We all listen to you and our studies proceed peacefully. But when you are gone, disagreements may arise over the precepts, how best to organize the sangha, or how to spread the teaching. If conflicts erupt, many could grow disheartened and even lose their faith in the path."

The Buddha consoled him. "Don't worry, Ananda. If arguments and conflicts arise in the sangha over the contents of the teaching such as the Four Establishments of Mindfulness, the Four Right Efforts, the Five Faculties, the Five Powers, the Seven Factors of Awakening, or the Noble Eightfold Path—that would be cause for worry. Disagreements over small matters concerning the practice of the precepts, sangha organization, and dissemination of the teaching are not worth worrying about."

Despite the Buddha's reassurances, Venerable Ananda remained unconvinced. Only recently he had learned that in Vesali, Venerable Sunakkhata, who had once been the Buddha's attendant, had abandoned the sangha out of personal dissatisfaction. He was organizing lectures at which he denounced the Buddha and the sangha. He exclaimed that the monk Gautama was no more than an ordinary man who possessed no special insight. He said that Gautama's teaching only spoke about liberating one's own self and showed no concern for society as a whole. Sunakkhata was sowing seeds of confusion. Venerable Sariputta was also aware of the situation and shared Ananda's concern.

Ananda knew that seeds of discontent were also being sown in Rajagaha. Several bhikkhus, under the leadership of Venerable Devadatta, were secretly trying to organize a new sangha, independent from the Buddha. Several capable bhikkhus were cooperating with Devadatta, including Venerables Kokalika, Katamoraka Tissa, Khandadeviputta, and Samuddadatta. Devadatta was one of the Buddha's brightest and most capable senior disciples. Brother Sariputta had often praised him before the people and had treated him as a special friend. Ananda could not understand why Devadatta had recently grown so jealous of others, especially the Buddha himself. Ananda knew that no one had disclosed these things to the Buddha yet. He was afraid he himself would have to be the one to inform the Buddha of these sad developments before long.

The next year, the Buddha returned to Savatthi for the rainy season. He dwelled at Jetavana. There he delivered the *Sutra on the Dharma Seal.*

"There is a wonderful teaching which I will speak to you about today. Please empty your minds of all other thoughts in order to calmly and peacefully hear, receive, and understand this teaching.

"Bhikkhus, certain Dharma seals are the signs of true Dharma. There are three seals which every teaching of mine bears. These are Emptiness, Signlessness, and Aimlessness. These three characteristics are the three gates which lead to emancipation. These Dharma seals are also known as the Three Gates of Emancipation, or the Three Liberation Gates.

"Bhikkhus, the first seal is Emptiness, *sunnata.* Emptiness does not mean non-existence. It means that nothing exists independently. Emptiness means empty of a separate self. As you know, the belief in being and the belief in non-being are both incorrect. All dharmas depend on each other for their existence. This is because that is, this is not because that is not, this is born because that is born, this dies because that dies. Thus, the nature of emptiness is interdependence.

"Bhikkhus, practice looking at the interdependent relationships of all dharmas in order to see how all dharmas are present in each other, how one dharma contains all other dharmas. Apart from one dharma, no other dharmas can exist. Contemplate the eighteen realms of the six sense organs, the six sense objects, and the six sense consciousnesses. Contemplate the five aggregates of body, feelings, perceptions, mental formations, and consciousness. You will see that no phenomenon, no aggregate, can exist independently. All depend on each other for existence. When you see this, you will see into the empty nature of all dharmas. Once you see the empty nature of all dharmas, you will no longer chase after or run away from any dharma. You will transcend attachment, discrimination, and prejudice towards all dharmas.

Contemplation on the nature of emptiness opens the first gate to freedom. Emptiness is the first Liberation Gate.

"Bhikkhus, the second seal is Signlessness, *animitta*. Signlessness means to transcend the confines of perception and mental discrimination. When people are unable to see the interdependent and empty nature of all dharmas, they perceive dharmas as being separate and independent phenomena. This exists apart from that, this is independent of all other dharmas. Looking at dharmas in such a way is like taking a sword of mental discrimination and cutting up reality into small pieces. One is then prevented from seeing the true face of reality. Bhikkhus, all dharmas depend on each other. This is in that, this fits within that, in the one are found the all. That is the meaning of the terms interpenetration and interbeing. This is in that, that is in this, this is that, that is this. Contemplate in this way and you will see that ordinary perception is full of error. The eyes of perception are unable to see as clearly and accurately as the eyes of understanding. The eyes of perception can mistake a rope for a snake. With the illuminating eyes of understanding, the true form of the rope reveals itself and the image of a snake disappears.

"Bhikkhus, all mental concepts such as existence, non-existence, birth, death, one, many, appearing, disappearing, coming, going, defiled, immaculate, increasing, and decreasing are created by perception and mental discrimination. From the view of the unconditioned absolute, the true face of reality cannot be confined within the prisons of such concepts. Thus all dharmas are said to be signless. Contemplate in order to dissolve all thoughts about existence, non-existence, birth, death, one, many, appearing, disappearing, coming, going, defiled, immaculate, increasing, and decreasing, and you will attain liberation. Signlessness is the second Liberation Gate.

"Bhikkhus, the third sign is Aimlessness, *appanihita*. Aimlessness means not chasing after anything. Why? Usually people try to avoid one dharma by chasing after another one. People pursue wealth in order to avoid poverty. The spiritual seeker rejects birth and death in order to attain liberation.

But if all dharmas are contained within each other, if all dharmas are each other, how can you run away from one dharma to pursue a different one? Within birth and death lies nirvana, within nirvana lies birth and death. Nirvana and birth and death are not two separate realities. If you reject birth and death in order to pursue nirvana, you have not yet grasped the interdependent nature of all dharmas. You have not yet grasped the empty and formless nature of all dharmas. Contemplate aimlessness in order to end once and for all your chasing and running away.

"Liberation and enlightenment do not exist outside of your own self. We need only open our eyes to see that we ourselves are the very essence of liberation and enlightenment. All dharmas, all beings, contain the nature of full enlightenment within themselves. Don't look for it outside yourself. If you shine the light of awareness on your own self, you will realize enlightenment immediately. Bhikkhus, nothing in the universe exists independently of your own consciousness, not even nirvana or liberation. Don't search for them elsewhere. Remember that the object of consciousness cannot exist independently from consciousness. Don't chase after any dharma, including Brahma, nirvana, and liberation. That is the meaning of aimlessness. You already are what you are searching for. Aimlessness is a wondrous gate that leads to freedom. It is called the third Liberation Gate.

"Bhikkhus, this is the teaching of the Dharma Seals, the teaching of the Three Gates of Emancipation. The Three Gates of Emancipation are wondrous and sublime. Devote yourselves wholeheartedly to studying and practicing them. If you practice according to this teaching, you will surely realize liberation."

When the Buddha finished giving this sutra, Venerable Sariputta stood up and bowed to the Buddha. All the other bhikkhus followed his example in order to show their deep gratitude to the Buddha. Venerable Sariputta announced to the community that there would be a special session to study the sutra the following day. He said that this sutra was immeasurably profound and they must devote their efforts to study, practice, and understand it. Venerable Svasti saw that this sutra was related to the *Sutra on Emptiness* which the Buddha had delivered the previous year. He saw how the Buddha was guiding his disciples from simple teachings towards ever more subtle and profound teachings. Svasti looked at the radiant and happy faces of such disciples as Mahakassapa, Sariputta, Punna, and Moggallana. Svasti remembered how the previous year they also followed Sariputta's example in bowing to the Buddha after he delivered the *Sutra on Emptiness*. He saw how deep the bond between Teacher and students was.

The next afternoon Venerables Yamelu and Tekula visited the Buddha at his hut. These two bhikkhus were brothers from the brahmana caste. They were well-known for their expertise in linguistics and ancient literature. When they recited the scriptures, their voices were clear as bells and as resonant as drums. They bowed to the Buddha, and he invited them to be seated.

Venerable Yamelu spoke, "Lord, we would like to speak to you concerning the question of language as it relates to the dissemination of the teaching. Lord, you usually deliver your talks in Magadhi, but Magadhi is not the native tongue of many bhikkhus, and the people in some of the regions where the bhikkus teach do not understand Magadhi. Thus, they translate the teaching into local dialects. Before we were ordained, we had the good fortune to study many dialects and languages. It is our observation that the sublime and subtle nuances of your teaching have been hampered by being translated into local dialects and idioms. We would like your permission to render all your teachings into the classical meter of the Vedic language. If all the bhikkhus studied and taught the teaching in one language, distortion and error could be avoided."

The Buddha was silent for a moment. Then he said, "It would not be beneficial to follow your suggestion. The Dharma is a living reality. The words used to transmit it should be the words used daily by the people. I do not want the teaching to be transmitted in a language that can be understood by only a few scholars. Yamelu and Tekula, I want all my disciples, both ordained and lay, to study and practice the Dharma in their native tongues. That way the Dharma will remain vital and accessible. The Dharma must be applicable to present life, and compatible with local culture."

Understanding the Buddha's intent, Venerables Yamelu and Tekula bowed to him and took their leave.

Chapter Sixty-Nine
Where Will the Buddha Go?

One day during a rainstorm, an ascetic named Uttiya came to visit the Buddha. Ananda led him into the hut and introduced him to the Buddha. The ascetic was invited to sit down, and Ananda offered him a towel to dry himself.

Uttiya asked the Buddha, "Monk Gautama, is the world eternal or will it one day perish?"

The Buddha smiled and said, "Ascetic Uttiya, with your consent, I will not answer that question."

Uttiya then asked, "Is the world finite or infinite?"

"I will not answer that question either."

"Well then, are body and spirit one or two?"

"I will not answer that question either."

"After you die, will you continue to exist or not?"

"This question too, I will not answer."

"Or perhaps you hold that after death you will neither continue to exist nor cease to exist?"

"Ascetic Uttiya, I will not answer that question either."

Uttiya looked confounded. He said, "Monk Gautama, you have refused to answer every question I've asked. What question will you answer?"

The Buddha replied, "I only answer questions that pertain directly to the practice of gaining mastery over one's mind and body in order to overcome all sorrows and anxieties."

"How many people in the world do you think your teaching can save?"

The Buddha sat silently. Ascetic Uttiya said no more.

Sensing that the ascetic felt that the Buddha didn't want to answer him or was unable to, Ananda took pity on the man and spoke up, "Ascetic Uttiya, perhaps this example will help you better understand my teacher's intent. Imagine a king who dwells in a strongly fortified palace surrounded by a wide moat and wall. There is only one entrance and exit to the palace which is guarded day and night. The vigilant guard will only allow persons he knows into the palace. No one else is granted permission to enter. The guard has furthermore made a careful check of the palace wall to make sure there are no gaps or cracks big enough for even a kitten to squeeze through. The king sits on his throne without concern for how many people enter the palace. He knows the guard will prevent all unwelcome guests from entering. It is similar for Monk Gautama. He is not concerned with the number of people who follow his Way. He is only concerned with teaching the Way which has the capacity to dissolve greed, violence, and delusion, so that those who follow the Way can realize peace, joy, and liberation. Ask my teacher questions about how to master the mind and body, and he will surely answer you."

Ascetic Uttiya understood Ananda's example, but because he was still entangled in questions of a metaphysical nature, he asked no more. He departed feeling somewhat unsatisfied with his encounter with the Buddha.

A few days later, another ascetic, named Vacchagota, came to visit the Buddha. He asked the Buddha questions of a similar nature. For instance, he asked, "Monk Gautama, could you please tell me whether or not there is a self?"

The Buddha sat silently. He did not say a word. After asking several questions and receiving no reply, Vacchagota stood up and left. After he was gone, Venerable Ananda asked the Buddha, "Lord, you speak about the non-self in your Dharma talks. Why wouldn't you answer Vacchagota's questions about the self?"

The Buddha replied, "Ananda, the teaching on the emptiness of self is meant to guide our meditation. It is not to be taken as a doctrine. If people take it as a doctrine, they will become entangled by it. I have often said that the teaching should be considered as a raft used to cross to the other shore or a finger pointing to the moon. We should not become caught in the teaching. Ascetic Vacchagota wanted me to hand him a doctrine, but I do not want him to become trapped by any doctrine, whether it be a doctrine of the self or the non-self. If I told him there was a self, that would contradict my teaching. But if I told him there was no self and he clings to that as a doctrine, it would not benefit him. It is better to remain silent than to answer such questions. It is better for people to think I do not know the answers to their questions than for them to become trapped in narrow views."

One day Venerable Anuradha was stopped by a group of ascetics. They did not want to let him pass until he answered their question. They asked him, "We have heard that Monk Gautama is a completely enlightened Master and that his teaching is subtle and profound. You are his disciple. Therefore, answer this—when Monk Gautama dies, will he continue to exist or will he cease to exist?"

The ascetics told Anuradha that he must select from one of the four following possibilities:

When he dies, Monk Gautama will continue to exist.

When he dies, Monk Gautama will cease to exist.

When he dies, Monk Gautama will both continue to exist and cease to exist.

When he dies, Monk Gautama will neither continue to exist nor cease to exist.

Bhikkhu Anuradha knew that none of these four responses was compatible with the true teaching. He remained silent. The ascetics did not want to accept his silence. They tried in vain to force him to select one of the four responses. At last, the Venerable said, "My friends, according to my understanding, none of these four responses can accurately express the truth concerning Monk Gautama."

The ascetics burst out laughing. One said, "This bhikkhu must be newly ordained. He doesn't possess the ability to answer our question. No wonder he's trying to avoid giving an answer. We'd better let him go."

A few days later, Venerable Anuradha presented the ascetics' question to the Buddha and said, "Lord, please enlighten us so that we can better answer such questions when they arise."

The Buddha said, "Anuradha, it is impossible to find Monk Gautama through conceptual knowledge. Where is Monk Gautama? Anuradha, can Gautama be found in form?"

"No, Lord."

"Can Gautama be found in feelings?"

"No, Lord."

"Can Gautama be found in perceptions, mental formations, or consciousness?"

"No, Lord."

"Well then, Anuradha, can Gautama be found outside of form?"

"No, Lord."

"Can Gautama be found outside of feelings?"

"No, Lord."

"Can Gautama be found outside of perceptions, mental formations, and consciousness?"

"No, Lord."

The Buddha looked at Anuradha. "Where then can you find Gautama? Anuradha, right this moment as you stand before Gautama, you cannot grab hold of him. How much less so after he dies! Anuradha, the essence of Gautama, like the essence of all dharmas, cannot be grasped by conceptual knowledge or in the categories of mental discrimination. One must see the dharmas in interdependent relation with all other dharmas. You must see Gautama in all the dharmas normally thought of as non-Gautama, in order to see the true face of Gautama.

"Anuradha, if you want to see the essence of a lotus flower, you must see the lotus present in all the dharmas normally thought of as non-lotus, such as the sun, pond water, clouds, mud, and heat. Only by looking in this way can we tear asunder the web of narrow views, the web of mental discrimination which creates the prisons of birth, death, here, there, existence, non-existence, defiled, immaculate, increasing, and decreasing. It is the same if you want to see Gautama. The ascetics' four categories of existence, non-existence, both existence and non-existence, and neither existence nor non-existence, are spiderwebs among spiderwebs which can never take hold of the enormous bird of reality.

"Anuradha, reality in itself cannot be expressed by conceptual knowledge or by written and spoken language. Only the understanding which meditation brings can help us recognize the essence of reality. Anuradha, a person who has never tasted a mango cannot know its taste no matter how many words and concepts someone else uses to describe it to him. We can only grasp reality through direct experience. That is why I have often told the bhikkhus not to lose themselves in useless discussion that wastes precious time better spent looking deeply at things.

"Anuradha, the nature of all dharmas is unconditioned and can be called suchness, *tathata*. Suchness is the wondrous nature of all dharmas. From suchness the lotus arises. Anuradha arises from suchness. Gautama arises from suchness. We can call someone who arises from suchness a *tathagata*, or 'one who thus comes.' Arising from suchness, where do all dharmas return? All dharmas return to suchness. Returning to suchness can also be expressed by the term tathagata, or 'one who thus goes.' In truth, dharmas do not arise from anywhere or go to any place, because their nature is already suchness. Anuradha, the truer meaning of suchness is 'one who comes from nowhere,' and 'one who goes nowhere.' Anuradha, from now on, I will call myself 'Tathagata'. I like this term because it avoids the discrimination that arises when one uses the words, 'I' and 'mine'."

Anuradha smiled and said, "We know that all of us arise in suchness, but we will reserve the name 'Tathagata' for you.

Every time you refer to yourself as 'Tathagata', we will be reminded how we all have the nature of suchness which has no beginning and no end."

The Buddha smiled too, and said, "The Tathagata is pleased with your suggestion, Anuradha."

Venerable Ananda was present at this conversation between the Buddha and Venerable Anuradha. He followed Anuradha out of the hut and suggested that they share the conversation with the rest of the community at the next day's Dharma discussion. Anuradha happily agreed. He said he would introduce the exchange by first recounting his meeting with the ascetics in Savatthi.

Chapter Seventy
The Quail and the Falcon

Although he had never been scolded or corrected by the Buddha, Bhikkhu Svasti was aware of his own shortcomings. Perhaps the Buddha refrained from saying anything critical of him because he could see Svasti's wholehearted efforts to be master of his six senses, even if his mastery was far from complete. Whenever Svasti saw another bhikkhu or bhikkhuni being corrected, he took it to heart as if he himself were the one at fault. This provided him with many opportunities to deepen his practice. He especially took to heart any correction and guidance the Buddha gave to Rahula. Rahula continued to make great strides in his practice, and that benefited Svasti's practice as well.

Once while sitting in a forest glade with Rahula, Svasti expressed how fortunate he felt to be a disciple of the Buddha. He said that because he had tasted true peace, joy, and freedom, he had no more desire for the life of the world. Rahula cautioned him, "While that may be true, don't give yourself too much credit too fast. The effort to continually observe and master the senses is the very foundation of the practice, and not even the most senior disciples can afford to grow lax in their practice."

Rahula told Svasti about Bhikkhu Vangisa, a monk renowned for his intelligence and gift with language. He was, in fact, a fine poet who had composed several gathas praising the Buddha, Dharma, and Sangha which had earned the

Buddha's compliments. When Vangisa first joined the sangha, he studied under the guidance of Bhikkhu Nigrodhakappa in Aggalava, just outside Savatthi. After Nigrodhakappa died, Vangisa went to dwell at Jetavana. One day while out begging with Ananda, Vangisa confided that his mind was troubled, and he asked for Ananda's assistance. Ananda learned that Vangisa was disturbed by the lust he felt for the young women who came to the monastery to bring food offerings. Ananda understood that as an artist, Vangisa was easily touched by beauty. Ananda appealed to that very sense in helping Vangisa see how he could use the beauty of the path of awakening in order to transcend his desires for the kind of fleeting beauty that creates only clinging and obstacles. Ananda showed him how to shine his awareness on the objects of his contemplation in order to see clearly the empty and impermanent nature of all dharmas. Practicing according to Ananda's instructions, Vangisa learned to master the six senses. He wrote a poem about this practice which was now well known to other monks. It went as follows:

> Even after donning the saffron robe,
> I chased after desires
> like a buffalo pining after the farmer's rice.
> How ashamed I felt!
> A mighty general's son
> gifted with bow and arrow
> might fend off the siege
> of even a thousand soldiers.
> Dwelling in Mindfulness,
> I will not be defeated,
> even before a throng of beautiful women.
> I follow the Lord
> who is a descendent of the sun.
> Serenely walking on this path
> all desire is released.
> Becoming master of my senses,
> I walk forth calmly.

Though met by countless obstacles
none can shake my peace.

Because Vangisa was a man gifted with intelligence and
talent, there were times when his pride got the better of
him, and he felt a quiet disdain for some of the other monks.
Luckily, thanks to his practice of mindfulness, he was able to
recognize this arrogance within himself. He composed a
gatha on this theme:

Disciples of Gautama,
overcome arrogance!
The path of pride
leads only to suffering.
The man who silently hides his arrogance
is on the road to hell
as surely as the man
all bloated up by pride.
Seek instead the happiness
of a peaceful heart.
Practice mindfulness
to realize the three knowledges.
True success can only come
when arrogance is subdued.

Thanks to his deep awareness, Vangisa was able to transcend many sorrows and obstacles, and to make great strides
on the path of transformation. He attained the fruit of
Never-Returner, confirmed by Venerable Sariputta. The day
his heart and mind were opened, Vangisa composed a poem to
express his gratitude to the Buddha:

Intoxicated by youthful dreams,
I wandered far and wide
through marketplaces and countryside,
until at last I met the Buddha!
All compassionate, he shared

the wondrous teaching with me.
My faith was awakened
and I donned the robes of a monk.
Dwelling in awareness,
focusing heart and mind,
I have attained the three knowledges,
thanks to the Awakened One!
Far and wide, the Lord
has sown the seeds of illumination.
Because all beings dwell in darkness,
he has shown the Way—
the Four Noble Truths,
the Noble Eightfold Path,
Tranquility, Joy, and Freedom.
His words so subtle and profound,
his noble life without blame,
skillfully, he leads all beings to liberation.
How deep my gratitude!

Once in a special teaching session held for the younger bhikkhus, Venerable Sariputta held Bhikkhu Vangisa up as an example. He told them that in the beginning of his practice, Vangisa was sometimes troubled by certain afflictions and states of mind; but thanks to determined practice, he overcame such states and attained great understanding. "Therefore," Sariputta told the young monks, "don't let yourself be caught in any mental complex, whether an inferiority or a superiority complex. Practicing mindfulness, you will be aware of everything that is going on inside yourself and nothing will be able to entangle you. Learning to master the six senses is a most wonderful method to make firm progress along the path."

Listening to Rahula talk about Vangisa made Svasti feel as if he knew Vangisa. Though he had met Vangisa, he had never had a real chance to speak with him. He resolved to find an occasion to get acquainted with Venerable Vangisa, for he knew he could learn much from Vangisa's spiritual experience.

Svasti remembered how the Buddha once used the image of the sea to explain the practice of mastering the six senses. The Buddha said, "Bhikkhus, your eyes are a deep ocean in which are concealed sea monsters, whirlpools, and perilous currents. If you don't proceed in mindfulness, your boat will be attacked and submerged by the sea monsters, whirlpools, and perilous currents. Your ears, nose, tongue, body, and mind are also deep oceans in which are concealed sea monsters."

Recalling those words, Svasti's understanding increased manifold. The six senses were indeed deep oceans whose hidden waves could rise at any moment to submerge one. Rahula's advice was well worth heeding—he should not rest on any laurels. The Buddha's teaching should be practiced continuously.

One afternoon, as he sat outside his hut at Jetavana monastery, the Buddha told the younger bhikkhus a story to remind them to observe and master their six senses and not allow themselves to be lost in forgetfulness. The Buddha recounted, "One day a falcon swooped down and caught a young quail in her talons. As she flew back into the sky, the quail began to cry. He chastised himself for wandering away from where his parents had told him to stay—'If only I had listened to my parents, I would not be in this predicament.'

"The falcon asked, 'And where did your parents tell you to stay, you runt?' The quail answered, 'In the newly plowed field.'

"To the quail's surprise, the falcon said, 'I can catch any quail I want anytime I want. I will return you to that field and offer you one more hour of life. I will be looking for you, and in just an hour I will catch you, break your little neck, and eat you at once.' And the falcon swooped down again and released the quail in the newly plowed field.

"Surprisingly, the young quail immediately climbed up on a mound of newly plowed earth and began to taunt the falcon.

'Hey, falcon, why wait an hour? Why don't you fly back down and try to catch me right now?'

"Angered, the falcon tucked her wings close to her sides and shot down at full speed. But the quail quickly ducked for cover in the furrow beneath the mound of earth, and the falcon missed the quail and landed with such force that she broke her breastbone and was killed instantly.

"Bhikkhus, you must dwell in mindfulness at all times and master your six senses. When you leave mindfulness, you enter the domain of Mara, and danger is unavoidable."

Svasti was encouraged by the number of sincere and talented young bhikkhus in the Buddha's sangha. One day he was invited with several other monks to the home of a layperson named Citta, who lived in the village Macchika-sanda. It was on this outing that Svasti learned how bright one of these young bhikkhus was. Lay disciple Citta was well known for his devotion to the teaching. Because of his large and generous heart, he was deeply loved by the people just as lay devotee Anathapindika was loved. Citta enjoyed inviting senior disciples to his home in order to offer them food and ask them questions on the Dharma. On this particular day, he had invited ten senior monks and two young monks, Svasti and Isidatta. After the monks were finished eating, Citta bowed to them respectfully and then asked if he could sit before them on a low stool.

He asked them the following question, "Respected Venerables, I have heard the *Brahmajala Sutra* in which the Buddha discusses the sixty-two false views of contemporary sects. I have also heard the questions raised by members of other sects concerning life, death, and the soul, such as: is the world finite or infinite, temporal or everlasting, are body and mind one or two, will the Tathagata still exist after his death or cease to exist, will he both exist and cease to exist, or will he neither exist nor cease to exist. Venerables, what gives rise to these esoteric kinds of views and questions?"

Not one of the bhikkhus ventured to answer Citta's question, even after he repeated it three times. Svasti was embarrassed, and felt his ears turning warm. Suddenly Isidatta spoke. He turned towards the senior bhikkhus and asked, "Respected elders, may I respond to lay disciple Citta's question?"

The senior monks answered, "Bhikkhu, you may answer his question if you wish."

Turning back towards Citta, Isidatta said, "Sir, such views and questions arise because people still cling to a false view of the self. If the idea of a separate self were abandoned, people would no longer have a need to cling to such views or ask such questions."

Citta was visibly impressed by the young bhikkhu's response. He said, "Please, Venerable, could you explain this more clearly."

"People without a chance to be exposed to and to study the Way of Awakening generally think of the body as being the same as one's self, or they think that the self is contained in the body and the body is contained in the self. Likewise, they consider feelings to be the same as the self, or they think that feelings are contained in the self and the self is contained in feelings. Such people hold the same views as regards their perceptions, mental formations, and consciousness. They are caught in a false view of self. It is precisely because they are caught in a false view of self that they become entrapped by the sixty-two false views discussed in the *Brahmajala Sutra* and by questions about the finite and infinite, temporal and everlasting, one and two, existing and ceasing to exist. Lay disciple Citta, such questions and views are rendered meaningless when, through dedicated study and practice, one breaks through the false view of self."

Increasingly impressed by the young bhikkhu, Citta respectfully asked Isidatta, "Venerable, where are you from?"

"I come from Avanti."

"Venerable, I have heard about a young man from Avanti named Isidatta who became a bhikkhu. It is said that he is remarkably bright and able. Though I have heard his name, I have never seen him. Have you ever met him?"

"Yes, Citta, I have met him."

"Then, Venerable, can you tell me where this talented young monk is at present?"

Isidatta did not answer.

In fact, Citta had already guessed that the young bhikkhu sitting before him was Isidatta. He asked, "Can it be that you yourself are Bhikkhu Isidatta?"

"Yes, sir," replied Isidatta.

Citta was overjoyed and exclaimed, "This is a great honor for me! Respected Venerable Isidatta, my mango grove and private residence in Macchikasanda are refreshing places equipped with every convenience. I hope you will come to visit us often. We offer you whatever you may need—food, robes, medicine, or a place to stay."

Isidatta did not say anything. The bhikkhus thanked Citta and departed. Svasti later heard that Isidatta never returned to Citta's home. Isidatta did not desire lavish praise or offerings, not even from such a well-respected man as Citta. Though Svasti did not meet Isidatta again for some time, the image of the bright and humble bhikkhu remained engraved on his mind. Svasti pledged to follow Isidatta's example and to seek him out whenever he had a chance to pass through Avanti.

Svasti knew how much the Buddha loved young bhikkhus who showed determination, wisdom, and concern for the welfare and happiness of others. The Buddha expressed how greatly he depended on these young monks to transmit the teaching to future generations. However, Svasti observed how devoted the Buddha was in teaching all the bhikkhus, regardless of their individual abilities. Some monks encountered more difficulties than others. There was one monk who abandoned the community six times but was still welcomed back by the Buddha for another effort. The Buddha never ceased to offer kindly encouragement to those monks who found it difficult to remember even such simple practices as the sixteen methods of observing the breath.

There was a monk named Bhaddali who lived at Jetavana. The Buddha was well aware of Bhaddali's shortcomings, but he chose to overlook them in order to provide the bhikkhu with an opportunity to transform himself. Bhaddali seemed incapable of following a number of monastic disciplines. For instance, during meals every bhikkhu was expected to remain seated until he had finished eating. Standing up during the meal for second helpings or to tend to other tasks was not allowed. This discipline was called One Sitting for Meals. Bhaddali never managed to remember this discipline. His behavior around the monastery was a frequent cause of distress to the other bhikkhus. The Buddha called him aside a number of times and taught him to ask himself this question every morning upon arising, "What can I do today to contribute to the community's happiness?" But after several months, Bhaddali appeared to have made little if any progress. A number of bhikkhus grew impatient with Bhaddali and spoke harshly to him. Aware of this, one day the Buddha addressed the community.

He said, "Bhikkhus, although an individual in the sangha may possess a number of serious flaws, there undoubtedly remains within him at least a few seeds of faith and love. We must relate to such an individual in a way that will protect and nurture those seeds of faith and love, lest they, too, perish. Take the example of a person who loses an eye in an accident. His family and friends will do everything in their power to protect his remaining eye, because they know how bleak his future will be if he loses it. Thus, bhikkhus, help protect the seeds of faith and love in your brother by treating him kindly."

Svasti was present when the Buddha spoke these words. He was deeply moved by the Buddha's loving attitude. He looked up and saw Ananda wiping away tears and knew that Ananda, too, had been touched.

Although the Buddha was kind-hearted and gentle, he could also be stern when the occasion called for it. A person who could not be helped by the Buddha was truly a person without a future. One day Svasti was present when a short but impressive conversation took place between the Buddha and a man called Kesi, who was a well-known horse trainer.

The Buddha asked Kesi, "Can you please explain to us how you go about training a horse?"

Kesi answered, "Lord, horses have different temperaments. Some are quite docile and can be trained by the simple use of gentle words. Others are more difficult and require a firm hand along with gentle methods. Others are still more stubborn and require the use of firm discipline alone."

The Buddha laughed and asked, "What do you do when you encounter a horse that won't respond to any of those three methods?"

"Lord, in that situation it is necessary to kill the horse. If it is allowed to live with the other horses, it will spoil them all. Lord, for my part, I would like to know how you train your disciples."

The Buddha smiled. He said, "I do the same as you. Some monks respond to gentleness alone. Others require firmness along with gentleness. Others can only make progress when given stern discipline."

"And what do you do in the case of a monk who doesn't respond to any of those methods?"

The Buddha said, "I do as you do. I kill him."

The horse trainer's eyes widened in alarm. "What? You kill him? I thought you were against killing."

The Buddha explained, "I do not kill him in the same way you kill a horse. When a person does not respond to any of the three methods we've just discussed, we refuse to let him join the sangha of bhikkhus. I do not accept him as my student. That is an extreme misfortune. Being refused the chance to practice the Dharma in community is to lose an opportunity that only arises once in a thousand lifetimes. What is that if not death to the spiritual life? It isn't just a pity for the person refused. It is as much a pity for me, for I feel great love and concern for that person. I never stop hoping that one day he will open himself up to the practice and come back to us."

Long ago, Svasti had heard the Buddha scold and counsel Rahula. He had also witnessed the Buddha correct a number of other bhikkhus. He now understood more deeply the profound love behind the Buddha's rebukes. Svasti also knew how much the Buddha loved him even though the Buddha never said so aloud. Svasti needed only to look into the Buddha's eyes to know.

That night, the Buddha received a guest, and Ananda asked Svasti to prepare tea. The guest was a warrior with proud and aristocratic bearing who traveled with a shining sword slung across his back. He dismounted his steed outside Jetavana and left his sword tucked in the saddle. Sariputta showed him to the Buddha's hut. He was a man of impressive height. His strides were long and he had a piercing gaze. Ananda told Svasti that the warrior's name was Rohitassa.

When Svasti entered the hut to serve tea, he found Rohitassa and Sariputta sitting before the Buddha on low stools. Ananda was standing behind the Buddha. After serving the three men tea, Svasti stood next to Ananda behind the Buddha. The men drank their tea in silence. After a long pause, Rohitassa spoke, "Lord, is there any world in which there is no birth, old age, sickness, or death? Is there any world in which beings never die? By what means of travel can one leave this world of birth and death behind in order to arrive at a world in which death does not exist?"

The Buddha answered, "There are no means of travel by which you can leave this world of birth and death, no matter how fast you might go, even if you travel at the speed of light."

Rohitassa joined his palms and said, "You speak the truth. I know for a fact that it is not possible to escape this world of birth and death through any means of travel, no matter how fast one is able to go. I can recall a past life in which I possessed supernatural powers and was able to fly through the air faster than an arrow. With one step I could leap from the Eastern Sea all the way to the Western Sea. I was determined to escape the world of birth, old age, sickness, and death, in order to find a world in which beings were no longer oppressed by birth and death. Day after day I traveled at great speed, never stopping to eat or drink, rest or sleep, urinate or defecate. For a hundred years I went at that great speed, but arrived nowhere, until one day I died by the side of a road. Lord, your words are indeed true! Truly one can never escape the world of birth and death by any means of travel, even if one can fly at the speed of light."

The Buddha said, "I did not say, however, that one cannot transcend the world of birth and death. Listen, Rohitassa, you can indeed transcend this world of birth and death. I will show you the path by which you may do so. In your very own body six feet tall, the world of birth and death has its origins, and in that same body are the means to transcend the world of birth and death. Contemplate your body, Rohitassa. Shine your awareness on the world of birth and death as it unfolds in your own tall body. Contemplate until you can see the truth of impermanence, emptiness, birthlessness, and deathlessness of all dharmas. Before you, the world of birth and death will dissolve and the world of birthlessness and deathlessness will reveal itself. You will be freed from every sorrow and fear. You do not need to travel anywhere in order to leave the world of suffering and death. You need only look deeply into the nature of your own body."

Svasti noticed how Sariputta's eyes glistened like stars as he listened to the Buddha. Warrior Rohitassa's face also radiated happiness. Svasti was profoundly moved. Who could fathom how wondrous and majestic the Buddha's teaching was? It was like a piece of epic music. More clearly than ever, Svasti saw how the key to liberation lay right in his own hand.

Chapter Seventy-One

The Art of Stringing a Sitar

When the retreat season ended, the Buddha returned south. He stopped by Deer Park in Isipatana, the place he had delivered his first Dharma talk on the Four Noble Truths thirty-six years earlier. Though it seemed like only yesterday, much had changed since then. Since the first turning of the wheel of Dharma, the Dharma had been carried throughout all the countries in the Ganga basin. The local people in Isipatana had built a stupa to commemorate the first turning, and a monastery had been built where many bhikkhus lived and practiced. After teaching the Dharma and encouraging the community there, the Buddha departed for Gaya.

He stopped by Uruvela to visit the ancient bodhi tree, which he found lovelier and greener than ever. Many huts were now scattered throughout the forest. King Bimbisara was also planning to build a stupa that would commemorate the spot where the Buddha attained Awakening. The Buddha stopped to visit the village children. They were no different from the children he met years ago. The buffalo boy Svasti was now forty-seven years old and a respected elder in the sangha. The village children gathered ripe papayas to offer to the Buddha. Every child in the village could recite the three refuges.

From Gaya, the Buddha headed northeast to Rajagaha. As soon as he reached the capital, he headed for Vulture

Peak. There he met Venerable Punna, who told him about his work teaching the Dharma on Sunaparanta island. Punna had just completed a retreat season there with several other bhikkhus. The number of people in Sunaparanta who had taken refuge in the Buddha, Dharma, and Sangha had already risen to five hundred.

Throughout the following days, the Buddha visited the spiritual centers scattered throughout the region. One night while sitting in meditation at one of the centers, he heard a monk chanting sutras. There was something disturbing about the voice, as though the monk was tired and discouraged. The Buddha could tell that the monk was encountering difficulties in his practice. The next morning he asked Venerable Ananda about it and learned that the monk chanting the sutras in the night was Sona. The Buddha remembered meeting Sona several years before in Savatthi.

Venerable Sona Kutikanna was ordained under the guidance of Venerable Mahakaccana and studied with him for several years on Pavatta mountain in the Kuraraghara region. Sona was a young man from a wealthy family. He was refined and intelligent but had a frail constitution. He had to make a great effort to endure the homeless life of a bhikkhu, in which he ate only one meal a day and slept beneath the trees. But his devotion to the practice never wavered. After a year, he was brought by his teacher to meet the Buddha in Savatthi.

That first time in Savatthi, Buddha asked Sona, "Sona, are you enjoying good health? Are you experiencing any difficulties in your practice, in begging, or in spreading the Dharma?"

Sona answered, "Lord, I am very happy. I am not experiencing any difficulties."

The Buddha instructed Ananda to prepare a place for Sona to sleep that night in the Buddha's hut. Venerable Ananda placed another bed in the hut. That night the Buddha sat in meditation outside until three in the morning. Aware of that, Sona was unable to fall asleep. When the Buddha entered the hut, he asked Sona, "Aren't you asleep yet?"

"No, Lord, I am still awake."

"Aren't you sleepy? Well then, why don't you recite some gathas you have memorized."

Venerable Sona recited the sixteen gathas contained in the *Sutra on the Full Awareness of Breathing*. His voice was as clear as a bell. He did not stumble over any word or leave any word out. The Buddha praised him,

"You recite most beautifully. How many years has it been since you were ordained?"

"Lord, it has been a little more than a year. I have the experience of only one retreat season."

That was the first time the Buddha and Sona met. Now, when the Buddha heard Sona's chanting, he knew that Sona had overexerted himself. He asked Ananda to accompany him to Sona's hut. Seeing the Buddha, Sona stood up at once to greet him. Buddha asked both Sona and Ananda to be seated beside him, and then he asked Sona, "Before you became a monk, you were a musician, were you not? You specialized in the sixteen- string sitar, didn't you?"

"Yes, Lord, that is correct."

The Buddha asked Sona, "If you play the sitar while the strings are slack, what is the result?"

Sona answered, "Lord, if the strings are slack, the sitar will be out of tune."

"And what if the strings are too taut?"

"Lord, if the strings are too taut, the strings are more likely to break."

"And if the strings are just right, neither too slack nor too taut?"

"Lord, if the strings are just right, the sitar will provide fine music."

"Just so, Sona! If one is idle or lazy, one will not make progress in the practice. But if one tries too hard, one will suffer fatigue and discouragement. Sona, know your own strength. Don't force your body and mind beyond their limits. Only then can you attain the fruits of practice."

Venerable Sona stood up and bowed to the Buddha to express his gratitude for the Buddha's insight.

One afternoon, physician Jivaka visited the Buddha. He found the Buddha returning from Bamboo Forest and asked if he might walk up with him to his hut on Vulture Peak. Jivaka watched with admiration as the Buddha climbed the stone steps. The Buddha, now seventy-two years old, was as healthy and energetic as ever. He walked with relaxed, leisurely steps, one hand carrying his bowl, the other lifting the corner of his robe. Venerable Ananda walked in the same manner. Jivaka offered to take the Buddha's bowl, and the Buddha handed it to him with a smile. He said, "But you know, the Tathagata has climbed this mountain hundreds of times, always carrying his own bowl without difficulty."

The carefully carved stone steps that wound up the mountainside had been a gift from King Bimbisara, Jivaka's father. When they climbed the last of them, the Buddha invited Jivaka to sit with him on a large rock outside his hut. Jivaka inquired about the Buddha's health and travels. Then he looked first at Venerable Ananda, and then at the Buddha. In a solemn voice, he said, "Lord, I feel I must tell you about the situation here. Events taking place in the sangha are directly related to the current political situation in the kingdom. I believe you should know what is happening."

The physician told the Buddha that it had become clear that Venerable Devadatta desired to replace the Buddha as the leader of the sangha. He already had considerable support among many bhikkhus, as well as among the ruling elite. Venerable Kokalika was his chief advisor. He also had the backing of Venerables Katamoraka Tissa, Khandadeviputta, and Samuddadatta, all of whom had large numbers of students. Venerable Devadatta was both intelligent and eloquent. He was deeply respected by many bhikkhus and lay disciples. He had not come out and stated directly that he was opposed to the Buddha or the Buddha's senior disciples, but he made frequent allusions to the Buddha's advancing years, questioning whether he still possessed the ability to guide the sangha. He had even insinuated that the Buddha's approach to the teaching was too outdated to meet the needs of young people. Devadatta enjoyed support from several wealthy disciples. Prince Ajatasattu, for reasons Jivaka was unable to understand, was Devadatta's most devoted supporter. As much as King Bimbisara revered the Buddha, Ajatasattu revered Devadatta. He had a large spiritual center built for Devadatta on Gayasisa mountain, the very place where the Buddha had delivered the *Fire Sutra* to the Kassapa brothers and their one thousand disciples. The prince personally brought food offerings to the center every few days. Merchants and politicians, wanting to get in the good graces of the prince, brought offerings and attended Devadatta's Dharma talks as well. Devadatta's influence was growing daily. Already three to four hundred bhikkhus had pledged their support to him.

Jivaka looked at the Buddha and then lowered his voice, "Lord, I do not consider the things I have just recounted sufficient to cause worry on their own, but there is one thing that does concern me greatly—I have learned that Ajatasattu is impatient to assume the throne in order to implement his own agendas. He feels that our father has monopolized the throne for too long, in the same way that Venerable Devadatta is impatient for you to pass the mantle of leadership on to him. It is, in fact, my belief that Venerable Devadatta has planted some dangerous thoughts in the prince's head. Lord, I receive this impression every time I visit the palace to tend after the royal family's health. If something unexpected were to happen to King Bimbisara, you and your sangha could be implicated. Please, Lord, take heed."

The Buddha answered, "Thank you, Jivaka, for telling the Tathagata about the situation. It is important to know what is going on. Don't worry. I will see to it that the sangha is not dragged into any unfortunate circumstances."

Jivaka bowed to the Buddha and returned down the mountain. The Buddha instructed Ananda not to speak to anyone about what Jivaka had shared.

Ten days later, the Buddha gave a Dharma talk to a gathering of three thousand disciples at Bamboo Forest. King Bimbisara was among those present. The Buddha spoke about the Five Powers necessary to nourish the fruits of enlightenment. They are confidence, energy, mindfulness, concentration, and true understanding.

When the Buddha had finished speaking and before anyone else had a chance to ask him any questions, Venerable Devadatta stood and bowed to the Buddha. He said, "Lord, you are now advanced in years. Your health is no longer what it once was. You deserve to rest undisturbed and to lead a life free of any irritations for the final years of your life. The task of leading the sangha is too heavy for you, Lord. Please retire. I would be willing to serve as leader of the bhikkhus."

The Buddha looked at Devadatta. He answered, "Devadatta, thank you for your concern, but the Tathagata still possesses good health and strength adequate to lead the sangha."

Venerable Devadatta turned to the community. Three hundred bhikkhus stood up and joined their palms. Devadatta said to the Buddha, "There are many other bhikkhus who agree with me. Please, Lord, have no worries. I have the ability to lead the sangha. Allow me to relieve you of your burden."

The Buddha said, "Enough, Devadatta, say no more. There are several senior disciples who possess abilities greater than yours, and I have not asked any of them to assume the leadership of the sangha. How much less would I be inclined to transfer the leadership to you. You do not yet possess the ability to lead the community of bhikkhus."

Venerable Devadatta felt humiliated before the great gathering. His face turned red, and he sat back down in anger.

The following day at Vulture Peak, Venerable Ananda confided to the Buddha, "Lord, I feel great pain over my brother
Devadatta's actions. I am afraid that he will seek some form
of revenge against you since you criticized him in front of the
community. I am afraid a schism may occur in the sangha.
With your permission, I would like to speak privately with
Devadatta and and offer him some counsel."

The Buddha said, "Ananda, I spoke severely to Devadatta
before the king and community, because I wanted to make it
clear that I have not chosen Devadatta to succeed me as
leader of the bhikkhus. Any actions he undertakes now will
be in his own name. Ananda, if you think that speaking with
him will help him calm down, please do so."

A few days later Jivaka paid a visit to the Buddha. He
informed the Buddha that he had heard that Devadatta
was plotting to create a great division in the sangha, but by
what means, he did not yet know.

Chapter Seventy-Two
Quiet Resistance

It was the day of the Buddha's weekly Dharma talk at Bamboo Forest. A large crowd was assembled to hear him, including King Bimbisara and Prince Ajatasattu. Venerable Ananda noticed that the number of bhikkhus attending from other centers was even greater than at the two previous Dharma talks. Venerable Devadatta was there, sitting between Venerables Sariputta and Mahakassapa.

Once again, as soon as the Buddha was finished speaking, Venerable Devadatta stood up and bowed to the Buddha. He said, "Lord, you teach the bhikkhus to live a simple life free of desires and to use only what is truly needed. I would like to propose five new rules which would make our commitment to simple living greater.

"First, bhikkhus should dwell in the forests and never be allowed to sleep in villages or towns.

"Second, bhikkhus should beg only and never accept invitations to eat in the homes of lay disciples.

"Third, bhikkhus should sew their robes from discarded scraps and rags and never receive robes as offerings from lay disciples.

"Fourth, bhikkhus should sleep only beneath the trees and not in huts or buildings.

"Fifth, bhikkhus should eat only vegetarian food.

"Lord, if bhikkhus followed these five rules, they would succeed in living a simple life of few desires."

The Buddha answered, "Devadatta, the Tathagata cannot accept your rules as mandatory. Any bhikkhu who wishes to dwell only in the forests has permission to do that. But it is fine for others to live in huts, monasteries, villages, and cities. Any bhikkhu who wishes to only beg for his food may refuse invitations to eat in the homes of lay disciples. But others should feel free to accept such invitations as they provide occasions to help share the teaching. Any bhikkhu who wishes to sew his own robes from scraps and rags is free to do so. But it is fine for others to accept robes from lay disciples, as long as bhikkhus do not possess more than three robes. Any bhikkhu who wishes to sleep only beneath the trees is welcome to do so. But it is all right for others to sleep in huts and buildings. Any bhikkhu who wishes to eat only vegetarian food may do so. But others may accept food offerings containing meat when they are sure the animal was not killed expressly for them. Devadatta, under the present order, bhikkhus have many opportunities to make contact with the laity. They are able to share the teaching with those who are just becoming acquainted with the Way of Awakening."

Venerable Devadatta asked, "Then you do not accept these five rules?"

The Buddha answered, "No, Devadatta, the Tathagata does not accept them."

Devadatta bowed and sat back down. His mouth was turned up in a self-satisfied smile.

That night as the Buddha rested in his hut at Bamboo Forest, he said to Ananda, "The Tathagata understands Devadatta's intentions. I believe there will soon be a serious split in our community."

Not long after that, Venerable Ananda met Venerable Devadatta in Rajagaha. They stopped to talk along the side of the road. Devadatta informed Ananda that he was setting up his own sangha and would hold his own precepts recitations, confession ceremonies, retreat seasons, and Pavarana Days for his followers, separate from the Buddha's sangha. Deeply saddened, Venerable Ananda informed the Buddha of Devadatta's decision. At the next confession ceremony that took place at Bamboo Forest, Ananda noticed that several hundred bhikkhus who normally attended were absent. He knew they were attending the ceremony at Devadatta's center instead.

When the ceremony was over, several bhikkhus went to the Buddha's hut to speak with him. They said, "Lord, bhikkhus who have sided with Devadatta are approaching many of us, exhorting us to join Venerable Devadatta's sangha. They claim his rules are more upright than yours. They hold up your refusal to accept Venerable Devadatta's five rules as proof. They claim that monastic life at Bamboo Forest is too soft, not much different from life as a layperson. They say you only talk about living simply but won't institute the five rules that would assure that the bhikkhus lived such a life. They say you are hypocritical. Lord, we were not swayed by their arguments. Our faith rests with your wisdom. But many young bhikkhus who lack experience in the practice, especially those originally ordained by Devadatta, are drawn to the more austere practice of the five rules. They are leaving the sangha to follow Venerable Devadatta. We felt we should inform you."

The Buddha answered, "Please do not give this matter too much thought. The most important thing is your own practice of the noble and pure life of a monk."

Several days later Jivaka visited the Buddha on Vulture Peak to inform him that Devadatta now commanded a following of more than five hundred bhikkhus. They were all dwelling at Devadatta's Gayasisa headquarters. Jivaka also informed the Buddha of secret political stirrings in the capital in which Devadatta was playing a key role. Jivaka suggested that the Buddha make a clear statement that Devadatta was no longer considered a member of the Buddha's sangha.

News of Venerable Devadatta's independent sangha spread quickly. The bhikkhus were asked about it everywhere they went. Venerable Sariputta instructed them to answer all questions by simply saying, "Those who sow bad seeds reap bad fruits. Causing the community to break is the most serious violation of the teaching."

One day while speaking to several bhikkhus, the Buddha mentioned that Jivaka had counselled him to make a formal announcement that Venerable Devadatta was no longer considered a member of the Buddha's sangha. Sariputta reflected on Jivaka's suggestion and then said, "Lord, we often publicly praised Venerable Devadatta's ability and virtue in the past. How will it look if we now denounce him?"

The Buddha asked, "Sariputta, in the past when you publicly praised Devadatta, were you speaking the truth?"

"Yes, Lord, I was speaking the truth when I praised Venerable Devadatta's ability and virtue."

"Will you be speaking the truth now if you denounce brother Devadatta's actions?"

"Yes, Lord."

"Then there is no problem. The important thing is to speak the truth."

At a gathering of lay persons some days later, the bhikkhus announced to the people that the Venerable Devadatta had been expelled from the Buddha's sangha and that henceforth the sangha could not assume responsibility for Venerable Devadatta's actions.

Venerables Sariputta and Moggallana remained curiously silent throughout these events. They did not even answer the laity's questions. Venerable Ananda noticed their reticence and said to them, "Brothers, you have not offered any views on Venerable Devadatta's actions. Perhaps you have some plan of your own?"

They smiled and Venerable Moggallana said, "That is correct, brother Ananda. We will serve the Buddha and the sangha in our own way."

Many of the laity gossiped about the schism and blamed it on jealousy and petty feelings. Others understood that there must be deeper unrevealed reasons for the Buddha to denounce Venerable Devadatta. Their faith in the Buddha and the sangha did not waver.

One stormy morning, the people in the capital were shocked to learn that King Bimbisara was abdicating the throne in favor of his son, Prince Ajatasattu. The coronation ceremony for the new king was scheduled to take place ten days later on the day of the full moon. The Buddha was concerned that he did not learn of these plans directly from King Bimbisara. The king had always consulted with the Buddha in the past before making major decisions. His concern that something was amiss was confirmed when Jivaka paid him a visit some days later.

The Buddha and Jivaka did walking meditation together along a mountain path. They took slow, quiet steps while observing their breath. After a time, the Buddha invited Jivaka to sit with him on a large rock. Jivaka informed the Buddha that Prince Ajatasattu had placed King Bimbisara under house arrest. The king was confined to his chambers. No one but Queen Videhi was allowed to see him. The king's two most trusted advisors had also been placed under arrest because the prince feared they would try to prevent his coronation from taking place. Their families were falsely informed that they needed to remain at the palace for several days in order to assist with important political matters.

Jivaka told the Buddha that the only reason he knew about these events was because he had been called to tend to an illness of the queen's. She told him how a month earlier, the imperial guards had caught the prince about to enter the king's chambers late one night. Finding his behavior suspicious, they searched him and discovered a sword concealed under his robes. They led him into the king's chambers and told the king of their discovery. The king looked at his son and asked, "Ajatasattu, why were you carrying a sword into the royal chamber?"

"It was my intention to kill you, Father."

"But why would you want to kill me?"

"I want to be king."

"Why must you kill your own father to be king? If you but asked me, I would have abdicated in your favor at once."

"I did not think you would do that. I have obviously made a grave error and beg you to forgive me."

The king asked his son, "Who put you up to this?"

Prince Ajatasattu did not answer at first, but after his father's persistent questioning, he confessed that the idea had been Venerable Devadatta's. Although it was the middle of the night, the king summoned his two most trusted advisors to ask for their counsel. One advisor said that trying to assassinate the king was a crime punishable by death and therefore the prince and Venerable Devadatta should both be beheaded. He even demanded the deaths of all the bhikkhus.

The king disagreed. "I cannot kill Ajatasattu. He is my own son. As for the bhikkhus, they have already made it clear that they cannot be held responsible for the actions of Venerable Devadatta. The Buddha had true foresight in this matter. Suspecting Venerable Devadatta capable of harmful acts, he disavowed Venerable Devadatta's relation to his sangha. But I do not wish to kill Venerable Devadatta either. He is the Buddha's own cousin and has been a respected bhikkhu for many years in the past."

The second advisor exclaimed, "Your compassion has no equal, your Majesty! You are a worthy student of the Lord Buddha. But how do you propose to deal with this matter?"

The king said, "Tomorrow I will let it be known to the people that I am abdicating the throne in favor of my son, Prince Ajatasattu. His coronation can take place in ten days."

"But what of his crime of attempted assassination?"

"I forgive both my son and Venerable Devadatta. Hopefully, they will learn something from my forgiveness."

The two advisors bowed low to their king, as did Prince Ajatasattu. The king ordered the guards to keep the entire incident secret. The next day, after hearing the king's announcement, Venerable Devadatta hurriedly made his way to the capital. He requested an audience with the prince. Later the prince told the queen that Venerable Devadatta had come to assist him in planning the coronation ceremony. But all the queen knew was that two days after her son's meeting with the bhikkhu, her husband and his two closest advisors were placed under house arrest. Jivaka ended by saying, "Lord Buddha, I only pray that the prince will release the king and advisors after his coronation has taken place."

The next day, a royal messenger arrived with an invitation to the Buddha and his bhikkhus to attend the coronation ceremony. Soldiers were already busy decorating the city gates and streets with flags and lanterns. The Buddha learned that Venerable Devadatta planned to attend the ceremony accompanied by six hundred of his own bhikkhus. The Buddha summoned Venerable Sariputta and said, "Sariputta, I will not attend the coronation ceremony. It is my wish that none of our bhikkhus attend, either. We cannot lend any sign of support to this cruel and unjust affair."

The absence of the Buddha and all his bhikkhus was blatantly noticeable on the day of the coronation, causing questions to rise in the people's minds. Before long, they learned the truth that King Bimbisara and his advisors had been placed under house arrest. There grew among the people a quiet but steadfast resistance to the new regime. Although Venerable Devadatta called himself a leader, the people began to notice differences between how his bhikkhus handled themselves and how the bhikkhus of the Buddha did. The people began to refuse to give any food offerings to Devadatta's followers. Their refusal to support Devadatta was simultaneously a condemnation of the new king.

King Ajatasattu was infuriated when he was told of the people's quiet refusal to lend him support. But he did not dare move against the Buddha or his sangha, for he was wise enough to know that if he did so, a mighty protest would well up among the people, and from the neighboring kingdoms, where the Buddha was held in great esteem. He knew that King Pasenadi of Kosala might even send soldiers if he heard that the Buddha had been arrested or harmed in any way. The king summoned Venerable Devadatta for further counsel.

Chapter Seventy-Three
Hidden Rice

Late one night, while sitting in meditation on Vulture Peak, the Buddha opened his eyes to see a man half-concealed behind a nearby tree. The Buddha called to him. Beneath the bright moonlight, the man came forward, laid a sword at the Buddha's feet, and prostrated himself as if making an offering.

The Buddha asked, "Who are you and why have you come here?"

The man exclaimed, "Allow me to bow before you, Teacher Gautama! I was ordered to come and kill you but I cannot do it. I raised this sword in my two hands more than ten times while you were meditating, but I was unable to take even one step towards you. I cannot kill you, but now I am afraid that my master will kill me. I was trying to decide what to do when you called to me. Allow me to bow before you!"

The Buddha asked, "Who gave you orders to come kill the Tathagata?"

"I dare not tell you my Master's name!"

"Very well, you need not tell me his name. But what did he tell you to do?"

"Master, he told me which path to climb up the mountain and he showed me a different path to return by after completing my mission."

"Do you have a wife and children?"

The man exclaimed, "Teacher Gautama, I was ordered to kill you, but I cannot do it!"

"No, Teacher, I am not yet married. I have only an aged mother."

"Then listen to me, and follow my instructions carefully. Return home at once and escape tonight with your mother across the border into Kosala. You and your mother can find a new life there. Do not return by the road your master showed you. If you take that route, you are sure to be ambushed and killed yourself. Go now!"

The man prostrated himself once more and then hurriedly left, leaving the sword behind.

The next morning, Venerables Sariputta and Moggallana came to speak with the Buddha. They said, "We believe it is time the two of us paid a visit to the other side. We want to help our brothers who, out of ignorance, have taken a wrong turn. We request your permission to be gone for a period of time."

The Buddha looked at his two disciples and said, "Go if you feel you must, but take special care. Do all you can to protect your own lives."

Just at that moment, Venerable Sariputta noticed the sword lying on the ground. He looked into the Buddha's eyes as if to question him. The Buddha nodded and said, "Yes, last night a soldier came here with orders to kill the Tathagata, but the Tathagata has offered him guidance instead. Leave the sword there. When Jivaka calls, I will ask him to dispose of it."

Moggallana looked at Sariputta and said, "Perhaps it would be better not to leave the Buddha in such circumstances. What do you think, my brother?"

Before Sariputta could respond, the Buddha said, "Do not worry. The Tathagata is capable of avoiding any dangers that arise."

That afternoon several bhikkhus from Bamboo Forest came to see the Buddha. They were so distraught, they were unable to speak. Tears rolled down their cheeks. The Buddha asked them, "What is the matter? Why are you crying?"

One bhikkhu wiped his tears and answered, "Lord, we have just come from Bamboo Forest. On the road we met brothers Sariputta and Moggallana. When we asked them where they were headed, they said they were crossing over to Gayasisa. We are so upset we cannot hold back our tears. More than five hundred other bhikkhus have abandoned the sangha, but we never expected your two most esteemed disciples to forsake you."

The Buddha smiled and comforted the bhikkhus by saying, "Bhikkhus, do not grieve. The Tathagata trusts Sariputta and Moggallana. They will not betray the sangha."

Eased, the bhikkhus sat quietly at the Buddha's feet.

The following day, Jivaka invited the Buddha for a meal offering at his Mango Grove. Venerable Ananda accompanied the Buddha. When they were finished eating, Jivaka informed them that Queen Videhi happened to be visiting. He wondered if the Buddha would mind meeting with her. The Buddha understood that Jivaka had secretly arranged this meeting to take place, and he asked Jivaka to summon the former queen.

After she bowed to the Buddha, the queen began to sob. The Buddha let her ease her pain and then he gently said, "Please tell me everything."

The queen said, "Lord, King Bimbisara's life is in grave danger. Ajatasattu plans to starve him to death. He won't allow me to bring any more food to my husband."

She told the Buddha that when the king had first been placed under house arrest, she had been allowed to bring him food each day. Then one day the guards confiscated the tray of food she was bringing to the king before allowing her to enter his chambers. She told the Buddha how, even though she wept, Bimbisara had consoled her and told her that he bore no hatred towards their son for his actions. He said he would rather suffer hunger than have the country plunged into war. The next morning, the queen hid small rice balls in her hair while also carrying a platter of food. The guards took away the platter, but the rice in her hair went undetected. She managed to feed her husband in such a manner for several days. But when the king did not die, Ajatasattu ordered the guards to more thoroughly search the queen. They discovered the hidden rice, and she was no longer able to bring him food that way.

Three days later she devised another plan. She mixed a paste of milk, honey, and flour which she spread over her body after bathing and drying herself. When the paste was dry, she put on her clothes. When the guards found no rice in her hair, they allowed her to enter the king's chamber. Once inside, she undressed and scraped off the paste to feed him. She had fed her husband twice now in this manner, but she feared she would soon be discovered and forbidden to visit him at all.

The former queen began to sob again. The Buddha sat silently. After a long moment, he asked about the king's state of health, both physical and spiritual. The queen said that although he had lost a lot of weight, his strength was holding up, and his spirit was most elevated. He expressed no feelings of hatred or regret. He continued to smile and carry on a conversation as if nothing had happened. He was using his time as a prisoner to practice meditation. There was a long corridor in his chamber where he did walking meditation. The room also had a window which faced Vulture Peak. He gazed at the mountain everyday for long periods and did his sitting meditation at the same window.

The Buddha asked the queen whether or not she had been able to send news to her brother King Pasenadi. She replied that she had no means to do so. The Buddha said he would send a bhikkhu to Savatthi and ask King Pasenadi to help her any way he could.

The queen thanked the Buddha. She then confided how before Prince Ajatasattu was born, the royal astrologers predicted he would betray his father. One day during her pregnancy she was suddenly seized with a bizarre urge to bite King Bimbisara's finger and suck his blood. She was frightened and shocked by her desire, unable to believe she could give rise to so terrible a thought. From the time she was a little girl, she had always been afraid of the sight of blood and could not even bear to watch a fish or chicken slaughtered. Yet on that day she desired nothing more than to taste her husband's blood. She struggled against her urge with all her strength until she finally burst into tears. Overcome with shame, she covered her face in her hands but would not tell the king what was disturbing her. One day not long after that, King Bimbisara accidentally cut his finger while peeling a piece of fruit. Unable to control herself, the queen grabbed his finger and sucked the drops of blood. The king was startled but he did not stop her. Then the queen collapsed to the floor and sobbed. Alarmed, the king helped her up and asked her what the matter was. She told him of her strange and terrible desire. She told him how she had struggled against it but had finally been defeated. She knew that the baby growing within her was the source of her violent urge.

The royal astrologers suggested the baby be aborted or killed at birth. King Bimbisara could not agree to such a thing and neither could the queen. When the prince was born, they named him Ajatasattu which means "the enemy not born."

The Buddha advised the queen to visit her husband only once every two or three days to prevent arousing Ajatasattu's suspicions. She could spend a longer time with him on the days she did visit him. He also suggested that the king eat only a small amount of the nourishing paste at a time in order to save some for the days the queen did not visit. After offering these suggestions to the queen, the Buddha bid farewell to Jivaka and returned to Vulture Peak.

Chapter Seventy-Four
Cry of the Elephant Queen

Venerables Sariputta and Moggallana returned to Bamboo Forest after spending a little over a month at Gayasisa. The bhikkhus joyously welcomed them back. They asked the two venerables about the situation at Gayasisa, but Sariputta and Moggallana only smiled. A few days later, more than three hundred bhikkhus from Devadatta's sangha returned to Bamboo Forest. The bhikkhus at Bamboo Forest were overjoyed and they greeted their Gayasisa brothers warmly. Four days later Venerable Sariputta took an exact count of the brothers who had returned from Gayasisa and learned there were three hundred eighty in all. He led them together with Venerable Moggallana to Vulture Peak to have an audience with the Buddha.

As he stood outside his hut, the Buddha watched the bhikkhus being led up the mountain by his two senior disciples. Other bhikkhus who lived on Vulture Peak came out of their huts to greet the returning monks. Sariputta and Moggallana left the monks for a moment in order to speak privately with the Buddha. They bowed to the Buddha, who invited them to sit down. Venerable Sariputta smiled and said, "Lord Buddha, we have brought back nearly four hundred bhikkhus."

The Buddha said, "You have done well. But tell me, how were you able to open their eyes?"

Venerable Moggallana explained, "Lord, when we first arrived, Brother Devadatta had just finished eating and was preparing to give a Dharma talk. He looked very much as though he were trying to imitate you. When he looked up and saw us approaching, he appeared enormously pleased. He invited Sariputta to sit next to him on the Dharma platform. But Sariputta refused and chose to sit by one side instead. I sat on the other side. Devadatta then addressed the other bhikkhus. He said, 'Today Venerable Sariputta and Venerable Moggallana have joined us. They were my close friends in the past. Let me take this chance to invite Venerable Sariputta to give the Dharma talk today.'

"Devadatta turned to Sariputta and joined his palms. My brother accepted the invitation to speak. He spoke about the Four Noble Truths in a most beautiful way. All the bhikkhus listened as if spellbound. But I noticed Devadatta's eyes growing heavy as if he wanted to fall asleep. No doubt he was tired from all his recent activities. Halfway through the Dharma talk, he was fast asleep.

"We stayed at Gayasisa for more than a month and participated in all the activities there. Every three days, Brother Sariputta gave a Dharma talk. He instructed the bhikkhus with all his heart. Once I noticed Bhikkhu Kokalita, Devadatta's chief advisor, whisper something to Devadatta, but Devadatta seemed to pay him little attention. I suspect Kokalita was warning him not to trust us. Devadatta, however, was glad to have someone assume responsibility for teaching the Dharma, especially when it was someone as capable as my brother Sariputta.

"One day, after delivering a discourse on the Four Establishments of Mindfulness, Sariputta said, 'This afternoon, my brother and I will be leaving you to return to the Buddha and the sangha he leads. Dear brothers, there is only one fully enlightened Master and that is the Teacher Gautama. The Buddha founded the sangha of bhikkhus. He is the source for all of us. I know that you would be warmly welcomed back by the Buddha if you returned. Dear brothers, there is nothing more painful than seeing a community divided. I have met only one true Master in my life and that is the Buddha. We will depart from you today, but should any of you decide to return to the Buddha, please come to Bamboo Forest. We will meet you there and take you to meet with the Buddha on Vulture Peak.'

"That day, Devadatta was in the capital on business, but Venerable Kokalita, who had been hostile to us since our arrival, stood up to protest. He even hurled curses at us, but we simply stood up and pretended not to hear. We silently took our bowls and extra robes and left Gayasisa to return to Venuvana. We stayed in Venuvana for five days. Three hundred and eighty bhikkhus from Gayasisa followed shortly."

Venerable Sariputta asked, "Lord, do these bhikkhus need to be re-ordained? If necessary, I will organize an ordination ceremony for them before they meet with you."

The Buddha said, "That is not necessary, Sariputta. It will be adequate for them to make a confession before the community."

The two senior disciples bowed and rejoined the waiting bhikkhus.

Over the next few days, thirty-five more bhikkhus left Gayasisa. Venerable Sariputta arranged a confession ceremony for them and then presented them to the Buddha. Venerable Ananda spoke to the thirty-five newest arrivals and asked them about the situation at Gayasisa. They told him that after Venerable Devadatta had returned from Rajagaha and learned that nearly four hundred bhikkhus had abandoned him to return to the Buddha, his face turned scarlet in anger. He refused to speak to anyone for several days.

Ananda asked, "What did Brothers Sariputta and Moggallana say to you that made you want to leave Brother Devadatta and return to the Buddha?"

One of the bhikkhus answered, "They never spoke a critical word against Venerable Devadatta or the Gayasisa sangha. They simply taught the Dharma with all their hearts. Most of us have only been ordained two or three years and still lack stability and depth in our practice. When we heard Brother Sariputta's Dharma talks and received personal instruction from Brother Moggallana, we saw how marvelous and sublime the teaching of the Buddha truly is. The presence of Venerables Sariputta and Moggallana with their profound understanding and virtue was like the presence of the Buddha himself. We realized that although Venerable Devadatta speaks with great skill, he could not compare with them. After Venerables Sariputta and Moggallana departed, many of us discussed these things and reached the decision to return to the Buddha."

Ananda asked, "What did Bhikkhu Kokalita do when you left?"

"He was enraged. He cursed us, but that only made us all the more determined to leave."

One afternoon as the Buddha stood on the mountain slope admiring the evening sky, he suddenly heard a shout from below, "Watch out, Lord! A boulder is about to crash behind you!"

The Buddha looked back to see a boulder the size of a cattle cart crashing down the mountain towards him. It was difficult to move out of the way in time as the mountain path was suddenly covered with sharp and jutting stones. By a stroke of luck, the boulder was blocked by two other rocks on the mountainside just before reaching the Buddha. But the impact of rock against rock sent a fragment flying which pierced the Buddha's foot. Blood gushed from his wound and stained his robes. Looking up, the Buddha saw a man at the top of the mountain running quickly away.

His wound was very painful. He folded his sanghati in four and placed it on the earth. He sat down on it in a lotus position and began to concentrate on his breath in order to calm the pain. Bhikkhus came running towards him. One exclaimed, "This is surely the work of Devadatta!"

Another said, "Brothers, let us divide ourselves into patrols to guard the mountain and protect the Lord Buddha. Let's not lose any time!"

Everyone ran about in circles, disturbing the previously calm evening. The Buddha said, "Brothers, please do not shout. Nothing warrants such noise. The Tathagata does not need to be guarded or protected. Please return to your huts. Ananda, send novice Cunda for physician Jivaka."

They obeyed the Buddha's wishes. Jivaka came up to Vulture Peak in no time at all and asked that the Buddha be carried in a palanquin down to the mango grove.

Within a few short days, people in the capital learned of the two attempts on the Buddha's life. They were shocked and dismayed. Not only that, but they received the announcement that King Bimbisara had died. Through unknown channels, the people learned how he died under house arrest. Agony filled the people's hearts. They looked towards Vulture Peak as a symbol of moral resistance. As they grieved for the king, their admiration for the Buddha deepened. Though the Buddha had chosen to remain silent about recent events, his silence had been well understood by the people.

King Bimbisara was sixty-seven years old when he died. He was five years younger than the Buddha. He had taken the three refuges with the Buddha when he was just thirty-one years old. Having ascended to the throne at the age of fifteen, he then reigned for fifty-two years. It was he who rebuilt the capital of Rajagaha after it had been destroyed by fire. Throughout his reign, Magadha had enjoyed continuous peace with the exception of one short war with the kingdom of Anga. King Brahmadatta of Anga lost the war and Anga temporarily fell under the jurisdiction of Magadha. When King Taxila Pukkusati later assumed the throne in Anga, King Bimbisara maintained close and friendly relations with him to prevent future conflicts. Thanks to that, the new king also became a disciple of the Buddha. King Bimbisara had always understood the importance of maintaining good relations with neighboring kingdoms. He married Princess Kosaladevi, the younger sister of King Pasenadi of Kosala, and made her his queen. He also took wives from the Madra and

Licchavi dynasties. His elder sister was married to the king of Kosala.

King Bimbisara showed his deep love and respect for the Buddha by having a stupa built in the royal gardens which contained the Buddha's hair and fingernails. Incense and candles were regularly lit around the foot of the stupa to express gratitude for the Buddha's teaching. The king entrusted Shrimati, a lady-in-waiting at the palace, with the stupa's upkeep. Shrimati tended all the flowers and plants around the stupa and kept the area well swept.

Just ten days after the boulder was hurled at the Buddha, he and several bhikkhus were begging in the capital, when Venerable Ananda looked up to see an elephant charging towards them. It appeared to have escaped from the royal stables. He recognized that it was the elephant named Nalagiri, infamous for its violent behavior. Ananda could not understand how the royal keeper could have allowed it to escape. Panic-stricken, people ran for cover. The elephant raised its trunk, lifted its tail and ears, and headed straight for the Buddha. Ananda grabbed the Buddha's arm to lead him to safety, but the Buddha would not budge. He stood calmly, unperturbed. Some bhikkhus cowered behind him while others fled. People shouted at the Buddha to save himself. Ananda held his breath and stepped forward to place his body between the Buddha and Nalagiri. At that very moment, to Ananda's surprise, the Buddha let forth a majestic cry. It was the cry of the Elephant Queen the Buddha had befriended long ago in Rakkhita Forest in Parileyyaka.

Nalagiri was but a few yards from the Buddha when he heard the resounding cry, and he came to a sudden halt. The mighty elephant knelt on all fours and lowered his head to the ground as if to bow to the Buddha. The Buddha gently stroked Nalagiri's head and then, holding the elephant's trunk in one hand, led an obedient Nalagiri back to the royal stables.

The people applauded and cheered. Ananda smiled. He thought back to the days when they were young. The

The Buddha gently stroked Nalagiri's head.

young Siddhartha had known no equal in the martial arts. He excelled at everything—archery, weightlifting, swordsmanship, horseracing—and today, the Buddha treated an elephant on a rampage as though he were an old and docile friend. The bhikkhus and a large crowd followed the Buddha and the elephant back to the stables. When they arrived, the Buddha gave the keeper a stern look, but then spoke in a compassionate voice, "The Tathagata does not need to know who ordered you to release this elephant. But you should understand the seriousness of your action. Dozens, even hundreds, of people could have been killed. You must never allow such a thing to happen again."

The keeper bowed before the Buddha. The Buddha helped him back to his feet, and then joined the bhikkhus to resume begging.

The Buddha and all his bhikkhus attended King Bimbisara's funeral. The ceremony was an event of great solemnity and beauty. The people grieved the passing of their beloved monarch and showed up in dense crowds to pay their final respects. More than four thousand bhikkhus were present.

When the funeral was over, the Buddha spent the night at Jivaka's Mango Grove before returning to Vulture Peak. The physician informed him that the former queen Videhi had been forbidden to visit the king at all during the past month. The king passed from this life all alone. They found him lying down before his favorite window. His eyes were turned towards Vulture Peak when he took his last breath.

Shortly after the king's funeral, Jivaka brought Prince Abhayaraja, son of King Bimbisara and his wife Padumavati, to see the Buddha. The prince requested to take vows as a bhikkhu. He told the Buddha that since his father's death, he had lost all enthusiasm for a life of wealth or fame. He had heard many of the Buddha's Dharma talks and felt drawn to the path of enlightenment. He desired nothing more than to lead the peaceful, unburdened life of a bhikkhu. The Buddha accepted Prince Abhayaraja into the sangha of bhikkhus.

Chapter Seventy-Five
Tears of Happiness

Ten days later, the Buddha put on his outer robe, took his begging bowl, and left the city of Rajagaha. He headed north across the Ganga, stopped along the way to visit Kutagara monastery, and then made his way to Savatthi. It would soon be the rainy season again, and he needed to return to Jetavana to prepare for the annual retreat. Venerables Ananda, Sariputta, Moggallana, and three hundred other bhikkhus accompanied him.

When they reached Savatthi, the Buddha walked directly to Jetavana. Many bhikkhus and bhikkhunis had gathered to await his arrival. They had heard of events in Magadha and were relieved to see the Buddha unharmed and in good health. Bhikkhuni Khema was present. She now served as abbess to the bhikkhunis.

King Pasenadi came to see the Buddha the moment he learned of his arrival. He asked the Buddha about the situation in Rajagaha and listened as the Buddha recounted everything, including his meeting with Queen Videhi, King Pasenadi's own sister. The Buddha told him that while she maintained a calm composure, he knew her heart was filled with grief and sorrow. King Pasenadi told the Buddha that he had already sent a delegation to Rajagaha to ask Ajatasattu, his nephew, to explain the imprisonment of King Bimbisara. A month had already passed but no response had been received. King Pasenadi sent further word that if the new king deemed it necessary, he could come to Savatthi in person to explain the situation. King Pasenadi informed the Buddha that in order to demonstrate his opposition to the events in Magadha, he had reclaimed the territory he offered to Magadha many years ago on the occasion of his sister's marriage to King Bimbisara. This land was located close to the city of Varanasi in Kasi.

The first day of the retreat season arrived. All the spiritual centers and monasteries in the region were filled to overflowing with bhikkhus and bhikkhunis. Every ten days, the Buddha gave a Dharma talk at Jetavana to all the monks and nuns. These talks always took place following the noon meal. Monks and nuns who walked from the more distant centers did not have enough time to go begging if they wanted to arrive in time for the discourse. Lay disciples in the city worked hard to assure there was always enough food waiting for these monks and nuns.

The first Dharma talk the Buddha delivered that season was on the subject of happiness. He told the assembly that happiness is real and can be realized in the very midst of daily life. "First of all," the Buddha said, "happiness is not the result of gratifying sense desires. Sense pleasures give the illusion of happiness, but in fact they are sources of suffering.

"It is like a leper who is forced to live alone in the forest. His flesh is wracked by terrible pain day and night. So he digs a pit and makes a fierce fire, and he stands over it to seek temporary relief from his pain by toasting his limbs over the fire. It is the only way he can feel any comfort. But, miraculously, after a few years, his disease goes into remission, and he is able to return to a normal life in the village. One day he enters the forest and sees a group of lepers toasting their limbs over hot flames just as he once did. He is filled with pity for them, for he knows that in his healthy state he could never bear to hold his limbs over such fierce flames. If someone tried to drag him over the fire he would resist with all his might. He understands that what he once took to be a comfort, is actually a source of pain to one who is healthy."

The Buddha said, "Sense pleasures are like a pit of fire. They bring happiness only to those who are ill. A healthy person shuns the flames of sense desires."

The Buddha explained that the source of true happiness is living in ease and freedom, fully experiencing the wonders of life. Happiness is being aware of what is going on in the present moment, free from both clinging and aversion. A happy person cherishes the wonders taking place in the present moment—a cool breeze, the morning sky, a golden flower, a violet bamboo tree, the smile of a child. A happy person can appreciate these things without being bound by them. Understanding all dharmas as impermanent and without a separate self, a happy person does not become consumed even by such pleasures. A happy person thus lives in ease, free from all worry and fear. Because he understands that a flower will soon wilt, he is not sad when it does. A happy person understands the nature of birth and death of all dharmas. His happiness is true happiness, and he does not even worry about or fear his own death.

The Buddha told the assembly that some people believe it is necessary to suffer in the present in order to have happiness in the future. They make sacrifices and endure hardships of body and mind, thinking they can acquire happiness in the future. But life exists only in the present moment. That kind of sacrifice is a waste of life. Other people think that if you want peace, joy, and liberation in the future, you must practice self-mortification in the present. They practice austerities, starve themselves, and inflict pain on their minds and bodies. The Buddha taught that such practices cause suffering for the person in both the present and the future. Still others contend that because life is so fleeting, they should not concern themselves with the future at all. They may try to satisfy all their sense desires in the present. The Buddha explained that clinging to sense pleasures this way causes suffering in both the present and the future.

The path the Buddha taught avoided both extremes. He taught that the most intelligent way is to live in a way that fosters happiness for both the present and the future. The way of liberation does not force austerities on the body in the hope of attaining future happiness. A bhikkhu creates happiness for himself and for all those around him in the present moment by the way in which he eats his daily meal, meditates, and practices the Four Establishments of Mindfulness, the Four Limitless Meditations, and the Full Awareness of Breathing. Eating only one meal a day keeps his body healthy and light, and allows more time for spiritual practice. Living in ease and freedom, he is better able to help others. Bhikkhus remain celibate and childless, not as a practice of austerity, but as a means of being more free to help others. The bhikkhu is able to see the happiness that is present in each moment of daily life. If he feels his chastity deprives him of happiness, he is not living the spirit of the teaching. A bhikkhu who follows the teaching of celibacy according to its true spirit radiates ease, peace, and joy. Such a life brings happiness in both the present and future.

After the Dharma talk, lay disciple Punnalakkhana asked the Buddha if she could speak to him. She told the Buddha that her husband, Sudatta Anathapindika, had fallen gravely ill. He was in such great pain he was unable to attend the Dharma talk. His condition was steadily worsening. He feared he would die before having a chance to see the Buddha one last time.

The next day the Buddha, together with Venerables Sariputta and Ananda, went to visit Sudatta. Sudatta was deeply moved to see them. His face was pale and drawn and he could barely sit up. The Buddha said to him, "Sudatta, your entire life has been filled with meaning and happiness. You have relieved the suffering of countless others, moving the people to bestow upon you the name of Anathapindika, 'the one who cares for the poor and abandoned.' Jetavana monastery is one of your many fine accomplishments. You have constantly contributed to efforts to spread the Dharma.

You have lived according to the teaching and have thus created true happiness for yourself, your family, and many others. You can rest now. I will ask Venerable Sariputta to visit you often and provide you special guidance. Don't try to come to the monastery. You should reserve your strength."

Sudatta joined his palms in gratitude.

Fifteen days later, the Buddha gave a Dharma talk on lay life. He told the laity how they could realize true happiness in their daily lives. He reviewed the principle of living for "peace in the present, peace for the future" which he had presented in his previous Dharma talk to the monks and nuns. He also said, "A bhikkhu lives a celibate life in order to enjoy peace and joy in the present moment. Such a life assures future happiness as well. But homeless bhikkhus are not the only ones who can enjoy such happiness. Lay disciples living in the world can follow the principles of the teaching to foster true happiness. First of all, do not let a desire for wealth cause you to become so consumed by your work that you prevent happiness for yourself and your family in the present moment. Happiness is foremost. A look filled with understanding, an accepting smile, a loving word, a meal shared in warmth and awareness are the things which create happiness in the present moment. By nourishing awareness in the present moment, you can avoid causing suffering to yourself and those around you. The way you look at others, your smile, and your small acts of caring can create happiness. True happiness does not depend on wealth or fame."

The Buddha recalled a conversation he had had with a merchant named Sigala several years previously in Rajagaha. One morning, the Buddha left Bamboo Forest with his begging bowl just as daylight was breaking. He came upon a young man on a path just outside the city. Sigala was bowing to the six directions of East, West, South, North, Down, and Up. The Buddha stopped and asked him the purpose of his bowing. Sigala said that his father had taught him as a child to bow to the six directions every morning. He liked to obey his father's wishes, but he did not actually know the purpose for the ritual.

The Buddha told him, "Bowing is a practice which can foster happiness for both the present and the future." He told Sigala that as he bowed to the East he could contemplate gratitude to his parents. When he bowed to the South, he could contemplate gratitude to his teachers. Bowing West, he could contemplate love for his wife and children. Bowing to the North, he could contemplate love for his friends. Bowing down, he could contemplate gratitude to his co-workers. Bowing up, he could contemplate gratitude to all wise and virtuous persons.

The Buddha taught Sigala the five precepts and how to look deeply at things in order to avoid acting out of greed, anger, passion, or fear. The Buddha told Sigala to avoid the six actions which lead to ruin—abusing alcohol, wandering through city streets late at night, frequenting places of gambling, visiting places of depravity, loitering with persons of poor character, and succumbing to laziness. In addition, he told Sigala how to determine who was worthy of being considered a good friend. He said, "A good friend is constant. Whether you are rich or poor, happy or sad, successful or unsuccessful, a good friend is one whose feelings for you do not waver. A good friend listens to you and shares your sufferings. He shares his own joys and sorrows with you, while regarding your joys and sorrows as his own."

The Buddha continued his Dharma talk by saying, "True happiness can be realized in this very life, especially when you observe the following:

"1. Foster relations with people of virtue and avoid the path of degradation.

"2. Live in an environment that is conducive to spiritual practice and builds good character.

"3. Foster opportunities to learn more about the Dharma, the precepts, and your own trade in greater depth.

"4. Take the time to care well for your parents, spouse, and children.

"5. Share time, resources, and happiness with others.

"6. Foster opportunities to cultivate virtue. Avoid alcohol and gambling.

"7. Cultivate humility, gratitude, and simple living.

"8. Seek opportunities to be close to bhikkhus in order to study the Way.

"9. Live a life based on the Four Noble Truths.

"10. Learn how to meditate in order to release sorrows and anxieties."

The Buddha praised lay disciples who lived the teaching in their daily lives within their families and society. He made special mention of Sudatta Anathapindika. He said that Sudatta was an exemplar of one who devoted all his efforts to creating a life full of meaning, service, and happiness. Sudatta's heart was truly deep. His entire life had been guided by the teaching. The Buddha said that people who owned far greater wealth than Sudatta would not find it easy to match the happiness he had created for others. Sudatta's wife, Punnalakkhana, was moved to tears by the Buddha's praise of her husband.

She stood up and respectfully addressed the Buddha, "Lord, a wealthy person's life is often very busy, especially when he owns many things. I think that maintaining a small and modest vocation would be more conducive to spiritual practice. When we see the bhikkhus, free of home and family, who own little more than a bowl, we long for a more simple, carefree life ourselves. We would like to live a leisurely life, too, but we are bound by so many responsibilities. What can we do?"

The Buddha answered, "Punnalakkhana, bhikkhus have responsibilities too. A celibate life requires a bhikkhu to live mindfully by the precepts day and night. A bhikkhu devotes his life to others. Lay disciples, the Tathagata wishes to suggest a way by which you can taste the life of a bhikkhu twice a month or so. We shall call this practice the Eight Observances for the Laity. Twice a month you can come to the temple and follow these practices for a day and a night. Like the bhikkhus, you will eat only one meal. You can practice sitting and walking meditation. For twenty-hours you can enjoy a celibate, aware, concentrated, relaxed, peaceful, and joyous life as if you were a monk or nun. When the day is over, you can return to your secular life, observing the five precepts and three refuges as usual.

"Lay disciples, the Tathagata will inform the bhikkhus about the Eight Observances for the Laity. These special days of practice can be organized at temples or even in your own homes. You can invite bhikkhus to your homes to administer the eight observances and to offer teaching on your day of practice."

Punnalakkhana was pleased with the Buddha's suggestion. She asked, "Please, Lord, what are the eight observances?"

The Buddha answered,"Do not kill, do not steal, do not engage in sexual activity, do not lie, do not use alcohol, do not adorn yourself with jewelry, do not sit or lie on a fancy bed, and do not use money. These eight observances can prevent forgetfulness and confusion. Eating only one meal on your day of practice will allow more time for your practice."

The people were happy with the Buddha's suggestion for special days of practice for the laity.

Ten days later, a servant from Sudatta's household came to inform Venerable Sariputta that Sudatta's illness had taken a turn for the worse. Sariputta asked Ananda to join him and together they walked into the city. They found Sudatta lying on his bed. A servant pulled two chairs close to the bed for the bhikkhus.

Knowing that Sudatta was suffering greatly in his body, Venerable Sariputta advised him to practice contemplating on the Buddha, the Dharma, and the Sangha, to ease the pain. "Lay disciple Sudatta, let us contemplate together on the Buddha, the Enlightened One; on the Dharma, the Way of Understanding and Love; and on the Sangha, the Noble Community which lives in harmony and awareness."

Knowing that Sudatta did not have much longer to live, Venerable Sariputta told him, "Lay disciple Sudatta, let us contemplate as follows—my eyes are not me, my ears are not me, my nose, my tongue, my body, and my mind are not me."

Sudatta followed Sariputta's instructions. Then Sariputta continued, "Now let us continue to contemplate—that which I see is not me, that which I hear is not me, that which I smell, taste, touch, and think are not me."

Sariputta then showed Sudatta how to contemplate on the six sense consciousnesses—seeing is not me, hearing is not me, smelling, tasting, touching, and thinking are not me."

Sariputta continued, "The element earth is not me. The elements water, fire, air, space, and consciousness are not me. I am not bound or restrained by the elements. Birth and death cannot touch me. I smile because I have never been born and I will never die. Birth does not give me existence. Death does not take existence away."

Suddenly Sudatta began to weep. Startled to see tears roll down the lay disciple's cheeks, Ananda asked him, "Are you upset, Sudatta, because you are unable to follow the contemplation?"

Sudatta answered, "Venerable Ananda, I am not upset at all. I am able to follow the contemplation without difficulty. I weep because I am so deeply moved. For more than thirty years I have had the honor of serving the Buddha and the bhikkhus. But I have never heard a more sublime and profound teaching than this teaching today."

Ananda said, "Sudatta, the Lord Buddha frequently offers this kind of teaching to the bhikkhus and bhikkhunis."

"Venerable Ananda, lay disciples are also able to understand and practice such a teaching. Please ask Lord Buddha to share this teaching with the laity."

Sudatta died later that day. Venerables Sariputta and Ananda remained with him and continued to recite sutras over his body. Anathapindika's family was a model for all other families. All the members of his family took refuge in the Buddha and devoted themselves to studying and applying the Dharma in their daily lives. A few days before his death, Sudatta learned that his youngest daughter, Sumagadha, was sharing the teaching with people in Anga. She had married a man from Anga who was a governor and a devout follower of the unclothed ascetics. When he asked her to visit the ascetics with him, she diplomatically declined. Over time, her solid understanding of the Buddha's Way touched her husband and opened the hearts of many people in their region.

The Fruits of Practice

Just as the retreat season was ending, the sangha learned that war had broken out between Kosala and Magadha. Magadha's army, led by King Ajatasattu Videhiputta himself, had crossed over the Ganga into Kasi, a region under Kosala's jurisdiction. The king and his generals led an enormous battalion of elephants, horses, carts, artillery, and soldiers. Because it all happened so quickly, King Pasenadi was unable to inform the Buddha of his departure to Kasi. He asked Prince Jeta to explain the situation in his place.

The Buddha already knew that after King Pasenadi learned how Ajatasattu killed his own father to usurp the throne, King Pasenadi showed his opposition by reclaiming a district near Varanasi he had formerly presented to King Bimbisara. For nearly seventy years this district had brought in revenues of over a hundred thousand gold pieces to Magadha, and King Ajatasattu was not about to give it up. So he called his soldiers into battle.

Venerable Sariputta instructed all the bhikkhus and bhikkhunis to remain in Savatthi. It was too dangerous to travel with a war raging. He also asked the Buddha to remain in Savatthi until peace was restored.

Two months later the people of Savatthi received the disheartening news that their army had suffered defeat in Kasi. King Pasenadi and his generals were forced to retreat back to the capital. The situation was fraught with tension, but thanks to a strong system of defense, Savatthi did not fall, even though Ajatasattu's generals attacked day and night. Then, thanks to a brilliant plan devised by General Bandhula, King Pasenadi was able to mount a major counter-offensive. This time Kosala scored the decisive victory. King Ajatasattu and all his generals were captured alive. More than a thousand soldiers were taken prisoner. Another thousand had either been killed or fled. In addition, Kosala confiscated large numbers of elephants, horses, army carts, and supplies of artillery.

The war had raged for more than six months. The people of Savatthi organized a victory celebration. After dismantling his army, King Pasenadi visited the Buddha at Jetavana. He described the terrible cost of the war and said that Kosala had acted in self-defense when King Ajatasattu attacked their borders. He added that he believed King Ajatasattu had been wrongly influenced by his advisors.

"Lord Buddha, the king of Magadha is my own nephew. I cannot kill him, nor do I have any desire to put him in prison. Please help me find a wise course of action."

The Buddha said, "Your majesty, you are surrounded by loyal friends and aides. It is no surprise that you came out the victor in this war. King Ajatasattu is surrounded by bad elements and so he has gone astray. The Tathagata suggests you treat him with all the respect due a king of Magadha. Take time, as well, to guide him as your own nephew. Strongly impress on him the importance of surrounding himself with friends and aides of good and loyal character. Then you can send him back to Magadha with proper ceremony. The possibility of lasting peace depends on your skill in handling these matters."

The Buddha called for a young bhikkhu named Silavat and introduced him to King Pasenadi. Bhikkhu Silavat was originally a prince, one of King Bimbisara's sons, and King Ajatasattu's half-brother. Silavat was a wise and bright man who had studied the Dharma as a lay disciple under the guidance of Venerable Moggallana from the age of sixteen.

After the changes that took place in Magadha, he asked Moggallana to allow him to be ordained, and he was sent to Jetavana in Savatthi to further his studies. Venerable Moggallana knew that although Silavat harbored no desire for the throne, it would nonetheless be safer for him to be out of King Ajatasattu's jealous reach.

King Pasenadi asked the young bhikkhu to describe the situation in Rajagaha. Silavat told the king all he had seen and heard before he left Magadha. He also informed the king that someone had been sent from Magadha to try and kill him, but he had been able to effect a change of heart in the assassin. That man was now an ordained bhikkhu himself living in a center close to the capital. King Pasenadi bowed to the Buddha and returned to his palace.

Shortly afterwards, King Ajatasattu was released and allowed to return to Magadha. Using love to ease the wounds of hatred, King Pasenadi gave his own daughter, Princess Vajira, in marriage to Ajatasattu. Ajatasattu was now his son-in-law as well as his nephew. King Pasenadi also promised to return the district near Varanasi as a wedding gift. King Pasenadi had wholeheartedly followed the spirit of the Buddha's counsel.

With the war over, bhikkhus and bhikkhunis once again took to the road to spread the teaching. King Pasenadi ordered the construction of a new monastery on the outskirts of the capital and named it Rajakarama.

The Buddha remained in Kosala for the following two years, passing the retreat seasons at Jetavana and the rest of the time teaching throughout the region. From time to time he received news from Magadha from bhikkhus who had come from there. They told him that after the Buddha left Magadha, Venerable Devadatta ceased to enjoy the good graces of King Ajatasattu. Of the more than one hundred bhikkhus still with Devadatta at that time, eighty had returned to the Buddha's sangha at Bamboo Forest. Devadatta was more and more isolated. He had recently fallen ill and was unable to leave Gayasisa. Since the end of the war, King

Ajatasattu had not paid him even one visit. King Ajatasattu did not pay any visits to Bamboo Forest either. He only maintained relations with leaders of other religious sects. Nonetheless, the sangha continued to spread the Dharma unimpeded. The laity and bhikkhus in Magadha hoped that the Buddha would return to visit them. Vulture Peak and Bamboo Forest seemed empty without him. Jivaka awaited his return as well.

That winter Queen Mallika of Kosala died. Deeply grieved, King Pasenadi came to the Buddha for comfort. The queen had been his closest friend, and he loved her with all his heart. She was a faithful disciple of the Buddha, a radiant spirit who understood the deeper reaches of the Dharma. Even before the king met the Buddha, the queen had shared her understanding of the Way with him. The king recalled how one night he had a disturbing dream which he feared was a warning that misfortune would befall him. Placing his faith in the brahmans, he asked them to sacrifice several animals in order to ask the gods for protection. The queen dissuaded him from doing so. She had often served as a close advisor to the king on political matters, helping him find solutions to problems that beset the country. She was one of the Buddha's most devoted lay disciples. Because she loved to study the Dharma, she built a Dharma discussion hall in a park with many beautiful tinduka trees. She often invited the Buddha and his senior disciples to give Dharma discourses and lead discussions there. She also opened the hall to leaders of other religious sects to use.

Suffering from the loss of his companion for more than forty years, the king came to the Buddha. As he sat quietly next to the Buddha, he felt peace slowly return to his heart. He had been following the Buddha's suggestion to spend more time meditating. The Buddha reminded him of their previous conversation in which they discussed the importance of living according to the teaching in order to create happiness for those around one. The Buddha encouraged the king to reform the system of justice and economics in the country. He said corporal punishment, torture, imprisonment, and execution were not effective means for stopping crime. Crime and violence were the natural result of hunger and poverty. The best way to assist the people and provide for their security was to concentrate on building a healthy economy. It was essential to provide food, seeds, and fertilizer to poor farmers until they could become self-sufficient and productive. Loans should be provided to small merchants, retirement funds should be set up for those no longer able to work, and the poor should be exempted from taxes. All manner of coercion and oppression against manual laborers must cease. People should be free to select their own jobs. Ample opportunities for training should be made available to help people master the trades they chose. The Buddha said that a correct economic policy should be based on voluntary participation.

Venerable Ananda was sitting close to the Buddha during this conversation with the king. He was thus able to preserve the Buddha's ideas on politics and economics in the *Kutadanta Sutra*.

Late one afternoon Ananda found the Buddha sitting outside the Visakha Dharma hall. His back was turned to the sun. Ananda found it curious. The Buddha was usually fond of watching the sun set. He asked the Buddha about it, and the Buddha replied that he was letting the sun warm his back. Ananda approached and began to massage the Buddha's back. He knelt down to massage his legs as well. As he massaged the Buddha's legs, he remarked, "Lord, I have been your attendant for the past fifteen years. I remember how firm your skin was in the past and how it had such a healthy glow. But now your skin is wrinkled and your leg muscles have grown soft. Why, I can count all your bones!"

The Buddha laughed. "If you live long enough, you grow old, Ananda. But my eyes and ears are as sharp as ever. Ananda, do you miss Vulture Peak and the groves at Bamboo Forest? Wouldn't you like to climb Vulture Peak again and watch the sun set?"

"Lord, if you would like to return to Vulture Peak, please let me accompany you."

That summer the Buddha returned to Magadha. He walked leisurely, breaking the long trek into several short trips. He stopped all along the way to visit sangha centers. He taught the bhikkhus at each center and delivered talks to the laity. He passed through the kingdoms of Sakya, Malla, Videha, and Vajji, before he at last crossed the Ganga into Magadha. Before going on to Rajagaha, he stopped to visit the sangha center in Nalanda.

Bamboo Forest and Vulture Peak were as beautiful as ever. People from the capital and neighboring villages came to see the Buddha in droves. Nearly a month passed before the Buddha was free to accept Jivaka's invitation to visit his Mango Grove. Jivaka had built a new Dharma hall in the grove that was large enough to seat one thousand bhikkhus.

While they sat outside his hut at the Mango Grove, the Buddha listened to Jivaka recount events that had taken place in the Buddha's absence. Queen Videhi, he was pleased to learn, had found inner peace. She devoted time to meditation and had become a vegetarian. King Ajatasattu, on the other hand, was suffering from extreme mental anguish. He was haunted by his father's death and his mind could find no ease. His nerves were constantly on edge, and he was afraid to sleep at night because of the terrible nightmares he suffered. Many doctors and high-ranking priests from the sects of Makkhali Gosala, Ajita Kosakambali, Pakudha Kaccayana, Nigantha Nataputta, and Sanjaya Belatthiputta, had been summoned to try to cure him. Each priest hoped to effect a cure so that their particular sect would receive special patronage, but not one of them was able to help the king.

One day the king ate dinner with his wife, their son Udayibhadda, and his mother, the former queen Videhi. Prince Udayibhadda was almost three years old. Because the king catered to his son's every whim, the prince was an unruly and spoiled child. The prince demanded his dog be allowed to sit at the table with them. Though such a thing was normally forbidden, the king gave in to his son's wish. Feeling somewhat embarrassed, he said to his mother, "It is unpleasant having a dog sitting at the table, isn't it, but what else can I do?"

Queen Videhi answered, "You love your son and so you have allowed him to bring his dog to the table. There is nothing unusual about that. Do you remember how your own father once swallowed pus from your hand because he loved you?"

Ajatasattu did not recall the incident and asked his mother to tell him what had happened.

The queen said, "One day your finger became red and swollen. A boil formed underneath your fingernail. It caused you so much pain, you cried and fretted all day and night. Your father was unable to sleep out of concern for you. He lifted you onto his pillow and placed your infected finger in his mouth. He sucked on it to help relieve the pain. He sucked on your finger throughout four days and nights until the boil broke. He then sucked out the pus. He did not dare remove your finger from his mouth to spit out the pus for fear you would feel more pain. And so he swallowed the pus while continuing to suck on your finger. From this story, you can see how deeply your father loved you. You love your own son and that is why you have allowed him to bring his dog to the table. I can understand that very well."

The king suddenly clutched his head in his two hands and ran from the room, leaving his meal uneaten. After that night, his mental state worsened. At last, Jivaka was summoned to take a look at the king. Jivaka listened to Ajatasattu recount all his woes and how no priest or brahman had been able to help him. Jivaka sat without saying a word. The king asked, "Jivaka, why don't you say anything?"

Jivaka responded, "There is only thing to tell you. Teacher Gautama is the only person who can help you overcome the agony in your heart. Go to the Buddha for guidance."

The king did not speak for several minutes. Finally he muttered, "But I am sure Teacher Gautama hates me."

Jivaka disagreed. "Don't say such a thing. Teacher Gautama does not hate anyone. He was your father's teacher and closest friend. Going to him will be like going to your own father. See him and you will find inner peace. You will be able to restore all you have torn asunder. My ability to heal is not worth anything compared with the Buddha's ability to heal. He is not a medical physician but he is the king of all physicians. Some people call him the Medicine King."

The king agreed to think about it.

The Buddha remained at Vulture Peak for several months. He visited the sangha centers in the region and also agreed to spend a month at Jivaka's Mango Grove. It was there that Jivaka arranged for King Ajatasattu to meet with the Buddha. On a moonlit night, the king, seated on an elephant, proceeded to the grove accompanied by the royal family, his concubines, palace guards, and Queen Videhi. When they entered the grove, all was still. The king was seized with sudden panic. Jivaka had told him that the Buddha was dwelling in the grove with a thousand bhikkhus. If that was true, how could it be so quiet? Could it be a trick? Was Jivaka leading him to be ambushed? He turned to Jivaka and asked if this was all a plot in order for Jivaka to seek revenge. Jivaka laughed out loud. He pointed to the Dharma hall from which light was streaming through a round window.

Jivaka said, "The Buddha and all the bhikkhus are in there this very moment."

The king climbed down from his elephant and entered the hall, followed by his family and attendants. Jivaka pointed to a man sitting on a platform, his back supported against a pillar, and said, "There is the Buddha."

The king was deeply impressed by the attentive quiet. A thousand bhikkhus surrounded the Buddha in perfect silence. Not even a robe rustled. King Ajatasattu had only seen the Buddha a few times in his life, as he had never joined his father in attending the Buddha's regular Dharma talks.

The Buddha invited the king and royal family to be seated. The king bowed and then spoke, "Lord, I remember hearing you speak at the palace when I was a young boy. Tonight, I would like to ask you a question. What kinds of fruit does the spiritual life bear that hundreds, even thousands, abandon their homes to pursue it?"

The Buddha asked the king if he had ever asked any other teacher the same question. The king responded that he had, in fact, asked dozens of other teachers including Venerable Devadatta, but he had never received a satisfactory answer.

The Buddha said, "Your majesty, tonight the Tathagata will tell you the fruits which can be found in this teaching, fruits that can be enjoyed in this very moment, and fruits which can be reaped in the future. You need not seek lofty answers. Simply look and see these fruits as clearly as a mango held in your own hand.

"Your majesty, consider this example. A servant caters to all his master's whims and commands from sunup to sundown, until one day he asks himself, 'As my master and I are both human beings, why should I allow myself to be abused by him?' The servant decides to leave his life as a servant to enter the homeless life of a bhikkhu. He pursues a chaste, diligent, and mindful life. He eats but one meal a day, practices sitting and walking meditation, and expresses calm dignity in all his movements. He becomes a respected, virtuous monk. Knowing that he was formerly a servant, if you met him, would you call out to him and say, 'Here, fellow, I want you to serve me from sunup to sundown. Obey all my commands.'"

The king said, "No, Lord, I would not address him in such a way. I would respectfully greet him. I would make food offerings to him and assure that he received the full protection of the law afforded to monks."

The Buddha said, "Your majesty, that is the first fruit a bhikkhu reaps. He is liberated from racial, social, and caste prejudice. His human dignity is restored."

The king said, "Wonderful, Lord! Please tell me more."

The Buddha continued, "Your majesty, dignity is only the first fruit. A bhikkhu observes two hundred fifty precepts which enable him to dwell in calm peace. People who do not observe precepts are more easily misguided. They may commit such crimes as lying, drunkenness, sexual misconduct, stealing, and even murder. They bring cruel punishment on their minds and bodies by acting this way. They may be arrested and put in jail by the police and government officials. A bhikkhu observes the precepts of not killing, not stealing, not engaging in sexual misconduct, not lying, and not using alcohol. In addition, he observes more than two hundred other precepts which assure him a carefree life unknown to those who do not observe precepts. Precepts help prevent one from falling into error, thus assuring a carefree state. That is another fruit of spiritual practice which can be enjoyed right in the present moment."

The king said, "Wonderful, Lord! Please tell me more."

The Buddha continued, "Your majesty, a bhikkhu owns no more than three robes and a begging bowl. He has no fear of losing his possessions or being robbed. He knows he will not be attacked in the night by people who want to steal his wealth. He is free to sleep alone in the forest beneath a tree, relaxed and without worries. Freedom from fear is a great happiness. That is another fruit of spiritual practice which can be enjoyed right in the present moment."

The king trembled and he said, "Wonderful, Lord! Please tell me more."

The Buddha continued, "Your majesty, a bhikkhu lives simply. Though he eats only one meal a day, his bowl receives offerings from a thousand different homes. He does not chase after wealth or fame. He uses only what he needs and remains unattached to desires. Living in such carefree ease is a great happiness. That is another fruit of spiritual practice which can be enjoyed right in the present moment."

The king said, "Wonderful, Lord! Please tell me more."

The Buddha continued, "Your majesty, if you knew how to practice full awareness of breathing and how to meditate, you could experience the happiness of one who follows the path. It is the happiness that meditation brings. A bhikkhu observes the six sense organs and overcomes the five obstacles of the mind which are greed, hatred, ignorance, torpor, and doubt. He uses the full awareness of breathing to create joy and happiness that nourishes his mind and body and helps him to make progress on the path of enlightenment. The pleasant sensations which result from gratifying sense desires are no measure for the joy and happiness that meditation brings. The joy and happiness of meditation permeates mind and body, heals all anxiety, sorrow, and despair, and enables the practitioner to experience the wonders of life. Your majesty, that is one of the most important fruits of spiritual practice and one which can be enjoyed right in the present moment."

The king said, "Wonderful, Lord! Please tell me more."

The Buddha continued, "Your majesty, thanks to dwelling diligently in mindfulness and observing the precepts, the bhikkhu is able to build concentration which he can use to illuminate all dharmas. Thanks to his penetrating illumination, he sees the selfless and impermanent nature of all dharmas. Thanks to seeing the selfless and impermanent nature of all dharmas, he is no longer entangled by any dharma. He can thus cut through the ropes of bondage which bind most people—the ropes of greed, hatred, desire, laziness, doubt, false view of self, extreme views, wrong views, distorted views, and views advocating unnecessary prohibitions. Cutting through all these ropes, the bhikkhu attains liberation and true freedom. Your majesty, liberation is a great happiness and one of the greatest fruits of spiritual practice. There are bhikkhus sitting here tonight who have attained that fruit. This fruit, your majesty, can be attained right here in this life."

The king exclaimed, "Wonderful, Lord! Please tell me more."

The Buddha continued, "Your majesty, thanks to illuminating and seeing deeply into the nature of all dharmas, a bhikkhu knows that all dharmas are neither produced nor destroyed, neither defiled nor immaculate, neither increasing nor decreasing, neither one nor many, neither coming nor going. Thanks to this understanding, a bhikkhu does not discriminate. He regards all dharmas with complete equanimity, without fear or worry. He rides the waves of birth and death in order to save all beings. He shows all beings the Way so they too can taste liberation, joy, and happiness. Your majesty, being able to help others free themselves from the maze of desire, hatred, and ignorance is a great happiness. Such happiness is a sublime fruit of spiritual practice which begins to be realized in the present and extends to the future. Your majesty, in all of his contacts, a bhikkhu remembers his responsibility to guide others on the path of virtue and liberation. Bhikkhus do not engage in partisan politics but they contribute to building peace, joy, and virtue in society. The fruits of his spiritual practice are not for the bhikkhu's sole enjoyment and benefit. They are the people's and country's inheritance."

The king stood up and joined his palms in deepest respect. He said, "Most sublime Teacher! Lord! By the use of simple words, you have shown me the light. You have helped me see the true value of the Dharma. Lord, you have rebuilt that which was in ruins, revealed that which was concealed, shown the way to one who was lost, and brought light into the darkness. Please, Lord, accept me as your disciple, as you accepted my parents in the past."

The king prostrated himself before the Buddha.

The Buddha nodded his acceptance. He asked Venerable Sariputta to teach the three refuges to the king and queen. After they recited them, the king said, "As it is late, please allow us to return to the palace. I have an early morning audience."

The Buddha nodded again.

The encounter between the Buddha and King Ajatasattu benefited all those present. The king's mental torment rapidly improved. That same night he dreamed he saw his father smiling at him, and he felt that all that had been torn asunder was now made whole again. The king's heart was transformed, bringing great joy to all his people.

After that, the king visited the Buddha often on his own. He no longer came on an elephant accompanied by royal guards. He climbed the stone steps carved into the mountain just as his father, King Bimbisara, had done so often in the past. In his private meetings with the Buddha, King Ajatasattu was able to reveal his heart and confess his past crimes. The Buddha treated him as though he were his own son. He counselled the king to surround himself with men of virtue.

At the end of the retreat season, Jivaka asked the Buddha to allow him to enter the homeless life as a bhikkhu. The Buddha accepted him, and gave him the Dharma name of Vimala Kondanna. Bhikkhu Vimala Kondanna was permitted to continue to stay at the Mango Grove. There were about two hundred bhikkhus already in residence there. This was the place at which the Buddha was cared for following the accident on Vulture Peak. With so many mature mango trees, the Mango Grove monastery was a very pleasant place to stay. Bhikkhu Vimala Kondanna continued to grow medicinal herbs for the community of bhikkhus.

Chapter Seventy-Seven
Stars in Your Eyes

When the retreat season ended, the Buddha and Ananda traveled throughout Magadha. They stopped in many out-of-the-way places and at every local Dharma center, so the Buddha could offer teaching to both the bhikkhus and the laity. The Buddha frequently pointed out beautiful scenery to Venerable Ananda. The Buddha knew that because Ananda devoted such wholehearted attention to attending to the Buddha's needs, he sometimes forgot to enjoy the countryside around them.

Ananda had served as the Buddha's attendant for nearly twenty years. Thinking back over the years, he recalled how often the Buddha pointed to the landscape and exclaimed such things as, "Look how beautiful Vulture Peak is, Ananda!" or "Ananda, look how beautiful the plains of Saptapanni are!" Ananda fondly remembered the day the Buddha pointed to golden rice fields bordered by green grasses and suggested they use the same pattern to sew the bhikkhus' robes. Ananda saw that the Buddha knew how to truly enjoy beautiful things while never becoming caught by either the beautiful or ugly.

The following rainy season, the Buddha returned to Jetavana. Because King Pasenadi was on a journey, he did not see the Buddha until the retreat was half-over. Immediately after his arrival, he visited the Buddha and told him that he no longer liked to be confined to the palace. Now that he was advanced in years, he had delegated many of his royal tasks to trusted ministers so that he could travel with a small party. He wanted to see and enjoy the land of his own country and that of neighboring kingdoms. When he visited another country, he never expected a formal reception. He came as a simple pilgrim. His trips were also occasions to practice walking meditation. Leaving behind all thoughts and worries, he took leisurely steps while enjoying the countryside. He told the Buddha how much these trips refreshed his heart.

"Lord Buddha, I am seventy-eight years old, the same as you. I know that you also enjoy walking in beautiful places. But I'm afraid my travels do not serve others in the way your travels do. Wherever you go, you stop to teach and guide the people. You are like a shining light wherever you go."

The king confided to the Buddha a secret pain he carried in his heart. Seven years earlier when an attempted coup took place in the capital, he wrongly accused the commander-in-chief of the royal forces, General Bandhula, and had him executed. A few years later he learned that the general had not been involved. The king was overcome with regret. He did all he could to restore the general's good name and provided ample assistance to his widow. He also appointed the general's nephew, General Karayana, as the new commander-in-chief of the royal forces.

During the remainder of the retreat season, the king visited Jetavana every other day to attend Dharma talks and discussions, and sometimes simply to sit quietly by the Buddha's side. When the retreat season came to a close, the Buddha began traveling. The king, too, set out on another trip with a small traveling party.

The following year, the Buddha spent two weeks in Kuru after the retreat season. Then he followed the river down to Kosali, Varanasi, and Vesali before returning north.

One day while staying in Medalumpa, a small district in Sakya, the Buddha received an unexpected visit from King Pasenadi. It so happened that the king was traveling in the same region with Prince Vidudabha and General Karayana. The king learned from some local people that the Buddha was staying not far away in Medalumpa. As it was only a half day's journey from where the king was, he instructed General Karayana to drive their carriage there. There were three other carriages in their party. They left their carriages outside the park where the Buddha was dwelling, and the king and the general entered the park together. The king asked a bhikkhu where to find the Buddha's hut and the bhikkhu pointed to a small hut beneath a shady tree.

The door to the hut was closed. The king walked leisurely to the hut and before knocking cleared his throat. He removed his sword and crown and handed them to the general, requesting the general to take them back to the carriage and wait for him there. The door to the Buddha's hut opened. He was most happy to see the king and invited him in at once. Venerables Sariputta and Ananda were also there. They stood to greet the king.

The Buddha asked the king to be seated on the chair next to his own. Sariputta and Ananda stood behind the Buddha. To their surprise the king stood up again and then knelt down and kissed the Buddha's feet. Several times he said, "Lord, I am King Pasenadi of the kingdom of Kosala. I respectfully pay you homage."

The Buddha assisted the king back onto his chair and asked, "Your majesty, we are old, close friends. Why do you pay me such formal respects today?"

The king answered, "Lord, I am old. There are a number of things I wish to say to you before it is too late."

The Buddha regarded him kindly and said, "Please speak."

"Lord, I have total faith in you, the Enlightened One. I have total faith in the Dharma and in the Sangha. I have known many brahmans and practitioners of other sects. I have watched so many of them practice in an upright manner for ten, twenty, thirty, or even forty years, only to finally abandon their practice to return to a life of indulgence. But among your bhikkhus, I do not see anyone abandoning his practice.

"Lord, I have seen kings oppose other kings, generals plot against other generals, brahmans compete with other brahmans, wives berate husbands, children accuse their parents, brothers argue with brothers, and friends fight with friends. But I see the bhikkhus living in harmony, joy, and mutual respect. They live together like milk and water. Nowhere else have I witnessed such harmony.

"Lord, wherever I go, I see spiritual practitioners whose faces are lined with worry, anxiety, and hardship. But your bhikkhus look refreshed and happy, relaxed and carefree. Lord, all these things strengthen my faith in you and your teaching.

"Lord, I am a king from the warrior caste. It is within my power to order anyone's death or to condemn anyone to prison. Even so, during councils with my ministers, I am often interrupted. But in your sangha, even when a thousand bhikkhus are gathered, there is never so much as a murmur or the rustling of a single robe to disturb your speaking. That is marvelous, Lord. You do not need to wield a sword or threaten others with punishment to be paid absolute respect. Lord, this strengthens my faith in you and your teaching.

"Lord, I have watched famous scholars scheme together to come up with questions that will confound you. But when they meet with you and hear you expound the Dharma, their mouths fall open and they forget their useless questions. They express nothing but admiration for you. Lord, this also strengthens my faith in you and your teaching.

"Lord, there are two highly skilled horsemen named Isidatta and Purana who work in the palace. They receive their wages from me, but the respect they hold for me is nothing compared to the respect they hold for you. I once took them with me on one of my travels. We were caught in a storm one night and had to seek shelter in a tiny palm-leaf hut. For most of the night, the horsemen spoke about your teaching. When they finally went to sleep, they slept with their heads in the direction of Vulture Peak and their feet pointing to me! You don't give them any wages, Lord, but they regard you far more highly than they do me. This also strengthens my faith in you and your teaching.

"Lord, you came from the same warrior caste as me. We are both seventy-eight years old this year. I wanted to take this occasion to express my gratitude for the deep friendship we have shared. With your permission, I will now take my leave."

"Please, your majesty," said the Buddha, "take good care of your health."

He walked with the king to the door. When the Buddha turned back to Ananda and Sariputta, he saw them standing silently with their palms joined. He said, "Sariputta and Ananda, King Pasenadi has just expressed his innermost sentiments about the three gems. Please share these things with others to help them strengthen their own faith."

The next month, the Buddha returned south to Vulture Peak. Upon his arrival he received two sad announcements. King Pasenadi had died under disturbing circumstances, and Venerable Moggallana had been murdered by hostile ascetics just outside Bamboo Forest.

King Pasenadi did not die peacefully in his palace in Savatthi. He died in Rajagaha in circumstances hardly befitting a king. After visiting the Buddha that day in Medalumpa, the king walked back to his carriage. He was surprised to find only one carriage instead of the four he had left there. His attendant informed him that General Karayana had forced the others to return to Savatthi. The general still held the king's crown and sword. He told Prince Vidudabha to return at once to Savatthi and claim the throne as his own. The general said King Pasenadi was too old and weak to reign any longer. The prince was unwilling, but when General Karayana threatened to usurp the throne himself, the prince felt he had no choice but to obey the general's wishes.

King Pasenadi headed straight to Rajagaha intending to ask his nephew and son-in-law, King Ajatasattu, for assistance. The king was too upset to eat anything along the way and only drank a small amount of water. When they reached Rajagaha it was too late to disturb the palace. The king and his attendant checked into a local inn. That night the king fell suddenly ill and died in his attendant's arms before help could be sought. The attendant sobbed inconsolably over his king's sorry fate. When King Ajatasattu learned what had happened in the morning, he sent for King Pasenadi's body and ordered a solemn and majestic funeral be organized. When the funeral was over, he wanted to send soldiers to topple King Vidudabha, but he was discouraged by Bhikkhu Vimala Kondanna, formerly the physician Jivaka, who said that as King Pasenadi had already passed away and the new king was a rightful heir, there was no point in starting a war. Heeding this counsel, King Ajatasattu sent an envoy to Savatthi to express his recognition of the new king.

Venerable Moggallana was one of the Buddha's finest senior disciples, ranking with Sariputta and Kondanna. Many senior disciples had already passed away, including Kondanna, who had been among the Buddha's first five disciples. The Kassapa brothers had all died, and so had Abbess Mahapajapati. Bhikkhu Rahula had died at the age of fifty-one, shortly after his mother, Bhikkhuni Yasodhara died.

Venerable Moggallana was known for his fearless, upright character. He always spoke the truth directly and without compromise. Because of that, he had earned the hatred of others outside the sangha. The day of his death, he set out, accompanied by two disciples, quite early in the morning. Assassins were hiding just outside the monastery, waiting for him. When he appeared, they rushed out and began to beat him and the other two bhikkhus with large sticks. The bhikkhus were outnumbered and unable to defend themselves from the blows. Moggallana's two disciples were beaten and left by the side of the road. They cried out for help but it was too late. Venerable Moggallana let forth a cry that shook the forest. When other bhikkhus ran out of the monastery, Moggallana was dead and the assassins had disappeared.

Venerable Moggallana's body had already been cremated by the time the Buddha returned to Vulture Peak. An urn with his ashes had been placed just outside the Buddha's hut. The Buddha asked about Venerable Sariputta and was told that since Moggallana's murder, he had remained in his hut with the door closed. Sariputta and Moggallana had been like brothers, as close as a form and its shadow. The Buddha had not yet stopped to rest after his travels, but he proceeded at once to Sariputta's hut to console him.

As they walked to Sariputta's hut, Ananda reflected on how sad the Buddha must feel. How could he avoid feeling heartbroken when two of his closest friends had just died? The Buddha would console Sariputta, but who would console the Buddha? As if to answer Ananda's hidden thoughts, the Buddha stopped, looked at him, and said, "Ananda, everyone commends you for studying hard and possessing a phenomenal memory, but don't think that is enough. It is important to look after the Tathagata and the sangha, but it is not sufficient. Whatever time remains you, devote your efforts to breaking through birth and death. Learn to look at birth and death as mere illusions, like the stars one sees in one's eyes after rubbing them."

Venerable Ananda bowed his head and continued walking in silence.

The next day, the Buddha suggested a stupa be built for the Venerable Moggallana's relics.

Chapter Seventy-Eight
Two Thousand Saffron Robes

One afternoon as the Buddha was doing walking meditation along the mountain slope, two bhikkhus arrived carrying Venerable Devadatta on a stretcher. Venerable Devadatta's health had been poor for several years, and now, on the point of death, he wished to see the Buddha. He had only six remaining disciples, having lost even his most fervent supporters years earlier. His closest associate, Venerable Kokalika, died years before of an unusual skin disease. During Devadatta's final years at Gayasisa, he had much time alone to examine his actions.

When the Buddha was informed that Venerable Devadatta wished to see him, he returned to his hut at once in order to receive him. Venerable Devadatta was too weak to sit up. He had barely enough strength to speak. He looked at the Buddha and with great pain, joined his palms and spoke the words, "I take refuge in the Buddha." The Buddha gently placed his hand on Devadatta's forehead. That evening Venerable Devadatta died.

It was Summer and the skies were clear and blue. The Buddha was preparing to depart on a journey, when a messenger from King Ajatasattu arrived. It was Vassakara, the king's minister of foreign affairs. He had been asked by the king to inform the Buddha about the king's intentions to send his army to conquer Vajji, a country which lay north of the

Ganga. Before carrying out his attack, the king wanted to ask what the Buddha thought of his plans.

Venerable Ananda was also present, standing behind the Buddha and fanning him. The Buddha turned to Ananda and asked, "Venerable Ananda, have you heard whether or not the people of Vajji still regularly gather together in large numbers to discuss politics?"

Ananda answered, "Lord, I have heard that the people of Vajji often assemble in large numbers to discuss the political situation."

"Then Vajji still prospers, Ananda. And tell me, do you know whether or not they still display a spirit of cooperation and unity during their meetings?"

"Lord, I have heard they enjoy great cooperation and unity."

"Well then, Vajji still prospers. Ananda, do the people of Vajji still respect and follow the laws that have been enacted in their country?"

"Lord, I have heard that they respect and follow all their laws."

"Then it is certain Vajji still prospers. Ananda, do the people of Vajji respect and listen to worthy leaders?"

"Lord, I have heard that the people of Vajji respect and listen to worthy leaders."

"Then it is certain their country still prospers. Ananda, have you heard whether or not there is rape and other violent crime in Vajji?"

"Lord, there is almost no rape or other violent crime in their country."

"Then Vajji continues to prosper. Ananda, have you heard whether or not the people of Vajji still protect and maintain the shrines of their ancestors?"

"Lord, it is said that they protect and maintain the shrines of their ancestors."

"Then Vajji still prospers. Have you heard whether or not the people of Vajji respect, make offerings to, and study with spiritual teachers who have attained the Way?"

"Lord, they continue to respect, make offerings to, and study with spiritual teachers who have attained the Way."

"Ananda, it is then certain that Vajji still prospers. Ananda, some time ago the Tathagata had the opportunity to speak with Vajji's leaders about the seven practices which make a country prosper. They are called the Seven Practices of No-Regression. They include: gathering together for discussion, cooperation and unity, respecting laws that have been enacted, respecting and following worthy leaders, refraining from rape and other violent crimes, protecting the ancestral shrines, and respecting teachers who have attained the Way. As the people of Vajji continue to observe these seven practices, it is certain that their country still prospers. Because of that, the Tathagata believes it would be impossible for Magadha to defeat Vajji."

Minister Vassakara spoke, "Lord, if the people of Vajji observed only one of those seven practices, their country would prosper. Lord, I do not think King Ajatasattu can win a war with Vajji with power and weapons alone. He could only succeed if he sowed seeds of discord among Vajji's leaders. Thank you, Lord, for your counsel. I will return now to my duties."

After Vassakara departed, the Buddha turned to Ananda and said, "Vassakara knows how to scheme. The Tathagata fears that in the future, King Ajatasattu will indeed send his army to fight Vajji."

That afternoon, the Buddha asked Venerable Ananda to invite all the bhikkhus and bhikkhunis currently in Rajagaha to assemble at Vulture Peak. When, after seven days, they were all gathered, they numbered two thousand. It was a splendid sight to see so many saffron robes against the mountain.

The Buddha walked slowly from his hut down to the Dharma platform where the monks and nuns were gathered. He stepped up onto the platform, looked out over the community, smiled and said, "Bhikkhus and Bhikkhunis, the

Tathagata will teach you the Seven Methods to prevent the teaching and sangha from falling into decline. Listen!

"First, meet frequently in groups to study and discuss the Dharma. Second, always gather and disperse in a spirit of co-operation and unity. Third, respect and follow the precepts which have been enacted. Fourth, respect and follow the guidance of elders in the sangha who possess virtue and experience. Fifth, live a pure and simple life, unswayed by desire and greed. Sixth, cherish a calm and peaceful life. Seventh, dwell in mindfulness in order to realize peace, joy, and liberation, and to become a refuge and support to friends along the path.

"Bhikkhus and Bhikkhunis, if you live by these seven practices, the Dharma will flourish and the sangha cannot fall into decline. Nothing outside will be able to disturb the sangha. Only division and discord from within can cause the sangha to break. Bhikkhus and Bhikkhunis, when a lion king dies in the mountain forest, no animals dare eat its flesh. Only the worms in its own body devour it from within. Protect the Dharma by living according to these seven practices. Never become as worms which devour a lion's corpse from within."

The Buddha also counselled the monks and nuns to avoid wasting precious time by engaging in idle conversation, over-sleeping, pursuing fame and recognition, chasing after desires, spending time with people of poor character, and being satisfied with only a shallow understanding of the teaching. He reminded them of the Seven Factors of Awakening as the path every bhikkhu and bhikkhuni should travel—mindfulness, investigating dharmas, energy, joy, ease, concentration, and letting go. He also repeated the teachings on impermanence, emptiness of self, non-attachment, liberation, and overcoming desire and greed.

The two thousand monks and nuns remained on Vulture Peak for ten days. They slept beneath trees, in caves and huts, or by mountain streams. The Buddha gave them a Dharma talk every day. On the tenth and final day, the Buddha told them they could return to their own centers.

After the bhikkhus and bhikkhunis departed, the Buddha turned to Venerable Ananda and said, "We will visit Bamboo Forest tomorrow."

After visiting Bamboo Forest, the Buddha and Ananda left Rajagaha and headed towards Ambalatthika, the refreshing park set aside long ago by King Bimbisara for followers of the Way. The bhikkhus often rested there on their way to Nalanda. Venerable Sariputta had once dwelled there with Rahula. The Buddha visited and instructed the bhikkhus living in Ambalatthika. He spoke about Precepts, Concentration, and Understanding.

The Buddha proceeded to Nalanda accompanied by a hundred bhikkhus. Venerables Ananda, Sariputta, and Anuruddha walked close by his side. When they reached Nalanda, the Buddha rested in Pavarika's mango grove.

The next morning, Venerable Sariputta sat for a long quiet moment by the Buddha's side. Finally, he said, "Lord, I am sure that in the past, present, or future, there is no spiritual teacher whose wisdom and attainment surpasses yours."

The Buddha said, "Sariputta, those words are as bold as a lion's roar. Have you met all the spiritual teachers in the past, present, and future that you dare make such a statement?"

"Lord, I have not met all the masters of the three realms, but there is one thing I know for certain. I have lived close by you for more than forty-five years. I have heard your teaching and I have observed the way you live. I know that you dwell constantly in awareness. You are a perfect master of your six senses. You never show any sign of the five obstacles of greed and desire, anger and hatred, forgetfulness, agitation, doubt, or suspicion. While there may be masters in the past, present, and future who attain to the same wisdom and awakening, I do not think anyone could surpass your understanding."

In Nalanda, the Buddha taught the bhikkhus more concerning Precepts, Concentration, and Understanding. He then
returned to Pataligama where he was welcomed by crowds of
bhikkhus and lay disciples. He was offered food and water,
after which he delivered a Dharma talk.

The next morning, Venerable Sariputta received news that
his mother was very ill. She was more than one hundred
years old. He requested permission to go visit her. The Buddha saw Venerable Sariputta off. Sariputta bowed to him
three times and then departed for Nala with the novice
Cunda.

As the Buddha and bhikkhus passed through the city
gates of Pataligama, they were met by two officials from
Magadha, Sunidha and Vassakara. They had been assigned
by King Ajatasattu to transform Pataligama into a major city.
They told the Buddha, "We plan to rename the city gate you
have just passed through 'Gautama Gate.' Allow us to accompany you to the ferry landing. We will name it 'Gautama
Ferry Landing.'"

The Ganga was so swollen from recent rains that the crows
could stand on the high upper banks and dip their beaks in
the water for a drink. Five rafts carried the Buddha and his
bhikkhus across the river. Venerable Ananda stood by the
Buddha's side. They looked out over the water towards
Vesali on the opposite shore.

Ananda remembered the time twenty-five years earlier
when the Buddha had been greeted by vast throngs of people
on that shore. At that time, Vesali was almost destroyed by
a plague. Young and old alike died in droves. There was
nothing even the best physicians in Vesali could do. Altars
were set up, but even ceaseless prayers did nothing to alter
the situation. Finally the people's thoughts turned towards
the Buddha. Governor Tomara traveled to Rajagaha and beseeched the Buddha to come to Vesali in hopes that his virtuous presence would turn the tragic tide. The Buddha agreed
to go. King Bimbisara and his queen, palace officials, and the
citizens of Rajagaha saw the Buddha off.

When the Buddha reached Vesali by boat, he found the shore crowded with altars, flags, and flowers to welcome him.

When the Buddha reached Vesali by boat, he found the shore crowded with altars, flags, and flowers to welcome him as though he were a savior. The people's cheers shook the air. Venerable Vimala Kondanna, the former Jivaka, and several senior disciples accompanied the Buddha. No sooner did the Buddha's foot touch the shore than thunder shook the sky, and it began to rain. It was the first rain after a long drought, and it brought cool relief and new hope. The Buddha and his bhikkhus were led to a park in the center of Kotigama. There the Buddha spoke about the Three Treasures. A few days later, the Buddha and his bhikkhus were invited to Vesali. They dwelled at Kutagara Monastery in Mahavana during their stay. Thanks to the Buddha's merit and Vimala Kondanna's skills, the spread of the plague was slowed until, at last, it disappeared. The Buddha remained in Vesali for six months.

Ananda's thoughts returned to the present as they reached the shore. The Buddha walked to Kotigama, where he was met by a large number of monks. He spoke about the Four Establishments of Mindfulness, and about Precepts, Concentration, and Understanding. After spending several days in Kotigama, the Buddha headed for Nadika. There he and his bhikkhus slept in a brick house called Ginjakavasatha.

In Nadika, the Buddha thought about the many disciples who had passed away in that same region. He thought of his sister Bhikkhuni Sundari Nanda, Bhikkhus Salha and Nadiya, lay disciple Sujata who had so long ago offered him milk, and lay disciples Kakudha, Bhadda, and Subhadda. At least fifty bhikkhus in the region had attained the fruits of Stream Enterer, Once Returner, and Never Returner. Bhikkhuni Nanda had attained the fruit of Returning Once More. Bhikkhus Salha and Nadiya had attained Arhatship.

The Buddha taught his disciples that whoever has faith in the Buddha, Dharma, and Sangha need only look into his or her own heart to know whether he or she had entered the stream of liberation. There was no need to ask anyone else. In Nadika, the Buddha taught the bhikkhus concerning Precepts, Concentration, and Understanding. He walked to Vesali where he rested in Ambapali's Mango Grove. There he spoke on contemplating the body, feelings, mind, and objects of mind.

When Ambapali heard that the Buddha was dwelling in the Mango Grove, she came at once to visit him. She invited him and the bhikkhus for a meal offering. After the meal, she asked to be ordained as a bhikkhuni, and she was accepted into the sangha of nuns.

The Buddha spoke more about Precepts, Concentration, and Understanding during his stay in Vesali. Afterwards, he visited Beluvagamaka village. As the rainy season was already underway, he decided to spend it there. It was the forty-fifth retreat season since the Buddha attained Awakening. He asked monks and nuns in the region to stay at Dharma centers in Vesali or in the homes of friends and relatives for the duration of the retreat.

Halfway into the retreat season, the Buddha fell gravely ill. Though he was in extreme pain, he did not utter any sound. Lying down, he continued to mindfully follow his breath. At first, his disciples feared he would not survive his illness, but to their joy, he slowly regained his strength. After many days, he was able to sit on a chair outside his hut.

Chapter Seventy-Nine
Sandalwood Tree Mushrooms

Venerable Ananda sat down next to the Buddha and spoke in a soft voice, "I never saw you so sick in all the years we have been together. I felt paralyzed. I couldn't think clearly or carry out my duties. The others did not think you would pull through, but I said to myself, the Lord Buddha has not yet given us his last testament. Surely he cannot enter nirvana yet. That thought kept me from the brink of despair."

The Buddha said, "Ananda, what else can you and the sangha expect from me? I have taught the Dharma fully and deeply. Do you think I have concealed anything from the bhikkhus? Ananda, the teaching is the true refuge. Every person must make the teaching his own refuge. Live according to the teaching. Every person should be a lamp unto himself. Ananda, the Buddha, Dharma, and Sangha are present in everyone. The capacity for enlightenment is the Buddha, the teaching is the Dharma, the community of support is the Sangha. No one can take away the Buddha, Dharma, and Sangha within you. Though heaven and earth may crumble, the Three Gems will remain intact within every person. They are the true refuge. When a bhikkhu dwells in mindfulness and contemplates his body, feelings, mind, and objects of mind, he is like an island unto himself. He possesses the truest refuge of all. No person, not even a great Master, can ever be a more stable refuge than your own island of mindfulness, the Three Gems within you."

By the end of the retreat, the Buddha's health was greatly restored.

One morning, novice Cunda who was Venerable Sariputta's attendant, came seeking Ananda. He informed Ananda that Sariputta had just died in Nala. He handed Ananda Venerable Sariputta's robe, begging bowl, and urn of ashes. He then covered his face and burst into tears. Venerable Ananda wept too. Cunda explained that after Sariputta returned to Nala, he cared for his mother until her death. After her cremation ceremony, he assembled his relatives and all the villagers, and gave them a teaching concerning the Dharma. He gave them the three refuges and showed them how to follow the practice. He then sat in a lotus position and passed into nirvana. Shortly before this, he told Cunda that he wanted his robe, bowl, and ashes carried back to the Buddha. He also wanted Cunda to ask the Buddha to allow Cunda to remain by the Buddha's side. Venerable Sariputta told Cunda that he wished to pass away before the Buddha did.

Venerable Ananda wiped away his tears and went with Cunda to find the Buddha. The Buddha gazed quietly at the robe, bowl, and ashes of his greatest disciple. He did not say anything. Then he looked up and gently patted Cunda's head.

Venerable Ananda said, "Lord Buddha, when I heard that our brother Sariputta was dead, I felt paralyzed. My eyes and mind grew hazy. I am deeply grieved."

The Buddha looked at Ananda and said, "Ananda, did your brother take away your precepts, concentration, understanding, and liberation when he died?"

Ananda quietly answered, "That is not the reason for my sadness, Lord. When brother Sariputta was alive, he lived the teaching with his whole being. He taught, guided, and encouraged the rest of us. With brothers Sariputta and Moggallana gone, the sangha feels empty. How could we not feel sad?"

The Buddha said, "Ananda, so many times I have reminded you that with birth there is death. That which comes together must separate. All dharmas are impermanent. We should not become attached to them. You must transcend the world of birth and death, arising and dissolving. Ananda, Sariputta was a great branch that fulfilled his duty in helping nourish the tree. That branch is still present in the tree. The tree is the community of bhikkhus practicing the teaching of enlightenment. If you but open your eyes and look, you will see Sariputta in yourself, in the Tathagata, in the community of bhikkhus, in all the people Sariputta taught, in novice Cunda, and along every path Sariputta traveled to spread the teaching. Open your eyes, Ananda, and you will see Sariputta everywhere. Don't think Sariputta is no longer with us. He is here and will always be.

"Ananda, Sariputta was a bodhisattva, an enlightened person who used his Understanding and Love to guide other beings to the shore of enlightenment. Among the bhikkhus, Sariputta earned praise for his great wisdom. He will be remembered by future generations as a bodhisattva of great understanding. Ananda, among the bhikkhus, there are many bodhisattvas who, like Sariputta, have taken the Great Vow. Bhikkhu Punna, Bhikkhuni Yasodhara, lay disciple Sudatta are bodhisattvas of great compassion who lived the vow to help all beings, never afraid of suffering or hardship. Bhikkhuni Yasodhara and disciple Sudatta have passed away, but Venerable Punna continues to work courageously and energetically to serve all beings. The Tathagata thinks of Venerable Moggallana and knows he was a bodhisattva of great courage and energy. Few can compare with him. Venerable Mahakassapa with his simple, humble life, is a bodhisattva of simple living. Venerable Anuruddha is a bodhisattva of great effort and diligence.

"Ananda, if future generations continue to study and practice the path of liberation, bodhisattvas will continue to appear in this world. Ananda, faith in the Buddha, Dharma, and Sangha is faith in the future of the community. In the future there will be other bodhisattvas as great as Sariputta,

Moggallana, Punna, Anuruddha, Yasodhara, and Anathapindika. Ananda, do not grieve over brother Sariputta's death."

That noon along the banks of the Ganga, near Ukkacela
hamlet, the Buddha serenely announced Venerable Sariputta's
death. He urged the bhikkhus to devote all their efforts to
become more like Sariputta, who took the Great Vow to help
all other beings. He said, "Bhikkhus, you should take refuge
in yourself and be an island unto yourself. Do not rely on
anything else, and you will not be drowned by the waves of
sorrow and despair. You should take refuge in the Dharma
and take the Dharma as the island."

One morning, the Buddha and Ananda entered Vesali to
beg. They took their food and ate it in a nearby forest. After
that, the Buddha said, "Ananda, we should return to Capala
temple to rest this afternoon."

Along the way to Capala temple, the Buddha stopped several times to admire the landscape. He said, "Ananda, Vesali
is so beautiful. Udena temple is so lovely. All the temples
such as Gotamaka, Sattambaka, and Bahuputta are beautiful.
The temple in Capala where we will soon rest is also a very
pleasant place."

After making a place for the Buddha to rest, Venerable
Ananda went outside to practice walking meditation. While
he was walking, the earth suddenly quaked beneath his feet.
Both his mind and body were shaken. He quickly returned to
the temple and found the Buddha sitting there peacefully.
Ananda told him of the tremor he had just felt.

The Buddha said, "Ananda, the Tathagata has made his
decision. In three months, I will pass away."

Venerable Ananda felt his arms and legs go numb. His
eyes blurred and his head spun. He knelt before the Buddha
and begged him, "Please, Lord, do not die so soon. Please
have pity on all your disciples."

The Buddha did not answer. Ananda repeated his
words three times. The Buddha then said, "Ananda, if you
have faith in the Tathagata, you will know that my decisions
are timely. I have said I will pass away in three months.

Ananda, invite all the bhikkhus in this region to gather at Kutagara Dharma hall in Great Forest."

Seven days later, one thousand five hundred bhikkhus and bhikkhunis gathered in Kutagara Dharma hall. The Buddha sat on the Dharma platform. He looked out over the community and said, "Bhikkhus and Bhikkhunis! All that the Tathagata has transmitted to you, you must carefully and skillfully study, observe, practice, and verify for yourselves in order to transmit it to future generations. Living and practicing the Way should continue to assure the peace, joy, and happiness of all beings.

"Bhikkhus and Bhikkhunis, the essence of the Tathagata's teaching can be found in the Four Establishments of Mindfulness, the Four Right Efforts, the Four Bases of Spiritual Strength, the Five Faculties, the Five Powers, the Seven Factors of Awakening, and the Noble Eightfold Path. Study, practice, realize, and transmit these teachings.

"Bhikkhus and Bhikkhunis, all dharmas are impermanent. They are born and die, they arise and dissolve. Make great efforts to attain liberation. In three months, the Tathagata will pass away."

One thousand five hundred monks and nuns silently listened to the Buddha and absorbed his direct teaching. They understood this would be their last chance to see and hear the Buddha give a Dharma talk. Knowing that the Buddha would pass away soon, everyone felt anguish.

The next morning, the Buddha went into Vesali to beg, and then he ate in the forest. Afterwards, he and several bhikkhus departed from Vesali. Looking back at the city with the eyes of an elephant queen, the Buddha said to Venerable Ananda, "Ananda, Vesali is so beautiful. This is the last time the Tathagata will look upon it." The Buddha then turned around. Looking straight ahead, he said, "Let us head towards Bhandagama."

That afternoon, the Buddha offered Dharma teaching to three hundred bhikkhus in Bhandagama about Precepts, Concentration, Understanding, and Liberation. After several days of rest there, the Buddha proceeded on to Hatthigama, Ambagama, and Jambugama. He instructed the bhikkhus in all these places. They next traveled to Bhoganagara where the Buddha rested in Ananda temple. Many bhikkhus in the region came to receive his teaching. He told the bhikkhus how necessary it was to verify the teaching for themselves.

"Whenever someone speaks about the teaching, even if he claims that it comes directly from recognized authorities, do not be hasty to accept his words as the Tathagata's authentic teaching. Compare what he says to the sutras and precepts. If it contradicts the sutras and precepts, discard what he says. But if his words are in accord with the sutras and precepts, accept and practice what he says."

The Buddha went on to Pava, where he rested in the mango grove that belonged to a lay disciple named Cunda, a blacksmith's son. Cunda invited the Buddha and the nearly three hundred bhikkhus traveling with him to take a meal in his home. Cunda's wife and friends served all the bhikkhus, while Cunda personally served the Buddha a special dish he had prepared. It was a dish of mushrooms picked from a sandalwood tree and was called *sukara maddava.*

When he had finished eating, the Buddha told Cunda, "Dear Cunda, please bury whatever remains of the mushrooms and do not allow anyone else to eat them."

When everyone was finished eating, the Buddha gave a Dharma talk. Then he and the bhikkhus rested in the mango grove. That night, the Buddha was seized with violent stomach cramps. He was unable to sleep all night. In the morning, he took to the road with the bhikkhus, and headed towards Kusinara. All along the way, his stomach cramps worsened until he was forced to stop and rest beneath a tree. Venerable Ananda folded the Buddha's extra sanghati and placed it beneath the tree for the Buddha to rest upon. The Buddha asked Ananda to fetch some water for him to ease his thirst.

Ananda said, "Lord, the stream here is filled with muddy water because a caravan of cattle carts recently passed by. Please wait until we reach the Kakuttha River. The water there will be clear and sweet. I will fetch you water there for both washing and drinking."

But the Buddha said, "Ananda, I am too thirsty. Please get me some water here."

Ananda did as he was told. To his surprise, when he scooped up the muddy water into a jug, it turned perfectly clear. After he drank the water, the Buddha lay down to rest. Venerables Anuruddha and Ananda sat close by. The other bhikkhus sat in a circle around the Buddha.

At that very moment, a man from Kusinara happened to walk by. When he saw the Buddha and the bhikkhus, he bowed down low. He introduced himself as Pukkusa, a member of the Malla clan. He had once been a disciple of Master Alara Kalama, the same teacher the young Siddhartha had studied with. Pukkusa had heard a great deal about the Buddha. He bowed again and then offered the Buddha two new robes. The Buddha accepted one and then asked Pukkusa to offer the other robe to Venerable Ananda. Pukkusa asked to be accepted as a disciple. The Buddha spoke to him of the teaching and gave him the refuges. Overjoyed, Pukkusa thanked the Buddha and then took his leave.

The Buddha's robe was travel-worn and stained, and so Ananda helped him change into the new robe. Then the Buddha stood up and, together with the bhikkhus, continued to walk toward Kusinara. When they reached the banks of the Kakuttha River, the Buddha bathed and drank more water. Then he headed for a nearby mango grove. He asked Bhikkhu Cundaka to fold his extra robe and place it on the ground for him to lie upon.

The Buddha called Venerable Ananda and said, "Ananda, the meal we ate at lay disciple Cunda's home was the Tathagata's last meal. People may accuse Cunda of serving me an unworthy meal, so I want you to tell him that the two meals I treasure the most in my life were the one I ate just before attaining the Way and my last meal before passing into Nirvana. He should feel nothing but happiness for having served me one of those meals."

To Ananda's surprise, when he scooped up the muddy water into a jug, it turned perfectly clear.

After resting a short while, the Buddha stood up and said, "Ananda, let us cross the Hirannavati River and enter the forest of sal trees which belongs to the Malla people. That forest, at the entrance to Kusinara, is most beautiful."

Chapter Eighty

Be Diligent!

It was dusk by the time the Buddha and the bhikkhus reached the forest of sal trees. The Buddha asked Ananda to prepare a place between two sal trees for him to lie down. The Buddha lay on his side, his head facing north. All the bhikkhus sat around him. They knew that the Buddha would pass into nirvana that same night.

The Buddha looked up at the trees and said, "Ananda, look! It is not yet spring, but the sal trees are covered with red blossoms. Do you see the petals falling on the Tathagata's robes and the robes of all the bhikkhus? This forest is truly beautiful. Do you see the western horizon all aglow from the setting sun? Do you hear the gentle breeze rustling in the sal branches? The Tathagata finds all these things lovely and touching. Bhikkhus, if you want to please me, if you want to express your respect and gratitude to the Tathagata, there is only one way, and that is by living the teaching."

The evening was warm and Venerable Upavana stood over the Buddha to fan him, but the Buddha asked him not to. Perhaps the Buddha did not want his splendid view of the setting sun obstructed.

The Buddha asked Venerable Anuruddha, "I do not see Ananda, where is he?"

Another bhikkhu spoke up, "I saw brother Ananda standing behind some trees weeping. He was saying to himself, 'I have not yet attained my spiritual goal and now my teacher is dying. Who has ever cared more deeply for me than my teacher?'"

The Buddha asked the bhikkhu to summon Ananda. The Buddha tried to comfort Ananda. He said, "Don't be so sad, Ananda. The Tathagata has often reminded you that all dharmas are impermanent. With birth, there is death; with arising, there is dissolving; with coming together, there is separation. How can there be birth without death? How can there be arising without dissolving? How can there be coming together without separation? Ananda, you have cared for me with all your heart for many years. You have devoted all your efforts to helping me and I am most grateful to you. Your merit is great, Ananda, but you can go even farther. If you make just a little more effort, you can overcome birth and death. You can attain freedom and transcend every sorrow. I know you can do that, and that is what would make me the most happy."

Turning to the other bhikkhus, the Buddha said, "No one has been as good an attendant as Ananda. Other attendants in the past sometimes dropped my robe or bowl to the ground, but never Ananda. He has taken care of all my needs from the tiniest detail to the largest tasks. Ananda always knew when and where a bhikkhu, bhikkhuni, lay disciple, king, official, or practitioner from a different religious sect, should meet with me. He arranged all meetings most effectively and intelligently. The Tathagata believes that no enlightened master in the past or future could have an attendant more talented and devoted than Ananda."

Venerable Ananda wiped his tears and said, "Lord, please don't pass away here. Kusinara is just a small town of mud dwellings. There are so many more worthy places like Sampa, Rajagaha, Savatthi, Saketa, Kosambi, or Varanasi. Please Lord, select such a place to pass away so that more people will have a chance to see your face one last time."

The Buddha replied, "Ananda, Kusinara is also important, even if it is no more than a small town of mud dwellings.

The Tathagata finds this forest most agreeable. Ananda, do you see the sal flowers falling about me?"

The Buddha asked Ananda to go into Kusinara and announce to the Mallas that the Buddha would pass into nirvana in the grove of sal trees at the night's last watch. When the Malla people heard this news, they hastily made their way to the forest. An ascetic named Subhadda was among them. While the people took turns bowing to the Buddha, Subhadda asked Venerable Ananda if he could have an audience with the Buddha. Ananda refused, saying the Buddha was too tired to receive anyone. But the Buddha overheard their conversation and said, "Ananda, let ascetic Subhadda speak with me. The Tathagata will receive him."

Ascetic Subhadda knelt before the Buddha. He had long felt drawn to the Buddha's teaching but had never met him before. He bowed and said, "Lord, I have heard about spiritual leaders such as Purana Kassapa, Makhali Gosala, Ajita Kesakambali, Pakudha Kaccayana, Sanjaya Belatthiputta, and Nigantha Nataputta. I would like to ask if, according to you, any of them attained true enlightenment."

The Buddha answered, "Subhadda, whether or not they attained enlightenment is not a necessary thing to discuss now. Subhadda, the Tathagata will show you the path by which you yourself can attain enlightenment."

The Buddha spoke to Subhadda about the Noble Eightfold Path. He concluded by saying, "Subhadda, wherever the Noble Eightfold Path is truly practiced, you will find people who have attained enlightenment. Subhadda, if you follow this path, you, too, can attain enlightenment."

Ascetic Subhadda felt his heart suddenly opened. He was filled with great happiness. He asked the Buddha to accept him as a bhikkhu. The Buddha asked the Venerable Anuruddha to perform the ordination ceremony right then and there. Subhadda was the last disciple received by the Buddha.

After Subhadda's head was shaved, he received the precepts and was given a robe and bowl. The Buddha then looked at all the bhikkhus sitting around him. Many bhikkhus from the vicinity had arrived and so there were now nearly five hundred. The Buddha spoke to them.

"Bhikkhus! If you have any doubts or perplexity concerning the teaching, now is the time to ask the Tathagata about it. Don't let this opportunity pass by, so that later you will reproach yourselves, saying, 'That day I was face to face with the Buddha but I did not ask him.'"

The Buddha repeated these words three times, but no bhikkhu spoke.

Venerable Ananda exclaimed, "Lord, it is truly wonderful! I have faith in the community of bhikkhus. I have faith in the sangha. Everyone has clearly understood your teaching. No one has any doubts or perplexity about your teaching and the path to realize it."

The Buddha said, "Ananda, you speak from faith, while the Tathagata has direct knowledge. The Tathagata knows that all the bhikkhus here possess deep faith in the Three Gems. Even the lowest attainment among these bhikkhus is that of Stream-Enterer."

The Buddha looked quietly over the community and then said, "Bhikkhus, listen to what the Tathagata now says. Dharmas are impermanent. If there is birth, there is death. Be diligent in your efforts to attain liberation!"

The Buddha closed his eyes. He had spoken his last words. The earth shook. Sal blossoms fell like rain. Everyone felt their minds and bodies tremble. They knew the Buddha had passed into nirvana.

Reader, please put your book down here and breathe lightly for a few minutes before continuing.

The Buddha had passed away. Some bhikkhus threw up their arms and flung themselves on the ground. They wailed, "The Buddha has passed away! The Lord has died! The eyes of the world are no more! Who can we take refuge in now?"

While these bhikkhus cried and thrashed about, other bhikkhus sat silently, observing their breath and contemplating the things the Buddha had taught them. Venerable Anuruddha spoke up, "Brothers, do not cry so pitifully! The Lord Buddha taught us that with birth there is death, with arising there is dissolving, with coming together there is separation. If you understand and follow the Buddha's teaching, you will cease to make such a disturbance. Please sit up again and follow your breathing. We will maintain silence."

Everyone returned to his place and followed Venerable Anuruddha's counsel. He led them in reciting sutras they all knew by heart which spoke about impermanence, emptiness of self, non-attachment, and liberation. Calm dignity was restored.

The Mallas lit torches. Sounds of chanting echoed impressively in the dark night as everyone placed his full awareness on the words in the sutras. After a lengthy recitation, Venerable Anuruddha gave a Dharma talk. He praised the Buddha's attainments—his wisdom, compassion, virtue, concentration, joy, and equanimity. When Venerable Anuruddha finished speaking, Venerable Ananda recounted beautiful episodes from the Buddha's life. Throughout the night, the two venerables took turns speaking. The five hundred bhikkhus and three hundred lay disciples listened quietly. As torches burned down, new ones were lit to take their places until dawn broke.

Chapter Eighty-One
Old Path White Clouds

W hen day broke, Venerable Anuruddha said to Venerable
Ananda, "Brother, go into Kusinara and inform the authorities that our Master has passed away so that they may begin
the necessary arrangements."

Venerable Ananda put on his outer robe and entered town.
The Malla officials were holding a meeting to discuss local
matters. When they learned the Buddha had passed away
they expressed deep sorrow and regret. They put aside all
other work in order to make arrangements for the Buddha's
funeral. By the time the sun was perched above the trees, everyone in Kusinara knew of the Buddha's death in the forest
of sal trees. Many beat their chests and sobbed. They regretted they had not been able to look upon and bow to the Buddha before his death. People came to the forest bearing flowers, incense, musical instruments, and cloth streamers. They
prostrated and placed flowers and incense around his body.
They performed special songs and dances, and draped colorful
streamers throughout the forest. People brought food offerings
to the five hundred bhikkhus. Before long the sal forest had
the atmosphere of a festival. Occasionally, Venerable Anuruddha invited the sound of the large bell to call people back
to silence. He then led everyone in reciting passages from the
sutras.

For six days and nights, the people of Kusinara and nearby
Pava came to offer flowers, incense, dance, and music. Man-

For six days and nights, the people of Kusinara came to the sal forest to offer flowers, incense, dance, and music to the Buddha.

darava blossoms and other flowers soon thickly carpeted the area between the two sal trees. On the seventh day the Malla authorities bathed themselves in water perfumed with incense, put on ceremonial garments, and carried the Buddha's body into town. They passed through the town's center and out the East gate to Makuta-Bandhana temple, the main temple of the Mallas.

The town officials had planned a funeral fit for a king. The Buddha's body was wrapped in many layers of cloth and then placed in an iron coffin which was placed in another, larger iron coffin. It was then placed on a great funeral pyre of fragrant wood.

The moment to light the pyre had come. Just as the authorities approached with their torches, a messenger on horseback rode up and asked them to wait. He informed them that Venerable Mahakassapa and five hundred bhikkhus were on their way to the funeral from Pava.

Venerable Mahakassapa had been teaching the Dharma in Campa. He learned of the Buddha's imminent death in Vesali and that the Buddha was traveling north. The venerable immediately set out to find the Buddha. Everywhere he went, other bhikkhus asked to join him. By the time he reached Bhandagama, there were five hundred bhikkhus with him. When they reached Pava, they met a traveler coming from the opposite direction with a sal flower tucked in his shirt. The man informed them that the Buddha had already passed away in the sal forest near Kusinara six days earlier. With that news, Mahakassapa's search came to an end, and he led his bhikkhus towards Kusinara. They met a man on horseback who agreed to gallop ahead to inform Venerable Anuruddha that they were on their way to attend the funeral.

At noon, Venerable Mahakassapa and the five hundred bhikkhus reached Makuta-Bandhana temple. The Venerable placed the end of his robe over his right shoulder, joined his palms and solemnly walked around the altar three times. He faced the Buddha and prostrated along with the five hundred bhikkhus. After they completed their third bow, the pyre was lit. Everyone, bhikkhus and laity alike, knelt down and joined their palms. Venerable Anuruddha invited the bell to sound and led everyone in reciting passages on impermanence, emptiness of self, non-attachment, and liberation. It was a most majestic sound.

When the fire died down, perfume was poured over the ashes. The coffin was lowered and opened up, and the authorities placed the Buddha's relics into a golden jar, which was placed on the temple's main altar. Senior disciples took turns guarding the relics. News of the Buddha's death had been sent several days earlier to other cities, and delegations from neighboring kingdoms arrived to pay their respects. They were given a share of the Buddha's relics to be kept in stupas. There were representatives from Magadha, Vesali, Sakya, Koliya, Bulaya, Pava, and Vetha. They divided the relics into eight portions. The people of Magadha would build a stupa in Rajagaha, the people of Licchavi would build one in Vesali, the people of Sakya would build one in Kapilavatthu, the Buli people in Allakappa, the Koliya people in Ramagama, the Vetha people in Vethadipa, and the Mallas in both Kusinara and Pava.

After the delegations returned to their own countries, all the bhikkhus returned to their own locales to practice and teach. Venerables Mahakassapa, Anuruddha, and Ananda brought the Buddha's begging bowl back to Bamboo Forest.

A month later, Venerable Mahakassapa organized an assembly of bhikkhus in Rajagaha with the purpose of compiling all the sutras and precepts that the Buddha had given them. Five hundred bhikkhus were to be selected based on their standing and experience in the sangha. The assembly was to begin at the beginning of the retreat season and last for six months.

Venerable Mahakassapa had been considered the fourth highest-ranking disciple of the Buddha after Venerables Kondanna, Sariputta, and Moggallana. He was especially regarded for his simple living and humility. He had been deeply trusted and loved by the Buddha. Everyone in the sangha had heard about the time twenty years earlier when Mahakassapa sewed his own sanghati from several hundred scraps of discarded cloth. Once he folded this sanghati and invited the Buddha to sit upon it. The Buddha remarked how soft a cushion it made and Venerable Mahakassapa offered the robe to the Buddha. The Buddha accepted it with a smile and offered his own sanghati to Mahakassapa in return. Everyone also knew that Mahakassapa was the one monk who smiled the time the Buddha silently lifted up a lotus flower at Jetavana. Mahakassapa had thus received the Buddha's transmission of the Dharma treasure.

King Ajatasattu sponsored the assembly. Because Venerable Upali was highly regarded for his thorough knowledge of the precepts, he was invited to recite them all for the assembly, as well as recount the specific conditions and situations that gave rise to each of the precepts. Venerable Ananda was to be invited to repeat all of the Buddha's Dharma talks, including the details concerning the time, place, and situation that gave rise to each talk.

Naturally, Venerables Upali and Ananda could not be expected to remember every detail, and so the presence of five hundred respected bhikkhus was of great help. During the special gathering, all the precepts were compiled and given the name *Vinaya pitaka,* the basket of discipline. The basket of compiled Dharma talks was named *Sutra pitaka.* The sutras were divided into four categories, based on their length and subject matter. Venerable Ananda shared with the assembly that the Buddha had told him that after the Buddha's death, they could discard the lesser precepts. The other bhikkhus asked Ananda whether the Buddha had stated clearly which precepts he meant, but Ananda admitted he had not thought of asking the Buddha that question. After lengthy discussion, the bhikkhus decided to preserve all the precepts for both bhikkhus and bhikkhunis.

Remembering the Buddha's words, they agreed not to render the sutras into the classical meter of the Vedic language.

Ardhamagadhi was the primary language the sutras and precepts had been given in. The assembly agreed to encourage the translation of the sutras into other languages to enable people to study them in their native tongues. They also decided to increase the number of *bhanaka*, bhikkhus whose role it was to recite the sutras in order to transmit them for both present and future generations.

When the assembly adjourned, all the bhikkhus returned to their own places of practice and teaching.

* * *

Along the banks of the Neranjara River, Venerable Svasti stood to watch the flowing waters. Young buffalo boys on the opposite shore were preparing to lead their buffaloes across the shallow river. Each boy carried a sickle and a basket, just as Svasti had done forty-five years earlier. He knew that the boys would fill their baskets with fresh kusa grass while the buffaloes grazed.

The Buddha had bathed in this same river. There was the bodhi tree, more green and healthy than ever. Venerable Svasti slept beneath that beloved tree during the night. The forest was no longer the place of solitude it had once been. The bodhi tree was now a place where pilgrims visited, and much of the forest had been cleared of brush and thorns.

Venerable Svasti felt grateful that he had been one of the five hundred bhikkhus invited to attend the assembly. He was now fifty-six years old. His closest friend on the path, Venerable Rahula, had died five years earlier. Rahula had been an embodiment of devoted and diligent effort. Though he was the son of royalty, he lived in utmost simplicity. He was a modest man, and though his accomplishments in spreading the teaching were great, he never spoke about them.

Venerable Svasti had been with the Buddha on his last journey from Rajagaha to Kusinara. He was present during the final hours of the Buddha's life. On the road from Pava

Venerable Svasti watched the young buffalo boys cross the Neran-jara River.

to Kusinara, Svasti remembered how Venerable Ananda asked the Buddha where he was heading. The Buddha simply said, "I'm heading north." Svasti felt he understood. Throughout his life, the Buddha had traveled without thinking about his destination. He had taken each step mindfully, enjoying the present moment. Like an elephant prince returning to its native land when it knows its time has come, the Buddha headed north in the last days of his life. He didn't need to reach Kapilavatthu or Lumbini before he passed into nirvana. To head north was sufficient. Kusinara itself was the Lumbini Gardens.

Drawn homeward in a similar way, Venerable Svasti had returned to the banks of the Neranjara the night before. This was his own home. He still felt like the eleven-year-old who tended another man's buffaloes to feed his younger siblings. Uruvela village was the same as ever. Papaya trees still grew before every house. The rice fields were still there, the gentle river flowed as before. Water buffalos were still led and bathed by young buffalo boys. Though Sujata no longer lived in the village and his own siblings had started families of their own and moved away, Uruvela would always be Svasti's home. Svasti thought back to the first time he saw the young monk Siddhartha doing walking meditation in the forest. He thought of the many meals the village children had shared with Siddhartha beneath the cool shade of the pippala tree. These images of the past could live again. When the buffalo boys crossed over to his side, he would introduce himself. Every one of those boys was Svasti. Just as long ago he had been given a chance to enter the path of peace, joy, and liberation, he would show the path to these young boys.

Venerable Svasti smiled. A month earlier in Kusinara, he had listened to Venerable Mahakassapa tell about an encounter he had with a young bhikkhu named Subhada who traveled with him from Pava. When Subhada learned that the Buddha had already passed away, he remarked glibly, "The old man is gone. From now on, we are free. No one will scold or reproach us any more." Venerable Mahakassapa was shocked at the young bhikkhu's foolish comment, but he did not say anything.

Venerable Mahakassapa did not scold the young Subhada, but he did not mince words with Venerable Ananda, even though Ananda was a deeply respected senior disciple. Venerable Ananda's presence at the assembly was considered essential in order to accurately compile all the sutras. Nonetheless, just three days prior to the assembly, Venerable Mahakassapa told Venerable Ananda that he was seriously considering barring Ananda from the gathering. The reason he gave was that although Venerable Ananda had a solid grasp of the teaching, he had not yet attained true realization. The other bhikkhus feared Ananda would be insulted by Mahakassapa's comments and perhaps even leave, but Ananda simply retired to his own hut and closed the door. He remained there three days and nights deep in meditation. Just before dawn on the day of the assembly, Venerable Ananda attained the Great Awakening. After practicing sitting meditation all night long, he finally decided to rest. As his back touched his sleeping mat, he attained enlightenment.

That morning when Venerable Mahakassapa met Venerable Ananda, he looked into Ananda's eyes and knew at once what had happened. He told Ananda he would see him at the assembly.

Svasti looked up and saw the white clouds floating across the blue sky. The sun had risen high, and the green grass along the riverbanks sparkled in the morning light. The Buddha had walked on this very path many times as he traveled to Varanasi, Savatthi, Rajagaha, and countless other places. The Buddha's footprints were everywhere, and with each mindful step, Svasti knew he was walking in the footsteps of the Buddha. The Buddha's path was at his feet. The same clouds the Buddha had seen were in the sky. Each serene step brought to life the old path and white clouds of the Buddha. The path of the Buddha was beneath his very feet.

The Buddha had passed away, but Venerable Svasti could see his presence everywhere. Bodhi seeds had been planted throughout the Ganga basin. They had taken root and given rise to healthy trees. No one had heard of the Buddha or the Way of Awakening forty-five years before. Now saffron-robed monks and nuns were a common sight. Many Dharma centers had been established. Kings and their families had taken the refuges, as had scholars and officials. The poorest and most oppressed members of society had found refuge in the Way of Awakening. They had found liberation for their lives and spirits in the Way. Forty-five years before, Svasti was a poor, untouchable buffalo boy. Today he was a bhikkhu who had transcended all the barriers of caste and prejudice. Venerable Svasti had been greeted respectfully by kings.

Who was the Buddha that he had been able to effect such profound change? Venerable Svasti asked himself that question as he watched the buffalo boys busily cutting kusa grass along the shore. Though many of the Buddha's senior disciples had passed away, there remained bhikkhus of great effort and attainment. Many of these monks were still young. The Buddha was like the seed of a mighty bodhi tree. The seed had cracked open in order for strong roots to take hold in the earth. Perhaps when people looked at the tree, they no longer saw the seed, but the seed was there. It had not perished. It had become the tree itself. The Buddha taught that nothing passes from existence to non-existence. The Buddha had changed form, but he was still present. Anyone who looked deeply could see the Buddha within the sangha. They could see him in the presence of young bhikkhus who were diligent, kind, and wise. Venerable Svasti understood that he had a responsibility to nurture the Dharma body of the Buddha. The Dharma body was the teaching and the community. As long as the Dharma and the Sangha remained strong, the Buddha would remain present.

Venerable Svasti smiled as he watched the buffalo boys cross to his side of the river. If he didn't continue the Buddha's work by bringing equality, peace, and joy to these children, who would? The Buddha had initiated the work. His disciples would have to continue it. The bodhi seeds that the Buddha sowed would continue to put forth roots throughout the world. Venerable Svasti felt as if the Buddha had sown ten thousand precious seeds in the earth of his own heart. Svasti would tend those seeds carefully to help them grow into strong, healthy bodhi trees. People said that the Buddha had died, yet Svasti saw that the Buddha was more present than ever. He was present in Svasti's own mind and body. He was present everywhere Svasti looked—in the bodhi tree, the Neranjara River, the green grass, the white clouds, and the leaves. The young buffalo boys were themselves the Buddha. Venerable Svasti felt a special relation to them. In a moment, he would strike up a conversation with them. They too could continue the Buddha's work. Svasti understood that the way to continue the Buddha's work was to look at all things with awareness, to take peaceful steps, and to smile with compassion, as the Buddha had done.

The Buddha was the source. Venerable Svasti and the young buffalo boys were rivers that flowed from that source. Wherever the rivers flowed, the Buddha would be there.

Appendix

Appendix
Chapter Contents & Sources

Abbreviations used for sutras
Transliteration of Chinese is from Taisho Revised Tripitaka

T.	Taisho Revised Tripitaka
Tch'ang	Tch'ang A Han King (T. 1) Dirghagama)
Tchong	Tchong A Han King (T. 25) (Madhyagama)
Tsa	Tsa A Han King (T. 99) (Samyuktagama)
Tseng	Tseng Yi A Han King (T. 125) (Ekottaragama)
SV.	Sutta-vibhanga
Para.	Parajika-pali
Mv.	Mahavagga
Cv.	Cullavagga
Kh.	Khandhaka
D.	Digha-nikaya
M.	Majjhima-nikaya
S.	Samyutta-nikaya
A.	Anguttara-nikaya
Kh.	Khuddaka-nikaya
Khp.	Khuddaka-patha
Ud.	Udana
Iti.	Itivuttaka
Sn.	Sutta-nipata
Dh.	Dhammapada
Thag.	Theragatha
Thig.	Therigatha
Jat.	Jatakapali
Vin.	Vinaya

A note from the author

In researching and writing this book, I have drawn almost exclusively from the texts of the so-called "Lesser Vehicle," purposefully using very little from Mahayana texts in order to demonstrate that the more expansive ideas and doctrines associated with Mahayana can all be found in the earlier Pali *Nikayas* and Chinese *Agamas*. One need only read these sutras with an open mind to see that all sutras are sutras of Buddhism, whether they belong to the Northern or Southern Tradition.

Mahayana sutras offer a more liberal and broad way of looking at and understanding the basic teachings of Buddhism. This has the effect of preventing the reification of the teachings, which can come about from a narrow or rigid way of learning and practice. Mahayana sutras help us discover the depths of the *Nikaya* and *Agama* texts. They are like a light projected onto an object under a microscope, an object that has somehow been distorted by artificial means of preservation. Of course the *Nikayas* and the *Agamas* are closer to the original form of the Buddha's teachings, but they have been altered and modified by the understanding and practice of the traditions that have passed them down. Modern scholars and practitioners should be able to restore original Buddhism from the available texts of both the Southern and Northern Traditions. We need to be familiar with the texts of both traditions.

I have avoided including the many miracles that are often used in the sutras to embellish the Buddha's life. The Buddha himself advised his disciples not to waste time and energy on acquiring or practicing supernatural powers. I have, however, included many of the difficulties the Buddha encountered during his life from both the larger society and his own disciples. If the Buddha appears in this book as a man close to us, it is partly thanks to recounting such difficulties.

I have used the Pali version of most people and place names and technical Buddhist terms, as Pali is easier to pronounce. But I have used the Sanskrit version of those names and terms that are already familiar to Westerners, such as Siddhartha, Gautama, Dharma, sutra, nirvana, karma, atman, and bodhisattva. Many of the Pali-Sanskrit equivalents are listed at the end of the appendix.

Chapter Contents & Sources

Book One
Chapter One: Walking Just to Walk
Summary: The Buddha stops by Uruvela village along the Neranjara River in order to bring Svasti back to Bamboo Forest Monastery in Rajagaha for ordination. Svasti becomes acquainted with Rahula.
Sources: Fo Chouo Fou Yao King (T. 186), Fo So Hing Tsan (T. 192), Fo Pen Hing Tsi King (T. 190), Fo Chouo Fang Nieou King (T. 123), Lalitavistara, Buddhacarita.
Additional note: The young boy who cut kusa grass named Svastika is mentioned in Lalitavistara, T. 186, and T. 187. A French translation of the Lalitavistara by P. Foucaux can be found in the Annales du Musée Guimet, Volume VI (1884) and Volume XIX (1892).

Chapter Two: Tending Water Buffaloes
The Buddha delivers the Sutra on Tending Water Buffaloes. Svasti confides to Rahula that he is homesick. Rahula tells Svasti that Venerable Ananda wishes to meet him.
Culagopalaka Sutta (M. 34); Mahagopalaka Sutta (M. 33); A. 11, 18; Fo Chouo Fang Nieou King (T. 123) (Tseng 43, 6); Fang Nieou King (Tseng 49, 1).
The contents of the Sutra on Tending Water Buffaloes in this chapter were drawn from T. 123. Details about tending water buffaloes are also mentioned in Tseng 43, 6; Tseng 49, 1; M. 34 and M. 33.

Chapter Three: An Armful of Kusa Grass
Svasti meets Siddhartha for the first time and makes him a gift of kusa grass to use as a meditation cushion.
Fo Chouo Fou Yao King (T. 186); Fang Kouang Ta Tchouang Yen King (T. 186); Lalitavistara; Buddhacarita; Fo Chouo Fang Nieou King (T. 123).

Chapter Four: The Wounded Swan
Svasti meets Sujata for the first time. Siddhartha tells them the story about the swan shot down by Devadatta's arrow.
Fo Chouo Fou Yao King (T. 186); Fo Pen Hing Tsi King (T. 190); Lalitavistara; Buddhacarita.

Chapter Five: A Bowl of Milk

Sujata meets Siddhartha for the first time after finding him collapsed by the river shore.

Fo So Hing Tsan (T. 192); Fo Chouo Fou Yao King (T. 186); Fang Kouang Ta Tchouang Yen King (T. 187); Lalitavistara, Buddhacarita.

Buddhacarita mentions a girl named Nandabala who offers the Buddha a bowl of milk. Perhaps Nandabala and Sujata were the same person.

Chapter Six: Beneath a Rose-Apple Tree

Prince Siddhartha is born. Asita Kaladeva visits the palace. Siddhartha attends the ritual plowing of the fields. He sits in meditation for the first time.

Acchariyabbhuta Sutta (M. 123); Mahapadana Sutta (D. 14); Nalaka Sutta (Sn. III, 11); Fo So Hing Tsan (T. 192); Fo Chouo Fou Yao King (T. 186); Fang Kouang Ta Tchouang Yen King (T. 187); Fo Pen Hing Tsi King (T. 190): Buddhacarita.

Fo So Hing Tsan (T. 192), the translation of Buddhacarita-kavya Sutta, is referred to in abbreviated form as Buddhacarita. The author was Ashvaghosha. The Buddhacarita was translated in 1893 by E. B. Cowell and was printed in Volume XLVI of The Sacred Books of the East. Fo So Hing Tsan was also translated into English by S. Beal under the name The Romantic Legend of Sakya Buddha, published in London in 1875.

In the Southern Tradition, Queen Mahamaya's dream of being pregnant and the birth of Siddhartha are recorded in M. 123, as well as D. 14. The visit of the hermit Asita is recounted in Sn. III, 11.

Chapter Seven: White Elephant Prize

Siddhartha furthers his studies. He reacts against the philosophy and lifestyle of the brahmans. Siddhartha attends the martial arts competition organized by Dandapani.

Fo Chouo Fou Yao King (T. 186); Fang Kouang Ta Tchouang Yen King (T. 187); Fo Pen Hing Tsi King (T. 190); Lalitavistara, Buddhacarita.

Chapter Eight: The Jewelled Necklace

Siddhartha encounters Yasodhara in a poor hamlet. Queen Gotami presents the kingdom's young women.

Fo Chouo Fou Yao King (T. 186); Fo Pen Hing Tsi King (T. 190); Lalitavistara; Buddhacarita.

Chapter Nine: The Path of Compassion

Siddhartha and Yasodhara celebrate their marriage. They take a journey throughout the kingdom. Queen Gotami and Yasodhara join efforts to assist the needy.

A. III, 38; Fo Chouo Fou Yao King (T. 186); Fo Pen Hing Tsi King (T. 190); Fang Kouang Ta Tchouang Yen King (T. 187); Lalitavistara, Buddhacarita.

The fact that Siddhartha is given three palaces by his royal father is recorded in A. III, 38.

Chapter Ten: Unborn Child

Siddhartha begins studies to prepare for the throne. Yasodhara announces that she is pregnant.

Fo Chouo Fou Yao King (T. 186); Fo Pen Hing Tsi King (T. 190); Fang Kouang Ta Tchouang Yen King (T. 187); Lalitavistara; Buddhacarita.

Chapter Eleven: Moonlight Flute

Siddhartha plays the flute while Anuruddha listens. Yasodhara gives birth to Rahula.

Fo Chouo Fou Yao King (T. 186); Fo Pen Hing Tsi King (T. 190); Fang Kouang Ta Tchouang Yen King (T. 187); Lalitavistara; Buddhacarita.

Chapter Twelve: Kanthaka

On a spring outing, Siddhartha encounters a sick man who dies. Yasodhara has three dreams which announce Siddhartha's departure. Siddhartha asks his father for permission to become a monk. The king refuses. Siddhartha leaves in the middle of the night after a party.

Fo Chouo Fou Yao King (T. 186); Fo Pen Hing Tsi King (T. 190); Lalitavistara, Buddhacarita.

Chapter Thirteen: Beginning Spiritual Practice

Siddhartha crosses the Anoma River and tells Channa to return with Kanthaka carrying his hair, necklace, and sword. Siddhartha trades his princely garments with a hunter for a monk's robe and then meets a monk. The monk leads Siddhartha to the spiritual center of Master Alara Kalama. Siddhartha learns to beg and to practice sitting meditation, the four dhyanas, and three of the formless concentrations.

Fo Chouo Fou Yao King (T. 186); Fo Pen Hing Tsi King (T. 190); Lalitavistara; Buddhacarita; Pasarasi Sutta (M. 126); Mahasaccaka Sutta (M. 36).

Siddhartha's studies of meditation with Master Kalama, his attainment of the Realm of No Materiality, and his departure from Master Kalama are recorded in M. 26 and Tchong 204. They are also mentioned in M. 36, M. 85, M. 100, Tsa 110, and Wou Fen Liu (T. 1421).

Chapter Fourteen: Crossing the Ganga

Siddhartha leaves Master Alara Kalama and crosses the Ganga (Ganges River) into Magadha in search of another spiritual teacher. He encounters a number of spiritual seekers from different sects. He meets King Bimbisara. Siddhartha finds his way to the spiritual center of Addaka Ramaputta.

Fo Chouo Fou Yao King (T. 186); Fo Pen Hing Tsi King (T. 190); Lalitavistara, Buddhacarita; Pabbajja Sutta (Sn. III, 1); Pasarasi Sutta (M. 26); Mahasaccaka Sutta (M. 36); Bodhirajakumara Sutta (M. 85), Tsa 107.

Siddhartha meeting King Bimbisara is recorded in Sn. III, 1.

Chapter Fifteen: Forest Ascetic

Siddhartha attains the Realm of Neither Perception Nor Non-Perception under the guidance of Master Ramaputta. Having not attained his goal with this Master either, Siddhartha departs for Dangsiri mountain for a period of self-mortification. He abandons self-mortification and begins to eat and drink normally again. He is abandoned by his five friends. Gautama practices beneath the pippala tree.

Fo Chouo Fou Yao King Z (T. 186); Fo Pen Hing Tsi King (T. 190); Pabbajja Sutta (Sn. III, 1); Pasarasi Sutta (M. 26); Mahasaccaka Sutta (M. 36); Bodhirajakumara Sutta (M. 85); Bhayabherava Sutta (M. 4), Wou Fen Liu (T. 1421).

Siddhartha's attainment of the Realm of Neither Perception Nor Non-Perception is recorded in M. 26. His efforts to control fear are mentioned in M. 4 and Tseng 23, 31. His self-mortification practices are mentioned in M. 36, as well as in M. 85, M. 100, and Wou Fen Liu (T. 1421).

Chapter Sixteen: Was Yasodhara Sleeping?

Svasti asks Bhikkhuni Pajapati details about the Buddha's life before and after he became a monk.

Fo Chouo Fou Yao King (T. 186); Fo Pen Hing Tsi King (T. 190); Lalitavistara, Buddhacarita; Fang Kouang Ta Tchouang Yen King (T. 187).

Chapter Seventeen: Pippala Leaf

Beneath the pippala tree, Gautama contemplates on the nature of the emptiness, impermanence, and interdependence of all things.

Fo Chouo Fou Yao King (T. 186); Fo Pen Hing Tsi King (T. 190); Lalitavistara; Buddhacarita; Fang Kouang Ta Tchouang Yen King (T. 187), Tsa 287, Tseng 38.4.

Siddhartha's discovery of the nature of interdependence of all things is recorded in S. XII, 65, Tsa 287, and in many other sutras.

Chapter Eighteen: The Morning Star Has Risen

Gautama contemplates on the nature of dependent co-arising and the birthless and deathless nature of all things. He attains the six abhijñas and transcends birth and death. He attains Total Awakening. That morning, Svasti pays him a visit.

Fo Chouo Fou Yao King (T. 186); Lalitavistara; Buddhacarita; Fang Kouang Ta Tchouang Yen King (T. 187); Mahasaccaka Sutta (M. 36); S. XII, 65; XXII, 26; Pasarasi Sutta (M. 26); Dhammapada 153-154; Ud. I, 1-3.

The passage "Oh jailkeeper..." is recorded in Dh. 153-154.

Chapter Nineteen: Tangerine of Mindfulness

The village children visit Gautama bringing with them a basket of tangerines, fresh coconut, and palm sugar. Gautama teaches the children about mindfulness. The children give him the name "Buddha," his path "The Way of Awakening," and the pippala tree the "bodhi tree."

Lalitavistara; Nian Tchou King (Tchong 98); Satipatthana Sutta (M. 10).

Ideas concerning mindfulness are drawn from M. 10 and Tchong 98.

Chapter Twenty: The Deer

The Buddha tells the children a past-life tale concerning the friendship between a deer, a turtle, and a magpie.

Cheng King (T. 154); Jataka (Kh. 10); Siuan Tsi Po Yuan King (T. 200); Purnamukhavadanashataka; Lieou Tou Tsi King (T. 152).

Chapter Twenty-One: The Lotus Pond

The Buddha visits a lotus pond and reflects on how to teach the Way to others. He meets the monk Upaka and inquires about the Masters Kalama and Ramaputta. He bids farewell to the village children and heads for Varanasi in search of his five friends.

Fo Chouo Fou Yao King (T. 186); Fo Pen Hing Tsi King (T. 190); Lalitavistara; Fang Kouang Ta Tchouang Yen King (T. 187); Vin. Mv. Kh. 1; S. VI, 1.

Comparing people's characteristics to parts of the lotus is contained in Vin. Mv. Kh. 1.

Chapter Twenty-Two: Turning the Wheel of Dharma
The Buddha teaches the Way to his five friends in the Deer Park.

Lalitavistara; Buddhacarita; Vin. Mv. Kh. 1; S. LVI, 11; Pasarasi Sutta (M. 26); Fo Chouo Tchouan Fa Louen King (T. 109); Fo Chouo Pa Tcheng Tao King (T. 112).

The encounter between the Buddha and the five friends who practiced self-mortification with him is recounted in Vin. Mv. Kh. 1 and S. LVI, 11.

Chapter Twenty-Three: Dharma Nectar
The Buddha ordains Yasa and instructs Yasa's parents in the five precepts for lay disciples.

Vin. Mv. Kh. 1; Fo Chouo Fou Yao King (T. 186); Fang Kouang Ta Tchouang Yen King (T. 187).

Yasa's ordination is recounted in Vin. Mv. Kh. 1.

Chapter Twenty-Four: Taking Refuge
Fifty-four of Yasa's friends ask to be ordained. The Buddha sends his disciples out to teach the Dharma. The Buddha formalizes the ritual for ordination.

Vin. Mv. Kh. 1; Sseu Fen Liu (T. 1428); Fang Kouang Ta Tchouang Yen King (T. 187); Lalitavistara.

Most of the details contained in this chapter are contained in Vin. Mv. Kh. 1.

Chapter Twenty-Five: Music's Lofty Peaks
The Buddha converts thirty young men by his flute playing.

Vin. Mv. Kh. 1; Sseu Fen Liu (T. 1428); Fang Kouang Ta Tchouang Yen King (T. 187); Lalitavistara; Fo Chouo Fou Yao King (T. 186).

The episode between the Buddha and the thirty young men is recounted in Vin. Mv. Kh. 1.

Chapter Twenty-Six: Water Rises, Too
The Buddha discusses with Kassapa the nature of the universe and the principle of interdependence. The Buddha spends the night in the altar room. At night the altar room burns down. The Buddha explains emptiness to Kassapa and how it is not the same as nihilism.

Vin. Mv. Kh. 1; Sseu Fen Liu (T. 1428); Fang Kouang Ta Tchouang Yen King (T. 187); Lalitavistara; Fo Pen Hing Tsi King (T. 190).

The Buddha's ordination of the three Kassapa brothers is told in Vin. Mv. Kh. 1.

Chapter Twenty-Seven: All Dharmas Are on Fire
The Buddha teaches Kassapa the Four Noble Truths and explains why it is not necessary to have a separate self in order to attain liberation. The three Kassapa brothers and their nine hundred disciples ask to be ordained by the Buddha. The Buddha delivers the Fire Sutra.

Vin. Mv. Kh. 1; Fo Pen Hing Tsi King (T. 190); Fo Chouo Fou Yao King (T. 186); S. XXXV, 28.

The Fire Sutra is contained in Vin. Mv. Kh. 1. Also look at S. XXXV, 28.

Chapter Twenty-Eight: Palm Forest
The Buddha together with a thousand bhikkhus returns to Rajagaha. King Bimbisara and his family and attendants visit the Buddha and listen to him deliver a Dharma discourse.

Vin. Mv. Kh. 1; Lalitavistara; Fo Pen Hing Tsi King (T. 190); Fang Kouang Ta Tchouang Yen King (T. 187).

Chapter Twenty-Nine: Dependent Co-Arising
Many people come to Palm Forest to request to be ordained or to be accepted as lay disciples. Venerable Kondanna gives a discourse on the Three Gems. Thanks to meeting Assaji, Sariputta and Moggallana ask to be ordained by the Buddha.

Vin. Mv. Kh. 1, 23, 1 ff.; Lalitavistara; Fo Chouo Fou Yao King (T. 186).

The gatha recited by Assaji to Sariputta is in Vin. Mv. Kh. 1, 23, 5.

Book Two
Chapter Thirty: Bamboo Forest
The Buddha and his bhikkhus partake of a meal at the palace. The Buddha speaks of the five precepts as principles of living which can build long-lasting peace and prosperity for the kingdom. The Buddha tells the children a past-life tale about a plumeria tree. King Bimbisara offers Bamboo Forest to the Buddha and his sangha.

Vin. Mv. Kh. 1; Jataka (Kh. 10); Siuan Tsi Po Yuan King (T. 200); Purnamukhavadanashataka; Lieou Tou Tsi King (T. 152); Cheng King (T. 154).

The invitation to the palace and King, Bimbisara's offering of Bamboo Forest are both recounted in Vin. Mv. Kh. 1.

Chapter Thirty-One: I Will Return in the Spring
The community of bhikkhus organizes a retreat season at Bamboo Forest. Kaludayi is sent by King Suddhodana to invite the Buddha to return home. Kaludayi asks to be ordained.

Vin. Mv. Kh. 1; Fo Chouo Fou Yao King (T. 186); Fang Kouang Ta Tchouang Yen King (T. 157); Lalitavistara; Thag.

Kaludayi being sent by King Suddhodana to invite the Buddha to return is mentioned in Thag. (527-33).

Chapter Thirty-Two: The Finger Is Not the Moon
The Buddha teaches Dighanakha about attachment to views and the nature of feelings. The Dharma discourse brings about Sariputta's awakening, and Dighanakha asks to be ordained. A rumor to stain the Buddha's reputation circulates in the capital.

Dighanakha Sutta (M. 74); Tch'ang Tchao Fan Tche Ts'ing Wen King (T. 584).

Chapter Thirty-Three: Beauty That Does Not Fade
Ambapali and Jivaka visit the Buddha. The Buddha teaches his bhikkhus concerning beauty and ugliness.

S. 47, 1; Tsa 622; Mahaparinibbana Sutta (D. 16); Vin. Mv Kh. 6; Jivaka Sutta (M. 55).

Chapter Thirty-Four: Reunion
The Buddha returns to Kapilavatthu. King Suddhodana enters the city to greet the Buddha. The Buddha explains the meaning and purpose of begging to the king. Rahula asks the Buddha for his inheritance. The Buddha and his attendant

are invited to the palace for a meal. The Buddha tells the story of his spiritual search.

Vin. Mv. Kh. 1; Fang Kouang Ta Tchouang Yen King (T. 187); Lalitavistara.

Chapter Thirty-Five: Early Morning Sunshine
The Buddha and his sangha are invited to a meal at the palace together with guests of King Suddhodana. The Buddha gives a discourse on the Four Noble Truths and how to meditate in order to transcend suffering. Gotami and Yasodhara visit the Buddha at Nigrodha Monastery.

Vin. Mv. Kh. 1.

Chapter Thirty-Six: Lotus Vow
Yasodhara invites the Buddha and Kaludayi to a meal at the palace. The Buddha meets with children in a poor village and tells them the past-life story of Megha and the young woman who gave him lotus flowers to offer to the Enlightened Master Dipankara.

Siuan Tsi Po Yuan King (T. 200); Fo Pen Hing Tsi King (T. 190); Purnamukhavadanashakata; Jataka (Kh. 10); Cheng King (T. 154).

Chapter Thirty-Seven: A New Faith
Nanda and Rahula join the sangha. King Suddhodana criticizes the Buddha for allowing Rahula to become a monk. The Buddha gives a discourse on politics and the way of virtue.

Vin. Mv. Kh. 1; Sseu Fen Liu (T. 1428).

The king's words to the Buddha, "Master, I suffered unbelievably when you abandoned home to become a monk...the pain is like a knife cutting into my skin, flesh, bone, and marrow..." have been taken almost verbatim from Vin. Mv. Kh. 1.

Chapter Thirty-Eight: O, Happiness!
Six princes of the Sakya clan leave home and ask to be ordained along with a barber. The Buddha spends the retreat season at Bamboo Forest. Venerable Baddhiya tastes the joys of the Dharma. Mahakassapa is ordained.

Vin. Cv. Kh. 7; Ud. 11, 10; Sseu Fen Liu (T. 1428).

Baddhiya's experiencing the joys of the Dharma are mentioned in Vin. Cv. Kh. 7.

Chapter Thirty-Nine: Waiting for Daybreak

The merchant Sudatta goes to meet the Buddha before daylight. Sudatta invites Sariputta to go with him to Savatthi in order to prepare for the Buddha's arrival to teach the Dharma in the kingdom of Kosala.

Vin. Cv. Kh. 6; S. X, 8; Tsa 592 and 593.

Sudatta's first encounter with the Buddha is described in Vin. Cv. Kh. 6.

Chapter Forty: Cover the Land in Gold

Sudatta purchases Prince Jeta's grove in order to build a monastery for the bhikkhus. Venerable Sariputta returns to accompany the Buddha. The Buddha teaches the Dharma to the Licchavi princes.

Vin. Cv. Kh. 6; S. X, 8; Sseu Fen Liu (T. 1428).

Chapter Forty-One: Has Anyone Seen My Mother?

The Buddha spends the retreat season at Jetavana. Other religious sects disagree with the Buddha concerning the subject of love.

Piyajatika Sutta (M. 87), Tchong 216 (T. 26).

Chapter Forty-Two: Love Is Understanding

King Pasenadi visits the Buddha and receives teaching about Love and Understanding.

Piyajatika Sutta (M. 87); Ud. VI, 4; Metta Sutta (Sn. I, 8), Tchong 216 (T. 26).

The passage in which the Buddha speaks to the king about a young prince, a small snake, a spark of fire, and a young monk is found in S. III, 1.

Chapter Forty-Three: Everyone's Tears Are Salty

The Buddha invites the nightsoil carrier, Sunita, to join the sangha of bhikkhus. King Pasenadi comes to ask the Buddha why he has accepted an untouchable into the sangha.

Fo Pen Hing Tsi King (T. 190); Fang Kouang Ta Tchouang Yen King (T. 187); Lalitavistara.

Chapter Forty-Four: The Elements Will Recombine

Nanda misses his betrothed. The Buddha returns to Vesali for the retreat season. King Suddhodana, on his deathbed, asks the Buddha to return. The Buddha speaks to his father about birth and death and assists him in choosing a successor.

After the funeral, Queen Pajapati asks to be ordained. The Buddha refuses her request.

Ud. 111, 2; Vin. Cv. Kh. 10; A. VII, 51; Fang Kouang Ta Tchouang Yen King (T. 187); Sseu Fen Liu (T. 1428).

The Buddha's refusal to allow Gotami to be ordained is mentioned in Vin. Cv. Kh. 10 and in T. 1428. Additional references can be found in A. VII, 51 and A. VIII, 53.

Chapter Forty-Five: Opening the Door

Mahapajapati and women comrades demonstrate their intention and ability to lead the homeless life. Eight Rules are created as a prerequisite for women to be ordained.

Ud. 111, 2; Vin. Cv. Kh. 10; A. VIII, 51-53; Tchong 116 (T. 26); Tchong 130 (T. 26); Sseu Fen Liu (T. 1428); Wou Fen Liu (T. 1421).

Detailed accounts of Mahapajapati and her women comrades' efforts to be accepted into the sangha are recorded in Vin. Cv. Kh. 10; T. 1428 and T. 1421.

Chapter Forty-Six: A Handful Of Sirnsapa Leaves

The Buddha deals with Bhikkhu Malunkyaputta and esoteric questions. After dispute and division in the sangha at Kosambi, the Buddha goes to the forest alone. He creates the six principles for community harmony.

Vin. Mv. Kh. 10; Upakkilesa Sutta (M. 128); Culamalunkya Sutta (M. 63); Tchong 205 (T. 26); Tchong 221 (T. 26); S. 56, 31; Tsa 404; Fo Chouo Tsien Yu King (T. 94); Culagosinga Sutta (M. 31); Kosambiya Sutta (M. 48); Tchong 72 (T. 26).

The episode with Bhikkhu Malunkyaputta can be found in M. 63 and Tchong 221 (T. 26). Division in the sangha is recorded in Vin. Mv. Kh. 10 and M. 128. The harmonious community life of Anuruddha, Kimbila and Nandiya is recounted in M. 128, Tchong 72 (T. 26), and Vin. Mv. Kh. 10.

Chapter Forty-Seven: Follow the Dharma

The Buddha spends the retreat season in Rakkhita Forest and befriends an elephant matriarch. The Buddha returns to Savatthi. His senior disciples ask him how to receive the bhikkhus from Kosambi.

Vin. Mv. Kh. 10; Ud- IV, 5; Upakkilesa Sutta (M. 128).

The Buddha's befriending of the elephant is recorded in Vin. Mv. Kh. 10. Look also at Ud. IV, 5. The repentance and reconciliation among the bhikkhus from Kosambi is recorded in Vin. Mv. Kh. 10.

Chapter Forty-Eight: Covering Mud with Straw

The Buddha's senior disciples establish the Seven Practices of Reconciliation.

Vin. Mv. Kh. 10; Sseu Fen Liu (T. 1428).

The Seven Practices of Reconciliation are the final items in the precepts of the bhikkhus, in both the Southern and Northern traditions.

Chapter Forty-Nine: Earth's Lessons

Rahula recounts for Svasti how the precepts were developed. The Buddha encounters a farmer who accuses the bhikkhus of eating without working. The Buddha teaches Rahula concerning Right Speech, Right Mindfulness, and the Four Limitless Meditations.

Ambalatthikarahulovada Sutta (M. 61); Maharahulovada Sutta (M. 62); Vin. Sv. Para. I; A. VIII, 11; Kasibharadvaja Sutta (Sn. I, 4); Cularahulovada Sutta (M. 147); Tchong 14 (T. 26); Tsa 897 (T. 99); Tchong 200 (T. 26).

The farmer's accusations that the Buddha does not plow or sow seeds is taken from Sn. I, 4 and S. VII, 11. The Buddha's instruction to Rahula can be found in M. 62, M. 147, Tseng 17, 1 (T. 125), and Tchong 200 (T. 26).

Chapter Fifty: A Handful of Bran

There is a famine in Veranja. The Buddha speaks to Sariputta concerning how to know when the precepts are complete. Svasti feels homesick. The Buddha teaches Meghiya concerning the Four Establishments of Mindfulness.

Vin. Sv. Para. 1; Ud. IV, 1; A. IX, 3; Tsa 897 (T. 99); Sseu Fen Liu (T. 1428).

The Buddha's instruction to Meghiya can be found in Ud. IV, 1 and A. IX, 3. According to the Southern Tradition, the complete precepts number 227 for bhikkhus and 311 for bhikkhunis. According to the Northern Tradition which relies most on Sseu Fen Liu (T. 1428) of the Dharmagupta tradition, there are 250 precepts for bhikkhus and 358 for bhikkhunis.

Chapter Fifty-One: The Treasure of Insight

Rahula receives full ordination. The Buddha gives Rahula teaching concerning contemplation of the eighteen realms of existence. The Buddha delivers the Sutra on Knowing the Better Way to Live Alone. The Buddha teaches about Compassion to a group of children. The Buddha lifts a lotus before the community as a means of opening them to the direct experience of life's wonders.

S. XXI, 10; Metta Sutta (Sn. I, 8); Ud. V, 4; Bhaddekaratta Sutta (M. 131); Ananda Bhaddekaratta Sutta (M. 132); Mahakaccana Bhaddekaratta Sutta (M. 133); Tseng 49, 10 (T. 125); Tchong 165, 166, 167 (T. 26); and Fo Chouo Tsouen Chang King (T. 77).

The meeting between the Buddha and a group of children harming crabs can be found in the Metta Sutta, Sn. I, 8. The Sutra on Knowing the Better Way to Live Alone is from M. 131. Also look at M. 132, M. 133, Tchong 165, 166, 167 (T. 26), and T. 77.

Chapter Fifty-Two: Fields of Merit

The Buddha mediates and brings to resolution the conflict between Sakya and Koliya, and then spends the retreat season in Kapilavatthu. The Buddha returns to Vulture Peak. He suggests a new way of sewing bhikkhus' robes to Ananda. Lay disciple Lady Visakha pays a visit. The senior disciples suggest that Ananda serve as the Buddha's full-time attendant, and they ask the Buddha to return to Savatthi every year for the retreat season.

Vin. Mv. Kh. 8; Ud. VIII, 8; Sseu Fen Liu (T. 1428).

The Buddha's idea to sew robes as fields of merit is mentioned in Vin. Mv. Kh. 8. Lay disciple Lady Visakha is mentioned in Vin. Mv. Kh. 8, Ud. VIII, 8 and T. 1428.

Chapter Fifty-Three: Dwelling in the Present Moment

The Buddha delivers the Satipatthana Sutta. He converts Angulimala.

Satipatthana Sutta (M. 10); Mahasatipatthana Sutta (D. 22); Angulimala Sutta (M. 86); Nian Tan King (Tchong 81); Nian Chu King (Tchong 98) (T. 26); Tseng 12, 1 (T. 125); Yang Kiue Mo Lo King (T. 120).

The Satipatthana Sutta is transmitted in three documents: M. 10, Tchong 98, and Tseng 12, 1 (T. 125). It is the fundamental sutra on meditation. M. 10 is from the Theravada tradition, Tchong 98 is from the Sarvastivada tradition, and Tseng 12, 1 is of the Mahasanghika tradition. The story of Angulimala is told in M. 86. In the Chinese canon, in addition to T. 120, there are several other sutras which mention Angulimala.

Chapter Fifty-Four: Dwell in Mindfulness
The intellectual Upali abandons the Nigantha sect in order to follow the teaching of the Buddha. Jetavana Monastery is disturbed by false accusations.
Upali Sutta (M. 56); Lalitavistara; Tchong 133 (T. 26); Fo Chouo Fou Yao King (T. 186).

Chapter Fifty-Five: Appearance of the Morning Star
The Buddha cares for a bhikkhu who has dysentery. Bhikkhuni Dhammadinna delivers a discourse on Emptiness to lay disciples Visakha and Sudatta and is praised by the Buddha. The stories of Bhikkhunis Patacara and Uppalavanna are recounted.
Vin. Mv. Kh. 8; AV. 123-124; Culavedalla Sutta (M. 44); Tchong 210 (T. 26); Sseu Fen Liu (T. 1428).
Patacara's poem can be found in the Therigatha. The lay disciple named Visakha who listened to Bhikkhuni Dhammadinna's discourse was a male disciple and not Lady Visakha. Uppalavanna's story is recounted in T. 1428. See also Thig.

Book Three
Chapter Fifty-Six: Full Awareness of Breathing
The Buddha delivers the Sutra on the Full Awareness of Breathing. Angulimala is beaten by an angry mob.
Anapanasati Sutta (M. 118); Angulimala Sutta (M. 86); Tsa 1077 (T. 125); Tseng 17, 1 and 38, 6 (T. 125); Fo Chouo Ta Nyan Pan Cheou Yi King (T. 602), Tsa 1077 (T. 125).
The general outline of the Sutra on the Full Awareness of Breathing in this chapter is taken from M. 118. The version in T. 602 of the Chinese canon is not so clear or precise. The attack on Angulimala is recounted in M. 86.

Chapter Fifty-Seven: The Raft Is Not the Shore
The Buddha delivers the Simile of the Snake Sutra. Venerable Bhanda gives a Dharma talk at the bhikkhunis' monastery. The Buddha ordains the young untouchable woman Prakriti.
S. LIV, 9; Alagaddupama Sutta (M. 22); Sseu Fen Liu (T. 1428); Tchong 200 (T. 26).
The examples of catching a snake and using a raft to cross the river, as well as the Buddha's teaching that one must study and practice intelligently, unbound by narrow views and

ignorance, like the man who carries the raft around on his head, can all be found in M. 22. The story about Bhanda is taken from T. 1428.

Chapter Fifty-Eight: A Handful of Precious Earth
Children offer a handful of earth to the Buddha. The Buddha tells them the past-life story of Visvantara. The physician Jivaka asks the Buddha about vegetarianism.

Jivaka Sutta (M. 55); Avadanashataka; Purnamukhavadanashataka.

Jivaka's questions about vegetarianism are from M. 55.

Chapter Fifty-Nine: The Net of Theories
Bhikkhuni Subha is almost violated by a strange man. The Buddha delivers the Brahmajala Sutta.

Samannaphala Sutta (D. 2); Brahmajala Sutta (D. 1); Tch'ang 21 (T. 1); Thig.

To find the story of bhikkhuni Subha, read Thig. The names and ages of the leaders of the various religious sects of the time are recorded in D. 2, and here and there in many other sutras. Their philosophies are mentioned in D. 1.

Chapter Sixty: Lady Visakha's Grief
The Buddha discusses with Sonadanda the fundamental characteristics necessary to make a brahman. Lady Visakha expresses a wish for many children and grandchildren. Venerable Ananda promises to plant a bodhi tree at Jetavana.

Vasettha Sutta (M. 98); Ud. VIII, 8; Tch'ang 22 (T. 1); Sonadanda Sutta (D. 4).

Venerable Moggallana explains in brief the philosophies of the various contemporary religious sects to Venerable Svasti.

The encounter with Sonadanda is recounted in D. 4, as well as mentioned in M. 98. The story of Lady Visakha's drenched hair is from Ud. VIII, 8.

Chapter Sixty-One: The Lion's Roar
The Buddha gives the teaching on dependent co-arising. The young woman Cinca falsely accuses the Buddha. The Buddha delivers the Sutra on the Lion's Roar.

Ud. IV, 8; S. XII, 2; Culasihanada Sutta (M. 11); A. IV, 33; Mahanidana Sutta (D. 15); Yuan K'i King (T. 124); Lalitavistara; Tchong 97 (T. 26); Tsa 684 (T. 125); Jou Lai Che Tseu Heou King (T. 835); Fo Chouo Fou Yao King (T. 186).

Dependent co-arising is taught in many sutras. The substance of the Sutra on the Lion's Roar in this chapter has been taken from M. 11.

Chapter Sixty-Two: Sariputta's Roar
Venerable Sariputta is falsely accused out of jealousy. The Buddha delivers the Kalama Sutra.

Kalama Sutta (A. III, 65); Sariputtasihanada Sutta (A. IX, 11).

The incident of jealousy leading to Sariputta being falsely accused can be found in A. IX, 11. The Kalama Sutra is like the charter of Buddhist teaching concerning freedom of thought. It is also called Kesamutta Sutta. The story of Kokalika is found in S. 6, 1, 10.

Chapter Sixty-Three: All the Way to the Sea
The Buddha waits for a farmer to eat before beginning his Dharma talk. The Buddha speaks about a piece of driftwood floating towards the sea. Svasti is asked to guide and look after a young buffalo tender who joins the sangha.

S. XXXV, 200.

The Buddha's words about the piece of driftwood are taken from S. XXXV, 200.

Chapter Sixty-Four: The Round of Birth and Death
The Buddha delivers the Sutra on the Eight Realizations of the Great Beings. Venerable Vakkali dies. The Buddha teaches about beginninglessness and endlessness.

A. VIII, 30; S. XII, 15; S. XXII, 87; S. VX, 1; Tchong 74 (T. 26); Tsa 1265 (T. 125) ; Tseng 26, 10 (T. 125); Tseng 42, 6 (T. 125); Fo Chouo A Na Liu Pa Nien King (T. 46); Fo Chouo Pa Ta Jen Kiao King (T. 779).

The Eight Realizations of the Great Beings in this chapter are taken from T. 779. They are also mentioned in several other sutras, both Southern and Northern. The story about Venerable Vakkali's death is recounted in S. XXII, 87, in Tsa 47 (T. 125), and Tseng 19 (T. 99). The Buddha's thoughts concerning beginninglessness and endlessness at the end of this chapter are from S. XV, 1. The parable of the arrows and the Buddha's teaching on feelings are found in S. XXXVI, 1, 6. His teaching concerning the contemplation on feelings at the moment of dying is taken from S. XXXVI, 1, 7.

Chapter Sixty-Five: Neither Full nor Empty

The Buddha teaches concerning emptiness, birthlessness, and deathlessness.

S. XXXV, 85; Culasunnata Sutta (M. 121); Mahasunnata Sutta (M. 122); Tsa 232 (T. 99); Fo Chouo Wou Yun Kiai K'ong King (T. 102); Tao Hing Pan Jo King (T. 224); Pan Jo Po Lo Mi To Sin King (T. 251); Ta Fang Kouang Fo Houa Yen King (T. 278).

The section in which Ananda asks about the nature of the world and the Buddha's response are taken from S. XXXV, 84. The section in which Ananda asks what the Buddha means when he says that all the dharmas are empty, is taken from S. XXXV, 85. The example given by the Buddha of the Dharma hall, the sangha of bhikkhus, the market, water buffaloes, and the village, is taken from M. 121, whose contents are basically the same as Tsa 232 (T. 99). The following explanations are all based on the principle of interdependence and emptiness of self. All the ideas in this chapter concerning birthlessness, deathlessness, interpenetration, and interbeing spoken of in the Prajñaparamita Sutra and the Avatamsaka Sutra are the natural and inevitable expansion of the Buddha's original teaching on dependent co-arising, selflessness, and emptiness.

Chapter Sixty-Six: Four Mountains

The Buddha delivers the Ullambana Sutra on filial piety. The Buddha encourages King Pasenadi to devote more time to spiritual practice in his old age. The Buddha tells a story about blind men and an elephant.

Ud. VI, 4; S. III, 25; Fo Chouo Yu Lan Pen King (T. 685); Fo Chouo Hiao Tseu King (T. 687); Fo Chouo Fou Mou Ngen Nan Pao King (T. 684).

The Yu Lan Sutra does not exist in the Pali canon. To find the story of the four mountains, see S. III, 3, 5. The Vietnamese Emperor Tran Thai Tong was inspired by this sutra to write his piece "Four Mountains, Preface and Gathas," in the work Khoa Hu Luc (Treatise on Emptiness). The story about the blind men and the elephant is from Ud. VI, 4.

Chapter Sixty-Seven: Ocean Poet

Venerable Punna asks the Buddha's permission to spread the Dharma in a region that is known for its violence and lack of civilization. The Buddha talks about the eight characteristics of the sea.

Punnovada Sutta (M. 145); S. XXXV, 63-64; Tsa 311 (T. 99);
A. VIII, 19; Fa Hai King (T. 34); Fo Chouo Hai Pa T6 King (T.
35).

The eight characteristics of the sea are recounted in A. VIII,
19. Also look at T. 35.

Chapter Sixty-Eight: Three Wondrous Gates

The Buddha speaks about the problem of division in the
sangha. He delivers the Sutra on the Dharma Seal. The two
venerables Yamelu and Tekula ask permission to translate the
sutras into classical meter but are refused by the Buddha.

Vin. Cv. Kh. 5; Samagama Sutta (M. 104); Pasadika Sutta (D.
29); Tsa 80 (T. 99); Fo Chouo Tcheng Fa Yin King (T. 103); Fo
Chouo Fa Yin King (T. 104).

The Buddha's words concerning the problem of division are
taken from M. 104. The contents of the Sutra on the Dharma
Seal used in this chapter are taken from T. 104. The two venerables asking permission to translate the sutras is mentioned
in Vin. Cv. Kh. 5.

Chapter Sixty-Nine: Where Will the Buddha Go?

Some ascetics ask the Buddha philosophical questions but
are met by silence. Thanks to Venerable Anuradha, the Buddha
receives a new name, the Tathagata.

S. XLIV, 2; Aggivaccha Sutta (M. 72); Alagaddupama Sutta
(M. 22); A. X, 95; S. XIV, 10; Tsa 106 (T. 99); Iti IV, 13.

The incident of the Buddha refusing to answer the ascetic
Uttiya's questions is taken from A. X, 95. The incident con-
cerning the ascetic Vacchagotta is taken from S. XIV, 10. The
incident with Anuradha is mentioned in S. XLIV, 2.
Concerning the title of Tathagata, look at M. 22 and M. 72; Iti.
IV, 13, and A. IV, 23.

Chapter Seventy: The Quail and the Falcon

Rahula tells Svasti about Bhikkhu Vangisa, a poet. The
Buddha compares the six sense organs to an ocean filled with
sea monsters and whirlpools. The Buddha tells the story of
the falcon and the quail, suggesting that bhikkhus be protected by mindfulness. Svasti recalls the story of Bhikkhu
Isidatta and Layperson Citta. The Buddha suggests a tender
way to deal with weak members of the sangha that will preserve the remaining good seeds in them. There is a conversation between the Buddha and Kesi, a horse trainer. The war-

rior Rohitassa asks the Buddha how to get out of the world of birth and death.

Tsa 1208-1221 (T. 99); S. VIII 1, 1-12; S. XLVII, 1, 6; Tsa 24, 15 (T. 99); S. SLI, 2-3; Tsa 570 (T. 99); Tchong 194 (T. 26); M. 65.

The story of Vangisa is told in Tsa 1208-1221 (T. 99) and Tchong 192 (T. 26). The story of Isidatta is found in S. XLI, 2-3, and Tsa 570 (T. 99). The conversation between the Buddha and the horse trainer is found in A. IV, 12, 110. The story of Rohitassa is seen in Tseng 43, 1 (T. 125), A. VI, 45, Tsa 1307, and S. II, 3, 6.

Chapter Seventy-One: The Art of Stringing a Sitar

The Buddha encourages Venerable Sona to take good care of his health. Jivaka informs the Buddha about Venerable Devadatta's and the Prince Ajatasattu's ambitions. Devadatta asks the Buddha to transfer the leadership of the sangha to Devadatta.

Ud. V, 6; Vin. Mv. Kh. 5; A. VI, 55; Vin. Cv. Kh. 7; Tchong 123 (T. 26), Tsa 254 (T. 99); Sseu Fen Liu (T. 1428).

The Buddha's questions to Sona about stringing a sitar are mentioned in Vin. Mv. Kh. 5. Also see A. VI, 55. Devadatta's request to be given the leadership of the sangha is recounted in T. 1428 and Vin. Cv. Kh. 7

Chapter Seventy-Two: Quiet Resistance

Devadatta proposes five new rules and organizes an independent sangha. King Bimbisara abdicates his throne in favor of his son, Prince Ajatasattu. The Buddha and his sangha do not attend the new king's coronation.

Vin. Cv. Kh. 7; Vin. Sv. Sangh. 10; Sseu Fen Liu (T. 1428).

Devadatta's proposal for five new rules and his setting up an independent sangha are recorded in Vin. Cv. Kh. 7. See also Vin. Sv. Sangh. 10. Prince Ajatasattu's attempted assassination of King Bimbisara is recorded in Vin. Cv. Kh. 7 and T. 1428.

Chapter Seventy-Three: Hidden Rice

The first attempt on the Buddha's life is unsuccessful. Venerables Sariputta and Moggallana leave for Gayasisa. The Buddha meets with Queen Videhi.

Vin. Cv. Kh. 7; Sseu Fen Liu (T. 1428).

The attempt on the Buddha's life and the departure of Venerables Sariputta and Moggallana for Gayasisa can be found in Vin. Cv. Kh. 7 and T. 1428.

Chapter Seventy-Four: Cry of the Elephant Queen

Venerables Sariputta and Moggallana lead four hundred bhikkhus back to the Buddha's sangha. The Buddha receives an injury in a second attempt on his life. The Buddha pacifies the elephant Nagagiri and thus survives the third attempt on his life.

Vin. Cv. Kh. 7; Sseu Fen Liu (T. 1428).

The return of bhikkhus under the guidance of the two elder disciples is recorded in Vin. Cv. Kh. 7. The hurling of a boulder and the releasing of a violent elephant in attempts to kill the Buddha are recorded in Vin. Cv. Kh. 7 and T. 1428.

Chapter Seventy-Five: Tears of Happiness

The Buddha departs from Magadha and returns to Savatthi for the retreat season. The Buddha delivers the Singala Sutta. Lay disciple Sudatta falls gravely ill. The Buddha creates the Eight Observances for the Laity. Venerables Sariputta and Ananda visit Sudatta and offer him teaching.

Magandiya Sutta (M. 75); Culadhammasammadana Sutta (M. 45); Singala Sutta (D. 31); Anathapindikovada Sutta (M. 143); Tchong 135 (T. 26); Tsa 1031 and 1032 (T. 99); Tseng 51, 8 (T. 125); Fo Chouo Che Kia Yue Viet Lieou Fang Li King (T. 16); Fo Chouo Pa Koan Tchai King (T. 89).

For the section on sense pleasures and the leper roasting himself on a fire in the forest, look at M. 75. The four kinds of happiness are described in M. 45. The episode of Sudatta's tears when he listens to the two venerables teach the Dharma is taken from M. 143. See also Tchong 28 (T. 26).

Chapter Seventy-Six: The Fruits of Practice

War erupts between Kosala and Magadha. Queen Mallika passes away. The Buddha speaks to King Pasenadi about politics and virtue. The Buddha returns to Vulture Peak. Jivaka arranges for King Ajatasattu to meet the Buddha. The Buddha delivers the Sutra on the Fruits of a Bhikkhu's Practice.

S. XLVIII, 41; Kutadanta Sutta (D. 5); Samannaphala Sutta (D. 2); Tch'ang 27 (T. 1).

King Ajatasattu's invasion of Kosala is recorded in S. III, 14-15. The Buddha's suggestions concerning how the law should deal with conflict and crime is taken from D. 5, although in this sutra the Buddha was not speaking to either King Pasenadi or King Bimbisara but rather to a brahmana named Kutadanta. Jivaka's invitation to King Ajatasattu to go meet the Buddha is spoken of in D. 2 and Tch'ang 27 (T. 1).

Chapter Seventy-Seven: Stars in Your Eyes
The Buddha returns to Savatthi for the retreat season. King Pasenadi praises the Buddha and the Sangha. Upon his return to Vulture Peak, the Buddha learns of the deaths of King Pasenadi and Venerable Moggallana.

Dhammacetiya Sutta (M. 89), Tchong 213 (T. 26).

King Pasenadi's visit to the Buddha and his praises are recorded in both M. 89 and Tchong 213 (T. 26).

Chapter Seventy-Eight: Two Thousand Saffron Robes
Venerable Devadatta repents. King Ajatasattu explores the idea of invading Vajji. The Buddha delivers his talk on the seven practices to assure the strength and continuation of the sangha. Venerable Sariputta praises the Buddha. The Buddha spends the retreat season in Beluvagamaka village and falls seriously ill.

Mahaparinibbana Sutta (D. 16); Tch'ang 2 (T. 1); Fo Pan Ni Yuan King (T. 5); Mahavastu.

King Ajatasattu's sending an envoy to the Buddha to ask his counsel concerning his plans to invade Vajji is mentioned in D. 16 and Tch'ang 2 (T. 1). The section about the people of Vesali asking the Buddha to come from Rajagaha to help them during the plague is recorded in Mahavastu.

Chapter Seventy-Nine: Sandalwood Tree Mushrooms
The Buddha speaks about the nature of the Three Gems. The Buddha receives news that Venerable Sariputta has died in Nala. The Buddha leaves Vesali and crosses the Ganga to head north. He is offered his last meal by Cunda. The Buddha enters the forest of sal trees in Kusinara.

S. XLVII, 1, 9; Tsa 638 (T. 99); Mahaparinibbana Sutta (D. 16); Tch'ang 2 (T. 1); Fo Pan Ni Yuan King (T. 5).

All the details in this chapter have been taken from D. 16 and T. 5.

Chapter Eighty: Be Diligent!
The Buddha praises Venerable Ananda. Ascetic Subhadda is the last person ordained by the Buddha. The Buddha passes into Nirvana.

Mahaparinibbana Sutta (D. 16); Tch'ang 2 (T. 1); Fo Pan
Ni Yuan King (T. 5).

The details in this chapter were all taken from D. 6 and
T. 5.

Chapter Eighty-One: Old Path White Clouds

The people of Kusinara offer the Buddha incense, flowers,
and music. Venerable Mahakassapa leads five hundred
bhikkhus to the Buddha's funeral. Several delegations from
different kingdoms receive relics of the Buddha to place in
stupas. Mahakassapa organizes a council to compile all the
precepts and sutras in Rajagaha. Venerable Svasti returns to
Uruvela and gazes at the shore of the Neranjara River and
the white clouds in the sky.

Mahaparinibbana Sutta (D. 16); Tch'ang 2 (T. 1); Fo Pan
Ni Yuan King (T. 5).

Details concerning the Buddha's funeral and the dividing
of his relics are taken from D. 16 and T. 5.

Sanskrit Equivalents of Pali Names and Places

Pali	Sanskrit
Ajita Kesamkambali	Ajita Keshakambala
Anathapindika	Anathapindada
Ajatasattu	Ajatasatru
Assaji	Ashvajit
Bhadda Kapilani	Bhadra Kapila
Bhaddiya	Bhadrika
Bhadda Kapilani	Bhadrakapila
Channa	Chandaka
Dighanakha	Dirghanakha
Gayasisa	Gayashiras
Gijjhakuta	Gridhrakuta
Isipatana	Mrigadava
Kaludayi	Kalodayin
Kapilavatthu	Kapilavastu
Kassapa	Kashyapa
Kosambi	Kaushambi
(Annata) Kondanna	(Ajnata) Kaundinya
Kusinara	Kushinagari
Mahanarna	Mahanaman
Maha Pajapati	Mahaprajapati
Makkhali Gosala	Maskari Goshaliputra
Moggallana	Maudgalyayana
Neranjara	Nairanjana
Nigrodha	Nyagrodha
Nigantha Nataputta	Nigrantha-jnatiputra
Pakudha Kaccayana	Kakuda Katyayana
Pataliputta	Pataliputra
Punna	Purna, Purnamaitrayaniputra
Purana Kassapa	Purana Kashyapa
Rajagaha	Rajagriha
Rarnagarna	Rarnagrama
Sanjaya Balatthiputta	Sanjayin Vairatiputra
Sariputta	Shariputra
Savatthi	Shravasti
Siddhattha	Siddhartha
Uppalavanna	Utpalavarna
Uruvela	Uruvilva
Uddaka Rarnaputta	Udraka Rarnaputra
Vappa	Dashabala Kashyapa
Veranja	Vairanti
Vesali	Vaishali

Shantum Seth, a student of Thich Nhat Hanh, organizes pilgrimages, "In the Footsteps of the Buddha," each winter in India and Nepal. The group visits the sites associated with the Buddha's life, going at a pace slower than tourists usually do, which allows the pilgrim to be mindful, have discussions, and listen to stories of the Buddha's life and teachings, many from *Old Path White Clouds.* It is also an opportunity to explore and understand the subtleties of Indian life that have changed little since the time of the Buddha. For further information and a free brochure, please contact:

Shantum Seth
309-B Sector 15 A
Noida 201301
India
Email: shantum@ivpas.unv.ernet.in

PARALLAX PRESS

Parallax Press publishes books and tapes on Buddhism and related subjects for contemporary readers. We carry all books by Thich Nhat Hanh. For a copy of our free catalog, please write to:

Parallax Press
P. O. Box 7355
Berkeley, CA 94707
www.parallax.org